P9-DDY-069

®

References for the Rest of Us! ®

COMPUTER BOOK SERIES FROM IDG

Are you intimidated and confused by computers? Do you find that traditional manuals are overloaded with technical details you'll never use? Do your friends and family always call you to fix simple problems on their PCs? Then the . . .*For Dummies*® computer book series from IDG Books Worldwide is for you.

. . .*For Dummies* books are written for those frustrated computer users who know they aren't really dumb but find that PC hardware, software, and indeed the unique vocabulary of computing make them feel helpless. . . .*For Dummies* books use a lighthearted approach, a down-to-earth style, and even cartoons and humorous icons to diffuse computer novices' fears and build their confidence. Lighthearted but not lightweight, these books are a perfect survival guide for anyone forced to use a computer.

> *"I like my copy so much I told friends; now they bought copies."*
> **Irene C., Orwell, Ohio**

> *"Quick, concise, nontechnical, and humorous."*
> **Jay A., Elburn, Illinois**

> *"Thanks, I needed this book. Now I can sleep at night."*
> **Robin F., British Columbia, Canada**

Already, hundreds of thousands of satisfied readers agree. They have made . . .*For Dummies* books the #1 introductory level computer book series and have written asking for more. So, if you're looking for the most fun and easy way to learn about computers, look to . . .*For Dummies* books to give you a helping hand.

IDG BOOKS WORLDWIDE
™

MORE DOS FOR DUMMIES®

by Dan Gookin

IDG Books Worldwide, Inc.
An International Data Group Company

Foster City, CA ◆ Chicago, IL ◆ Indianapolis, IN ◆ Braintree, MA ◆ Southlake, TX

MORE DOS For Dummies®

Published by
IDG Books Worldwide, Inc.
An International Data Group Company
155 Bovet Road, Suite 310
San Mateo, CA 94402

Text *and art* copyright ©1994 by IDG Books Worldwide. All rights reserved. No part of this book may be reproduced or transmitted in any form, by any means (electronic, photocopying, recording, or otherwise) without the prior written permission of the publisher.

Library of Congress Catalog Card No.: 93-80872

ISBN: 1-56884-046-2

Printed in the United States of America

10 9 8 7 6 5

1B/QZ/QS/ZW

Distributed in the United States by IDG Books Worldwide, Inc.

Distributed by Macmillan Canada for Canada; by Computer and Technical Books for the Caribbean Basin; by Contemporanea de Ediciones for Venezuela; by Distribuidora Cuspide for Argentina; by CITEC for Brazil; by Ediciones ZETA S.C.R. Ltda. for Peru; by Editorial Limusa SA for Mexico; by Transworld Publishers Limited in the United Kingdom and Europe; by Al-Maiman Publishers & Distributors for Saudi Arabia; by Simron Pty. Ltd. for South Africa; by IDG Communications (HK) Ltd. for Hong Kong; by Toppan Company Ltd. for Japan; by Addison Wesley Publishing Company for Korea; by Longman Singapore Publishers Ltd. for Singapore, Malaysia, Thailand, and Indonesia; by Unalis Corporation for Taiwan; by WS Computer Publishing Company, Inc. for the Philippines; by WoodsLane Pty. Ltd. for Australia; by WoodsLane Enterprises Ltd. for New Zealand.

For general information on IDG Books Worldwide's books in the U.S., please call our Consumer Customer Service department at 800-762-2974. For reseller information, including discounts and premium sales, please call our Reseller Customer Service department at 800-434-3422.

For information on where to purchase IDG Books Worldwide's books outside the U.S., contact IDG Books Worldwide at 415-655-3021 or fax 415-655-3295.

For information on translations, contact Marc Jeffrey Mikulich, Director, Foreign & Subsidiary Rights, at IDG Books Worldwide, 415-655-3018 or fax 415-655-3295.

For sales inquiries and special prices for bulk quantities, write to the address above or call IDG Books Worldwide at 415-655-3200.

For information on using IDG Books Worldwide's books in the classroom, or ordering examination copies, contact the Education Office at 800-434-2086 or fax 817-251-8174.

For authorization to photocopy items for corporate, personal, or educational use, please contact Copyright Clearance Center, 222 Rosewood Drive, Danvers, MA 01923, or fax 508-750-4470.

Limit of Liability/Disclaimer of Warranty: Author and Publisher have used their best efforts in preparing this book. IDG Books Worldwide, Inc., and Author make no representation or warranties with respect to the accuracy or completeness of the contents of this book and specifically disclaim any implied warranties of merchantability or fitness for any particular purpose and shall in no event be liable for any loss of profit or any other commercial damage, including but not limited to special, incidental, consequential, or other damages.

Trademarks: MS-DOS is a registered trademark of Microsoft Corporation. All brand names and product names used in this book are trademarks, registered trademarks, or trade names of their respective holders. IDG Books Worldwide is not associated with any product or vendor mentioned in this book.

is a trademark under exclusive license to IDG Books Worldwide, Inc., from International Data Group, Inc.

About the Author

Dan Gookin got started with computers back in the post slide rule age of computing: 1982. His first intention was to buy a computer to replace his aged and constantly breaking typewriter. Working as slave labor in a restaurant, however, Gookin was unable to afford the full "word processor" setup and settled on a computer that had a monitor, keyboard, and little else. Soon his writing career was underway with several submissions to fiction magazines and lots of rejections.

The big break came in 1984 when he began writing about computers. Applying his flair for fiction with a self-taught knowledge of computers, Gookin was able to demystify the subject and explain technology in a relaxed and understandable voice. He even dared to add humor, which eventually won him a column in a local computer magazine.

Eventually Gookin's talents came to roost as a ghost writer at a computer book publishing house. That was followed by an editing position at a San Diego computer magazine. During this time, he also regularly participated on a radio talk show about computers. In addition, Gookin kept writing books about computers, some of which became minor bestsellers.

In 1990, Gookin and IDG Books connected on an outrageous book idea: a long overdue and original idea for the computer book for the rest of us. What became *DOS For Dummies* blossomed into an international bestseller with hundreds and thousands of copies in print and many translations.

Today, Gookin still considers himself a writer and computer "guru" whose job it is to remind everyone that computers are not to be taken too seriously. His approach to computers is light and humorous yet very informative. He knows the complex beasts are important and can help people become productive and successful. Gookin mixes his knowledge of computers with a unique, dry sense of humor that keeps everyone informed — and awake. His favorite quote is "Computers are a notoriously dull subject, but that doesn't mean I have to write about them that way."

Gookin's titles for IDG Books include the best-selling *DOS For Dummies*, 1st and 2nd Editions; the *Microsoft MS-DOS 6.2 Upgrade For Dummies*; *WordPerfect For Dummies*, 1st and 2nd Editions; *Word For Windows 6 For Dummies*; *WordPerfect 6 For Dummies*; *PCs For Dummies*, *Word For Windows For Dummies*, and the *Illustrated Computer Dictionary For Dummies*. All told, he's written over 30 books on computers and contributes regularly to *DOS Resource Guide, InfoWorld*, and *PC Computing Magazine*. Gookin holds a degree in Communications from the University of California, San Diego, and currently lives with his wife and boys in the as-yet-untamed state of Idaho.

ABOUT IDG BOOKS WORLDWIDE

Welcome to the world of IDG Books Worldwide.

IDG Books Worldwide, Inc., is a subsidiary of International Data Group, the world's largest publisher of computer-related information and the leading global provider of information services on information technology. IDG was founded more than 25 years ago and now employs more than 7,700 people worldwide. IDG publishes more than 250 computer publications in 67 countries (see listing below). More than 70 million people read one or more IDG publications each month.

Launched in 1990, IDG Books Worldwide is today the #1 publisher of best-selling computer books in the United States. We are proud to have received 8 awards from the Computer Press Association in recognition of editorial excellence and three from Computer Currents' First Annual Readers' Choice Awards, and our best-selling ...*For Dummies*® series has more than 19 million copies in print with translations in 28 languages. IDG Books Worldwide, through a joint venture with IDG's Hi-Tech Beijing, became the first U.S. publisher to publish a computer book in the People's Republic of China. In record time, IDG Books Worldwide has become the first choice for millions of readers around the world who want to learn how to better manage their businesses.

Our mission is simple: Every one of our books is designed to bring extra value and skill-building instructions to the reader. Our books are written by experts who understand and care about our readers. The knowledge base of our editorial staff comes from years of experience in publishing, education, and journalism — experience which we use to produce books for the '90s. In short, we care about books, so we attract the best people. We devote special attention to details such as audience, interior design, use of icons, and illustrations..And because we use an efficient process of authoring, editing, and desktop publishing our books electronically, we can spend more time ensuring superior content and spend less time on the technicalities of making books.

You can count on our commitment to deliver high-quality books at competitive prices on topics you want to read about. At IDG Books Worldwide, we continue in the IDG tradition of delivering quality for more than 25 years. You'll find no better book on a subject than one from IDG Books Worldwide.

John J. Kilcullen

John Kilcullen
President and CEO
IDG Books Worldwide, Inc.

WINNER
Eighth Annual
Computer Press
Awards 1992

WINNER
Ninth Annual
Computer Press
Awards 1993

IDG Books Worldwide, Inc., is a subsidiary of International Data Group, the world's largest publisher of computer-related information and the leading global provider of information services on information technology. International Data Group publishes over 250 computer publications in 67 countries. Seventy million people read one or more International Data Group publications each month. International Data Group's publications include: **ARGENTINA:** Computerworld Argentina, GamePro, Infoworld, PC World Argentina; **AUSTRALIA:** Australian Macworld, Client/Server Journal, Computer Living, Computerworld, Digital News, Network World, PC World, Publishing Essentials, Reseller; **AUSTRIA:** Computerwelt, PC TEST; **BELARUS:** PC World Belarus; **BELGIUM:** Data News; **BRAZIL:** Annuário de Informática, Computerworld Brazil, Connections, Super Game Power, Macworld, PC World Brazil, Publish Brazil, SUPERGAME; **BULGARIA:** Computerworld Bulgaria, Networkworld/Bulgaria, PC & MacWorld Bulgaria; **CANADA:** CIO Canada, ComputerWorld Canada, InfoCanada, Network World Canada, Reseller World; **CHILE:** Computerworld Chile, GamePro, PC World Chile; **COLUMBIA:** Computerworld Colombia, GamePro, PC World Colombia; **COSTA RICA:** PC World Costa Rica/Nicaragua; **THE CZECH AND SLOVAK REPUBLICS:** Computerworld Czechoslovakia, Elektronika Czechoslovakia, PC World Czechoslovakia; **DENMARK:** Communications World, Computerworld Danmark, Macworld Danmark, PC World Danmark, PC World Danmark Supplements, TECH World; **DOMINICAN REPUBLIC:** PC World Republica Dominicana; **ECUADOR:** PC World Ecuador, GamePro; **EGYPT:** Computerworld Middle East, PC World Middle East; **EL SALVADOR:** PC World Centro America; **FINLAND:** MikroPC, Tietoverkko, Tietoviikko; **FRANCE:** Distributique, Golden, Info PC, Le Guide du Monde Informatique, Le Monde Informatique, Reseaux & Telecoms; **GERMANY:** Computer Business, Computerwoche, Computerwoche Extra, Computerwoche Focus, Electronic Entertainment, GamePro, I/M Information Management, Macwelt, PC Welt; **GREECE:** GamePro, Macworld & Publish; **GUATEMALA:** PC World Centro America; **HONDURAS:** PC World Centro America; **HONG KONG:** Computerworld Hong Kong, PCWorld Hong Kong, Publish in Asia; **HUNGARY:** ABCD CD-ROM, Computerworld Szamitastechnika, PC & Mac World Hungary, PC-X Magazine; **INDIA:** Computerworld India, PC World in Asia; **INDONESIA:** InfoKomputer PC World, Komputek Computerworld, Publish in Asia; **IRELAND:** ComputerScope, PC Live!; **ISRAEL:** PC World 32 BIT, People & Computers; **ITALY:** Computerworld Italia, Computerworld Italia Special Editions, Lotus Italia, Macworld Italia, Networking Italia, PC Shopping, PC World Italia, PC World/Walt Disney; **JAPAN:** Macworld Japan, Nikkei Personal Computing, SunWorld Japan, Windows World Japan; **KENYA:** East African Computer News; **KOREA:** Hi-Tech Information/Computerworld, Macworld Korea, PC World Korea; **MACEDONIA:** PC World Macedonia; **MALAYSIA:** Computerworld Malaysia, PC World Malaysia, Publish in Asia; **MEXICO:** Computerworld Mexico, GamePro, Macworld, PC World Mexico; **MYANMAR:** PC World Myanmar; **NETHERLANDS:** Computable, Computer! Totaal, LAN Magazine, Macworld, Net Magazine; **NEW ZEALAND:** Computer Buyer, Computerworld New Zealand, MTB, Network World, PC World New Zealand; **NICARAGUA:** PC World Costa Rica/Nicaragua; **NIGERIA:** PC World Africa; **NORWAY:** Computerworld Norge, Computerworld Privat, CW Rapport Klient/Tjener, CW Rapport Nettverk & Telecom, CW Rapport Offentlig Sektor, IDG's KURSGUIDE, Macworld Norge, Multimedia World, PC World Ekspress, PC World Nettverk, PC World Norge, PC World's Produktguide, Windows Spesial; **PAKISTAN:** Computerworld Pakistan, PC World Pakistan; **PANAMA:** GamePro, PC World Panama; **PARAGUAY:** PC World Paraguay; **P. R. OF CHINA:** China Computerworld, China Infoworld, Computer & Communication, Electronic Product World, Electronics Today, Game Camp, PC World China, Popular Computer Week, Software World, Telecom Product World; **PERU:** Computerworld Peru, GamePro, PC World Profesional Peru, PC World Peru; **POLAND:** Computerworld Poland, Computerworld Special Report, Macworld, Networld, PC World Komputer; **PHILIPPINES:** Computerworld Philippines, PC Digest, Publish in Asia; **PORTUGAL:** Cerebro/PC World, Correio Informático/Computerworld, Mac•In/PC•In Portugal; **PUERTO RICO:** PC World Puerto Rico; **ROMANIA:** Computerworld Romania, PC World Romania, Telecom Romania; **RUSSIA:** Computerworld Rossiya, Network World Russia, PC World Russia; **SINGAPORE:** Computerworld Singapore, PC World Singapore, Publish in Asia; **SLOVENIA:** MONITOR; **SOUTH AFRICA:** Computing S.A., Network World S.A., Software World; **SPAIN:** Computerworld España, COMUNICACIONES WORLD, Dealer World, Macworld España, PC World España; **SWEDEN:** CAP&Design, Computer Sweden, Corporate Computing, MacWorld, Maxi Data, MikroDatorn, Nätverk & Kommunikation, PC/Aktiv, PC World, Windows World; **SWITZERLAND:** Computerworld Schweiz, Macworld Schweiz, PCtip; **TAIWAN:** Computerworld Taiwan, Macworld Taiwan, PC World Taiwan, Publish Taiwan, Windows World; **THAILAND:** Thai Computerworld, Publish in Asia; **TURKEY:** Computerworld Monitör, MACWORLD Turkiye, PC WORLD Turkiye; **UKRAINE:** Computerworld Kiev, Computers & Software Magazine, PC World Ukraine; **UNITED KINGDOM:** Acorn User, Amiga Action, Amiga Computing, Amiga, Appletalk, CD Powerplay, CD-ROM Now, Computing, Connexion, GamePro, Lotus Magazine, Macaction, Macworld, Open Computing, Parents and Computers, PC Home, PC Works, The WEB; **UNITED STATES:** Cable in the Classroom, CD Review, CIO Magazine, Computerworld, Computerworld Client/Server Journal, Digital Video Magazine, DOS World, Electronic, InfoWorld, I-Way, Macworld, Maximize, MULTIMEDIA WORLD, Network World, PC World, PUBLISH, SWATPro Magazine, Video Event, WebMaster; **URUGUAY:** PC World Uruguay; **VENEZUELA:** Computerworld Venezuela, GamePro, PC World Venezuela; and **VIETNAM:** PC World Vietnam
10/17/95

Acknowledgments

I'd like to acknowledge my agents, Matt Wagner (my favorite dramaturge) and Bill Gladstone, for all they've done in promoting my career and putting up with my whining. Also my wife, Sandy, who has to put up with my whining *before* I call Matt.

For IDG Books, I'd like to thank the usual gang: John Kilcullen, David Solomon, Mary "the bee" Bednarek, Tracy Barr, Corbin Collins, Leigh Davis, Jeremy Judson, Shawn MacLaren, Barb Potter, Diane Steele, and Darlene Cunningham.

I'd like to acknowledge the help of Richard A. Spears' *Slang and Euphemism* for providing some of the many synonyms for "gadget" in this book, and Mark Pumm for contributing to the book's accuracy.

To Jordan! To Simon the Boo! To Charlie Schuster too!

(The publisher would like to give special thanks to Patrick McGovern, without whom this book would not have been possible.)

Credits

Senior Vice President and Publisher
Milissa L. Koloski

Associate Publisher
Diane Graves Steele

Brand Manager
Judith A. Taylor

Editorial Managers
Kristin A. Cocks
Mary Corder

Product Development Manager
Mary Bednarek

Editorial Executive Assistant
Richard Graves

Editorial Assistants
Constance Carlisle
Chris Collins
Kevin Spencer

Production Director
Beth Jenkins

Production Assistant
Jacalyn L. Pennywell

Supervisor of Project Coordination
Cindy L. Phipps

Supervisor of Page Layout
Kathie S. Schnorr

Supervisor of Graphics and Design
Shelley Lea

Production Systems Specialist
Steve Peake

Reprint/Blueline Coordination
Tony Augsburger
Patricia R. Reynolds
Theresa Sánchez-Baker

Media/Archive Coordination
Leslie Popplewell
Melissa Stauffer
Michael Wilkey

Project Editor
Tracy L. Barr

Editor
Corbin Collins

Technical Reviewer
Stuart Stuple

Graphics Coordination
Gina Scott
Angela F. Hunckler

Production Page Layout
Valery Bourke
Mary Breidenbach
Sherry Gomoll
Todd Klemme
Drew R. Moore

Proofreaders
Charles A. Hutchinson

Illustrator
Drew R. Moore

Cover Design
Kavish + Kavish

Contents at a Glance

Cartoons at a Glance
By Rich Tennant

Table of Contents

Part III: Batch Files 'n' Stuff *245*

Chapter 17: Batch File Basics 247

Chapter 18: Batch File Command Roundup
(or "Yikes! Where Did I See That Before?") 263

Introduction

• •

*W*elcome to *MORE DOS For Dummies*, a book with more of the stuff you loved so much in the original *DOS For Dummies*. The idea here is that you wanted more information and, being an action-packed subject, DOS was ready for it. (*More* than ready! You should see the truly technical junk we yanked out at the last minute. Ho-boy!)

This book contains not only more information on the basic stuff you read about in *DOS For Dummies*, it also goes beyond the basics to open the door a crack at some of DOS's more quiet and anti-social moments. And it's all done with the same lighthearted, tongue-in-cheek style that's a favorite of millions of readers on planet earth and elsewhere.

About This Book

This book is a reference. Please don't read everything here front to back or cover to cover. Instead, think of a topic that piques your interest. Look it up in the index, turn to that page, and start reading. Every topic has its own section, and no section assumes that you've read anything else in the book. (In fact, if you want more information, you can use the references sprinkled liberally throughout.)

This book is organized into various sections or modules, each of which goes into detail on some DOS topic. The chapters cover general subjects; the sections get specific. Examples of some of the sections you'll find in *MORE DOS For Dummies* include

- ✔ The logic behind naming your hard drive C instead of A
- ✔ "My DOS Prompt Makes Me Want to Vomit!"
- ✔ "Who's the joker who put the BBDBAMEL and BBDBAMFB files in my directory?"
- ✔ The Command Prompt (in All Its Ugliness)
- ✔ Forbidden Information on Macros Named Like DOS Commands
- ✔ Solving AUTOEXEC.BAT Problems
- ✔ Untamed and Wildcards
- ✔ The Real Reason for Batch Files
- ✔ The Bizarre and Technical Nature of Command Line Parameters

Some sections contain tutorials, allowing you to follow along to see how something is done or show how DOS works. Most of the time, the information in each section is packed with useful examples or illustrations of how to get something done, fixed, or made better.

How to Use This Book

Like all *Dummies* books, this is a reference: Look up a topic that interests you — something you've seen in a magazine, a trick someone taught you, or a subject that caught your eye — in the Table of Contents. Turn to that page to read about how it works and see plenty of examples.

If you want to find any cross references or additional information, tips, or helpful hints, just scan over the check marks at the end of each section. Chances are, you'll find what you're looking for — and more.

And because this book is a reference, nearly all terms are defined right in the section they are discussed. If not, I direct you to the section that does define a term — and usually provides even more interesting, useful information.

Technical stuff is always clearly marked so that you can avoid it if it tends to make you ill.

In the tutorial sections and elsewhere, I may tell you to type something in. If you're supposed to type something in, it will appear as follows:

```
C:\>TYPE IN THIS STUFF
```

The DOS prompt appears as shown in the preceding: C:\>. Sometimes this prompt may change, just as it does on your screen. But regardless of what it changes to, it will always be appropriate to the subject of that part of the book. Don't let it freak you.

After you type what you're told to type, always press the Enter key. In case you're baffled, a description of what you're typing usually follows the instruction. More difficult stuff gets detailed explanations.

If you need more information, you'll be directed to the appropriate chapter and section. And if anything goes wrong, you'll be told what to do and how to remedy the situation.

Foolish Assumptions

Here are my assumptions about you:

- ✔ You have a PC. You have DOS. You dislike one or the other, yet you work with them somehow.

- ✔ You have this book's progenitor, *DOS For Dummies*. Quite a few concepts discussed here have more introductory treatment in that book. However, that doesn't mean this book skims over its topics or treats you with any less respect. *MORE DOS For Dummies* builds on *DOS For Dummies*.

- ✔ You have a recent version of DOS, at least version 5.0 or later. (I'm assuming this because, well, we *are* approaching the middle of the decade.) Earlier versions of DOS are covered in this book, but if you're mired with an antique version of DOS, you just can't do all the interesting things discussed here.

How This Book Is Organized

This book has five major sections, each of which is divided into three or more chapters. Inside each chapter are individual sections that pertain, for the most part, to the chapter subject. Aside from that level of organization, the book is really modular. You can start reading at any section. However, thanks to incredible pressure from the Computer Book Writing Guild and Junk Food Cooperative, I've outlined the entire book below:

Part I: The Eternal Game of DOS Futzing

This part of the book contains general information on configuring DOS, specifically the two popular files, CONFIG.SYS and AUTOEXEC.BAT. Other information, such as messing with the DOS prompt and using the DOSKey program, is also presented here. Hey, it's all futzing to me.

Part II: More Stuff

This section contains a few of the items *DOS For Dummies* readers requested more of: More on disks, drives, copying files, deleting, the DIR command, and items of that nature. Instead of technical information, the *more* offered here is in the details; stuff I left out of *DOS For Dummies* for space reasons or because I just wasn't in the mood that day.

Part III: Batch Files 'n' Stuff

The thing *DOS For Dummies* readers wanted more than anything else? Discounts at the book stores! Aside from that, batch files was the subject that came up most often. While batch file programming can be quite techy, this part of the book provides a gentle introduction plus a few chapters on some batch file-related things you may find interesting and even useful.

Part IV: Keeping Your Stuff Organized

DOS urges you to toss files around your hard drive with reckless abandon. Unfortunately, this does nothing for your sanity. This section describes how to best organize stuff on your hard drive. It also tells you how to maintain all your PC's disks so that the File not found error will be a thing of the past.

Part V: Shortcuts and Tips Galore

The book ends with a bunch of interesting suggestions, tips, and a few trick-or-treats. It's a bonus section! Awarded to all the loyal *DOS For Dummies* readers who appreciated the book and wanted *More DOS For Dummies*.

Icons Used in This Book

This alerts you to nerdy technical discussions you may want to skip (or read — for that nerd in all of us).

Any shortcuts or new insights on a topic are marked with this icon.

This icon provides a friendly reminder to do something.

This icon provides a friendly reminder *not* to do something.

A tutorial or step-by-step instructions for accomplishing some task is indicated by this icon.

Where to Go from Here

My advice: Scour the table of contents for what you wanted *more* of in *DOS For Dummies*. It's in here. Otherwise, use the index, or just pick a page and start reading. You're bound to find something that interests you. Remember that this book is modular in nature and everything is cross-referenced.

- ✔ Don't forget to browse the check marks that follow most sections. They contain useful information that shouldn't be overlooked.

- ✔ I apologize in advance for putting way too many tables in this book.

- ✔ This is not the "Dummies guy." He's the "Nerd Guy."

Part I
The Eternal Game of DOS Futzing

The 5th Wave   By Rich Tennant

In this part...

Futzing is from the Yiddish word *futz,* which means, well . . . that's not important right now. Figuratively speaking, to futz means to fool with, to mess with, to fiddle in a hopefully positive manner. This is what you must do when it comes to living with DOS and your PC. No, never is DOS content or happy. There is no Zen to DOS. You can't think positive and expect DOS to follow suit. Just using DOS means the way it behaves changes. To help straighten this bending attitude, you need to futz. And with DOS, the futzing is eternal.

Chapter 1
The Big Picture

Morning for the computer is a terrible thing. Humans, we have to put up with alarm clocks. Computers, they start the day with a jolt of electricity. You flip the switch, and some heavy duty voltage surges through Mr. PC's innards (which may not even be legal in your state). So when it comes time to think of who's in charge, just remember that you start the day being lulled into consciousness by a bleating alarm clock. Computers are electrocuted to life.

This chapter covers the down-and-gritties on how your computer starts its day, specifically how DOS blossoms to life. Bill Gates just doesn't utter "Let there be DOS." No, it's a bit more involved than that. Understanding these subtle nuances and, more importantly, the roles of the key files — COMMAND.COM, CONFIG.SYS, and AUTOEXEC.BAT — is important if you ever expect to know *MORE* about DOS.

The Big Turn-On

Your PC doesn't just exist. It actually comes to life in a series of steps each time you switch on the power. Most of these steps happen quickly; others are painfully slow. Some of the steps you have direct control over (which is why turning on a PC fits into the larger picture of DOS futzing).

To make this process easier to understand, I've divided the steps in which the computer comes to life into the following three stages:

✔ Quicker than you can say "Jack Robinson"

(Who *was* Jack Robinson? I give up. It takes the average person about one second to say it aloud, seven seconds while sedated.)

✔ Painfully slow and questionable acts

✔ DOS rears its ugly head

Just glancing at the following information is okay. Knowing it all in detail isn't important, but knowing what happens when — and how — can help you understand how other chapters in this part of the book fit into the Big Picture.

Quicker than you can say "Jack Robinson"

1. **Event:** The power switch is flipped.

   Comparable human experience: Alarm clock buzzing in ear; small child poking finger in parent's eye.

   What happens: Millions of volts of electricity suddenly come lurching into your PC's brain.

   What it means: The computer is experiencing serious awake-time.

If there isn't any power, obviously the computer won't turn itself on. Actually, the computer's a lot smarter than that. Its power supply — the thing that supplies the computer's guts with the juice — won't turn itself on if you're in a "brownout" or low-power situation.

2. **Event:** The initial "I'm all here" check takes place.

   Comparable human experience: Get out of bed, make sure arms, legs, and head are still attached regardless of the bizarre dream you were just having.

   What happens: The computer does a quick check of its vitals. It checks for the keyboard, microprocessor, monitor, and a few other things not worth mentioning.

   The disk drives also wind up as part of this step. Your hard drive(s) may click once; the floppy disks will make the "uhn-uhn" sound. Maybe you'll hear some chipmunk chatter or maybe some sirens, should a vital component try to escape — nothing out of the ordinary.

   What it means: If anything is missing, the computer either beeps or displays a cryptic message.

The purpose of this stage is to make sure that the computer has all its parts. If anything is missing or awry, an error message is displayed or the computer beeps, explaining the problem in Morse code.

All this happens very quickly — yes, quicker than you can say "Jack Robinson."

Everything so far has happened *before* DOS has loaded. In fact, it's just your own computer running amok at this stage. Your computer doesn't begin to sniff out DOS (which is on *d*isk — where the *D* in DOS comes from) until much later. So blame any boo-boos at this point on your PC manufacturer.

Painfully slow and questionable acts

3. Event: The start-up message appears.

Comparable human experience: Seeing self in mirror; hearing spouse call name; turning on TV to see Willard attempt another weather forecast.

What happens: The computer is okey-dokey so far, so the manufacturer displays the start-up and copyright information on-screen.

What it means: Nothing much. This message just provides distraction because watching a blank screen at this stage tends to make PC users nervous.

The start-up message you see is different for each computer make and model. Something like the following might show up:

```
BlechCo, Inc. Personal Computer Model IX
Copyright (C) 1994 Greed Industries
Messy Entrails 486 BIOS version 0.10
Some portions written by monkeys
```

This message just contains computer model and maker information, plus some copyright dates and version numbers.

4. Event: More checking with the Power-On Self-Test, or *POST,* occurs.

Comparable human experience: Weigh self on scale; inspect face for signs of same self seen last night in same mirror; grumble.

What happens: The computer does a quick inventory of all its memory (this step took forever on older models), and other vital components may perform self-tests. On some models, you may actually see the memory totals tally up. Some video systems display various "tests" on the monitor. Computers in Rumania show young gymnasts on the uneven parallel bars.

What it means: The computer is now making doubly sure everything works properly. This step is a good idea. After all, if something is amiss, it's better to know about it before you start work than be disappointed later.

- In the olden days (okay, back in the early '80s), many computers displayed nothing when you turned them on. They performed the same memory tests and other checks that today's PCs do, but they didn't provide any visual feedback. Often it took a few minutes for you to decide whether your computer was on and working or just being silly.

✔ Memory tests are often painfully slow — especially if you have a lot of memory. On some PCs, you can skip the memory tests by pressing the spacebar. I do this on my laptop to conserve battery power.

✔ 'Nother tip: Refer to Chapter 25 for information on turning off a memory test DOS does when its HIMEM.SYS memory control and domination program runs.

✔ If something is wrong, you'll see an error message displayed on-screen. Write this message down and call your PC hardware tech support hotline.

DOS rears its ugly head

Beep!

The last thing your PC does before it loads DOS is beep once. This beep means everything is okay, and it's actually a happy beep because DOS hasn't been placed into memory and controlling your PC's mind. Yes, it's like the merry Gungas singing down the trail before the evil Sithian warlord erased their memories and made them into toxic waste-guzzling proto-drones.

TECHNICAL STUFF

Stuff you don't need to read about horrible CMOS boo-boos

Sometimes, as the computer starts, you may see a message that claims you have a "checksum" or other type of error. The message may beg you to press the F1 key to continue (or "ignore") or F2 to run your PC's hardware setup program. When this happens, press F2.

What's going on is that your PC's battery backed-up memory needs checking. The memory keeps track of an inventory of your PC's innards: memory totals, disk drives, the date and time, and other stuff. When that battery backed-up memory doesn't match what your computer thinks it has, you see this error message. The error message appears whenever you upgrade, but most often this message may mean the battery has died (especially if your computer has lost track of the date and time). You can solve the problem by replacing the battery, which is something your guru would be more than happy to help with.

5. Event: Your PC attempts to find an operating system.

Comparable human experience: Looking for a pair of pants that fit.

What happens: Out of desperation, your PC begins to look for a control program on one of the computer's disk drives. It looks first to the A floppy drive (which is why you'll hear it crunch after the beep), and then it looks on your C hard drive.

What it means: The computer is dumb by itself and can't do anything (other than its self-test described earlier). It needs a control program. Just like your car needs a human to set the speed and direction and obey most of the traffic laws, your PC needs DOS — or some other operating system — in the driver's seat.

- If DOS isn't found on the floppy drive or hard drive, you'll see an error message. Often this message asks you to `insert DOS diskette` into your A drive and then press Enter. See? The PC is desperately looking for a control program here.

- Some PCs may slip into a *ROM routine,* which is computer talk for some fancy-schmancy program that begs for a DOS disk. Old IBM PCs and Compaq computers used to display the BASIC programming language on-screen. Old Tandy computers just sat there and wept.

- The computer first looks to load an operating system from drive A, primarily with respect to tradition. Before the days of hard drives, PCs just came with one or two floppy drives, A or B. When the hard drive (labeled C) was added, the computer's BIOS was updated to also look there for an operating system. Still, the order is drive A first, then drive C (the hard drive).

6. **Event:** Secret DOS files are loaded.

Comparable human experience: You listen to a subliminal message tape — one that instructs you on how to be a nicer person — on the way to work.

What happens: You see the `Starting MS-DOS` message on-screen. (With versions prior to DOS 6, you didn't see squat, and the disk drives just merrily churned away.)

What it means: The secret DOS files form the core of DOS. There are two of these files, which you can read about in the techy note nearby, if you're so inclined. The files' names are MSDOS.SYS and IO.SYS. If you're using PC DOS, an earlier version of MS-DOS, or Compaq DOS, then the files are named IBMDOS.COM and IBMBIO.COM. The important thing to remember here is that these two files are DOS's guts and vital to your PC's operation. Under no circumstances should you ever delete them from your disk.

The secret files are "invisible" on your disk, meaning that the DIR command doesn't display them (unless you do some serious arm twisting). However, you can finagle Windows or the DOS Shell program (or PC Shell or Norton or . . .) to display them. If you do display these files, don't delete them. They're important. Without them, the PC just won't start DOS.

Tedious material on how DOS is loaded

When a disk is found, the PC loads the first infinitesimal inch or so of the disk into memory. That first part of the disk is called the *boot sector*. It's actually a tiny program that does one of two things:

- If the disk doesn't contain DOS, the tiny boot sector program displays the `Non-system disk or disk error` error message. That's it.

- If the disk is a DOS disk, then the tiny program works to load DOS's secret file, named MSDOS.SYS (which may also be called IBMDOS.COM).

Or

If you're using DOS's DoubleSpace program (which, by the way, is not included in MS-DOS 6.21), a secret file named DBLSPACE.BIN, which does some disk compression magic, is loaded from disk, and then the file MSDOS.SYS (or IBMDOS.COM) is loaded from disk.

Why the teensy boot sector program? Because your computer is capable of running operating systems other than DOS. If your computer just ran DOS, then you couldn't chicken out and go with OS/2 or UNIX or any of the other zany operating systems that can run on any PC. By using a boot sector, the PC remains flexible — at least, that's the hope of everyone involved.

Stuff only a nerd would appreciate about the MSDOS.SYS and IO.SYS files

The file MSDOS.SYS is called the *DOS kernel*. Its job is to set up DOS on your computer and get the ball rolling. MSDOS.SYS is actually a program (like a COM or EXE program), and it controls the next few steps DOS takes to start on your PC.

The second file, IO.SYS, contains fundamental DOS stuff: it keeps track of the date and time, stores information on disk, and does other typical, boring DOS stuff that you'll never have to worry about unless Bill Gates phones you up and wants you to work for him as a DOS programmer at Microsoft.

Why not one file? Originally, DOS was designed to run on multiple computers, some of which weren't compatible with the original IBM PC. The IO.SYS file would be customized for each of those different systems. Since then, all computers are more or less IBM PC-compatible; however, the dual nature of DOS's secret start-up programs (some would call it schizophrenia) remains.

7. **Event:** CONFIG.SYS configures the system.

> **Comparable human experience:** Mother dresses you.

> **What happens:** You'll see some stuff displayed on the screen: some start-up messages and possibly other information that looks potentially serious but scrolls by too fast to be overtly threatening.

What it means: The CONFIG.SYS file contains instructions that tell DOS about your computer. There are two types of instructions: those that tell DOS how much memory it can use for working with disk drives and other esoteric items and those instructions that tell DOS how to control any strange *devices* that may have attached themselves to your PC.

- The CONFIG.SYS file contains special instructions that tell DOS how to configure itself.

- Chapters 6 through 8 dwell on the subject of CONFIG.SYS at great length.

- For what it's worth, it's the MSDOS.SYS program that hunts down the CONFIG.SYS file and obeys the instructions held therein.

8. Event: The DOS command processor takes over.

Comparable human experience: Finally at work, you start obeying the unwritten laws of human nature and play nice with the other kids.

What happens: The *command processor* is a fancy name for the COMMAND.COM program. This program produces the DOS prompt and is responsible for running your programs and carrying our DOS's most essential and secret commands.

What it means: You don't really talk to DOS when you use a PC. Instead, you talk with a program that takes your instructions and converts them into the basic grunts and squawks that the computer can understand. Translating your instructions is the role of the command processor, named COMMAND.COM on your disk.

- The command processor is a program that provides a *user interface* between you and DOS. Supposedly, the purpose of the user interface is to make life easier by allowing you to type in commands such as COPY and RENAME and FDISK instead of stuff that could be even more cryptic — and that's a really scary thought.

- Another name for the command processor, COMMAND.COM, is the *shell.* Like a sea shell protects gooey and highly edible creatures from aquatic predators, the COMMAND.COM shell protects you from the wilds of the computer.

- The command processor is also called the *command interpreter* because it interprets your commands for DOS itself and translates your whims into orders (most of the time).

- In DOS, the command processor is named COMMAND.COM. Do not delete this file! It's your only method of communicating your intentions to DOS.

9. Event: The AUTOEXEC.BAT file runs.

Comparable human experience: You have a to-do list and you actually have the time and motivation to do everything on that list.

What happens: A bunch of DOS commands or programs are run automatically when DOS starts. You see the results of this on your screen: lots of copyright messages and other mysterious stuff appears, and maybe some programs automatically pop up in your face.

What it means: Anything that's done automatically every time you start your PC is done by a special command in your AUTOEXEC.BAT file. For example, if Windows or a menu system always comes up when you first start your PC, it's because the command that starts Windows or displays a menu was placed inside the AUTOEXEC.BAT file.

- The purpose of the AUTOEXEC.BAT file is to have the computer *auto*matically *exec*ute a bunch of DOS commands each time it starts. The AUTOEXEC.BAT file saves you the trouble of having to repeatedly type the commands yourself — and saving time and preventing redundancy are what computers are all about.

- You can find detailed information on the AUTOEXEC.BAT file in Chapters 9 and 10.

- A bunch of DOS commands or program names stored in a file is called a *batch file*. Bunch = batch. Information on batch files is found in Part III of this book.

- If your system doesn't have an AUTOEXEC.BAT file, then DOS does one of two things when it starts. It either displays a copyright notice and then the command prompt, or it displays the copyright notice, asks you to enter the date and time, and then displays the command prompt.

Read this only if you're frustrated by the differences between CONFIG.SYS and AUTOEXEC.BAT

Both the CONFIG.SYS and AUTOEXEC.BAT files configure your system, so it's easy to confuse them. Each has its duties and plays a specific role in the way your PC starts. And the reason you should bother with this information is that it's up to you — yes, you sitting there reading this — to govern what goes into the CONFIG.SYS and AUTOEXEC.BAT files on your computer.

CONFIG.SYS's role in life is to tell DOS three things: how memory is used in the computer, how to deal with the disk drives, and whether to load special control programs called *drivers* for any extra goodies your PC may have. (Mice, tape backups, scanners, sound cards, CD-ROMs, and so on are examples of extra goodies.)

AUTOEXEC.BAT's role is primarily for convenience. Basically, it contains a list of commands that you would otherwise have to manually type in each time your PC starts. Unlike CONFIG.SYS, AUTOEXEC.BAT is designed to save you time and help you get started with whatever it is you do with your computer.

If you still have trouble knowing which is which, keep in mind that CONFIG.SYS's duties come first, when the computer is starting up. You need CONFIG.SYS to do its thing — manage memory and hook up your mouse and other goodies — before DOS is fully awake. The stuff AUTOEXEC.BAT does (like running start-up programs) comes later.

The computer starts when you flip the power switch, and the whole start-up shebang doesn't end until you see the command prompt:

```
C:\>
```

From that point on, you work. You tell DOS to do something, run a program, fiddle and play. When you're done, you turn the computer off.

The quick-and-dirty summary

Here, in the most basic of steps and in abbreviated form, is how your PC starts and loads DOS. This sequence happens every time you turn on (or reset) the computer:

1. The computer does its self-check.

2. The computer tries to load an operating system from disk.

3. DOS starts loading.

4. The commands stored in the CONFIG.SYS file are obeyed and other instructions are followed.

5. The command processor, COMMAND.COM, takes over.

6. The instructions held in the AUTOEXEC.BAT file are obeyed.

7. The command prompt appears and DOS is ready to play.

The big lesson to be learned here is that you have direct control over the results of two of the preceding steps. Both CONFIG.SYS and AUTOEXEC.BAT are files you can create and modify. By using them both correctly, you'll be happier with your PC; by understanding their roles, you'll avoid a lot of frustration that most DOS users suffer from.

The *important* point here is not to accidentally delete any of these files, including the "invisible" files MSDOS.SYS and IO.SYS. If these files go bye-bye, your PC won't start.

Easily forgettable optional titles for each of the seven steps

Here are the "nerd names" for some of the terms listed in this section:

1. The computer's self-check is called the *POST* (pronounced as in *deaf as a*). POST stands for Power-On Self-Test, the fancy term for "self check."

2. The computer loading an operating system from disk is referred to as the *bootstrap*. This is where the phrase *boot the computer* comes from. Essentially, the itty-bitty programs that load DOS "pull the PC up by its bootstraps." (You know, I'm really sick of that metaphor. How about, "The PC gets the tar kicked out of it by a boot." That sounds much more satisfying.)

3. DOS starts loading by running two files: MSDOS.SYS is called the *kernel* and IO.SYS is the *DOS BIOS*. No point in dwelling on these terms any further.

4. The CONFIG.SYS file is just CONFIG.SYS. Nothing new here.

5. The COMMAND.COM file is called the *command processor, command interpreter,* or sometimes even the *DOS shell.*

6. The AUTOEXEC.BAT is just AUTOEXEC.BAT (no fancy geek speak).

7. The command prompt is no more beautiful in the eyes of computer programmers. In fact, they often change the way their prompts look to sate their techno-power lusts.

And . . . On Turning the Computer Off

The computer starts its day when you flip the power switch. After you see the command prompt $(C:\>)$ on the screen, you work. You tell DOS to do something, you run a program, you finish the task you started yesterday, and then, when you're done, you turn the computer off.

You should turn the computer off only when you see the DOS prompt. That's because when the DOS prompt appears, DOS is *idle*. It sits and spins, toils not. At that point, it's safe to switch off the computer and put it to bed.

- ✔ Quit your programs and return to the delightful DOS prompt before switching off Mr. PC.

- ✔ Never ever turn off the computer when the disk drive light is on or blinking. Wait.

> ✔ There is a school of thought that you should leave the computer on all the time. I do. This does increase your electrical bill a teeny bit, but more importantly, it increases the life span of your computer a whole lot. Do, however, switch off the monitor when you're away from the PC. And if you're going to be away for an extended period of time (more than a weekend), then it's okay to switch off the computer. Otherwise, I recommend leaving it on all the time.

All them files on disk is DOS (very optional reading)

To come alive on your computer, DOS requires a handful of files. They're listed below, along with a technical explanation of each.

More information on file types is found in Chapter 11. Note that you have direct control over the CONFIG.SYS and AUTOEXEC.BAT files. That information is covered in Chapters 6 and 9. The other three files — MSDOS.SYS, IO.SYS, and COMMAND.COM — are very important to DOS. And the DoubleSpace files are important if you're using that program (MS-DOS 6.21 doesn't include DoubleSpace). You should never delete any of these files. If you do, your PC just won't start.

File name	File Type	What It Does
MSDOS.SYS	Program	Loads DOS on your PC
IO.SYS	Program	DOS's guts, the main DOS program
DBLSPACE.INI	Text	DoubleSpace (disk compression) information file (only needed if you use DoubleSpace)
DBLSPACE.BIN	Program	DoubleSpace control program (only needed if you use DoubleSpace)
CONFIG.SYS	Text	Configures memory and disk drives; loads special control programs called *device drivers*
COMMAND.COM	Program	Command processor; displays the DOS prompt and carries out various commands
AUTOEXEC.BAT	Text	Automatically runs DOS commands and programs each time you start the PC

Chapter 2
Messing with the DOS Prompt

• •

In This Chapter

▶ Looking at the command prompt

▶ Typing commands

▶ Fun keys at the command prompt

▶ Clearing the screen (without electrocution)

• •

DOS is dumb, dumb, dumb. Never for an instant think that DOS is smart or that your computer has some sort of cold, calculating intelligence. Nope, DOS is dumb. A case in point is the command prompt, where you type instructions for DOS to digest. Sometimes it looks like a grouping of random characters or, perhaps, some optical illusion. Is it supposed to be friendly, informative, what? In any case, the nice thing about the command prompt — and what you type there — is that it can be changed.

All basic DOS futzing begins with the command prompt. It doesn't need to be the boring C:\> or even the more dreadful C>. No, the prompt can be just about anything you want it to be. It can even be something else entirely (like Windows, for example). This chapter covers your basic DOS command prompt futzing.

The Command Prompt (in All Its Ugliness)

Figure 2-1 illustrates the command prompt, along with the various pieces and parts you may see on your screen. Confirm that your screen looks something like the prompt in the figure. You can also confirm that your command prompt *does not* look like Figure 2-2, which is what most people imagine they see when they first look at DOS.

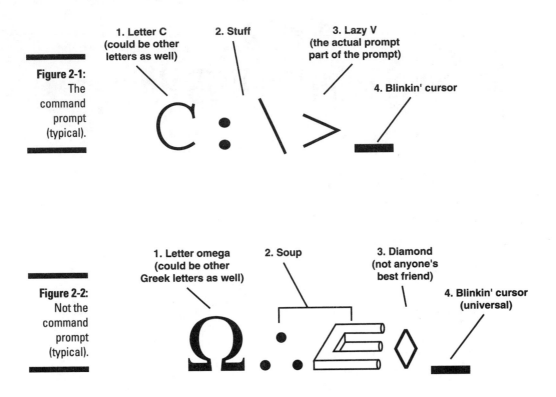

Figure 2-1:
The command prompt (typical).

1. **Letter C** (could be other letters as well)
2. **Stuff**
3. **Lazy V** (the actual prompt part of the prompt)
4. **Blinkin' cursor**

Figure 2-2:
Not the command prompt (typical).

1. **Letter omega** (could be other Greek letters as well)
2. **Soup**
3. **Diamond** (not anyone's best friend)
4. **Blinkin' cursor** (universal)

Please note the following items from Figure 2-1:

1. **Letter C**

   This letter may be some other letter, A through Z, but most often it's a C. The letter, C in this case, is how DOS tells you which disk drive you're using; in Figure 2-1 the poor hapless soul is using drive C.

2. **Stuff**

   What you see after the letter could be anything. Most often you'll see a colon and then a backslash. Sometimes — and this is totally arbitrary, depending on the fluctuation of Microsoft's stock price — you'll see more stuff in the Stuff section. This is the DOS *path*, which tells you which part of your disk drive you're using.

3. Lazy V

Actually, it's a "greater-than" symbol, the traditional computer prompt that translates as "type something here."

4. Blinkin' cursor

The cursor shows you where the stuff you type will appear on-screen. It blinks. Blink, blink, blink.

Your command prompt — the one you see on-screen — may look different from Figure 2-1. (Heck, you may be really unfortunate and see what's shown in Figure 2-2!) The ugliness isn't DOS being surly. No, a strange or unique-looking command prompt just means that someone else has bothered to change the way it looks. Yes, changing the command prompt is possible, and quite harmless, to do.

✔ The command prompt is also called the *DOS prompt*. Some people also call it *the prompt*. Prompt in this case has nothing to do with being on time.

✔ You use the command prompt to communicate with DOS. It's where you type commands for DOS to carry out and where you start programs and run applications.

✔ DOS names its disk drives after famous letters, A through Z. Refer to Chapter 15 for more information on disk drives and their letters.

✔ The *path*, which is often found in the middle part of the command prompt (between the letter and the > symbol) tells you which part of a disk drive you're using. Detailed information on the path is nestled in Chapter 16, which is required reading in this book.

✔ The best part about all these doodads — the things you see in your command prompt — is that they can be changed. Instructions are offered in the next chapter.

✔ The command prompt is produced by the COMMAND.COM program. When you type something at the prompt and press Enter, COMMAND.COM first converts all of what you typed into uppercase (ALL CAPS), checks it for special characters (such as >, <, or |), and then carries out the command. Refer to Chapter 20 for more information on the >, <, and | symbols and how they're used at the command prompt.

Typing Commands

DOS doesn't pay attention to anything you type until you press the Enter key on your keyboard. This step is important to remember, especially for lazy typists. You can type anything at the command prompt and DOS wouldn't mind — or care — until you press the Enter key.

Try typing the following, but don't press the Enter key:

```
C:\>EXPLODE LIKE A MILLION FIRECRACKERS
```

Obviously, this command is not one to take lightly, lest for some bizarre reason the computer suddenly decides to take you literally. The reason you can get away with this potential brush with fate (as well as typing in insults and questioning the computer's parentage) is that DOS won't hear your command until you press Enter.

If you do press Enter — and here is the dumb part — DOS won't understand what you typed. It will say something like:

```
Bad command or file name
```

This is DOS-speak for "huh?" Nothing nasty, just a basic "I don't understand you" in the charming way DOS does things.

Here's my point: Although DOS is fussy about what you type, you get an eternity — or until you press the Enter key — to change your mind and even *edit* your command (which is covered in the next section).

✔ What you type — the command — isn't heard by DOS until you press the Enter key. This is akin to God not hearing a prayer until you say "Amen," though the religious leaders I've consulted with tell me that's not the case when conversing with the Almighty.

✔ The thing you type *at* is the command prompt or DOS prompt. *What* you type is the command line.

✔ Watching what you type is important, but you don't have to pay much attention until just before you press Enter. If you check the command first, you'll have time to backspace and re-edit the command, if necessary. Then press Enter, and DOS will understand you. Hopefully.

✔ If you do type an insult (or something like the "explode" preceding command), just press the Escape key, marked Esc on your keyboard, to erase the command and start over.

✔ `Bad command or file name` errors happen when you mistype something. But don't be too quick to blame yourself. You know what you want; DOS is just slow on the uptake. Often, comparing what you actually typed with what you wanted to type yields the solution. Just try again at the next command prompt.

✔ So what does the "bad" mean in `Bad command or file name`? Does it mean *rotten?* Perhaps *naughty?* Maybe even *foul smelling and beyond reproach?* The point is, DOS doesn't understand. Your intent may be good, but DOS — in its callous little way — tells you you're bad. And that's too bad.

✔ How long is the command line? DOS lets you type up to 127 characters after the command prompt. Type any more and the PC *beeps* at you. (Okay, the DOS nerd purists claim that the true number is 128 characters. But that 128th "character" must be Enter. Any other key and *beep!*) This information is for trivial purposes only. No one in his right mind would have you type 127 characters at the DOS prompt (though I did it just to test this theory).

Editing what you type

Because DOS doesn't pay attention to your instructions until you press the Enter key, you have lots of time to change your mind or edit what you type. You use two main keys to edit: Backspace and Escape (Esc).

Fortunately, most of the things you type at the command prompt are short. Short means that editing them isn't an involved process. For example, to change the common typo DRI to the intended DIR command, you press the Backspace key and replace the RI with IR:

1. You type DRI when you mean to type DIR.

   ```
   C:\>DRI_
   ```

2. The cursor blinks after the I. Press Backspace once:

   ```
   C:\>DR_
   ```

No need to bother with this completely weird command line stuff

The command you type doesn't need to come right after the prompt. You can start any DOS command or program by typing one or more spaces or pressing the Tab key. For example,

```
C:\>DIR
```

is the same as

```
C:\> DIR
```

DOS ignores the leading spaces (or tab). In some instances, you can even start the line with a single equal sign:

```
C:\>=DIR
```

Any more than one equal sign and DOS pukes. I don't know why this is. It just is. Weird.

3. The I is erased. Press Backspace again:

```
C:\>D_
```

4. The R is erased. Now, type **IR** to make the complete DIR command:

```
C:\>DIR_
```

5. Press Enter to send the command to DOS for interpretation or ridicule.

   Unfortunately, most DOS commands are of the cryptic variety, which means you can never be quite sure you got it right until you press Enter to see whether it works.

   ✔ You can use the Backspace key to back up and erase your command. Backspace will gobble up the character to the left of the blinking cursor, moving the cursor back one "space."

   ✔ If you press and hold the Backspace key, the whole line gets erased.

   ✔ The Escape key (Esc) is used to erase the whole dang doodle command line and let you start over again. DOS usually displays a \ (backslash) character, and you start over on the next line. For example

```
C:\>DRI\

    _
```

   (The cursor sits below the D in the preceding line, at the "start" of a new line.) In some situations, pressing Escape may just erase the line, and no backslash is displayed.

```
C:\>_
```

   Don't let the inconsistency vex you.

   ✔ There's a whole hairy hoard of function keys you can use to edit the command line, although few people bother (see the sidebar "Other command line editing keys no one ever uses"). An advantage of knowing these keys is that you can use them when creating files with the COPY CON command in the old Edlin text editor and at other times. Refer to Chapter 13 for information on COPY CON.

Re-entering commands

The computer is a device that's supposed to ease drudgery, so anything you do with a computer that seems repetitive need not be that way. As a case in point, often you'll need to repeat a DOS command over and over. There are several ways to accomplish this task, three of which are listed here:

Other command line editing keys no one ever uses

There are other editing keys in addition to Backspace and Escape. I would go to the trouble of demonstrating them here, but the point is that no one ever uses them. Seriously, using them makes about as much sense as Granny wearing roller blades with her walker.

Because this book is supposed to be for intermediate-to-advanced users, I'm forced to list these editing keys here. I can't help it; it's a union-thing.

Key(s)	Function
F1, →	Move the cursor forward, displaying the next character in the template
F2,*n*	Display all the characters in the template, up to character *n*
F3	Redisplay the whole template all at once, thank you
F4,*n*	Delete all the characters in the template, up to character *n*
F5	Erase the template and start over

The big problem with using these keys is that you can't "see" what you're editing. DOS stores your previous command in a thing call the *template*. Yet, although DOS knows it's there, you can't see it; any text you "edit" is invisible on-screen.

The true solution to editing the command line is to use a handy utility called DOSKey. It's covered in Chapter 4.

✔ Retype the command.

This is the old, boring way of doing things. Yes, it works. But it doesn't save you all that time promised in the computer's brochure.

✔ Use the right-arrow key (→) or the F1 key.

These two keys perform the same function; they redisplay the previous DOS command line one character at a time.

To wit, type in the following command:

```
C:\>SHIFT
```

Press Enter. The SHIFT command does nothing, so nothing will happen. But after you press Enter, you'll see another command prompt:

```
C:\>
```

To repeat the same command — or any DOS command — press the F1 key:

```
C:\>S
```

You'll see the first letter of the previous command. Press the F1 key again (or press the → key instead — same thing) and you'll see the next letter, then the next, and the next again. Press and hold F1 to see the remainder of the command:

```
C:\>SHIFT
```

Press Enter, and you've retyped the same command again in a less-painful manner than by manually hunting and pecking for each key a second time.

✔ Use the handy F3 key.

This method is the best for retyping a command — no typing involved or woodpeckering of the F1 or → keys. Just press F3 at any command prompt, and you see the last command you typed. Press Enter and — zap! — DOS does the same thing all over again. Quick, convenient, and easy to do if you remember that the F3 key is the key to press.

✔ The F3 key automatically retypes the last DOS command. Press F3 and Enter, and DOS does it again.

✔ If you could create a stack of dollar bills equal to the size of the U.S. debt, you'd probably be able to get at least a $10,000 grant out of it.

Fun Keys at the Command Prompt

There is absolutely no reason you should know that your keyboard can do many more tricks than most human fingers will allow. For example, did you know that you can press the Enter key without ever touching it? Try this:

1. Type the following command at the DOS prompt:

```
C:\>DIR
```

Type **DIR**, but don't press the Enter key. Instead,

2. Press Ctrl-M.

Press and hold the Ctrl (Control) key and then tap the M key. It's like pressing Shift-M to get a capital *M,* though you're using the Ctrl key in place of Shift. Release both keys.

3. It worked just like the Enter key!

Yup. That's because Ctrl-M and the Enter key both *generate* the same character, which is called by the compu-jockeys *code 13.* So you can either use Ctrl-M or the Enter key at the DOS prompt, which is handy to know if you ever break or lose your right pinky. Otherwise, file this away under Useless Keyboard Stuff.

- Ctrl-M equals the Enter key. Cool.

- Ctrl-I equals the Tab key. Go ahead and try it at the DOS prompt: Type something and then press Tab. Press Ctrl-I, and you'll get another tab. Interesting.

- The Control key doppleganger for the Esc (Escape) key is Ctrl-[. That's the Ctrl key and the left bracket character, found near the P key on your keyboard.

- The Backspace key is duplicated by Ctrl-H, just in case you really did sever your pinky and needed a replacement key combo for that too.

- Having nothing to do with any of this, another fun key is Ctrl-T, which can only be used with the DOSKEY command covered in Chapter 4.

The ever-ready cancel key

DOS's cancel key is Ctrl-C or Ctrl-Break. Both key combinations are essentially the same. During my recent dealings with Microsoft, though, they told me that Ctrl-Break was better. Whatever. I use Ctrl-C.

The C in Ctrl-C means *cancel.* The command cancels any DOS command in action, or it forces DOS to ignore a command line and start over — just like pressing the Esc key. But unlike pressing the Esc key, you get another prompt.

Technically speaking, Ctrl-C (or Ctrl-Break) is the *Break* key. Why they spell it that way and not *brake* is beyond me. Anyhoo, DOS can occasionally be ignorant about the Ctrl-C key press. For example, DOS only pays attention to Ctrl-C when it's either reading something from the keyboard or writing something on-screen. In between those times, such as when DOS is reading or writing the disk, it ignores Ctrl-C. This condition can be bad, as anyone who's ever had a panic-driven motivation to stop the FORMAT command has discovered. To remedy this situation, you can use the BREAK command, covered in the next section.

Other fun keys to read about

Dickey. Donkey. Flunkey. Hickey. Hockey. Hokey. Honkey. Hookey. Jockey. Lackey. Latchkey. Malarkey. Mickey. Monkey. Okey-dokey. Passkey. Smokey. Turkey. Turnkey. Whiskey.

The BREAK command, covered in this section

The BREAK command is a real foot-stomper. It's a "pay attention, now" command as far as DOS is concerned. It tells DOS to keep a sharp eye on the keyboard for that event-stopping Ctrl-C key, allowing you to instantly halt nearly everything DOS does.

Type the following:

```
C:\>BREAK
```

Typed by itself, the BREAK command causes your computer to break. Just kidding. It displays one of two messages. You'll see either BREAK is on or BREAK is off. This tells you whether DOS's Ctrl-C eyeball is open or shut.

To switch on the hyperactive Ctrl-C keyboard monitoring, type the following command:

```
C:\>BREAK ON
```

Press Enter and DOS replies with . . . nothing! But when you type the BREAK command by itself again, you'll see the BREAK is on message displayed.

```
C:\>BREAK
BREAK is on
```

Having "break on" means that DOS will be attentive to your Ctrl-C desires. But it also means that your PC will run a bit slower at the DOS prompt. So when you feel a long stress-free stretch of work approaching, you can switch the break off with the following command:

```
C:\>BREAK OFF
```

Again, DOS responds with empty screen space when you press Enter. Type the BREAK command by itself at the next DOS prompt to ensure that break is, indeed, off:

```
C:\>BREAK
BREAK is off
```

> ✔ Most users don't bother with the BREAK command. However, if you have a fast PC, the slowdown induced by *break on* isn't noticeable. So leave it on if you like.
>
> ✔ The BREAK command has no effect when you run programs like Windows.
>
> ✔ Chapter 8 discusses the BREAK configuration command, which can be used in the mysterious CONFIG.SYS file.

Printing DOS commands and everything

The last fun key you can use at the DOS prompt is Ctrl-P, which is pronounced "control pee" as in what a bed wetter is constantly attempting. To try out Ctrl-P, do the following:

1. Turn on your printer.

   Make sure that your printer is stocked with paper and ready to print. This is important.

2. Press Ctrl-P.

   Press and hold the Ctrl (Control) key and type a **P** — just like you'd use the Shift and P keys to get a capital P. Release both keys.

3. Nothing happens.

   Well, not really. What you've just done activates DOS's "printer toggle." Ctrl-P is an on-off switch that tells DOS to display information on-screen and print that information on your printer.

4. Type the DIR command.

   ```
   C:\>DIR
   ```

   Press Enter. You'll see the DIR command's output on-screen as well as on the printer (see the following Tip if you have a laser printer).

   The stuff on-screen will continue to be printed until you press Ctrl-P again.

5. Press Ctrl-P again.

   This time the key combo shuts off the printing.

> ✔ This trick is a great one to use any time you need a transcript of your DOS activities.
>
> ✔ Don't forget to turn off printing with Ctrl-P; press it a second time to turn it off.
>
> ✔ Ctrl-P only prints what DOS displays, not the output from any of your programs. If the printer stops printing, DOS isn't in charge any more and something else — some other program — is running on your computer.

- If you have a laser printer, you won't see anything until a full sheet of paper has been printed. Laser printers don't tease you by printing one line at a time. To eject a sheet of paper before that happens, press your printer's *Eject* or *Form Feed* button. (You may have to take the computer off-line first; press the On-line or Select button to do so.)

- A command that both turns something on and off is called a *toggle*. Press Ctrl-P once to turn on printing, again to turn it off, again to turn it on again, and so on.

Cleaning the Screen without Risking Electrocution from Windex Dripping Down inside Your Monitor

Everyone commits DOS boo-boos from time to time. Occasionally, on a bad DOS day, you'll have a screen full of error messages and other nasty signs of DOS disaster. To unclutter the screen, I offer the CLS command.

```
C:\>CLS
```

Type **CLS** and press Enter; your screen clears. You are faced with a new, "blank" screen that you can quickly fill with more error messages if you like.

- CLS is pronounced See-El-Ess. Do not pronounce it *Kliss*.

- CLS probably stands for CLear the Screen. Or in French, *clear le screen*.

- After you type CLS, the contents of the screen are "wiped away," and you'll see another command prompt and blinking cursor— anxiously awaiting your next command — at the top of the screen .

- Even though CLS clears the screen, it's still a good idea to occasionally take a soft cloth and wipe away the *pixel dust* that accumulates on all PC monitors. If you must use Windex or another glass cleaner, spray it on the cloth first and then wipe your monitor. No, you don't have to turn off the monitor first. Just be careful and use a wee amount of Windex.

TECHNICAL STUFF

Only read this if you have an old, decrepit version of DOS

Some old, old versions of DOS erase the command line if you press Ctrl-U. This key combo does what the Esc key does, but it doesn't display the backslash character. Instead, the entire line gets erased, and you get to start over.

Newer versions of DOS display the thing when you press Ctrl-U. Ctrl-Y? Ctrl-I don't know.

Chapter 3
Changing the Dreary Prompt

• •

In This Chapter

▶ Changing the prompt

▶ Using the dollar-sign thingies

▶ Trying out the various prompts

▶ Amazing ANSI.SYS prompt (but not in this chapter)

• •

*I*t's not so much what you do at the prompt, but the prompt itself that can be a source of pain. Face it, it's ugly. I'm certain some doting programmer at Microsoft first created the repugnant little cuss and went around to show his peers. Shocked and appalled, they gazed at the screen. Swallowing hard, they commented, "It's just lovely, Bob." Then they plastered fake smiles on their faces, daintily minced out of the cubicle, and then dashed off to the head for a quick call to Uncle Ralph on the Big White Phone. Yeah, it probably went something like that.

Fortunately for all of us, that DOS programmer's supervisor insisted on adding a special command to change the prompt. He probably said something like, "Bob, it's great. What more can I say? But, hey, some people just don't appreciate art. What say you dream up a command — like a Prompt command — wherein those philistines can devise their own prompts? Huh, Bob? C'mon, be a sport!" And, lo, you have the topic of this chapter: the Prompt command and making the prompt look different. Better, sometimes.

My DOS Prompt Makes Me Want to Vomit!

The command prompt need not be eternally ugly. DOS tries its best to give you an informative command prompt automatically. For example,

```
C:\DOS>
```

The preceding command prompt not only shows you where on the screen to type the next DOS command, but it also tells you that you're *logged to* drive C and *using* the subdirectory named DOS. (Chapters 15 and 16 clue you in to the importance of those two items.)

```
D:\WP60\SPELLER>
```

The above prompt tells you that you're using drive D and the subdirectory \WP60\SPELLER. This is informative, albeit cryptic to anyone who's unfamiliar with drive and subdirectory concepts.

- ✔ You can change your prompt to almost anything using the Prompt command, covered in the next section.

- ✔ Drive letters and such are covered in Chapter 15; subdirectories are found in Chapter 16. Yes, you'll really appreciate the prompt even more after reading those two chapters.

Changing the look of the DOS prompt ("You really do look fifty years younger!")

To change the way your command prompt looks, you use the PROMPT command. It works like this: You type **prompt** followed by a space, and then type in what you want to see as your command prompt. For example,

```
C:\>PROMPT You rang?
```

The preceding command changes the prompt to read as follows:

```
You rang?
```

You can type just about any text after the PROMPT command to have that text as your DOS prompt. Here are some dandies I just thought up over a latté and chocolate biscotti. Please type them in to see how they affect your DOS prompt (if you like, and I'm not ordering you here — just a gentle suggestion — for fun):

```
PROMPT Now what?
PROMPT I promise to do this next:
PROMPT You again?
PROMPT Ready!
PROMPT Yes, Master?
PROMPT ?
PROMPT Huh?
```

Type in any of these commands to change your prompt accordingly, or be creative and think of your own clever prompt. Hey, use words they won't let me print in this book — stuff that will send the li'l old ladies shopping at Sam's Club into spinning conniption fits!

✔ The preceding PROMPT ? example is really silly: a single question mark, which isn't informative or friendly. Yet, that was the command prompt most users were faced with in the early, cro-magnon days of personal computing.

✔ Typing the PROMPT command by itself changes the DOS prompt to the old boring C> prompt. Try this for a major yawner, and then keep futzing with the PROMPT command to create something way more interesting.

✔ You cannot type the following characters as part of your new DOS prompt:

$ Dollar sign

= Equal sign

| The vertical bar/pipe thing

> Greater-than

< Less-than

The $ is used by the PROMPT command for something special, as shown in the next section. The other symbols are used by DOS for what's called *I/O redirection*, which is covered in Chapter 20.

✔ To make the prompt you create permanent, put a copy of the fancy PROMPT command into your PC's AUTOEXEC.BAT file. Refer to Chapter 10 for information on how to make a prompt permanent.

The prompt you create is stored in DOS's *environment*. Refer to Chapter 19 if you want to be bored by the environment.

The PROMPT command's dollar-sign characters

Text is okay as part of your command prompt. A *DOS For Dummies* fan wrote me a letter exclaiming how hilarious he thought it was to have DOS come at him with this prompt every day:

```
What is thy bidding?
```

This prompt puts the PC in its place but doesn't really grab you the way the PROMPT command can — providing you know about the secret *dollar-sign characters* and how to use them. But first a few soothing words of advice:

- Dollar-sign characters allow you to insert nifty things into your prompt — to really jazz it up, if that's your desire.
- There's no need to memorize the dollar-sign characters or what they do.

The dollar-sign characters allow you to put more than plain text into your command prompt. By using the dollar-sign characters, you can also have DOS display such interesting things as the date, time, disk drive you're using, subdirectory, number of traffic citations you have stuffed into your glove box, and your favorite color.

The whole heaving hoard or dollar-sign characters are shown in Table 3-1. (I had to list them all because of the Computer Book Writer's Guild Guidelines. You understand: It's a union thing.)

Table 3-1	Prompt Command Dollar-Sign Characters and What They Do
Dollar-Sign Character	*Displays*
$$	The dollar-sign character ($)
$_	A new line (same as pressing Enter)
$B	The pipe character (I)
$D	The current date
$E	The Escape code (used for special effects)
$G	The greater-than symbol (>)
$H	The Backspace "character" (to erase)
$L	The less-than symbol (<)
$N	The currently *logged* drive letter
$P	The current *path* (drive and subdirectory)
$Q	The equal sign character (=)
$T	The current time
$V	The DOS version number

You can mix and match the dollar-sign things with text to create interesting prompts such as the following:

```
MS-DOS Version 6.20 asks, What next?
```

The preceding prompt was created by the following PROMPT command:

```
PROMPT $V asks, What next?
```

Type that command and you'll get the wordy MS-DOS Version whatever prompt like the line shown here. When DOS displays the command prompt, it translates the $V dollar-sign character into the DOS version (MS-DOS 6.2 in this case) and then displays the rest of the prompt text as normal.

✔ The dollar-sign characters can be upper- or lowercase. Both $V and $v display the DOS version as part of the command prompt.

✔ To see a summarized list of all the dollar-sign commands at any time, type **PROMPT /?** at the command prompt. (For DOS versions prior to 5.0, just put a sticky note on this page.)

✔ The following dollar-sign characters produce a prompt that can change each time it appears:

$D, $N, $P, and $T

$D and $T display the date and time, which is changing constantly. $N displays the current drive letter, which changes as you change drives — ditto for $P, which changes as you change subdirectories (see the following examples).

For an enthusiastic explanation of why you need the $B, $G, and $L dollar-sign characters to display the |, >, and < symbols, refer to Chapter 20 on I/O redirection.

Multi-line prompts with the special $_ character

The $_ dollar-sign character allows you to create multi-line prompts. For example,

```
I'm only happy to serve!
What next:
```

This two-line prompt was created with the following PROMPT command. Type it in, if the prompt excites you:

```
C:\>PROMPT I'm only happy to serve!$_What next:
```

See the little $_ in there? That's what splits the prompt between two lines. So if you're hell-bent on using only text in your prompts and tire easily of long-winded text on the screen, use a few $_ things to break it up.

Speaking of breakups, how about this prompt command:

```
C:\>PROMPT John$_Paul$_George$_Ringo
```

Type it in if you like. I call the $_ in this command the "Yoko Ono dollar-sign character."

Because the point is breaking up long-winded text here, and because you probably didn't read this in Chapter 2, the maximum size of a prompt is 127 characters, and PROMPT takes up 6 characters. Gadzooks! Only a true nerd would use a prompt that long. Even so, $_ counts as two characters. Read the techy sidebar if you want to fry your neurons on the subject.

The $D-date and $T-time special characters in the PROMPT command

The following is an example that uses the $D and $T dollar-sign characters to display the current date and time:

```
Today is Fri 08-12-1994
At 11:22:36.18
Your command:
```

The preceding prompt displays the current date, the time, and the text Your command — not a bad prompt. This one isn't as hard to put together as it looks. Here is the PROMPT command that creates that prompt with all its dollar-sign characters:

```
C:\>PROMPT Today is $D$_At $T$_Your command:
```

The $D supplies the date, and $T supplies the time. The $_ characters "press Enter" at the end of each line. The end result is a three-line prompt with some text and the date and time interspliced.

TECHNICAL STUFF

Silly material about big, monster prompts

You can type up to 127 characters at the DOS prompt. But what if you really want a tremendously long prompt? Are you stuck out in the cold? Will Microsoft turn its back on you? Will anyone else alive really give a hoot?

Providing you have MS-DOS Version 6, you can create quite huge prompts, but you must do it in the CONFIG.SYS file in the following format:

    SET PROMPT=

Add the preceding line to your CONFIG.SYS file and follow the equal sign with whatever charac-

ters you want as your prompt. I don't know what the true maximum number of characters is; I typed a prompt 259 characters long and it worked (though it looked awful).

The only drawback to this trick is that you cannot change the prompt after your PC starts. If you try, you'll be using the PROMPT command at the DOS prompt, and it can only be 120 characters long, as described in this chapter.

Alas, the date and time displayed by the $D and $T characters are not updated. You see only the current date and time displayed when you press Enter to see a new prompt. (The date and time displayed are "frozen" in time.)

The special character dollar-sign characters

There are four "special" dollar-sign characters. These don't display fancy information or do weird things to the display. Instead, their job is to display characters that would otherwise cause DOS to choke until it was IBM-blue in the face.

Try the following PROMPT command:

```
C:\PROMPT <DOS is BOSS>
```

The File not found error occurs due to the special purposes of the < and > characters. (This is covered in Chapter 20.) Because these characters are special, you must use the $L and $G dollar-sign characters to represent them instead:

```
C:\>PROMPT $LDOS is BOSS$G
```

Never mind this information on the time and the $H dollar-sign character

When you use the PROMPT command's $H dollar-sign character to display the time, the prompt displays the time in the following format:

hours:minutes:seconds.hundredths

For example,

```
11:22:36.18
```

Now, let's be honest. Who really cares about the hundredths of seconds? Do you really need that value? Probably not. Instead, it just makes the current time look complex. So what most DOS-users-in-the-know do is take advantage of the $H dollar-sign character to "back up and erase" the extra hundredths of seconds value and the annoying period.

You can use the $H character to back up one space and erase the previous character in your DOS prompt. Try the following PROMPT command:

```
C:\>PROMPT $T
```

This PROMPT command creates a boring prompt that just displays the time. Now try this PROMPT command:

```
C:\>PROMPT $T$H$H$H
```

This PROMPT command displays the time, but the three $H's back up and erase the hundredths of seconds. Because no one needs to care about the seconds value either, most DOS users back up and erase it as well. This requires six $H's in the PROMPT command:

```
C:\>PROMPT $T$H$H$H$H$H$H
```

Finally, with six $H's following it, the $T in a PROMPT command displays only the current time, hours, and minutes. This is a useful trick because it keeps the prompt from looking complex, but wacky because it makes your PROMPT command long and involved.

(By the way, the U.S. Government spends about $28,539 every hundredth of a second.)

The preceding command may look funky, but it produces a prompt with the < and > characters, as in the following:

```
<DOS is BOSS>
```

I won't bother to question the logic of this prompt's message. The point here is that, if you want a < or > or even a $, |, or = in your prompt, you need the proper dollar-sign character.

✔ To stick a < in your prompt, use $L (L is for less-than).

✔ To stick a > in your prompt, use $G (G is for greater-than).

✔ To stick a $ in your prompt, use $$.

✔ To stick a | in your prompt, use $B (B must mean "bar").

✔ To stick an = in your prompt, use $Q (Q means "quickly put an equal sign here").

Choosing the correct dollar-sign character to use will most often be a problem when you want a single dollar sign in your prompt. Remember that you must specify two dollar signs so that only one will print: The command PROMPT THINK$$ displays a DOS prompt that reads *Think$*.

The undocumented, yet handy $A thing

One PROMPT command secret character I've always used and never seen documented is $A. Basically, this character does nothing but hold its own place. I use it to create DOS prompts that have an extra, comforting space after them. For example,

```
C:\>PROMPT $P$G
```

The preceding command creates the following DOS prompt:

```
C:\>DOS>_
```

Note that the cursor, and everything you type, starts right up against the > character. Yuck. Personally I prefer a more airy approach. Here is my prompt command:

```
C:\>PROMPT $P$G $A
```

A space follows the $G. The $A comes after the space. This command produces the following DOS prompt:

```
C:\>DOS> _
```

Ahhh. Note how the cursor blinks a space away from the > thing. In my opinion, this distance between the cursor and the > thing prevents the command line from looking too junky.

Sample Prompts Some People May Actually Use

Though there is great flexibility with the command prompt, few people bother to go gonzo with it. The problem is that involved prompts just make the screen look messy. So rather than waste your time here showing you what's possible, the following is a list of what's practical.

The all-time fave command prompt

```
C:\>PROMPT $P$G
```

The preceding PROMPT command creates the standard DOS 6 prompt. The $P displays the current disk drive letter and subdirectory and the $G displays the greater-than character:

```
C:\DOS>
```

Variations: You can also make other command prompt variations.

```
C:\>PROMPT ($P)
```

The preceding command also displays the current drive letter and subdirectory, but it's enclosed in parentheses:

```
(C:\DOS)
```

That's the way OS/2 displays its prompt. The following is the same deal but enclosed in less-than and greater-than angle brackets:

```
C:\>PROMPT $L$P$G
```

This makes the following prompt:

```
<C:\DOS>
```

Nice and cryptic, eh?

Date and time and such prompt

```
C:\>PROMPT $D$_$T$_$P$G
```

Although cryptic, the preceding prompt command is quite popular. It displays the date ($D), time ($T), and drive-subdirectory ($P) on three different lines thanks to the $_ dollar-sign character:

```
Fri 08-12-1994
11:22:36.18
C:\DOS>
```

Keep in mind that the current time (second line) doesn't update itself; you only see the current time when you see a new command prompt.

Quite a few DOS prompt zanies don't like the dot-hundredths display in the current time. To combat this, they add three backspace dollar-sign characters ($H) to the PROMPT command. This can make things quite hairy:

```
C:\>PROMPT $D$_$T$H$H$H$_$P$G
```

See the three $H's in there? Messy, messy. But the result is a wee bit nicer to read:

```
Fri 08-12-1994
11:22:36
C:\DOS>
```

Don't forget that you can also stick text in the prompt. For example, you can make the preceding prompt look like this:

```
Today is Fri 08-12-1994
It's now 11:22:36
And you're at C:\DOS>
```

Here is the monster PROMPT command that makes the preceding prompt possible:

```
C:\>PROMPT Today is $D$_$It's now T$H$H$H$_And you're at $P$G
```

Yikes! You should type the preceding command all on one line. Then again, if you think that prompt is a bit much, just stare in awe. My point is that you can mix text in with the dollar-sign goodies.

✔ Yes, at times DOS can certainly be loopy. It makes you almost completely forget the "serious nature" by which computers are sold.

✔ Additional "favorite prompts" are possible with the $E dollar-sign character. Refer to the next section on ANSI.SYS for the details.

Fun prompts done by a guy who went crazy one night

For a while there, it seemed like there was a PROMPT command revival craze. Everyone was coming up with clever prompt commands. The one I remember the most was the Bart Simpson prompt. But because he's a copyrighted character and my publisher is concerned about infringing on the copyright, consider the following DOS prompt:

```
  \
   \/\  Li'l Help!
   \ /\
   \./ \../\...(*)
```

The idea here (if you don't get it) is a ball rolling on the screen. The PROMPT command to create this is truly ugly. Don't even try to type this in:

```
C:\>PROMPT \$_ \/\  Li'l
Help!$_ \ /\$_  \./ \../\...(*)
```

This PROMPT command has been wrapped in this book to two lines; if you did dare to type the command in, it should be all on one line. And not only that, but five spaces need to follow the third $_ thingy.

How about this prompt:

```
 _ _ _ _ _ _
 /   \
 | . . |
 0 h D
 (_ _===_ _)
 ^^^ Speak to me!
```

Okay. It's supposed to be a large, ominous, floating head. (Ever see *Zardoz*?) I'm not an artist, and I don't play one on TV, but here is the PROMPT command to make the floating head prompt:

```
C:\>PROMPT _ _ _ _ _ _ _$_ /
\$_ $B . . $B$_ 0 h D$_
(_ _===_ _)$_ ^^^ Speak to me!
```

Again, there are a lot of spaces in there plus the $B dollar-sign things to represent the vertical bar characters. Type this in at your own peril.

I could go on. They pay me for this stuff. But the point is made. If you want to attempt this on your own, my recommendation is to use a text editor program (such as the DOS EDITOR) and create your prompt-graphic. Then translate it, line-by-line, into the proper PROMPT command. Those anxious to do this can sort out the details on their own time.

Fanciful Prompts with ANSI.SYS

The most mysterious PROMPT command dollar-sign character is $E. It represents the Escape character — the same "character" you get when you press the Escape key on your keyboard. This may sound strange, but the $_ dollar-sign character is used to represent the Enter character in a prompt — the same as pressing Enter on your keyboard. What's strange here is what you can do with the $E.

Basically, the $E doesn't do anything in a PROMPT command. However, if you're using a DOS *device driver* called ANSI.SYS, then you can use the $E to add color to your prompt or to make strange-looking prompts that would otherwise defy explanation.

- ✔ Refer to Chapter 21 for more information on using ANSI.SYS and the ANSI commands.

- ✔ The $E is always followed by a left-bracket ([) character when using ANSI commands, as in $E[. If your ANSI-fanciful prompt doesn't work, then it's probably because you forgot the [.

- ✔ If the ANSI.SYS device driver is not installed in CONFIG.SYS, then the $E dollar-sign character will have no effect on your prompt. (Though in some cases, it may display an arrow, as in ←).

- ✔ Yeah, most people tire of ANSI-inspired prompts just as they do with other prompts you can create using the standard dollar-sign characters. Chapter 21 has a few interesting examples to toss your way in any case.

Chapter 4
Command Line Headaches?
Take a DOSKey (and Call Me
in the Morning)

- -

In This Chapter

▶ Understanding DOSKey

▶ Installing DOSKey

▶ Editing the command line with DOSKey

▶ Working with multiple commands

▶ Using the command history

- -

*I*f you can't read the road signs, then danger looms as you drive. Fortunately, we humans can get glasses and see just like normal people are rumored to see. And when our ten thumbs drop a nut down into the bowels of some gizmo, we can use those long boingy-grabber things to retrieve it. In fact, for just about every human foible, a device exists that makes the situation better. The same thing holds true for our computers. You remedy DOS's distress with special-purpose computer programs called *utilities*.

Utilities are programs that do something DOS should do or something DOS tries to do and fails. The idea is that the utility can remove the misery from DOS. And a good place to start, misery-wise, is the command prompt — woe central for most of us. The utility in this case is called DOSKey.

Fifty Brief Words on DOSKey (Understanding DOSKey)

DOSKey is a special program — a utility — that gives you more control over the command prompt. With DOSKey, you can really edit the command line, easily recall old commands for reuse or editing, plus work with special firkins called *macros*. DOSKey helps make life easier at the DOS prompt.

✔ DOSKey is pronounced like *dahs-kee*, which is how the Germans say "the key" (*das key*) or, more accurately, how the Russians say DOS — *DOSSKI*.

✔ DOSKey comes with DOS; you don't have to buy anything else. Of course, DOSKey comes only with DOS versions 5.0 or later, so if you have an older version, you'll need to upgrade (or read the next note).

✔ Prior to DOS 5.0, many people enjoyed DOSKey-like command line editing by using such programs as DOSEdit and CED. These programs are available on DOS utility diskettes often sold in those twirly racks in the back of computer stores, in airports, and from "software galore"-like ads in the back of magazines.

✔ This book covers only DOSKey, not DOSEdit or CED.

✔ I use the word *firkin* to mean *thing,* as in thingamabob. A firkin is actually a small wooden container or a measurement equal to ¼ barrel. (I have to write this explanation, or my managing editor will assume *firkin* is some foul word in Latin, in which case she'd snip it from the text and replace it with something utterly dorky.)

✔ No, the 50 words only includes the initial paragraph. All this check mark stuff doesn't count.

Installing DOSKey

The easiest way to install DOSKey is to type the DOSKEY command at the prompt:

```
C:\>DOSKEY
```

Type in **DOSKEY** and press Enter. You may see the following displayed:

```
DOSKey Installed.
```

If you don't see the DOSKEY Installed message, that's okay. You either already have DOSKey installed on your system and just don't know it, or you may have a version of DOSKey that doesn't display the DOSKEY Installed message. No problem.

✔ If you get a Bad command or file name error, then one of three things happened: 1) You don't have DOS 5.0 or later; 2) You may have mistyped DOSKEY, so check your spelling and try again; 3) DOS doesn't know where to find the DOSKEY.COM program. In the last case, refer to Chapter 12 for information on finding lost files.

✔ DOSKey is named DOSKEY.COM and is tucked in your hard drive's \DOS subdirectory.

✔ For information on making DOSKey available each time you start your PC, refer to Chapter 10 on making AUTOEXEC.BAT work.

✔ I prefer installing DOSKey in its *insert* mode, which means that command line editing works like a word processor — any new text you type is inserted, and old text is pushed to the right. To start DOSKey in insert mode, use the following command:

```
C:\>DOSKEY /INSERT
```

The /INSERT option, or *switch,* tells DOSKey to start in the insert mode, which you'll probably find more pleasant than regular overtype mode.

Editing the Command Line with DOSKey

After you install DOSKey (see preceding section), editing your commands becomes much easier. The primary advantage is that you can "see" what you're editing. Without DOSKey, for example, you move the cursor backwards with the left arrow (←) and erase. With DOSKey, you move the cursor backwards and can still see the command line. This convenience is possible only with a computer.

Table 4-1 displays the keys you can use to edit the command line with DOSKey installed. This table is for reference purposes only, because I am a computer book author and I am required, by law in 49 states plus the District of Columbia, to list key commands in tables. Fortunately, you can refer to the tutorial in the next section if you need a sample run-through to hone your DOSKey editing skills. (Trust me, it's cinchy.)

Advanced nerdly information on freeing up DOSKey's memory

DOSKey, like all DOS programs, eats up memory—not a large amount, but usually about 4K or so. And if you have memory management software installed (see Chapter 25), that ain't all so bad. But sometimes you may want even more memory for DOSKey, especially when you create DOSKey macros or when you just become overwhelmingly greedy.

Normally, DOSKey sets aside about 512 bytes for use to hold the command history and macros. This value can be jostled up or down when you first install DOSKey by specifying the optional /BUFSIZE switch:

```
C:\>DOSKEY /BUFSIZE=1024
```

This command starts DOSKey — installing it and all that — but sets aside room for 1,024 (1K)

characters for the command history and macros. This is a good number to use if you ever see the dreaded `Insufficient memory` error. Even the following command is socially acceptable:

```
C:\>DOSKEY /BUFSIZE=2048 /INSERT
```

With this command, DOSKey's storage space has been boosted to 2,048 characters. Also note that the /INSERT option is also specified, which is perfectly okay.

You don't need to always specify funky computer numbers with the /BUFSIZE option. The smallest number you can use is 256, and the largest is something huge and obnoxious like 65,565 characters (or the number of people who have claimed to see Elvis alive last year).

Table 4-1	DOSKey's Editing Keys
Key	**What It Does**
Home	Moves to the start of the command line
End	Moves to the end of the command line
←	Moves back one character
→	Moves forward one character
Ctrl-←	Moves back one word
Ctrl-→	Moves forward one word
Backspace	Backs up and deletes the preceding character
Del	Deletes the character the cursor is blinking under
Ctrl-End	Deletes from the cursor to the end of the line
Insert	Switches between insert and overtype editing modes

✔ The *command line* is what you type at the DOS prompt — the command you send to DOS. You can edit the command line with DOSKey.

✔ The *cursor* is the blinking underline that appears on-screen and shows you where your text will next appear when you type.

✔ You can find more information on the DOS prompt, command line, and cursor in Chapter 2.

✔ Most of DOSKey's editing keys are the same as those you find in your favorite word processor. For example, Ctrl-End is the same key combination that you use in WordPerfect to delete to the end of the line. (I know it gives you great satisfaction that DOSKey and WordPerfect work kinda the same.)

✔ Yes, the primary advantage to all the key commands shown in Table 4-1 is that you can see what you're editing while your editing it. (You can go nuts with this advantage, however, as you see in the tutorial section that follows.)

✔ You can only edit the command line in this manner after you install DOSKey. Refer to the section "Installing DOSKey," which appears earlier in this chapter.

✔ You cannot use DOSKey to edit a file created with the COPY CON command. See Chapter 13 for more information on COPY CON.

For what it's worth: The ancient function key commands also can be used to edit the command line — even with DOSKey installed. (These commands are listed in a table in Chapter 2, in the sidebar "Other command line editing keys no one ever uses," if you care to look.)

The DOSKey editing tutorial

Today's DOSKey editing tutorial is brought to you by the keys ←, →, Backspace, Delete, Insert, Home, End — and the color Blue.

Please start DOSKey before trying this tutorial.

Start by entering the following DIR command, which lists files on disk (and it's covered in deep seriousness in Chapter 12, if you care to look):

```
C:\>DIR *>*
```

Type **dir**, * (asterisk), > (greater-than symbol, above the period key), and then another *. This DIR *.* command looks like you are holding down the Shift key the entire time you are typing (something I do all too often).

After you press Enter, you'll get a `Too many parameters - *` or similar error message. Yes, this command contains a goof — a common one — the > instead of a period. Dumb mistake, one that DOSKey fixes nicely if you follow these steps:

1. Press the F3 key to redisplay the command:

```
C:\>DIR *>*
```

The cursor is blinking at the end of the command line.

2. Press and hold down the ← key until the cursor is blinking below the > between the two asterisks.

Hey! The ← key does not erase. (If you press Backspace, it does erase — so be sure to press the left-arrow key instead.)

3. Type a period:

```
C:\>DIR *.*
```

If the > is overwritten by the period, fine. Otherwise, you have the insert mode on and have just inserted a period. Press the Delete key to remove the > from the command, if you have the insert mode on.

4. Press Enter to carry out the DIR command.

The cursor does not have to be at the end of the line when you press Enter. DOS "swallows the command whole" no matter which character the cursor is under.

✔ When you press the Insert key, you switch between overwrite and insert modes. In the overwrite mode, the cursor appears a bit larger than it does in the insert mode (though you can tell the difference only if you sit there and diddle with the Insert key).

✔ An elephant's appendix is nearly five feet long.

Pray no one is watching when you do this

Here's another DOSKey tutorial to try:

1. Type in another command. Maybe a long command, such as

```
C:\>ECHO MY BRAIN HURTS AND IT'S TIME FOR A SNACK
```

2. Don't press Enter.

3. Use the ← and → keys to move the cursor around.

   Press and hold down ← to move the cursor back to the start of the line. Then press and hold down → to move the cursor to the end of the line.

4. Back and forth, back and forth. Maybe try to make a humming sound while you're doing this. Hum up when you press → and then hum down when you press ←.

See how the cursor slides below the commands and doesn't erase? The same thing happens with the Ctrl-← and Ctrl-→ keys, but you move back and forth by "words" instead of characters.

DOSKey Mania with Multiple Commands on a Single Line

Imagine going to the kitchen to pile up on snacks, chips, and carbonated beverages and getting it all done in one trip. For a human, this feat would require growing a few extra limbs — an idea I've found attractive several times during my life. In DOS, multiple commands at a single prompt are possible with DOSKey.

With DOSKey installed, you can type in more than one command at the prompt by separating each command with the ¶ character.

You produce the ¶ character by pressing Ctrl-T. Ctrl-T works only with DOSKey installed. Press Ctrl-T and — blatt — you get a ¶. For example, type the following:

```
C:\>DIR *.COM ¶ DIR *.EXE
```

The preceding command line contains two DIR commands, the total output of each will list all the program files (COM and EXE files) in the current directory. This is a handy command that I use all the time to try and track down programs in the process of escaping my PC.

I first typed **DIR *.COM** and then a space. Then I pressed Ctrl-T. (Press and hold down the Ctrl, or Control, key and type a **T**; then release both keys.) The Ctrl-T produces the ¶ character. Then I typed another space and finally the **DIR *.EXE** command.

After you press Enter, DOS displays another DOS prompt at which the DIR *.COM command is "typed."

```
C:\>DIR *.COM
```

The output of that command follows. Then — as if the computer were typing by itself — another DOS prompt appears and the DIR *.EXE command is magically typed:

```
C:\>DIR *.EXE
```

Not given any time to think about it, that command's output appears. It's magical.

- ✔ You don't have to put a space before or after the ¶ character.

- ✔ If this exercise hasn't convinced you, try the following command line. Remember to press Ctrl-T between each command:

```
C:\>cls¶mode¶ver¶vol¶set
```

  This single command line runs five different DOS commands, one after the other: CLS, MODE, VER, VOL, and SET.

- ✔ The ¶ character is called the paragraph mark. It's used in editing to mean "put a paragraph (or new line) here." This mark sorta makes sense at the DOS prompt because each command is separated by a "new line." Oh, yeah, that's a stretch. But it *is* my job to make sense of all this somehow.

Don't press Ctrl-P to produce the ¶ character! When you press Ctrl-P, you activate DOS's "print everything" function. If your printer isn't on, you'll get a bunch of Write fault error writing to device PRN error messages. Heinous! Press Ctrl-P again to stop printing and then press A to answer the Abort, Retry? question.

And, Now, the Reasons Few People Bother with the Multiple Commands Trick

Few people use the ¶ trick for several valid reasons, not the least of which is "I just forgot about it."

The first reason to avoid the Ctrl-T trick is that you often want to view the output of one DOS command before typing in another. Using multiple commands via DOSKey is like trying to precision-aim a machine gun; most of the information DOS displays scrolls up the screen too fast for it to be useful.

The next reason is that if, for any reason, you want to stop DOS from its multiple command line fervor, you must press Ctrl-C to cancel *each* command. A single Ctrl-C (or Ctrl-Break) just doesn't cut it. If you type two commands separated by ¶, you have to press Ctrl-C twice to bring everything to a halt. (Ach! What the heck? Type Ctrl-C a zillion times, and it'll make you feel better.)

Finally, most DOS users resort to batch files when it comes to running several commands at once. In that light, the ¶ special treat is mostly an oddity.

- ✔ See Part III of this book for the lowdown on batch files.

- ✔ By the way, the ¶ trick doesn't work in batch files because the rule is that you can't include Ctrl-T as a multiple command character *inside* a batch file. The command character just doesn't work.

The Command History

With DOSKey installed, you also get the bonus of having DOS remember your last several command lines — just as if it were patiently taking notes. You also can reuse those commands over and over — like bad after-dinner speaker jokes. The official name for this trick that cuts down on your command line typing is the *command history*. I prefer to call it the *Super F3 Key*.

Recalling the preceding command (or "You look familiar, and your name is on the tip of my up-arrow key.")

Without DOSKey, you can redo any DOS command by pressing the F3 key. Simply press F3 and — zap! — there's the last DOS command you typed. The F3 shortcut still works when DOSKey is installed, but you'll probably find yourself using the up-arrow key (↑) more.

To see how DOSKey's command history works and how you can take advantage of the up-arrow command recall key, type the following DOS commands, pressing Enter after each one:

```
C:\>DIR
C:\>VOL
C:\>VER
C:\>SET
C:\>CD
```

These commands each display brief output, are (for the most part) nonviolent, and they're not too hairy to type.

1. To recall the CD command — the last command you typed — press the up-arrow key (↑).

2. You'll see the CD command displayed again — just like pressing F3 to recall the last command.

   Right now you can press Enter to redo the CD command. Or, using DOSKey's remarkable editing capabilities, you can edit the CD command, type something after it (such as CD \DOS) or press the Esc key to erase and start over. But no! This is a tutorial, so take the next step.

3. Press the up-arrow key (↑) again.

4. You'll see the SET command displayed. What the up-arrow key has done here is to recall the prior preceding command. In fact, each time you press the up-arrow key, you'll see the preceding DOS command displayed.

By pressing the up-arrow key, you can recall any old DOS command you've recently typed. If you don't see the command you want, press the up-arrow key again. After you find your command, press Enter to reuse the command or edit it by using DOSKey's editing keys (see Table 4-1, if you need to).

> ✔ Table 4-2 lists other keys, in addition to the up-arrow key, which you can use with DOSKey's command history. Please don't bother to memorize anything in Table 4-2. The most important key is the up-arrow key, plus maybe F8, which is covered in the next section.
>
> ✔ DOSKey remembers the last several command lines, typically the last 30 or so. The number of command lines it remembers depends on how long the commands were and how much sleep it got the night before.
>
> ✔ Eventually, you'll hit the up-arrow key and see the same command displayed over and over. Don't panic. You've just reached the "top" of the list of preceding commands; no more commands are stored in the command list. Oh, well, I guess you'll have to retype in your command the old manual way.
>
> ✔ Oops! If you press the up-arrow key one too many times, you can press the down-arrow key (↓) to recall the "next" DOS command.
>
> ✔ The PgUp and PgDn keys work to display the very first and very last command stored in the command history (see Table 4-2).
>
> ✔ If you're not familiar with the handy F3 key at the DOS prompt, refer to Chapter 2.
>
> ✔ Information on the SET command can be found in Chapter 19.

The F8 search-and-grab

Many times, you may want to recall a specific command, and most of the time, you'll know what it is. Because the computer's job is to make life easier, pressing the up-arrow key and hunting for your command seems kind of primitive. So what you need is the handy F8 key, which I call the *search-and-grab*.

1. To use the F8 key, start by typing the first part of your command at the DOS prompt. For example, say you wanted to recall an old VOL command. Type

```
C:\>V
```

You don't have to type in the whole command, just the first letter, sometimes just V will recall the command.

2. Anyway, after typing the first part of your command, press the F8 key.

3. DOSKey scans its command history and looks for any commands that match what you've typed so far. You may see the following:

```
C:\>VER
```

There. DOSKey has dug up the last matching V command. If VER is what you want, press Enter to reuse the command or edit it or whatever. Otherwise, you can search again by pressing F8 a second time. Maybe you'll see

```
C:\>VOL
```

If that's the command you want, great. If not, you can press F8 once more to keep looking for possible matches. And if you don't find what you're looking for, just retype the command. The process is painful, but it's the way humans did things in the eons before DOSKey.

To work DOSKey's F8 key, type in the first part of a previous DOS command — a command you want to reuse. Press F8. If you find your match, edit the command or press Enter to reuse it. If not, press F8 to search again.

All the command history keys (the rest of the story)

The most useful keys DOSKey offers for playing with the command history are the up-arrow and F8 keys. Other keys loom as well, though there's no point in memorizing them. The whole dang doodle is listed in Table 4-2 and the following text describes what each key does — strictly "only if you care" reading.

The F7 key: Do you want to see the entire command history — nay, a transcript of your entire DOS session, the work of your tired fingers busily typing? Press the F7 key. You may see something like this:

```
1: DIR
2: VOL
3: VER
4: SET
5: CD
```

If the list is longer, a handy More prompt appears on-screen; press the Enter key to see the rest of the list.

What the F7 key does is to display a numbered list of DOSKey's command history.

Another way to "press" the F7 key is to type the DOSKEY /HISTORY command, which displays the same list of commands, but without numbers or the handy More screen-pausing thing.

The F9 key: Here's another wacky thing: With the list displayed, you can recall any command line by its number by pressing the F9 key. You'll see

```
C:\>Line number:
```

Type the line number of the command you want — something like 15 — and press Enter. DOSKey erases its Line number prompt and replaces it with the command on that line number. Edit the command or press Enter to "execute" it.

The Alt-F7 key: Security-conscious users or folks who are just plain paranoid appreciate the Alt-F7 key. If you're concerned that someone else may sit at your PC and peruse the command history to see what you've been up to, press Alt-F7 to erase all the evidence. (Government employees use this key combination all the time, primarily to prevent taxpayers from realizing how much time they spend playing computer casino games.)

Table 4-2	DOSKey's Command History Keys
Key	*What It Does*
↑	Recalls preceding command from the command history
↓	Recalls next command from the command history
PgUp	Recalls the first (oldest) command in the history
PgDn	Recalls the most recent DOS command
F8	Searches the command history
F7	Displays a numbered command history list
Alt-F7	Erases the command history
F9	Recalls a command by its line number

Chapter 5

Another DOSKey Trick (But One Few Bother With)

In This Chapter

▶ Learning about DOSKey macros

▶ Typing in useful macro examples

▶ Naming your macros like DOS commands

▶ Using the dollar-sign thingies in macros

▶ Destroying macros

Another one of DOSKey's many tasks is to give you macro power at the DOS prompt. *Macro power* sounds like one of those powdered protein drinks with a picture of a guy on it who has so many muscles he must permanently walk around with clenched fists and both arms raised in the air. The description is close, but it doesn't have anything to do with DOSKey's macro power.

What DOSKey's macros allow you to do is think up abbreviations for longer DOS commands. The abbreviations allow you the luxury of being really terse (and cryptic) at the DOS prompt and saves you valuable typing calories because you can use the abbreviations rather than the longer commands — a handy feature. And, though I'll admit that few DOSKey fans use the macro feature, it's covered in this chapter for your reading and tootorialling enjoyment.

Holy Macro!

Macro is a word tossed about loosely in the computer industry. Oh, sometimes you may even hear a nerd use the official, long version: macro instruction (*makro in-struck-shun*). Ugh. Basically, a macro is a shortcut — a shorthand, a little dit that represents a longer thingamabob.

✔ To use DOSKey's macros, you must have DOSKey installed on your computer (refer to Chapter 4).

✔ DOSKey's macros must be *created*. The macros are li'l instructions you must type that tell DOSKey which shortcuts you're going to use. This must be done before you use the macro, or you can collectively stuff all your DOSKey macros into your PC's AUTOEXEC.BAT file (see Chapters 9 and 10 for the gories).

With macros, u cn typ lk ths

The idea behind a DOSKey macro is that it takes a long command and makes it easier to type. The command itself isn't shortened; a shortcut is created.

As an example, suppose that you just got this book and have discovered the joys of editing your PC's AUTOEXEC.BAT file. If so, you'll find yourself typing the following command a great deal:

```
C:\>EDIT C:\AUTOEXEC.BAT
```

The above command can be reduced to the following:

```
C:\>1
```

Type **1**, press Enter and — through the magic of a DOSKey macro — you've actually entered EDIT C:\AUTOEXEC.BAT. Such ease. Such elegance. Are you really using a computer?

The upside to macros is that you can really punch out some commands without having to worry about typos — or without living in fear that you'll lose all your fingers putting the chain on Justin's bike and be unable to manipulate the phone to dial 9-1-1. The downside is that the macros you create are your own shortcuts and won't be available on other PCs (unless you create them there as well). Enough talk! Time for a tutorial.

The DIR command seems short enough, but why not just type in a single **D** instead? This can be done by creating the D macro. Type the following DOSKey command at the prompt:

```
C:\>DOSKEY D=DIR /O /P
```

Type **DOSKEY**, a space, **D** (the name of the macro), = (an equals sign), then the command **DIR,** a space, **/O** (slash-O — the letter *O* and not a zero), a space, and finally **/P** (slash-P). The macro you're creating is going to be equivalent to the DIR command with its /O and /P options. Press Enter.

Nothing happens! Actually, because an error message didn't occur, you can assume that *something* happened. In this case, a DOSKey macro named "D" happened. To test the macro, type **D** and press Enter at the next convenient DOS prompt:

```
C:\>D
C:\>DIR /O /P
```

What you see almost immediately is a second DOS prompt and then the full command, typed out automatically for you. In the preceding, that's the DIR /O /P command, which displays a sorted directory on-screen a "page" at a time.

- ✔ The D macro is a shortcut for the longer DIR /O /P DOS command. The essence of DOSKey's macros is a shorter command that "types" a longer one.

- ✔ Yes, you still have to press Enter after typing the macro. You must always press Enter to send a command to DOS (though, in this case, you're sending a macro to DOSKey, which then sends the full command to DOS.)

- ✔ You can find more information on the DIR /O /P command in Chapter 12.

- ✔ To see a list of all the macros DOSKey has in store for you, refer to the section "Looking at your macros" later in this chapter.

- ✔ Okay, let's all create that 1 macro to edit AUTOEXEC.BAT. Type the following command:

  ```
  C:\>DOSKEY 1=EDIT C:\AUTOEXEC.BAT
  ```

Type **DOSKEY**, a space, the number **1** (the name of the macro), = (an equals sign), and then the command to edit AUTOEXEC.BAT: **EDIT** (which is the DOS Editor), a space, **C:** (the letter *C*, colon, backslash), **AUTOEXEC.BAT** (be sure to type the period between AUTOEXEC and BAT).

If you want to edit CONFIG.SYS with the 2 macro, use the following command to create it:

```
C:\>DOSKEY 2=EDIT C:\CONFIG.SYS
```

Making a macro: The instructions

Building a DOSKey macro is easy. Follow these steps:

1. Think of something that you type in all the time — something that takes a while to type in and that you'd really like to have a macro for so that you'd have to type in only *IG, POK,* or *NB* instead.

2. Fill in the blanks:

```
C:\>DOSKEY macro=command
```

For *macro* type in your handy shortcut. For *command*, type in the DOS command, complete with any options, just as you'd type it at the DOS prompt in normal life.

For example, to create a shortcut for the command to format a disk in drive A, you'd type the following:

```
C:\>DOSKEY F=FORMAT A:
```

3. Press Enter. The macro is locked into memory.

4. Repeat these steps as often as you like to create as many macros as you feel will better your life.

✔ There is no limit to the number of macros DOSKey can hold. Well, actually, that's not true. If you ever see the error message `Insufficient memory to store macro` or something to that extent, refer to the techy box "Advanced nerdly information on freeing up DOSKey's memory" near the start of Chapter 4 for some helpful information.

✔ After you get all your DOSKey macros created and are pleased with them, wouldn't it be a great idea if the computer automatically ran the macros for you each time it started? Turn to Chapter 10 on AUTOEXEC.BAT for more information.

✔ More information on the FORMAT command is concealed in Chapter 15.

✔ Take a gander at the section "More Mayhem: Dollar-Sign Thingies in DOSKey Macros" later in this chapter for additional information on creating DOSKey macros.

✔ The final section in this chapter deals with the timely subject of deleting DOSKey macros.

Ain't no such thing as part-time macros

DOSKey's macros are full commands only. They aren't abbreviations for pieces or parts of other commands. For example,

```
DOSKEY ALL=*.*
```

In the preceding, the ALL macro is created to represent the DOS filename wildcard *.* (star-dot-star), which probably makes you believe that the following command is possible:

```
C:\>DIR ALL
```

TECHNICAL STUFF

DOSKey macro naming rules

Everything has rules. I know this personally because I just took the driving test here in Idaho and —you know what?—a herd of sheep *does* have the right of way in this state. I did not know that. But that's why there are rules. They keep your PC from getting mad when you create a DOSKey macro, and they keep the lovely Idaho highways clear of sheep entrails.

The rules with DOSKey macros involve giving them proper names. Amazingly enough, you can give your macro just about any name, from a single letter or number to something obnoxiously long. For the nitpickers (and Idaho drivers), here are the definitive rules:

✔ The macro name can be from 1 to about 120 characters long. Obviously, shorter and more descriptive macro names are best. Single letter or number names are okay, provided you can remember what each one means.

✔ The macro name cannot contain a space.

✔ The macro name cannot contain any of the following characters:

. " / \ [ ] : * | < > + = ; , ?

(These are the same characters that are forbidden in a filename, too.)

✔ One weirdness: Macros can have the same names as DOS commands and other files on disk (see "Forbidden Information on Macros Named Like DOS Commands" later in this chapter).

Does DOSKey substitute *.* for ALL in the preceding? Nope! The ALL macro is equal to the "command" *.* (which isn't a command at all). So keep in mind that DOSKey macros can be set equal only to full DOS commands, not pieces or parts.

Looking at your macros

Creating DOSKey macros is easy, but some people go nuts with the process. Personally, I don't go nuts — otherwise I'd show you a basketful of examples here.

When you do become a DOSKey macro maniac, you'll need to know the following command:

```
C:\>DOSKEY /MACROS
```

After you type **DOSKEY**, followed by a space and then **/MACROS** (slash-MACROS), DOSKey lists all the macros you've created. For example,

```
D=DIR /O /P
1=EDIT C:\AUTOEXEC.BAT
2=EDIT C:\CONFIG.SYS
```

```
F=FORMAT A:
55MPH=DEL C:\IDAHO\SHEEP
H=DOSKEY /HISTORY
```

The macros are all listed as they were created: macro name, equals sign, DOS command. Cool.

✔ You also can type **DOSKEY /M** to list your macros. The /M is actually a shortcut for /MACROS. After all, the topic here is being lazy.

✔ The best way to have all your macros created for you automatically is to stick them in your PC's AUTOEXEC.BAT. Chapter 10 shows you how you can also use the DOSKEY /MACRO command with a batch file to automatically create your macros with a minimum of typing skills.

✔ Hey! Did anyone else see the H=DOSKEY /HISTORY macro? The DOSKEY /HISTORY command works just like pressing the F7 key (which I discussed in Chapter 4). With the H macro, you can do the same thing. Oh, computers can be so useful.

A sorry and sad note about DOSKey macros: They do not work in batch files. So while you can *create* them there, a DOSKey macro (such as the D macro) doesn't work in a batch file. Refer to Part III of this book for more information on batch files.

Forbidden Information on Macros Named Like DOS Commands

One strange thing you wouldn't expect about DOSKey macros is that you can give them names exactly the same as DOS commands. For example, you can have a DIR macro or a DEL, TIME, DATE, FDISK, or whatever macro. When you type that command at the prompt, the DOSKey macro will run — not the true DOS command. This sounds wacky, but there is a higher purpose.

For example, no one in his or her right mind wants to run the FDISK command, because this command is used only when first setting up your hard drives. If you use it after that, you run the risk of erasing all the information on your hard drives forever, and you'll spend serious time in purgatory if you even try — so don't bother. To avoid even the most daring user who's anxious to play *what if?*, you can create the following safe macro:

```
DOSKEY FDISK=CLS
```

This command creates the FDISK macro, which is equal to DOS's CLS command (which clears the screen — see Chapter 2). Press Enter after double-checking that you have everything in proper order.

Now, do the daring and type in the following:

```
C:\>FDISK
```

Ha! It only clears the screen. The FDISK macro has rendered DOS's potentially deadly FDISK command harmless.

- ✔ If you goofed, and after typing **FDISK** you see the actual, dreaded FDISK program displayed, just gingerly press the Escape key (labeled Esc on your keyboard). No harm done.

- ✔ Most DOSKey macros with names identical to DOS commands are created for safety purposes. For example, the following DEL macro runs the DEL command with its "safe /P" option. — a safe-delete utility — instead of the regular Delete command:

```
DOSKEY DEL= DEL $* /P
```

  In the preceding, the DEL macro is created, assigned to the DEL command with the /P option. Refer to Chapter 14 for more information on this option.

- ✔ You can assign the name of any DOS command to a DOSKey macro. When you type the DOS command name, the DOSKey macro "runs" instead.

- ✔ If you create a DOSKey macro with the same name as a DOS command and really want to run the command and not the macro, type a space at the DOS prompt before you type the command. The following command line, for example, runs the DIR macro, not the DIR command:

```
C:\>DIR
```

  But this command line

```
C:\> DIR
```

  runs the DIR command, not the DIR macro. (See the extra space? No? Look again.)

- ✔ You can use DOSKey macros to run batch file programs, just as the macros run other programs. Simply type the name of the batch file as the "command" part when you create the macro. Refer to Part III of this book for more information on batch files.

More Mayhem: Dollar-Sign Thingies in DOSKey Macros

A whole area of DOS, called I/O redirection, is quite droll and is covered in this book in Chapter 20. But one problem with I/O redirection is that it fouls up some other DOS commands, requiring the presence of dollar-sign thingies to iron out the difficulties. (You may have seen these thingies with the PROMPT command in Chapter 3; with DOSKey macros, you have the same trouble.)

The main problem lies in the following characters:

```
> >> < |
```

These characters are "forbidden," but they serve useful functions in DOS, so you may want to create a DOSKey macro that contains the characters. The problem is, you need to substitute dollar-sign thingies to get the characters to do what you want, or something unexpected may happen. (The same holds true with the PROMPT command.)

- Table 5-1 lists the dollar-sign thingies you can use when you create the command part of a DOSKey macro.

- Memorize these dollar-sign characters? What! Are you out of your gourd?

- Refer to Chapter 20 for more information on I/O redirection.

- The letters after the dollar sign command can be typed in either upper- or lowercase — so $G and $g are the same thing.

- You can find more information on the Ctrl-T (¶) command separator in Chapter 4.

- You may notice the strange $1, $2 through $9, and $* thingies in Table 5-1. These are given special attention in the section "The highly unusual $-number things," which follows.

An example of using >, >>, <, or | in a DOSKey macro

To see how these dollar-sign characters work, consider the following example:

```
C:\>DIR > PRN
```

Table 5-1   DOSKey Macro Dollar-Sign Command Characters

Dollar-Sign Command	Represents	Which Is
$g	>	The output-redirection symbol
gg	>>	The output-redirection/append symbol
$b	|	The pipe command
$l	<	The input-redirection symbol
$t	¶	The Ctrl-T DOSKey command separator
$$	$	The dollar-sign character by itself
$1	-	The first thing typed after the DOSKey macro
$2–$9	-	The second through ninth things typed after the DOSKey macro
$*	-	Everything typed after the DOSKey macro

The preceding command prints a directory, sending the output of the DIR command to the printer. To create a DOSKey macro named PD that does the same thing, you would use the following command:

```
C:\>DOSKEY PD=DIR $G PRN
```

The $G character in the macro command represents the > character in the "real" command. When DOS runs the macro, the $G becomes >, as it should be. But if you typed in a > instead of $G, something I-don't-know-what would happen, definitely something you don't want.

✔ Astute readers will read and appreciate Chapter 20 before trying out macros such as this with DOSKey.

✔ Don't forget that $T, which you can use to create DOSKey macros that burp up multiple DOS commands. How about the following:

```
C:\>DOSKEY PROGS=DIR *.COM $T DIR *.EXE
```

This creates the PROGS macro. It's set equal to two DOS commands. The first is DIR *.COM, which displays all the COM program files. The second is DIR *.EXE, which displays all the EXE program files. The $T is used to represent the ¶ command separator. (Had you used ¶ itself, DOS would believe you typed in two commands: a DOSKey macro command and DIR *.EXE.)

✔ The double dollar-sign thing is also important to remember. If you have a program or filename that has a dollar sign in it, then it must be specified twice in a DOSKey macro. For example,

```
DOSKEY F=FINANCE$
```

This macro should really read

```
DOSKEY F=FINANCE$$
```

The highly unusual $-number things (or "Talk about cryptic. Wowser!")

The most unusual dollar signs are the $1, $2 (up through $9), and $* doodads. These are used to represent items typed after the macro name at the DOS prompt. For example,

```
C:\COFFEE /CREAM /SUGAR /LICE
```

If COFFEE is the DOSKey macro, then the three items following it are called *options* or *parameters*. The first is /CREAM, /SUGAR is second, and /LICE is third.

These optional parameters happen a lot with various DOS commands and programs. You format a disk with

```
C:\>FORMAT A:
```

In the preceding, A: is the sole parameter. Or you can start WordPerfect with

```
C:\>WP POEM
```

where POEM is the optional parameter.

Quite a few commands have more than one option:

```
C:\>DIR \SHEEP /S /P
```

This DIR command is used to find a file on your hard drive (SHEEP is listed). DIR is the general file-finding command. In fact, you can find any file by using the following format:

```
C:\>DIR \filename /S /P
```

Replace *filename* with the name of the file you wanted to find. The word *filename* is a placeholder for something else you'd type in later.

Face it, DIR *FILENAME* /S /P is long and complex to type. Sure would be good to have a macro for it. Yes, indeedy. Problem: How do you get the ever-changing *filename* parameter into the macro? Answer: With the $1 dollar-sign thingy, used to represent the first item typed after the macro name.

Here's how it works. Suppose the macro is named WHEREIS (as in "Where is that file?"). To find a file, you'd probably type the following at the DOS prompt:

```
C:\>WHEREIS filename
```

The WHEREIS is your macro name and *filename* is a replaceable whatever to be filled in later. Because it appears first, right after the macro name, the $1 (dollar sign and one) code is used to represent it. Pulling everything together, here is the DOSKEY command to create the WHEREIS macro:

```
DOSKEY WHEREIS=DIR \$1 /S /P
```

First comes DOSKEY, then a space, then the macro name (WHEREIS), and an equal sign. The DIR command then follows with the $1 placeholder appearing where the filename would come.

Create this macro and then run it to see how it works. For example, to find the filename BLORF, you'd type in the following:

```
C:\>WHEREIS BLORF
```

Press Enter and DOSKey translates the macro, sticking the filename BLORF into the $1 placeholder on the next line:

```
C:\>DIR \BLORF /S /P
```

DOS continues its diligent look for the file, displaying the results on the next few lines or just coming back with the dreaded File not found error.

✔ Additional information on the $1, $2, and $* things is found in the techy sidebar "Potentially painful information on replaceable parameter dollar signs."

✔ A replaceable parameter is an option or other mysterious goody that appears after a command you type at the DOS prompt. The $1 through $9 dollar-sign things represent the first through ninth replaceable parameters in a DOSKey macro.

> ✔ I don't know about you, but $* certainly takes the cake for being cryptic, no? (Actually, if you think of * being a filename wildcard for everything, it sort of makes sense. Kinda.)

> ✔ More information on the find-a-file DIR command is found in Chapter 12.

If you're a network-nerdy type, you can use DOSKey's ability to disguise its macros as DOS commands *with* the replaceable parameter thing to prevent yourself from zonking out on network commands. For example,

```
DOSKEY COPY=NCOPY $*
```

In the preceding, the normal COPY command is assigned to the network NCOPY command. The $* thing represents all the options and whatnot that would follow COPY at the DOS prompt. Each one is carefully picked up and placed after the more desirable NCOPY command, and then the network does its stuff.

Wantonly Destroying Macros

DOSKey macros must be created every time you start your PC. Therefore, a sure fire way to get rid of them is to whack the reset button. I don't really recommend that, just as I wouldn't recommend shaving your head when you only need an ear-hair trim.

Getting rid of a DOSKey macro is as easy as creating it. The only difference is that you don't type anything after the equal sign. Type **DOSKEY**, a space, the macro name, and an equal sign. Then gently whack the Enter key to kill that macro.

For example, to get rid of the D macro, you type the following command:

```
C:\>DOSKEY D=
```

That's the DOSKEY command, a space, **D**, an equal sign, and then nothing. This effectively replaces the D macro with nothing. The computer sees this, notes the wasted space, and then removes D and its associated command — the whole dang doodle macro — from memory. Poof. It's gone.

To delete any DOSKey macro, just use the following format:

```
DOSKEY macro=
```

TECHNICAL STUFF

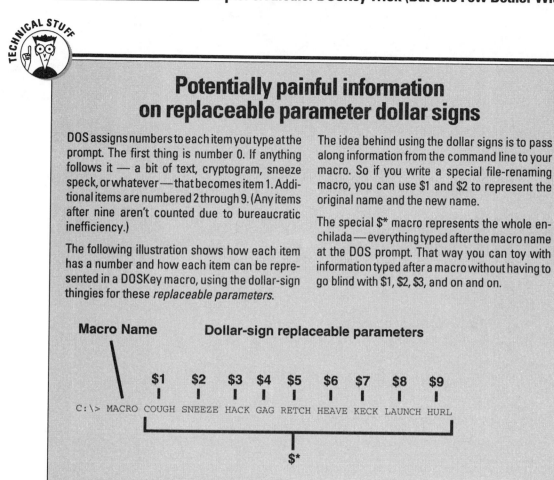

Potentially painful information on replaceable parameter dollar signs

DOS assigns numbers to each item you type at the prompt. The first thing is number 0. If anything follows it — a bit of text, cryptogram, sneeze speck, or whatever — that becomes item 1. Additional items are numbered 2 through 9. (Any items after nine aren't counted due to bureaucratic inefficiency.)

The following illustration shows how each item has a number and how each item can be represented in a DOSKey macro, using the dollar-sign thingies for these *replaceable parameters*.

The idea behind using the dollar signs is to pass along information from the command line to your macro. So if you write a special file-renaming macro, you can use $1 and $2 to represent the original name and the new name.

The special $* macro represents the whole enchilada — everything typed after the macro name at the DOS prompt. That way you can toy with information typed after a macro without having to go blind with $1, $2, $3, and on and on.

Macro Name   **Dollar-sign replaceable parameters**

| | $1 | $2 | $3 | $4 | $5 | $6 | $7 | $8 | $9 |

C:\> MACRO COUGH SNEEZE HACK GAG RETCH HEAVE KECK LAUNCH HURL

$*

Substitute the word *macro* in the preceding for the name of your macro. Press Enter and the macro's gone.

DOSKey has room for only so many macros. After you type too many, you'll see an Insufficient space type of error message. Refer to the techy box "Advanced nerdly information on freeing up DOSKey's memory" near the start of Chapter 4 for information on making more room for your macros. Or you can just delete some unused macros to free up more space.

Chapter 6
General Futzing Part I: CONFIG.SYS

*D*OS requires several programs to start its day (refer to Chapter 1). Of those, one of the most important is CONFIG.SYS. Oddly enough, CONFIG.SYS isn't even a program or a DOS file. No, it's a *text file* which you — yes, you, without even a doctorate in computer science — can and must edit. On second thought, *edit* is not the best word here; it's more like *toil*. You must toil with CONFIG.SYS. Work it raw. After all, it's your CONFIG.SYS file that helps make your PC do what it does best. Remember: Lousy CONFIG.SYS file means lousy PC performance; good CONFIG.SYS means you must be a programmer at Microsoft or some lofty computer book author.

The good news about CONFIG.SYS is that, once you understand what to do and what to avoid and get a few tiny things out of the way, you never have to bother with it again — that is, until you add some new piece of software or some hardware kajody to your system. Then it's toil and trouble all over again. This chapter is where you should turn when those moments arise.

CONFIG.SYS and the Big Picture

Face it, DOS is stupid when it comes to knowing how you run your computer. Just as DOS is starting its day (see Chapter 1), it must look for a file on disk named CONFIG.SYS to get things right. The CONFIG.SYS file contains a list of commands, which I call *configuration commands*. These commands tell DOS how to set itself up, how to use memory, and how to interact with various hardware goodies you may have attached to your PC.

✔ I suppose the name CONFIG.SYS comes from *configure system*, which implies setting up DOS and your computer to work well together.

✔ Insiders at Microsoft tell me that future versions of DOS won't have a CONFIG.SYS file. Instead, they'll come with a CONFOUND.SYS file and a companion FLUSTER.INI file.

What gets done in CONFIG.SYS?

There are two main jobs done in CONFIG.SYS:

First, CONFIG.SYS gives DOS information about how it's supposed to work. Most of this information deals with the disk drives; such as how many drives there are and how much memory to give DOS for working with disk drives. (You would think this could be handled automatically by a computer, but no.)

Second, CONFIG.SYS tells DOS and your computer's software about new and interesting devices attached to your computer. For example, if you have a sound card, CD-ROM player, tape backup unit, extra memory, a special type of hard drive, network thingamabob, a scanner, or any of a number of interesting devices, CONFIG.SYS tells DOS about it so that DOS and your programs can use those devices. This is perhaps the most important (and frustrating) part about CONFIG.SYS.

✔ Don't you think CONFIG.SYS should be fired from its two jobs?

☐ Yes ☐ No

Life without CONFIG.SYS (isn't as sweet as you'd imagine)

The ugly truth is that you don't really need a CONFIG.SYS file. Pop the champagne corks and kiss a nerd! DOS will start just fine without CONFIG.SYS. But the danger here is that DOS makes some inept assumptions about your PC when it starts. Only with a CONFIG.SYS file can you tell DOS precisely what to do and how to work. Especially in these days of multimedia computers, a CONFIG.SYS file is necessary to get everything inside your PC working together.

✔ *Sniff*. If you don't have a CONFIG.SYS on your PC, refer to the techy sidebar "But, *sniff*, I don't have a CONFIG.SYS file" later in this chapter.

CONFIG.SYS: The Guts

Unlike most of the haphazard ways DOS does things, there are some specific rules and regulations regarding CONFIG.SYS. Here they are in the order I thought of them:

- CONFIG.SYS must be in the root directory of your start-up disk, and it must be named CONFIG.SYS.

- CONFIG.SYS is a text file.

- CONFIG.SYS contains configuration commands.

- The root directory is the tippy-top, very first directory on a disk (see Chapter 16).

- The start-up disk, often called the *boot disk* by computer nerds, is either drive A or C on your computer. Most of the time it's drive C, your hard drive. (Refer to Chapter 15 for information on boot disks.)

- A text file is a file that contains readable text, often (hopefully) in your native tongue. Text files may be created or edited using a text editor, such as DOS's Editor, or any word processor.

    CONFIG.SYS doesn't really contain what most humans would call readable text. Even so, you'll probably end up changing your CONFIG.SYS files as you upgrade and use your PC.

- There are about 20-or-so configuration commands, depending on your version of DOS. These commands tell DOS how to configure itself, and they're minced around in Chapter 8.

- There is no need to memorize this list.

- Blank lines are okay in your CONFIG.SYS file. Like this:

- Be on the lookout for programs that modify your CONFIG.SYS file! Some install or setup programs may make their own modifications — sometimes without asking permission. Typically, these are good changes and help your PC and DOS understand whatever it was you just upgraded. However, keep a sharp eye out for IPS (Installation Program Stupidity). Some of the install or setup programs can really foul up a CONFIG.SYS file.

A Look at Your CONFIG.SYS File

The best way to view your CONFIG.SYS file is through lead shielding while wearing an asbestos suit. Some more daring users prefer to use the DOS Editor. You can also use the DOS Editor to change or modify your CONFIG.SYS file. For this exercise, however, it's look-only.

Follow these steps to gander at your PC's CONFIG.SYS file:

1. Type the following command:

```
C:\>EDIT C:\CONFIG.SYS
```

   That is, type **EDIT**, the DOS Editor command, then a space, and then the name of the file you're editing. In this case, you type **C**, a colon, backslash, then **CONFIG**, a period and **SYS**. Press Enter.

2. DOS digests the command and then displays a screen with the Editor and CONFIG.SYS all ready for editing (see Figure 6-1).

```
 ile  dit  earch  ptions                                             elp
┌─────────────────────────── CONFIG.SYS ────────────────────────────┐
│DEVICE=C:\DOS\HIMEM.SYS                                             ↑
│DEVICE=C:\DOS\EMM386.EXE NOEMS                                      │
│BUFFERS=15,0                                                        │
│FILES=30                                                            │
│DOS=UMB                                                             │
│LASTDRIVE=Z                                                         │
│FCBS=4,0                                                            │
│DEVICEHIGH /L:1,29120 =C:\UTIL\PROAUDIO\TSLCDR.SYS /D:MVCD001 /R /S:31
│REM  DEVICEHIGH /L:1,10208 =C:\UTIL\PROAUDIO\MVSOUND.SYS D:1 Q:7    │
│DEVICEHIGH /L:1,10208 =C:\UTIL\PROAUDIO\MVSOUND.SYS D:1 Q:3         │
│DEVICEHIGH /L:1,12048 =C:\DOS\SETVER.EXE                            │
│DOS=HIGH                                                            │
│NUMLOCK=OFF                                                         │
│SHELL=C:\DOS\COMMAND.COM C:\DOS\ /p                                 │
│STACKS=0,0                                                          │
│DEVICEHIGH /L:1,45120 =C:\UTIL\STACKER\STACKER.COM /P=5 D:          │
│DEVICEHIGH /L:1,5888 =C:\DOS\RAMDRIVE.SYS 1024 /E                   ↓
│↕                                                              →    │
└───────────────────────────────────────────────────────────────────┘
 MS-DOS Editor   <F1=Help> Press ALT to activate menus         00001:001
```

Figure 6-1:
A
CONFIG.SYS
file awaiting
editing in
the Editor.

3. Gander at thy CONFIG.SYS file! Notice that almost every command has the following format:

```
SOMETHING=SOMETHING ELSE
```

   This should be read "Please set *something* equal to *something else*." Typically, the *something else* is one or two numbers or a filename. And there may be other junk on the line as well. All in all, it's quite cryptic. Definitely touchy-not stuff.

   If your CONFIG.SYS file is particularly huge, you can use the PgDn (Page Down) key in the DOS Editor to see more of it.

4. To quit the Editor program, select the Exit command from the File menu. Press Alt, F, X on your keyboard (press each key individually), or — because the Editor is mouse-happy — you can use your PC's mouse to select the Exit menu item. If it asks you to save the changes, press N.

✔ The Editor program comes with DOS versions 5.0 and later. If you don't have the Editor, you can use the old EDLIN program. Because I detest EDLIN, I'm not writing anything here about how it works.

✔ The name following the EDIT command is CONFIG.SYS's *full pathname*: C:\CONFIG.SYS. That's C-colon for drive C (where CONFIG.SYS dwells) and then a backslash to represent the root directory. Refer to Chapter 16 for more information on pathnames.

✔ Oops! File not found error? Not every PC has a CONFIG.SYS file. Yes, they're optional. Your system runs better with one, so if your PC lacks a CONFIG.SYS, refer to the sidebar "But, *sniff*, I don't have a CONFIG.SYS file" for more information.

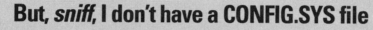

But, *sniff*, I don't have a CONFIG.SYS file

The quickest way to get a CONFIG.SYS file if you don't have one is to run DOS 6's MemMaker program. This program builds an adequate-to-mediocre CONFIG.SYS on your PC, which is at least a place to start. (To make sure this happens, press the F3 key right after MemMaker says your system's memory situation hasn't improved.)

The following is just such a CONFIG.SYS file, created on a 386 (or later) computer with MemMaker:

```
DEVICE=C:\DOS\HIMEM.SYS
DEVICE=C:\DOS\EMM386.EXE NOEMS
BUFFERS=15,0
FILES=8
DOS=UMB
DOS=HIGH
LASTDRIVE=E
FCBS=4,0
```

I suppose you could use the DOS Editor and create that CONFIG.SYS file by hand if you like. Or you can start with the following commands, which I feel are better than what MemMaker gives you:

```
REM My very own CONFIG.SYS file
DEVICE=C:\DOS\HIMEM.SYS
DOS=HIGH
FILES=20
BUFFERS=15
LASTDRIVE=Z
```

Use the tutorial instructions in the following section to create a CONFIG.SYS file on your computer. Place the preceding lines into this file. That should make you happy and end the CONFIG.SYS-envy your computer has with your friends' PCs.

Updating Your CONFIG.SYS File

The dirty thing about CONFIG.SYS is that it just can't be left alone. This is one of the worst aspects of DOS; whether you like it or not, CONFIG.SYS tinkering is required.

You should always start with a solid CONFIG.SYS file; something like those suggested in the sidebar "But, *sniff,* I don't have a CONFIG.SYS file" is fine. But after you create a CONFIG.SYS file, CONFIG.SYS requires modification. This usually happens in one of the following circumstances:

✔ You add some new piece of software, and its install or setup program fiddles with CONFIG.SYS.

✔ You add some new piece of hardware, and it requires a *device driver* so that DOS and your software can appreciate it.

✔ You read something in a book or magazine about "optimizing your PC" and decide you're hell-bent on modifying your CONFIG.SYS file.

✔ You're bored and, like my friend Tom, just want to tinker with CONFIG.SYS until your PC doesn't work right anymore.

Whatever the case, the following sections outline how you can add, remove, and modify commands and update CONFIG.SYS. The last step — resetting your computer — is quite important. Don't forget it!

✔ You update CONFIG.SYS by using a text editor program, such as the Editor program that comes with DOS. Refer to the preceding section, "A Look at Your CONFIG.SYS File," for more information on editing CONFIG.SYS.

✔ The best tool for updating CONFIG.SYS is a text editor, such as DOS's Editor. However, if you need to use a word processor, remember to save CONFIG.SYS back to disk as a plain text, DOS text, ASCII, or unformatted file.

✔ If you do use a word processor to edit CONFIG.SYS, turn the word-wrap feature off. This is best done by setting the right margin out to about 20 inches or so. The objective is to avoid having your word processor split long command lines in CONFIG.SYS, which would befuddle DOS to no end.

✔ It's a good idea to make a backup copy of CONFIG.SYS before you edit it to make changes. The following COPY command will back up CONFIG.SYS:

```
C:\>COPY C:\CONFIG.SYS C:\CONFIG.BAK
```

The backup copy—containing your original CONFIG.SYS file—is named CONFIG.BAK. (Some editors may automatically back up CONFIG.SYS for you; the DOS Editor isn't one of them.)

Adding a new command to your CONFIG.SYS file (pray you don't need to do this often)

The most important part about adding a new command to CONFIG.SYS is deciding where to put it. Where you put the command is important for only one type of command, the DEVICE command. Any other command, no matter what it is, can go just about anywhere and appear in any order in CONFIG.SYS. Here are the rules for adding a new command to CONFIG.SYS:

✔ Just stick the new command at the end of the file.

Edit CONFIG.SYS according to the instructions in the previous section. When the DOS Editor starts, press Ctrl-End (the Ctrl and End keys together). This moves the cursor to the end of the file, where you can type your new line.

✔ If you're adding a DEVICE configuration command, check your documentation to see whether you must place the command in a special location.

Generally speaking, your DEVICE configuration commands shout out their pecking order. Refer to the documentation telling you to stick the command in CONFIG.SYS, and it will beg to be put first, last, or after this or that. If you're confused, the following is typically how the DEVICE commands line up in CONFIG.SYS:

- **First:** Hard disk device drivers, such as the ASPI4DOS.SYS and other SCSI drivers. (Obviously, you'll need this driver right away because it controls your hard drive.)

- **Second:** Memory management device drivers (HIMEM.SYS, EMM386.EXE, QEMM.SYS, 386MAX.SYS, and so on).

- **Third:** Other device drivers, whatever: ANSI.SYS, sound drivers, CD-ROM drivers, network drivers. Some of these may jockey for position; for instance, the CD-ROM driver may come before the network driver. Double-check the documentation for any fussiness. (Look in the "Shooting trouble" section; some information there may help you.)

- **Last:** Some device drivers want to be last. Stacker usually comes last in CONFIG.SYS. One reason is that other commands may set up disk drives or RAM drives that you may want Stacker to squeeze and compress.

✔ When you're done, double-check what you type. Never be in a hurry. Then save CONFIG.SYS to disk and return promptly to the DOS prompt. At that point you need to reset your computer, which is covered in just a few pages.

✔ You can save a file in the DOS Editor by selecting the **S**ave command from the **F**ile menu; press Alt, F, S (press each key, one after the other — not together), or you can use your PC's mouse. Quit the Editor by selecting E**x**it from the **F**ile menu (press Alt, F, X, or use the mouse).

✔ Remember to always double-check what you typed, save CONFIG.SYS to disk, and then reset your computer to lock in the changes. Refer to the later section "The final and most important step to updating CONFIG.SYS" for more details.

✔ Each command you add to CONFIG.SYS appears on a line by itself. Even if the manual or book lists the command on two lines, don't split it in two; press the Enter key only at the end of the line. (Your editor should "shift to the right" as you type, allowing you to enter a very long line, if necessary.)

✔ The order of the commands in your CONFIG.SYS file, with the exception of the DEVICE configuration commands, isn't important. FILES, BUFFERS, STACKS, and so on can go anywhere. But DEVICE configuration commands may have to appear in a specific order.

Removing a command from CONFIG.SYS (the mean way)

To delete a command from CONFIG.SYS, use your text editor and get ready to operate. Firing up the DOS Editor for this purpose is covered in the section "A Look at Your CONFIG.SYS File" earlier in this chapter.

Use the up (↑) or down (↓) arrow keys to highlight the line you want to gut. Sometimes there's no "highlight," but the cursor hovers somewhere on the line you want to zap.

Delete the line! In the Editor, press Ctrl-Y (press and hold the Ctrl key and tap the Y key; then release both keys). The Ctrl-Y command may also work in other editors. You can also just keep woodpeckering the Delete key until the line is gone.

After it's gone, save CONFIG.SYS back to disk; then quit your editor, return to the DOS prompt, and reset the computer.

✔ The reasons you need to reset your computer are discussed in the section "The final and most important step to updating CONFIG.SYS" just a few paragraphs away.

✔ The Ctrl-Y command deletes a line of text in the DOS Editor.

✔ Why remove a command? You may have upgraded your system and no longer need an old "crutch" command or device driver. Or maybe you added something, such as a RAM drive, and then changed your mind. No problem. Happens all the time.

✔ It's a good idea to remove any duplicate configuration commands you may have lurking in your CONFIG.SYS file. For example, if you see two BUFFERS, FCBS, FILES, LASTDRIVE, or STACKS commands, you should probably delete one of them. Which one? Ask your guru for help, or refer to the section "Working Out the DEVICE Configuration Command" in Chapter 7, as well as the section on that command in Chapter 8.

✔ No, Robin, we should obey the speed limit. There's no point in breaking the laws we're trying to uphold and protect.

Removing a command in CONFIG.SYS (the nice way)

DOS mavens know a trick that enables them to disable a line in CONFIG.SYS without eviscerating it entirely. They use the REM configuration command. Take the following command, for example:

```
DEVICE=C:\DOS\ANSI.SYS
```

To disable this command, you could just delete it. Or you can earn bonus DOS smart-guy points and edit it to read as follows:

```
REM DEVICE=C:\DOS\ANSI.SYS
```

In the preceding, the word REM was typed, followed by a space, inserted squarely at the start of the line. This disables the command without deleting it. The result is that the command is gone but not forgotten.

- ✔ I refer to this technique as "remming a command."

- ✔ REM is actually a configuration command. You use REM to insert remarks or comments into your CONFIG.SYS file. When used as shown in the preceding example, REM leads DOS to believe that the old CONFIG.SYS command is really a comment. (Ha! Dumb ol' DOS.) Using REM has the same result as deleting the command, but it's more like putting the command in suspended animation or "on ice" (just like Walt Disney).

- ✔ The beauty here is that, to reenable the command, you just edit CONFIG.SYS and delete the REM at the start of the line. That reactivates the command with a minimum of typing, and you don't have to refer to the manual or a book to remember what the old command was.

- ✔ You can find more information about the REM command in the section "CONFIG.SYS Commands: The Top Five" in Chapter 8.

The final and most important step to updating CONFIG.SYS

After updating your CONFIG.SYS file, you need to — nay, *must* — reset your computer. Resetting your computer is necessary because DOS only reads CONFIG.SYS once, right after the computer starts. Even though you changed the file, to lock those changes in, you must reset your PC.

Make sure you're at the DOS prompt before you reset. Also, if you've been using Windows, the DOS Shell, DESQview, Software Carousel, or some menu system, quit before you reset the computer.

✔ Reset by either pressing the Ctrl-Alt-Delete keys all together, or you can press your PC's reset button (if it has one).

✔ Some nerdy people say *warm boot* the computer. This is the same thing as pressing the reset switch or Ctrl-Alt-Delete to reset. Whatever.

✔ Any time you work on CONFIG.SYS, whether to add or remove a command, you should take these three steps: 1) Double-check what you typed or removed. 2) Save the modified CONFIG.SYS file to disk. 3) Reset the computer.

Dealing with CONFIG.SYS Errors (without Gnashing Your Teeth)

During those rare moments when you must work on CONFIG.SYS, you'll find the occasional error. This is one of those aspects that makes DOS so painful. It's true. If it weren't, Apple Computer wouldn't figure CONFIG.SYS so prominently in its "reasons to buy a Macintosh" commercials.

CONFIG.SYS errors will startle you when you reset your computer. Your eyes will bulge as you watch them appear and scamper up the screen — too fast to see. That's if you're lucky. Often, with some CONFIG.SYS screw-ups, the PC decides not to start. That usually happens way after closing time, when every local nerd or guru has hit the drive-thru espresso stands for a latté-on-the-road before staying up all night for more hacking.

Shooting trouble

If you do encounter an error in your CONFIG.SYS file, take heart. Odds are really good the error's nothing more than a spelling mistake or typo. When you get the computer to start again, use your Editor to review your changes to CONFIG.SYS. Often you'll find the error quickly, and then you can edit, save, and reboot your computer, and everything will be fine. If not, try the following techniques:

✔ Just after you see the `Starting MS-DOS` message, press the F5 key.

The F5 key tells DOS to skip both your CONFIG.SYS and AUTOEXEC.BAT start-up files, and you are presented with nothing more than a boring DOS prompt when the computer starts. At that point, you can edit CONFIG.SYS without having anything foul up the PC or seize DOS in its tracks.

✔ If you have trouble figuring out where the problem is, then press the F8 key just after you see the Starting MS-DOS message.

The F8 key causes DOS to march through CONFIG.SYS one line at a time, asking you "yes or no?" for each command. Look at the following, for example:

```
DEVICE=C:\DOS\HIMEM.SYS [Y/N]?
```

Press Y to run the command; press N to skip it. So if you see something like this,

```
DEVICE=C:\DOS\HYRAM.SYS [Y/N]?
```

and you really meant to type HIMEM instead of HYRAM, you can press N to skip over it.

Or maybe you press Y but then see an error:

```
DEVICE=C:\SODA\COLA.SYS /FIZZ [Y/N]? Y

COLA.SYS (C) 1994 BelchSoft Inc.

Whoa! Error detected: There is no /FIZZ option.

Now I refuse to work properly.
```

In this example, you pressed Y to run the command but, lo, an improper option was specified. Oh, well. At least now you know where to find the problem and get it fixed.

✔ After you find a problem, you can press the Escape key (Esc) to tell DOS, "Okay, no more of the Y/N stuff. Just run the rest of CONFIG.SYS as is. Thanks."

✔ Pressing F5 skips over both CONFIG.SYS and AUTOEXEC.BAT. Pressing F8 trudges through CONFIG.SYS one line at a time, pressing Y or N to run or skip each command.

✔ There's no need to be overly aggressive when pressing the F5 or F8 keys; you have up to two seconds (which is really an eternity in computer time) to press either one after the Starting MS-DOS message.

✔ Alas, the F5 and F8 keys only work with DOS 6 or later.

✔ Hmmm. Wouldn't some *lemon cake* be good right about now?

✔ If you don't have DOS 6 (or later), your only troubleshooting option is to suffer. Actually, you should obtain a *boot disk* and start the computer using that. Refer to Chapter 15 for information on using a boot disk.

The (unfortunately) common errors

DOS does spit up some error messages when CONFIG.SYS runs. There are three of them — the common errors — you may encounter (but, hopefully, not that often):

```
Unrecognized command in CONFIG.SYS
```

This is a typo, no doubt. Something was stuck in CONFIG.SYS that shouldn't be there. (One time my sister, obviously drunk, typed *Hi, this is Jody* — right there in my CONFIG.SYS file!) Sometimes I'll mistakenly insert batch file commands in CONFIG.SYS when I'm also editing AUTOEXEC.BAT (or drunk). The solution here is to either step through CONFIG.SYS using the F8 key trick mentioned in the previous section or just review your last edits to the CONFIG.SYS file.

```
Error in CONFIG.SYS line xx
```

Something boo-booed at line number *xx* in your CONFIG.SYS file. Chances are it's a typo, but it could be that you typed the letter *O* when you meant to type zero, or maybe you put in a little *L* when a number 1 was needed, or maybe a value is too big. Fortunately, the line number is given. Because most editors list the line numbers right there on the screen, tracking down and fixing the problem is a cinch.

```
Bad or missing . . .
```

The dots above are replaced by the name of a file, most likely a device driver or other program name. What happened was that you specified the wrong location for that file. Sometimes this error may occur if you've just reorganized your hard drive and moved some files around. Oops! You also need to change their locations (actually *pathnames*) in CONFIG.SYS.

- ✔ In all of these situations, it's usually required that you edit the CONFIG.SYS file to patch up the error. Refer to the section "Updating Your CONFIG.SYS File" earlier in this chapter for the details.

- ✔ Again, DOS gets judgmental. I can understand a file *missing*, but how can it be *bad?*

- ✔ Other potential error messages are listed in the next section.

Specific errors and device driver errors

There are a few other errors you may see after you change your CONFIG.SYS file. These aren't as common as the three mentioned in the last section:

- ✔ Bad command or parameters

  This message means some of the options you typed are probably wrong. Check with the DOS manual or on-line help for all the options as well as the proper range of values you should specify with some configuration commands.

- ✔ Invalid country code or code page

  The frustrating numbers after the COUNTRY configuration command are obviously fouled up. This typically happens when you use the code for some fractured former Eastern European communist bloc nation.

- ✔ Error in COUNTRY command

  Yet another foul up with the COUNTRY command.

- ✔ Insufficient memory for COUNTRY.SYS file

  Golly, be thankful you live here and not somewhere else.

- ✔ Configuration too large for memory

  This is a doozy, like *Body too large for pants*: You've run out of memory, and the computer hasn't even started! The settings you've made and device drivers you've loaded in your CONFIG.SYS file are too big. You need to restart your PC with a boot diskette (see Chapter 15) and then edit some of the device drivers out of CONFIG.SYS.

- ✔ Invalid STACK parameters

  Someone stuck some strange numbers after the STACKS command, like

  ```
  STACKS=HI, THIS IS JODY
  ```

Finally, there are error messages particular to each device driver. For example, you may have unplugged your CD-ROM drive so the CD-ROM device driver panics and claims the drive is stolen. Lots of device drivers produce their own "out of memory" errors. And third party memory managers will come up with Not enough memory to load high; loading low instead, **or sometimes** I'm fed up and moving to Cleveland.

✔ Because these messages often scroll up the screen faster than you can see, it's a good idea to restart your computer and press the F8 key to step through CONFIG.SYS one line at a time. The section "Shooting trouble" has the details.

✔ For the record, my sister Jody does not drink, and I'm sure she'd be highly offended by my treatment of her in this chapter. She's really a good, decent person and a fine veterinarian. But she can be a bit testy when she has eyeball duty at the hospital.

Chapter 7

The Wacky World
of Configuration Commands

● ●

In This Chapter

▶ Understanding configuration commands

▶ Dealing with the command format

▶ Working out the DEVICE configuration command

▶ Reviewing DOS's many device drivers

▶ Deciding which device drivers you may need

▶ Adding a device driver to CONFIG.SYS

● ●

*T*he question isn't "What evils lurk in the heart of your CONFIG.SYS file?" No, the question is "Who cares?" or "If I do need to know, how much of it can I safely avoid?"

The answer to the first question is that *configuration commands* lurk in your CONFIG.SYS file. There are only 22 of them. Hey, some people innocently walk into a first-year French class only to discover that there are literally *thousands* of words they need to memorize. *Vous avez du bon chance!* But your luck is even better than you think. Because of the 22 configuration commands, there are only one or two commands you'll ever need to mess with. Regardless, this chapter has a few choice words to say about almost all of them.

Understanding Configuration Commands

Configuration commands are those grunts and squawks that appear in your CONFIG.SYS file. They tell DOS what to do with itself, how to configure itself, how to dress properly, and so on. There are 22 of them, but only five are worth mentioning, and of those, only one is what I consider important.

The five commands worth mentioning are BUFFERS, DEVICE, FILES, REM, and SHELL. The important one is DEVICE, which is covered in its own section a few pages away in this meaty chapter.

All the configuration commands, shown in a handy, table-like format

Table 7-1 lists all the configuration commands, current with MS-DOS 6.2. Please don't bother to memorize the contents of the table. (Even I looked them up in the on-line help before typing in the list.)

Table 7-1	CONFIG.SYS's Configuration Commands
Command	*What It Does*
BREAK	Breaks the computer (Not really! See Chapter 2)
BUFFERS	Makes DOS enjoy using the disk drives
COUNTRY	Sets up information for using DOS in other countries
DEVICE	Loads a special program called a *device driver*
DEVICEHIGH	Loads said device driver into *high memory*
DOS	Tells the computer where to stick DOS
DRIVPARM	Tells DOS about strange disk drives
FCBS	Sets up dealies called File Control Blocks (FCBs)
FILES	Makes DOS very happy about files
INCLUDE	Configuration menu command (advanced stuff)
INSTALL	Takes a program and sticks it into memory
LASTDRIVE	Lets DOS use just so many disk drives
MENUCOLOR	Configuration menu command
MENUDEFAULT	Configuration menu command
MENUITEM	Configuration menu command
NUMLOCK	Turns the numeric keypad on or off
REM	Allows for remarks and comments
SEIZE	Causes your PC to stop working at random points in time
SET	Creates an *environment variable* (see Chapter 19)
SHELL	Tells DOS which program to use as its shell
STACKS	Tells DOS how to neatly stack information in memory
SUBMENU	Configuration menu command
SWITCHES	Myriad optional stuff, tossed together

Each of the commands in Table 7-1 controls a different aspect of your computer's configuration. (And that's why they're called configuration commands, like duh.) Each of them is defined absolutely in your DOS manual and in your DOS 6's help system. Brief descriptions also appear in Chapter 8.

✔ The most important configuration command is DEVICE. It's covered, all by itself, in the section "Working out the DEVICE Configuration Command."

✔ There are actually 22 configuration commands. Only the truly disturbed would memorize them all. Table 7-1 lists everything; Chapter 8 provides more detail.

✔ Har, har. There is no SEIZE configuration command, though it often seems that way.

✔ In DOS 6, you can use the HELP command to find out even more information on the configuration commands, should you be so inclined. Type **HELP CONFIG** at the DOS prompt.

Basic configuration command format stuff

Overall, CONFIG.SYS's configuration commands have the following format. This is the way they appear in CONFIG.SYS — their presentation, so to speak:

```
COMMAND=VALUE
```

The *command* is the configuration command name, which can be in uppercase, lowercase, mixed case, mental case, or attaché case. The command is followed by an equal sign and then the *value*. The *value* part can be a filename, number, option, smudge, whatever; it all depends on what the configuration command needs to configure.

✔ Each configuration command appears on a line by itself in your CONFIG.SYS file. The line may get long, and it will definitely look cryptic — especially if you run memory management software on your PC.

✔ Most text editors, such as the DOS Editor, scroll right to let you edit and see ends of long lines.

✔ An equal sign doesn't really have to follow the configuration command. Older versions of DOS said that you could use either an equal sign or a space. However, to be consistent and because no one likes a spoilsport, I recommend that everyone use equal signs.

✔ Chapter 8 outlines recommended settings for each configuration command.

✔ Don't edit, modify, change, delete, mutilate, fold, or spindle any command in CONFIG.SYS unless you know what you're doing. Don't let Earl do it either because he *definitely* doesn't know what he's doing!

Working Out the DEVICE Configuration Command

The most popular CONFIG.SYS configuration command of all time is DEVICE. It won the PC World Most Favorite Configuration Command Annual Award 12 years straight before the NUMLOCK command usurped the title last year.

The DEVICE command appears over and over in CONFIG.SYS. That's okay; most PCs require a few device drivers to get themselves going, and the DEVICE configuration command is what's necessary to make that happen.

Of course, calling a configuration command *popular* is like saying "The shot that kids like the doctor to give them the most is the tetanus shot, followed by gamma globulin, with the rabies vaccine coming in a traditional last."

What does the DEVICE configuration command do?

The DEVICE configuration command loads special programs called *device drivers*. The device driver programs control specific hardware gilhooleys attached to your PC. Here is just a random sample of things a device driver may control:

Hard drives	Tape backup units	Computer mice
Scanners	Network hoses	Sound cards
CD-ROMs	The lawnmower	A video camera
Disk compression software	Smart-file erasing programs	A twitching muscle in your thigh

Only by putting a device driver in CONFIG.SYS with the DEVICE command can you get your computer and your software to use these and similar devices.

- ✔ Device drivers are special programs loaded into memory by CONFIG.SYS's DEVICE command.

- ✔ Most device drivers end with the SYS filename extension. Some end in COM, and there are a few EXE device drivers as well.

- ✔ Not every file that ends in SYS is a device driver! Two such files that come with DOS are COUNTRY.SYS and KEYBOARD.SYS. Also, the two "secret" DOS files, MSDOS.SYS and IO.SYS, are not device drivers. They are strange programs that you should not use with the DEVICE configuration command.

Don't bother with this info on why device drivers are necessary

It works like this: By itself, DOS only knows a few *devices.* These include your keyboard, disk drives, monitor, serial port, and printer port. That's about it. Any other devices you have connected to or living inside your PC require a device driver for DOS to know about them. The device driver software not only controls that specific bit of hardware, but it also allows DOS and other programs to use the hardware.

Things to remember about the DEVICE configuration command

The DEVICE command works like all other commands in CONFIG.SYS. First comes DEVICE, then an equal sign, and then the name of the device driver, followed by any options it may have. For example,

```
DEVICE=C:\DOS\SMARTDRV.EXE /DOUBLE_BUFFER
```

The preceding device driver is SMARTDRV.EXE; its *full pathname* (the long version of the filename) is C:\DOS\SMARTDRV.EXE. An option, /DOUBLE_BUFFER, follows the device driver name. Generally speaking, that's how it goes.

The only way to ensure that you have done everything properly is to save CONFIG.SYS, exit back to DOS from your editor, and then reboot the computer: Ka-chinka! Keep an eagle eye on the screen as the PC starts. Be wary of any error messages. Then test out the device driver (or the device it controls) to make sure that everything is working as expected. Fine-tuning may be required, but everything should work right the first time.

- ✔ Yes, due to the fact that you must always specify a full pathname to the device driver file, these commands can get quite long in CONFIG.SYS.

- ✔ Memory optimization software will often modify your DEVICE commands in CONFIG.SYS. That's okay! Refer to Chapter 25 for more information on how memory management may munge CONFIG.SYS.

- ✔ So that you can easily tell which changes work and which don't, make only one change at a time and then reboot. That way, if you have a problem all of a sudden, you'll know what caused it.

Rules for the DEVICE configuration command

Here are some important notes about using the DEVICE configuration command:

✔ **Get the device driver name right, all of it.**

You must always type in the full filename plus the extension. If the device driver is named SOUND.SYS, you must type in SOUND.SYS. If you don't, you get one of CONFIG.SYS's infamous errors.

Also, don't assume that the device driver ends in SYS. Many also end in EXE, and COM is also popular. And that's not ruling out any funky endings I haven't encountered.

✔ **Get the path right.**

The path is the long, C-colon-backslash thing that appears before the device driver name.

For example, if SOUND.SYS is in the SOUND subdirectory on drive C, the full pathname is as follows:

```
C:\SOUND\SOUND.SYS
```

If you don't specify the full pathname — or specify the wrong pathname — DOS tells you Bad or missing whatever.sys when the computer starts.

✔ **Get the options right.**

Many device drivers are followed by options. Make sure that you type them in correctly and, if required, in the proper order.

✔ **Save and reboot to test.**

A warning about duplicate DEVICE commands

The DEVICE configuration command is one of the few commands that can appear more than once in your CONFIG.SYS file. But, usually, the stuff that follows the DEVICE command must be unique. For example, I've seen a lot of systems that have two identical DEVICE commands in them, which is usually wrong. For example,

```
DEVICE=C:\DOS\HIMEM.SYS
DOS=HIGH
DEVICE=C:\DOS\HIMEM.SYS
```

In the preceding, the second DEVICE command is unnecessary: the first one does the job of starting the HIMEM.SYS device driver; the second one just takes up space — or worse. In some instances, the duplicate command may actually cause something stinky to happen. For example, two duplicate hard disk device drivers may cause you to "lose" your hard drives. That can be a pain.

The idea is to keep an eyeball on your entire CONFIG.SYS file as you add new commands, especially DEVICE commands.

✔ Be aware that there are exceptions! The RAMDRIVE.SYS (or VDISK.SYS) device driver can appear more than once in CONFIG.SYS when you're creating more than one RAM drive:

```
DEVICE=C:\DOS\RAMDRIVE.SYS 1024 /E
DEVICE=C:\DOS\RAMDRIVE.SYS 1024 /E
```

These commands look like duplicates, but they're really used to create two 1024K RAM drives. This is one of the rare (if not only) times such duplicate commands are allowed in CONFIG.SYS.

✔ Wanna create a RAM drive? Refer to Chapter 24.

A mercifully quick stroll through DOS's device drivers

Microsoft knows that you're curious about using the DEVICE configuration command in CONFIG.SYS. To please you, they've tossed in a few freebie device drivers with DOS (a few more than necessary). I've listed the lot in Table 7-2.

Device drivers you may find lurking in your CONFIG.SYS (or, "Hey, haven't I seen you around here before?")

What mayest thou see in thy CONFIG.SYS? On your PC, you may find the following device drivers:

SETVER.EXE: DOS's SETUP (installation) program often sticks the SETVER device driver in your CONFIG.SYS file.

HIMEM.SYS and EMM386.EXE: The HIMEM.SYS and EMM386.EXE device drivers cuddle together in CONFIG.SYS if you're using DOS's memory management capabilities.

RAMDRIVE.SYS or VDISK.SYS: If you're using a RAM drive, you'll often see the RAMDRIVE.SYS or VDISK.SYS device drivers doing their thing in CONFIG.SYS.

POWER.EXE or INTERLNK.EXE: Laptops may have the POWER.EXE or INTERLNK.EXE device drivers present.

Table 7-2	Device Drivers Included with DOS
Filename	*Its Function in Life*
ANSI.SYS	Controls the screen and keyboard for batch files and the DOS prompt
DBLSPACE.SYS	Makes DoubleSpace happy (MS-DOS 6.0 and 6.2)
DISPLAY.SYS	Configures something about code pages
DRIVER.SYS	Sets up floppy drives on weird computers
EGA.SYS	Supports fancy-schmansy stuff for old, EGA monitors
EMM386.EXE	DOS's second memory management device driver
HIMEM.SYS	DOS's first memory management device driver (and easier to pronounce)
INTERLNK.EXE	Provides brains for DOS's InterLink command
POWER.EXE	Configures supplies battery-saving smarts to some laptops (probably not the one you own, though)
PRINTER.SYS	Something about code pages for printers (this driver doesn't come with DOS 6 at all)
RAMDRIVE.SYS	Sets up a RAM drive on your PC (some DOSs use RAMDRIVE.SYS, the rest use VDISK.SYS)
SETVER.EXE	DOS's "version-fooling utility," which makes older DOS applications happy
SMARTDRV.EXE	Used in a few circumstances when your hard drive lusts after *double buffering* (see Chapter 5 on disk caching)
TWITCH.SYS	Controls your *vastus externus*, occasionally causing it to spasm in time to the Minute Waltz
VDISK.SYS	Sets up a RAM drive on your PC (some DOSs use VDISK.SYS, the rest use RAMDRIVE.SYS)

✔ You may see other device drivers as well, depending on your PC's hardware setup and your software's needs. However, device drivers relate mostly to third-party hardware and occasionally to software.

✔ Each one of DOS's device drivers has its own format, options, and other bangles you have to specify and include to get things to work right. A few of the more necessary ones are discussed elsewhere in this book. If not, they're just not important enough to bother with. (Or if you're daring, you can look up each in the DOS manual or the on-line help command included with DOS 6.)

- Refer to Chapter 11 for more information on the SETVER.EXE device driver.

- Information on memory management is found in detail in Chapter 25.

- Using DOS's RAMDrive device driver and RAMDRIVE.SYS (or VDISK.SYS) and general information about RAM drives are covered in Chapter 24.

- The DBLSPACE.SYS device driver is used when you install DOS's DoubleSpace disk-doubling software (available only in MS-DOS 6.0 and 6.2). The device driver helps DoubleSpace work with your computer's memory only; naturally, it has nothing to do with getting DoubleSpace to work.

Which device drivers do you really need?

Sometimes, certain device drivers can be a burden to your PC, unnecessary and even counterproductive. Because each device driver takes up a smidgen of precious memory, it's a good idea to be discriminating when choosing device drivers. Table 7-3 provides a list of some device drivers you may not actually need that you may have in your CONFIG.SYS.

Attached to your CONFIG.SYS file may be additional device drivers that aren't doing squat. Refer to your guru if you're curious about what they do. You can also trudge through your various computer manuals to see whether you can locate any of them or find out to which hardware devices or software programs they're attached.

As with anything in CONFIG.SYS, don't just randomly delete lines if you don't know what they do. The preceding situations are very specific. If they don't apply to you, don't delete the command.

If you're using Windows, you don't need the MOUSE.SYS or MOUSE.COM drivers. However, if you're running DOS software inside Windows and that software uses the mouse, you need a mouse driver. Use MOUSE.COM in AUTOEXEC.BAT.

Adding a Device Driver to CONFIG.SYS (an Example to Follow)

Adding a device driver to your CONFIG.SYS file works just like adding any other command. To ease you through the process, take the following tutorial:

1. Discover where your device driver likes to be placed.

Table 7-3	Device Drivers You May Not Need	
Driver Name	*What It Does*	*When You Don't Need It*
ANSI.SYS	Provides for fancy-looking prompts and a li'l bit of keyboard magic (see Chapter 21)	If you're running Windows on your system, you probably won't need ANSI.SYS; feel free to Ctrl-Y this file to kingdom come.
EMM386.EXE	DOS's memory management (second phase)	If you have an 80286 or 8088 PC, don't bother with EMM386.EXE. Also, you won't need it if you're using a third-party memory manager, such as QEMM or 386MAX.
HIMEM.SYS	DOS's main memory management device driver	If you have an 8088 PC or another memory manager (QEMM or 386MAX) installed, you don't need HIMEM.SYS.
MOUSE.SYS	Controls the mouse	You never need it! Use the MOUSE.COM program in your PC's AUTOEXEC.BAT file instead of this mouse device driver.
RAMDRIVE.SYS (or VDISK.SYS)	Creates a RAM drive on your PC	Although I think RAM drives are handy, if you're low on memory, it's best to let your programs use it instead of wasting it on a RAM drive. (How much is too low? With anything less than 2MB of memory, you shouldn't bother with a RAM drive.)
SMARTDRV.EXE	Provides a service known as *double buffering*, which is only necessary on a few PCs	Refer to the section on disk caches in Chapter 23 to see whether you need this command in your CONFIG.SYS file.
SMARTDRV.SYS	Disk caching	You never need this! SMARTDRV.SYS is the older version of the SMARTDrive disk cache program and has since been replaced with SMARTDRV.EXE in both MS-DOS 6 and Windows 3.1 or later. Refer to Chapter 23 for information on using SMARTDRV.EXE and delete the line containing this offending command from your CONFIG.SYS file.

For this example, I'll use the ANSI.SYS device driver. The DOS manual says this about ANSI.SYS:

> *Non curo. Mea nil refert.*

So it can go anywhere. (To be honest, most of the complex device drivers install themselves, though a manual may offer a preference. You should read the documentation, skim it, or at least claim you did.)

2. Edit CONFIG.SYS. Fire up your editor and edit the CONFIG.SYS file. Editing CONFIG.SYS by using the DOS Editor is covered in Chapter 6, but here's the command you'd type to edit CONFIG.SYS:

```
C:\>EDIT C:\CONFIG.SYS
```

3. Locate the exact spot for the DEVICE command. If an exact spot isn't necessary, just stick it at the end of the file. (Press Ctrl-End in the Editor.)

4. Obtain a snow-white lamb and examine it for blemishes. Whoa! Wait a second. Wrong operating system.

5. Type in the device command. For the most part, you'll be following an example, such as

```
DEVICE=C:\DOS\ANSI.SYS
```

Be careful with these examples! They assume the proper *pathname* for your device driver. In the preceding, I'm assuming that ANSI.SYS is in the DOS directory (which is probably where it lives). To avoid being wishy-washy, most manuals are conveniently vague:

```
DEVICE=pathname\ANSI.SYS
```

The manuals expect you to replace the italicized *pathname* in their example with the full pathname. (Refer to Chapter 16 for information on pathnames.)

6. Double-check the command. Equal sign okay? Backslashes in the proper spots? Jots and titles? *Device* spelled okay? Great.

Some manuals may break up a long configuration command on two lines; don't do that in CONFIG.SYS! Type your command all on the same line.

7. Save CONFIG.SYS back to disk.

8. Exit the Editor.

9. When you're safely back at the DOS prompt, reset your computer.

10. Watch the screen to make sure that no new, startling errors occur.

✔ Refer to Chapter 6 for a detailed description of updating your CONFIG.SYS file, in the section conveniently titled "Updating Your CONFIG.SYS File."

✔ Chapter 6 also has a few more details on using the DOS Editor to accomplish the CONFIG.SYS editing task.

✔ Refer to Chapter 21 for more information on the ANSI.SYS device driver (or return there if you were originally sent here from there).

✔ Donuone Latine loquebar?

Chapter 8

The Dry and Boring Configuration Command Summary

· ·

In This Chapter

▶ Looking at the five popular CONFIG.SYS commands

▶ Shielding your eyes from the rest of the commands

· ·

*T*he purpose of this chapter isn't to teach you all the CONFIG.SYS configuration commands. Heavens, no! Instead, this chapter is offered as an answer to the observation: "What the heck is that in my CONFIG.SYS file?" Although I can't describe what everything in CONFIG.SYS is or what it does (because, for the most part, little of it is important), I can shed some light on the more bizarre things you may find in your PC's CONFIG.SYS file. This chapter opens the hood on CONFIG.SYS, separating the grease and dirt (the majority) from the pretty parts (the minority).

CONFIG.SYS Commands, the Top Five

The typical CONFIG.SYS file may be several lines long but usually contains only a handful of configuration commands. Chief among them is the DEVICE command, which is covered in detail in Chapter 7. The others rounding out the "Top Five" are BUFFERS, FILES, REM, and SHELL. Odds are really good you'll see these scattered about your CONFIG.SYS file.

The BUFFERS configuration command

What it does: Sets aside memory storage (which is what a "buffer" is) that allows DOS to more efficiently access your disk drives.

Typical appearance:

```
BUFFERS=15
```

Suggestion: If you're using a disk cache, such as the SMARTDrive cache that comes with DOS or Windows, then you don't even need to specify this command in your CONFIG.SYS file. Indeed, I recommend not specifying the BUFFERS command and instead turning to the section on disk caches in Chapter 23.

The DEVICE configuration command

What it does: Loads a special program, called a device driver, into memory. It is by this program that your computer, DOS, and your software can access and use a particular device, or "thing" attached to or inside your PC.

Typical appearance:

```
DEVICE=C:\DOS\HIMEM.SYS
```

The DEVICE configuration command is followed by an equal sign and then the complete *pathname* for the device driver. Any options belonging to the driver may appear after the pathname on the same line.

Suggestion: Refer to the section on device drivers in Chapter 7 for the lowdown.

A variant of the DEVICE configuration command is DEVICEHIGH. This does the same thing as the standard DEVICE command but is used in DOS's memory management and has typical "computer sneeze" following it, such as

```
DEVICEHIGH /L:1,45120 =C:\STACKER\STACKER.COM /P-5 D:
```

See all the junk after DEVICEHIGH in the preceding? That's typical. The stuff following the equal sign is just a device driver pathname plus some options. It's important that you never mess with the numbers and options between DEVICEHIGH and the equal sign. If you do, then refer to Chapter 25 for information on running DOS's MemMaker program.

The FILES configuration command

What it does: Tells DOS how many files it can work with at once. This is serious stuff. Before DOS starts, it must set aside space to work with, oh, so many files.

If you have a system running Windows or some database or just a lot of programs, then you may actually encounter the `Not enough file handles available` error. If so, the FILES configuration command is the place to fix it.

Typical appearance:

```
FILES=32
```

Suggestion: The number following the FILES command and its equal sign shouldn't be too high. Anything up to 50 is okay. Over 50 and you're wasting memory. My advice is to set the value to at least 20 to start:

```
FILES=20
```

If, in your PC travels, you encounter a `Not enough file handles` type of error, edit CONFIG.SYS and stick a higher number by the FILES configuration command.

The REM configuration command

What it does: Allows you to stick remarks, comments, suggestions, or rude utterances into your CONFIG.SYS file. The idea here is that you can use REM to write notes to yourself about your CONFIG.SYS file. DOS ignores any line in CONFIG.SYS that starts with REM followed by a space. (Yes, DOS does occasionally ignore things on purpose.)

Typical appearance:

```
REM This is my CONFIG.SYS file
REM Which I wrote on 12/14/94
REM God bless America
```

Suggestion: I always use REM to add the most recent date that I updated my CONFIG.SYS file. If you work for a large company, you should stick your name in CONFIG.SYS, using a REM to let people know which CONFIG.SYS files you've been messing with.

Another purpose for the REM command is to disable configuration commands without deleting them. For example,

```
REM DEVICE=C:\DOS\ANSI.SYS
```

In the preceding, REM is used in front of a DEVICE configuration command. The net effect here is that DOS ignores the DEVICE configuration command when the PC starts. Dumb ol' DOS just thinks it's a comment you wrote to yourself.

Instead of the REM command, you can use a single semicolon (;). Put that at the start of a line, and DOS ignores the rest. For example,

```
;Don't mess with this file
```

or

```
;DEVICE=C:\DOS\ANSI.SYS
```

The last example is used to disable a command without deleting it. Computer people find semicolons to be so much more high-tech than bulky words like REM.

The SHELL configuration command

What it does: Tells DOS which program to use as the *command interpreter.* Normally, that program is COMMAND.COM, DOS's command interpreter. However, by using the SHELL configuration command, you can tell DOS to use another program as the command interpreter (which few people do).

Typical appearance:

```
SHELL=C:\COMMAND.COM /P
```

Any time you use the SHELL command with COMMAND.COM, you need to specify the /P option (as shown above). This tells COMMAND.COM to run your PC's AUTOEXEC.BAT file (covered in the next chapter). Without /P, DOS ignores AUTOEXEC.BAT whether you have it or not.

Suggestion: DOS normally finds your COMMAND.COM file in drive C's root directory and uses it as is. However, by using the SHELL configuration command in CONFIG.SYS, you can specify a few options with COMMAND.COM and customize the way your PC works.

One popular format is as follows:

```
SHELL=C:\COMMAND.COM /P /E:1024
```

This format ends with a special option, /E:1024. That tells DOS to set aside 1,024 bytes for storage space in DOS's *environment*. You discover what to do with the environment in Chapter 19. If you were referred here from there, then it's the /E switch you need to specify to get a larger environment. Everyone else: Ignore this information.

CONFIG.SYS Commands, the Other Ugly 11 (or So)

Most of the following commands will rarely, if ever, appear in your CONFIG.SYS file. If they ever do, look them up here to see how they work. The full-on, hard-core, technical description of these babies is covered in nerdier books, as well as in the DOS manual and the on-line HELP command.

The BREAK configuration command (or "Should really be BRAKE, but I don't make this stuff up")

The same BREAK command you can enter at the DOS prompt (see Chapter 2) can be used in your CONFIG.SYS file. Just stick an equal sign between either

```
BREAK=ON
```

to turn on Ctrl-Break monitoring, or

```
BREAK=OFF
```

to keep it off (which is dumb because it's automatically off anyway).

The COUNTRY configuration command (or "If it's Tuesday, this must be somewhere else")

This command controls certain country- and culture-specific items, such as how backwards the date format is (month-day-year versus day-month-year), the currency symbol, whether you put the comma after the thousands or ten thousands place in a number, and whether you use a comma or period. This is country-specific stuff, things liberals and out-of-touch college professors wail about daily.

Naturally, DOS is very United States-centric. For folks in other lands or for Americans just tired of the American way of doing things, you can use the COUNTRY command to refocus DOS to your *own* way of doing things.

The vague and general format for the COUNTRY configuration command is as follows:

```
COUNTRY=xxx,[[yyy],C:\DOS\COUNTRY.SYS]
```

The *xxx* and *yyy* things are placeholders for secret code numbers representing the country you seek to adapt DOS to. The brackets and commas are added merely for confusion's sake.

Yeah, if you really want to mess with this command, I'm forcing you to go to the DOS manual or on-line help.

The DOS configuration command (or "Couldn't they've thought up a more clever name for this one?")

You may actually encounter the DOS configuration command. It's used with PC memory management, which is covered in detail in Chapter 25. You may see one of the following commands in your CONFIG.SYS file:

```
DOS=HIGH
DOS=UMB
DOS=HIGH,UMB
```

The DOS command has a dual purpose: First, it tells DOS where to stick itself, either HIGH or LOW, and second, it works with things called UMBs, which is what I believe they yell at the batter in most major league baseball games (*UMB-Batter*). With respect to UMB, you'll see either UMB or NOUMB after the DOS configuration command's equal sign.

The DRIVPARM configuration command (or "Are we being cryptic here or what?")

The only time you need to use the DRIVPARM command is when a disk drive (or tape drive) manual tells you about it. Otherwise, it's safe to avoid this baby.

What DRIVPARM is trying to say is "Drive parameters." It's a way of telling DOS about an unusual disk drive or tape drive attached to your PC. There are many options and this guy can get very cryptic. No sense messing around here.

The FCBS configuration command (or "They've been telling us to ignore this one for seven years now, and we finally get the hint")

The initials *FCBS* stand for *File Control Blocks* although they're also an acronym for a saying popular with NBC television executives who are upset over letting David Letterman move to CBS.

The FCBS command, like the more popular FILES configuration command, is used to tell DOS about the files it can open. On any system other than a networked PC, this command can be ignored. On a networked PC, the FCBS command is used with DOS's SHARE command to prevent several programs from mucking up a single file at the same time. So the bottom line is this: If you don't follow any of this at all, forget about the FCBS command.

The INSTALL configuration command (or "The only command whose name actually has something to do with what it does")

This command actually does something similar to its name! It's used to install a program into memory. Normally, you would install the program (or *load* it) in your AUTOEXEC.BAT file (which is the subject of the next chapter). But some folks are impatient. That's why the INSTALL configuration command lets you load the file early, in CONFIG.SYS.

Only a few circumstances should occasion using the INSTALL command. If your software manual says that it's okay, then I guess it's okay. Otherwise, INSTALL should be used only with the following DOS commands: GRAFTABL.COM, GRAPHICS.COM, KEYB.COM, NLSFUNC.EXE, and SHARE.EXE. You can also use it with DOS's FASTOPEN.EXE command, though I don't recommend using that command at all. (If you see it in your CONFIG.SYS file, delete that line at once!)

The LASTDRIVE configuration command (or "Why isn't this the LSTDRV command?")

This command is funky and somewhat useful. It tells DOS how many drive letters it can use. Normally, this isn't a problem. If you have 18 hard drives, DOS gives you drive letters C through U for them. Otherwise, DOS gives you drive letters C, D, and E and nothing more. So, if you want to create some RAM drives or maybe use some Stacker drives or fool with the SUBST command, you need to set DOS's scopes a bit higher.

The most common version of the LASTDRIVE configuration command is as follows:

```
LASTDRIVE=Z
```

This tells DOS that it can use all the drive letters it wants to, from C on up through drive Z. This is the command I stick in all my CONFIG.SYS files, should I ever suddenly decide I need that drive W and can't live without it.

Presidential Election Campaign. Do you want $3 to go to this fund?

☐ Yes   ☐ No

Note: Checking "Yes" will not change your tax rate or reduce your refund.

The NUMLOCK configuration command (or "Oops! Did I forget to bring in the cat last night?")

This command is handy but often unnecessary. What the NUMLOCK configuration command does is switch your PC's numeric keypad on or off. Normally, when a PC starts, the numeric keypad is turned on — you press the keys and you get numbers and the arrow keys don't work. The following command in CONFIG.SYS changes that:

```
NUMLOCK=OFF
```

The OFF part of the command turns off your numeric keypad. This is a handy thing to have, especially if you find yourself whacking the Num Lock key every time you start Mr. PC.

Your PC may be able to turn off the Num Lock key automatically without your having to bother with the NUMLOCK configuration command. Check your PC's hardware setup program to see if there is a Num Lock or Numeric keypad option. If so, you can switch the keypad on or off at that point.

The SET configuration command (or "Did you know that this word has more definitions than any other in the English language?")

Full details on the SET command are offered in Chapter 19. But generally speaking, most DOS users prefer to use SET in AUTOEXEC.BAT instead of CONFIG.SYS. But you can have it both ways. AUTOEXEC.BAT is covered in the next chapter.

I believe the idea behind having the SET command in CONFIG.SYS as well as AUTOEXEC.BAT is that someday Microsoft may do away with AUTOEXEC.BAT as we know it. When that fateful day arrives, we'll only have CONFIG.SYS to contend with, and DOS book authors the world over will have one less chapter to write.

The STACKS configuration command (or "Stacks of what?")

A *stack* is a storage area in memory. The reason it's called a *stack* (and not a *storage area in memory)* is that programmers use it to stack various items, like values, one atop the other. Then they pull out values from the middle and try not to topple the whole stack. Often they mutter *Jen-ga, Jen-ga* while doing this.

In my travels, I've seen two versions of this command in various CONFIG.SYS files:

```
STACKS=9,256
```

This command is preferred by the Windows setup program. However, a DOS guru would look at that and say, "Hmmm, you're creating nine stacks of 256 bytes apiece. Interesting move, but I feel the following command would save you a bit of memory."

```
STACKS=0,0
```

This command tells DOS not to mess around with any stacks. Although that seems risky, it works with most programs. In fact, the only time you should change the numbers back to 9,256 is if you ever see a `Stack Overflow` type of error message (or if Windows whines about it).

The SWITCHES configuration command (or "The final grab-bag of all configuration commands")

This configuration command is one of those that Microsoft can't make up its mind about. Four different things can follow the SWITCHES command, each of which controls a different aspect of your PC.

The four options that can appear together or individually after the SWITCHES configuration command are /F, /K, /N, and /W.

```
SWITCHES=/F
```

This tells DOS to skip over the two-second pause after the `Starting MS-DOS` message is displayed. Yes, there really is a two-second pause. (This is a DOS 6-only thing.)

Some computer books claim the SWITCHES=/F command is the fast DOS start command. The fools! It just skips over the two-second pause. I use it on all my PCs, and I don't notice DOS taking any particularly shorter amount of time to get off its lardy butt.

```
SWITCHES=/K
```

Strange one. This command may be required by some ancient DOS programs that don't *read* certain keys on the new 101 enhanced keyboards. For example, if you're running a program and notice that it doesn't quite get it when you press the arrow keys between the typewriter keys and numeric keypad on your keyboard, then you should use the preceding command in CONFIG.SYS.

```
SWITCHES=/N
```

The /N switch prevents you from using F5 or F8 to skip over your CONFIG.SYS file when the PC starts. (This skipping aspect was mulled over in Chapter 6.)

```
SWITCHES=/W
```

The final incarnation of the SWITCHES command is the /W switch. This option is only necessary if you're using Windows 3.0. Later versions of Windows — ack, don't bother.

The "multi-boot" configuration commands (which you can merrily skip over)

Some people go so nutso with their CONFIG.SYS files that they actually have two or three of them on their PCs. To sate these awkward lusts, DOS 6 uses five different commands that let you store several CONFIG.SYS files or *boot options* all at once:

- ✔ Include
- ✔ MenuColor
- ✔ MenuDefault
- ✔ MenuItem
- ✔ SubMenu

I mention these commands here out of niceness. Quite frankly, I've written three chapters now on CONFIG.SYS and I'm sick of it. Heavier computer books cover these commands and are even nice enough to show you examples. For everyone else, let's be pleased that the CONFIG.SYS configuration command tour is over. You now have my permission to sit in front of the TV for an hour and wolf down a pint of Haägen Dazs ice cream. Belch freely.

Chapter 9

General Futzing Part II: AUTOEXEC.BAT

· ·

In This Chapter

▶ Fitting AUTOEXEC.BAT into the big picture

▶ Finding AUTOEXEC.BAT

▶ Editing AUTOEXEC.BAT

▶ Solving AUTOEXEC.BAT problems

· ·

Contrary to popular myth, AUTOEXEC.BAT is not one of DOS's vital start-up files. It's not like CONFIG.SYS (covered in Chapter 6). Without a CONFIG.SYS file, DOS makes a bunch of drunken assumptions and configures your PC likewise. No AUTOEXEC.BAT file? No biggie. DOS just starts. But let's not depress the chap too much here. No sense in trashing a worthy friend, which is what AUTOEXEC.BAT can be if you know how to work it.

There is an advantage to having and using an AUTOEXEC.BAT file. This chapter covers AUTOEXEC.BAT and how it fits into the big picture. Just like the store clerk promised: AUTOEXEC.BAT is a true DOS time-saver.

AUTOEXEC.BAT and the Big Picture

The idea behind using AUTOEXEC.BAT is to save yourself time. I can sum it up in one simple sentence but have written the following instead:

> *AUTOEXEC.BAT contains all the commands and stuff you'd normally type at the DOS prompt each time you start your computer.*

That's about it. So suppose you type the following three commands each time you start your PC:

```
C:\>PROMPT $P$G
C:\>PATH=C:\WINDOWS;C:\DOS
C:\>WIN
```

All you need to do is fire up the DOS Editor, type those three commands, each on a line by itself, and then save the file to disk as C:\AUTOEXEC.BAT. The next time DOS starts, it reads AUTOEXEC.BAT and automatically types out those command lines for you. Ack! Who'd'a believed it could be this easy?

▶ You can look at it this way: AUTOEXEC.BAT is the file that *auto*matically *exec*utes (or runs) each time DOS starts.

▶ The AUTOEXEC.BAT file contains DOS commands, just as you'd type them at the prompt. However, each command appears on a line by itself. When DOS starts, it reads AUTOEXEC.BAT and carries out the commands listed there one after the other, top to bottom.

▶ Any command you normally type when you start your computer can be placed into your AUTOEXEC.BAT file. Doing so saves you the trouble of having to type that command each time the computer starts.

▶ AUTOEXEC.BAT is a text file. Plain text. Boring old text. Just a bunch of stuff you type and can read — almost like English.

▶ AUTOEXEC.BAT is a batch file, which the astute reader can tell because it ends with the BAT filename extension. Batch files are covered in Part III of this book.

▶ Yeah, even though AUTOEXEC.BAT is a batch file, it doesn't need to work like one. AUTOEXEC.BAT is more of a "stack of commands" that run when DOS first starts.

Nerdy trivialities you can skip over about AUTOEXEC.BAT

Actually, AUTOEXEC.BAT isn't a part of DOS's start-up. (Refer to the section "Life without AUTOEXEC.BAT" to see how your computer would fire up without it.) Instead, it's the COMMAND.COM file that tells DOS to seek out AUTOEXEC.BAT and carry out its instructions. So, in a way, you can look at AUTOEXEC.BAT as a blessing from DOS. Without it, you'd be stuck typing in those same commands each time your PC started.

Life without AUTOEXEC.BAT

Here's how your computer would start without an AUTOEXEC.BAT file:

```
Starting MS-DOS...

Current date is Thu 11-11-1993
Enter new date (mm-dd-yy):
Current time is 1:01:32.39p
Enter new time:

Microsoft(R) MS-DOS(R) Version 6.20
   (C)Copyright Microsoft Corp 1981-1993.


C:\>
```

You'd see the Starting MS-DOS message (for DOS versions 6 and later) and then . . . you'd be asked to enter the current date and time, ala the DATE and TIME commands. Then DOS spits up a copyright notice, and you see the boring DOS prompt. This is definitely not a lively way to start Mr. PC's day.

✔ Essentially, DOS marches through the DATE and TIME commands before the PC starts. These commands are covered in *DOS For Dummies*, the original. Unless you have a very ancient PC, the date and time displayed will be more-or-less accurate (at least within this decade).

✔ Even if you have the most subtle trace of an AUTOEXEC.BAT file on your PC, you won't see the preceding information displayed. Instead, DOS will carry out, to the letter, the instructions in your AUTOEXEC.BAT file.

✔ The *Corp* in Microsoft Corp. is an abbreviation for *corporation*, not *corpse*.

"But my AUTOEXEC.BAT file doesn't run!"

There are a few things to check if your AUTOEXEC.BAT doesn't appear to be working:

✔ **Is the file named AUTOEXEC.BAT?**

Check the spelling. For some reason, many people find AUTOEXEC hard to spell (or at least hard to type).

✔ **Is the file in the root directory of your boot disk?**

For most of us, that's drive C, root directory. If you boot from a disk in drive A (or somewhere else), then the C:\AUTOEXEC.BAT file won't work.

✔ **Are you using the SHELL configuration command in CONFIG.SYS?**

You need to specify the /P option with COMMAND.COM. Refer to Chapter 8 on the various configuration commands for the precise format.

✔ **Is your AUTOEXEC.BAT file, in fact, a collection of commands that you would normally type each time your computer starts, or is it just random characters or a love poem to your aquarium?**

AUTOEXEC.BAT must contain instructions — DOS commands — that the computer understands. Refer to the section "Editing Your AUTOEXEC.BAT File" for more information on how to view your AUTOEXEC.BAT file's contents.

Which commands can AUTOEXEC.BAT contain? Anything you'd type on the command line. Weird stuff? No, that causes errors.

✔ The last section in this chapter deals with AUTOEXEC.BAT problems when it's running. Refer to "Solving AUTOEXEC.BAT Problems" for more help.

✔ I don't know about where you are, but here it's snowing like the whole heavenly host has dandruff.

Where Is Your AUTOEXEC.BAT File?

Your AUTOEXEC.BAT must be in a specific location on disk for it to work properly. That location is technically referred to as the root directory of your boot disk, which is the disk used to start DOS on your computer.

In most cases, the boot disk is drive C, your computer's first hard drive. If you have some other setup, such as a special laptop computer or other funky disk drive apparatus, then another disk drive may be used to start the computer.

If you start your computer using a floppy disk in drive A, then AUTOEXEC.BAT must be in the root directory of that disk.

✔ A boot disk is any disk drive used to start your computer. For most of us, that's drive C, though the computer can also start from a floppy disk inserted into drive A.

✔ Refer to Chapter 1 for more information on how your computer and DOS start their happy day.

✔ What's the *root directory*? Turn to Chapter 16 to find out.

Editing Your AUTOEXEC.BAT File

Changing your PC's AUTOEXEC.BAT file isn't something you'll be doing every day. Usually, you'll modify it only under a few circumstances: You add some new software; you want to take advantage of some command; you've changed some hardware on your PC and need to add commands to take advantage of it; or you read a book and discover some interesting way to get something done in AUTOEXEC.BAT.

Whatever the reason, you modify AUTOEXEC.BAT by using a text editor or word processor. Most people use the Editor program that comes with DOS. To wit,

```
C:\>EDIT C:\AUTOEXEC.BAT
```

The preceding command edits your AUTOEXEC.BAT file. Type **EDIT**, a space, the letter **C**, a colon, a backslash, and then **AUTOEXEC**, a period, and **BAT**. Double-check everything and then press Enter. A few microprocessor wiggles later, you'll see your AUTOEXEC.BAT file on-screen. The file will look similar to the file shown in Figure 9-1. You're now ready to tinker.

To save your work in the Editor, press Alt-F, S. Press and hold the Alt key and press F; then release both keys. This activates the File menu. Then press S to select the **S**ave command. You can also poke at these commands and menu items using a mouse, if you have one.

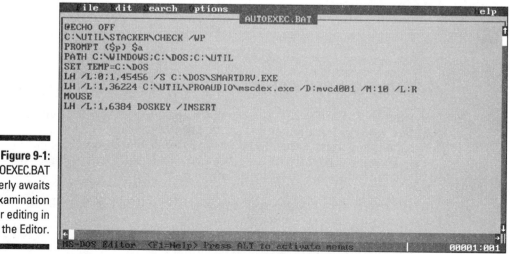

Figure 9-1:
AUTOEXEC.BAT
eagerly awaits
examination
or editing in
the Editor.

To quit the Editor, press Alt-F, X. This selects Exit from the File menu and safely deposits you back at the DOS prompt. Before you move on, be sure to check the section titled "The final and most important step" just a few pages away.

- Okay. So if you chicken out and don't want to save your changes, just quit the Editor: press Alt-F, X. A message appears claiming `Loaded file is not saved. Save it now?` Press N for No (you're chickening out here). This plops you back at the DOS prompt without altering your AUTOEXEC.BAT file.

- Many of the glorious commands listed in your AUTOEXEC.BAT file are mentioned elsewhere in this book. Please make liberal use of the index to look up items that may cause you to grit your teeth.

- Oops! The Editor only comes with DOS versions 5 and later. If you're stuck with an earlier version of DOS, you can use the crummy old EDLIN editor. Or just save yourself time and pain, and upgrade to the latest version of DOS — preferably one that comes with a copy of *DOS For Dummies* as the unauthorized DOS manual.

- If you use a word processor to create or edit AUTOEXEC.BAT, be sure to save the file back to disk as a plain text or unformatted DOS text or ASCII file.

- Another word processor tip: Set your right margin to 14 inches or so. Doing so circumvents the automatic *word wrap* feature that would otherwise split long lines of text. You don't want long lines to be cut up, and setting a wide right margin is the easiest way to do that in a word processor.

- If you've run memory management software on your PC, you'll probably see many, many strange commands and funky little numbers and such. Don't mess with them! Those commands carry out special memory management instructions in AUTOEXEC.BAT.

Adding a new command to AUTOEXEC.BAT

The commands in AUTOEXEC.BAT are magically "typed in" by DOS, one after the other when your computer first starts. Therefore, where you put a new command is important. Generally speaking, I like sticking things at the end of the file. Unless you read somewhere that a command should have a specific location, the end's as good a place as any.

To add a new command to the end of your AUTOEXEC.BAT by using DOS's Editor program, follow these steps:

1. Start the DOS Editor (as described in the preceding section).

2. Press Ctrl-End.

Press and hold the Ctrl key, press the End key, and then release both keys. Doing so moves the cursor to the end of the file, where you'll be adding the new command.

3. If the cursor isn't on a blank line (it's at the end of a line of text already in AUTOEXEC.BAT), press the Enter key.

4. Type in your new command.

   Double-check what you type. If you've been misusing your cough syrup, have a friend double-check it.

5. Save AUTOEXEC.BAT (see the instructions in the preceding section).

6. Quit the Editor.

7. Reset your computer. (Press Ctrl-Alt-Delete or whack your PC's reset switch.)

   The final step, resetting your computer, is necessary to lock in the changes you made in AUTOEXEC.BAT. (Refer to the section "The final and most important step" later in this chapter for the details.)

✔ Most commands you add in AUTOEXEC.BAT can go anywhere. Some are persnickety. For example, the old and very popular SideKick program demanded to be the very last thing in AUTOEXEC.BAT.

✔ Usually the last item in AUTOEXEC.BAT will be a program you want to run when your PC first starts. For example, most people end AUTOEXEC.BAT with the WIN command, which starts Windows. If that's your case, you might want to add your new command *before* the last line in AUTOEXEC.BAT.

✔ If you're adding the PATH command, check to see whether one is already in AUTOEXEC.BAT. If so, then you only need to edit the PATH command already there. Refer to Chapter 22 for more information on the PATH command.

Removing a command from AUTOEXEC.BAT

Oh, Jiminy Christmas, messing with AUTOEXEC.BAT is something you must seriously avoid if you can. However, there are times when you may need to remove a command. For example, your PC may be free of its networking shackles, in which case you can freely delete the network setup commands festering inside your PC's AUTOEXEC.BAT file.

To delete a command in AUTOEXEC.BAT, fire up a text editor like the DOS Editor and edit AUTOEXEC.BAT. (Editing instructions are in the section — you guessed it — "Editing Your AUTOEXEC.BAT File," earlier in this chapter.)

Locate the command (the line of text) you want to rip out. Use the up- or down-arrow keys to highlight that line.

Zap it! In the Editor, press Ctrl-Y (press and hold the Ctrl key and tap the Y key; release both keys). The Ctrl-Y command may also work in other editors, though you can always use the Delete key to gobble up the line one character at a time.

After surgery, save your AUTOEXEC.BAT file back to disk and then quit the editor. The commands to quit the DOS Editor are listed in the section "Editing Your AUTOEXEC.BAT File." Before you're done, please read the section "The final and most important step."

✔ The keyboard command to delete a line of text in the DOS Editor is Ctrl-Y.

✔ Why delete a line? Primarily for efficiency's sake. If there's something in AUTOEXEC.BAT your computer doesn't need, snip it out. Doctors do this all the time with people. They remove appendixes, gall bladders, and other things they decide we can live without.

✔ Only remove a command when you're absolutely certain you don't need it. Your guru may give you direction in this, or there may be instructions in some dusty documentation you've found.

✔ It's a good idea to make a backup copy of AUTOEXEC.BAT before you edit it. The following COPY command backs up AUTOEXEC.BAT:

```
C:\>COPY C:\AUTOEXEC.BAT C:\AUTOEXEC.BAK
```

The backup copy — containing your original AUTOEXEC.BAT file — is named AUTOEXEC.BAK in the preceding. (Some editors may automatically back up AUTOEXEC.BAT for you; the DOS Editor isn't one of them.)

Using REM to disable a command

A better way to remove a command is to disable it. Disabling a command is akin to unhooking a car battery to prevent your teenage daughter from eloping with that no-good Kyle; just as the car is still in the driveway but can't go anywhere, a disabled command lies dormant in AUTOEXEC.BAT, present but unheard.

To disable any command in AUTOEXEC.BAT, you use the handy REM batch file command. Just type **REM** and a space before the offending line. So, for example, you would fire up the Editor and move the cursor to the following line:

```
C:\NORTON\SMARTCAN
```

Then type **REM** and a space at the start of the line:

```
REM C:\NORTON\SMARTCAN
```

This command is now disabled in AUTOEXEC.BAT; it won't run when the computer starts. However, unlike just whacking it out of existence, you can re-enable the command by simply snipping away the REM. (Just as you can re-connect the car battery to finally rid yourself of a teenage daughter.)

- ✔ The batch file REM command allows you to insert remarks or comments into any batch file. Because AUTOEXEC.BAT is a batch file, REM works in there, too. For example, you could stick the following command into AUTOEXEC.BAT:

```
REM I wrote this all by myself
```

  DOS sees the REM command when AUTOEXEC.BAT runs, but it ignores the rest of the line.

- ✔ See Part III of this book for more information on batch files. (But keep in mind that REM is about the only true batch file command that winds its way into AUTOEXEC.BAT.)

- ✔ Kyle's not a bad kid, just irresponsible.

The final and most important step

DOS only heeds the instructions in your PC's AUTOEXEC.BAT file once — when the PC first starts (or when you reset). Therefore, whenever you change or edit AUTOEXEC.BAT, you need to save it back to disk and then reset your computer to see whether the changes worked. Follow these steps:

1. Double-check your work in AUTOEXEC.BAT.

2. Save AUTOEXEC.BAT back to disk.

3. Quit the Editor.

4. Reset your PC.

- ✔ You reset the PC either by pressing the Ctrl-Alt-Delete keys all at once or by gently whacking the reset button.

- ✔ On the off chance that you're using Windows, DESQview, Software Carousel, the DOS Shell, or some other type of menu system, don't bother to reset until you've quit that program as well.

✔ After the computer resets, pay special attention to the screen. If you see any errors when AUTOEXEC.BAT runs, such as `Bad command or file name` or `File not found`, refer to the last section in this chapter for some help.

✔ Now that I'm done, I can tell you that the next section is the last section of this chapter. There.

Solving AUTOEXEC.BAT Problems

You'll encounter two types of problems with AUTOEXEC.BAT: general batch file boo-boos and problems with the commands in AUTOEXEC.BAT. If you keep in mind that AUTOEXEC.BAT is merely a collection of DOS commands listed line by line, one after the other, just as you'd type them, then you can solve most of the problems by editing and looking over AUTOEXEC.BAT. Otherwise, the following sections should unmuddle things for you.

The general batch file boo-boos

Your AUTOEXEC.BAT file shouldn't produce any outrageous batch files error messages. If it does, then you're tinkering far beyond what's recommended in this book; refer to Part III for more information on batch files. Otherwise, you'll probably see one of two common DOS error messages produced:

✔ `Bad command or file name`

✔ `File not found`

Yeah, these are typical DOS error messages, commonly seen at a DOS prompt near you. Why do they happen in AUTOEXEC.BAT? Same reason: Typing mistakes. Because AUTOEXEC.BAT essentially types commands for you, if you've mistyped something in AUTOEXEC.BAT, it carries through with your mistake.

For example, you may want to start the DOSKey program (explained in Chapter 4) and type **DOKSEY** (or maybe even **DONKEY**) inside AUTOEXEC.BAT. Easy fix: Edit AUTOEXEC.BAT and change your typing. That's how it's done.

The hard part is tracking down the errors because AUTOEXEC.BAT doesn't stop after any boo-boo it makes. For example, you may see the following on your screen:

```
Bad command or file name
Bad command or file name
C:\>
```

This is not a good way to start your computing day. The solution is to double-check everything in AUTOEXEC.BAT; spy out typos particularly.

Another common error deals with the placement of DOS's PATH command in AUTOEXEC.BAT. Before you set DOS's search path, you must specify *full pathnames* to all your commands. Therefore, you either need to move the PATH command to the start of AUTOEXEC.BAT or edit in all the complete pathnames. Refer to Chapter 22 for information on the PATH command; Chapter 16 discusses pathnames.

Problems with commands

The double-edged sword of trouble also slices when it comes to goofing up DOS commands and other programs in AUTOEXEC.BAT. Consider the following, for example:

```
NOISE /UNBEARABLY_LOUD
```

Suppose NOISE is a command on your computer and you've typed an option after that command, /UNBEARABLY_LOUD. Unfortunately, the option is really 7 (a number instead of the words *unbearably loud*). Because of this, the NOISE command produces a mysterious error when AUTOEXEC.BAT runs:

```
NOISE 3.2
(C)Copyright 1994 TinEar Labs, Inc.
Error: Unrecognized option
You should feel ashamed
```

Fortunately, you can see that it's the NOISE program that spit up the error. Some programs are truly rude and only display the error message — or just some number. Only the eagle-eyed DOS user can spot these errors as they scroll up the screen.

The fortunate thing about this type of error is that it usually appears right after you add or change the command in AUTOEXEC.BAT. This is why you should immediately reset your computer after you modify and save AUTOEXEC.BAT.

The 5th Wave   By Rich Tennant

"I'm waiting for my AUTOEXEC file to run, so I'm gonna grab a cup of coffee, maybe make a sandwich, check the sports page, regrind the brake drums on my truck, balance my checkbook for the past 12 years, learn Swahili..."

Chapter 10
Making AUTOEXEC.BAT Work

● ●

In This Chapter

▶ Listing tasks for AUTOEXEC.BAT

▶ Starting AUTOEXEC.BAT properly

▶ Setting up your hardware

▶ Ending AUTOEXEC.BAT properly

● ●

*A*UTOEXEC.BAT's job: To run a bunch of DOS commands each time you start your computer.

Your job: To think of everything you normally type at the DOS prompt when you start your computer, and then put those commands — line by line — into AUTOEXEC.BAT. The computer does the rest.

This chapter lists some things you may want to accomplish in the typical AUTOEXEC.BAT. There are some definite things that get done there, plus some options and other goodies you may want to accomplish. This chapter lists them all, though other chapters in this book may offer AUTOEXEC.BAT suggestions as well.

✔ For information on editing your AUTOEXEC.BAT file, refer to Chapter 9.

✔ Additional tasks to be done in AUTOEXEC.BAT include using the PATH command, which is covered in Chapter 22, and the SMARTDrive disk cache, covered in Chapter 23.

A Possible To-Do List for AUTOEXEC.BAT

The following is a list of items, more or less in order, that should be done in the typical AUTOEXEC.BAT file. Nothing is truly required here; these are only my suggestions. But they're awfully darn good suggestions — except for maybe the one about not taking off your muddy boots after you enter the house because your wife will gladly shampoo the rug for you.

There are about 100 million PCs in the world, each complete with its own individual user who wants something useful to happen. Listing all the potential AUTOEXEC.BAT files would be, well, loopy. Therefore, use the following sections as a guide and reference to your own AUTOEXEC.BAT file.

The At-Echo Off thing

Nearly all AUTOEXEC.BAT files start with the following batch file command:

```
@ECHO OFF
```

That's the at-sign, ECHO, a space, and then the word OFF. A nice and cryptic way to start AUTOEXEC.BAT — some nerd hors d'oeuvres for your PC's start-up banquet.

What the @ECHO OFF does is to prevent the commands in AUTOEXEC.BAT from appearing on your screen as DOS automatically types them. Instead, only the output from the commands appears. The end result — the part you need to care about — is that the screen looks cleaner when the computer starts; there aren't as many weird characters and such.

- ✔ The @ECHO OFF can be in either upper- or lowercase.
- ✔ It's absolutely safe to have @ECHO OFF as the first command in your AUTOEXEC.BAT file. Even other, snooty commands that claim they must go first can follow it. Indeed, @ECHO OFF is the first peck in the AUTOEXEC.BAT pecking order.
- ✔ Part III of this book has more information on batch file commands, such as @ECHO OFF.
- ✔ Why can't they just spell it *orderves*?

Creating the DOS search path

The search path, which is a very handy thing to have, is a list of subdirectories in which DOS can hunt down programs. Setting up a proper search path means you can type **WP**, and DOS magically hunts down WordPerfect and runs it for you. Such a time-saver! The downer is that you must create the search path, which can be a bit tricky.

You create the DOS search path by using the PATH command, which is covered in Chapter 22. As a preview, here is what a typical PATH command may look like in an AUTOEXEC.BAT file:

```
PATH=C:\WINDOWS;C:\DOS;C:\UTIL
```

This command requires some serious introspection and a knowledge of hieroglyphics. Regardless, it essentially tells DOS to look for programs in the C:\WINDOWS directory, then in C:\DOS, and then in C:\UTIL. Other doodads have been added to the command primarily to make it appear more impressive.

- ✔ The PATH command should be one of the first commands in AUTOEXEC.BAT; after the DOS search path is set, DOS can easily find other programs and DOS commands you mention in AUTOEXEC.BAT.
- ✔ The full details on the PATH command are divulged in Chapter 22.
- ✔ Refer to Chapter 16 for information on subdirectories.
- ✔ With DOS 6 and later, a PATH is automatically set when the computer starts. Typically, the path lists your DOS directory, either C:\DOS or C:\MSDOS — if you installed DOS into a directory with that name.

Building a better prompt

Another AUTOEXEC.BAT favorite, usually cuddling with the PATH command, is the PROMPT command. This command allows you to create an interesting and potentially fun DOS prompt. For example,

```
PROMPT ($P)
```

Well, that may not be major giggles on the fun scale, but it creates a more exciting prompt than C>. Blech!

- ✔ The PROMPT command is covered in detail in Chapter 3. You might also want to check out Chapter 21, which describes how to add color and pizzazz to the DOS prompt.

- ✔ With DOS versions 6 and later, the PROMPT command is preset as follows:

```
PROMPT $P$G
```

So, theoretically, if you're using DOS 6 and have this command in your AUTOEXEC.BAT, it's redundant.

Bother with the network

Those computers shackled to a network will have their networking commands in AUTOEXEC.BAT. Usually, these commands fire up the network brains and then automatically connect your computer with computers and printers elsewhere on the network.

The following is a list of networking commands on my own computer, which is equipped with the LANtastic network operating system:

```
AEX IRQ=15 IOBASE=300 VERBOSE
AILANBIO
REDIR BEAST LOGINS=3
SERVER
NET LOGIN/WAIT \\BEAST BEAST
NET LOGIN/WAIT \\BEHEMOTH BEAST
NET LOGIN/WAIT \\UNICORN BEAST
NET USE LPT1: \\BEAST\@PRINTER
NET LPT TIMEOUT 10
```

This is definitely impressive stuff, but it's all automatically typed for me when my PC starts, connecting my system with other computers in the office — an ideal chore for an AUTOEXEC.BAT file.

✔ Sometimes the position of the networking commands is crucial. For example, if you have commands in AUTOEXEC.BAT that download printer fonts to your network printer, you should be connected to the network printer before you do that.

✔ The networking commands in CONFIG.SYS usually set up the network adapter device drivers; in AUTOEXEC.BAT, the commands that control the network and connect you to other computers are run.

Configure your printer, CD-ROM card, sound card, and so on

Primarily these types of commands are particular to whatever hardware goodies (call them *peripherals*) you may have attached to your PC. Something like the following gets done:

1. You configure your printer, download fonts, set an emulation mode, set up your FAX/modem, and so on.

   I don't have any examples for this because the printer I bought is just too stupid and unpopular to have anything as luxurious as downloadable fonts.

2. You set up your CD-ROM drive.

You usually do this through a program called MSCDEX.EXE, which stands for the Microsoft CD-ROM Extension. Here's how the command looks in my AUTOEXEC.BAT file:

```
C:\DOS\MSCDEX.EXE /D:MVCD001 /M:10 /L:R
```

The MSCDEX.EXE program came with DOS 6, which is in my C:\DOS directory. The option /D:MVCD001 means something and the /M:10 option means something else. Refer to the handy tip below for what /L:R means.

- I suppose there may be other CD-ROM control programs out there besides MSCDEX.EXE. Heaven help us.

- I haven't a clue what the options are that follow MSCDEX.EXE, yet I'm wise enough not to mess with them — except for the /L option. That option sets the drive letter for your CD-ROM drive, giving it forever the drive letter R. The reason for doing this is that otherwise DOS gives the CD-ROM drive the "next" drive letter. So if you have hard drive C and a RAM drive D, the CD-ROM would be E. But if you decided you didn't need a RAM drive, then the CD-ROM drive would become drive D. That tends to mess up installed software that assumes the CD-ROM to be E. So instead of bothering with this nonsense, I set /L:R, which makes my CD-ROM drive forever letter R. (Refer to the LASTDRIVE configuration command in Chapter 8 if you plan on doing this.)

- Hopefully, the program that set up and installed your CD-ROM software places the proper MSCDEX.EXE command in your AUTOEXEC.BAT file.

- If you're running a network, placement of the CD-ROM driver may be important in AUTOEXEC.BAT. In my case, I must put the command that starts MSCDEX.EXE *after* the command that starts my network. Under other circumstances, the order may be reversed. (An error message tells you which way is wrong.)

- Another command to put after MSCDEX.EXE: the command that starts the SMARTDrive disk cache. Installing the command here is really only necessary with MS-DOS 6.2 and later. If you start MSCDEX.EXE before SMARTDrive, it improves your CD-ROM drive's performance. (More info on SMARTDrive is offered in Chapter 23.)

- A device driver in your CONFIG.SYS is also required to connect your CD-ROM drive. That's the program that actually controls the hardware. The MSCDEX.EXE program is what makes the CD-ROM your E drive or whatever.

3. Load the program that controls your sound card.

As with the CD-ROM drive, there will typically be a device driver in CONFIG.SYS that says *hello* to the sound card, and then maybe a program in AUTOEXEC.BAT that makes the sound card work. Again, I don't have an example of this, but I do have a cool suggestion.

Some sound cards have programs that come with them to make noise. For example, mine has the PLAYFILE command, which plays a recorded sound file through the speakers. But the best trick is when your sound card has a program that makes the computer talk. For example, the TALKER program may make your computer say something like

```
TALKER I HATE YOU!
```

The preceding command would make the computer belch out *I hate you* every time it started. I suppose more pleasant messages are possible.

4. Fire up the mouse driver.

This is usually done by the MOUSE command. For example,

```
C:\MOUSE\MOUSE
```

Most mouse drivers are named MOUSE. Some may have different names (I don't suppose there's a RAT device driver out there). Whatever. Just list the command that starts the mouse, plus any options, in AUTOEXEC.BAT. That will wake up the mouse and make it useful for those DOS programs that appreciate mice.

- Oh, I could write a cheap joke here about a "mouse driver," but I won't.

- You don't need a mouse driver if you're running Windows. However, if you're running DOS programs in Windows, *and* those programs can use a mouse, then you need the MOUSE driver in AUTOEXEC.BAT.

- Please use the MOUSE.COM (or MOUSE.EXE) command in AUTOEXEC.BAT and not the MOUSE.SYS device driver in your CONFIG.SYS file.

5. And so on and so forth.

There must be a jillion other programs you can run that say "hello" to various pieces of hardware connected to your PC. As a word of advice, only run those programs you absolutely need. For example, if you're not going to use your scanner for a while, don't bother starting its little program in AUTOEXEC.BAT. That will save you precious computer memory.

Setting other stuff

A common DOS command that wends its way into AUTOEXEC.BAT is the SET command. You need to set various items for special programs and such.

One item to set in AUTOEXEC.BAT is the location of your temporary files directory — the place where DOS can stow all its clutter. Some people prefer to use drive C's root directory for this task, placing the following command into their AUTOEXEC.BAT files:

```
SET TEMP=C:\
```

This command tells DOS to store its temporary files (TEMP) into C:\, drive C's root directory. (Crypto-matic, eh?) I prefer the following:

```
SET TEMP=C:\TEMP
```

This tells DOS to shove its stuff into the TEMP directory on drive C. Another approach is

```
SET TEMP=F:
```

This tells DOS to put temporary files on drive F, which I'm assuming to be a RAM drive. This is an ideal location for temporary or junk files because the computer automatically erases a RAM drive's contents when you reset. The only caveat here is that the RAM drive needs to be quite large, typically 500K or more to accommodate all the junk files DOS spins off.

- ✔ Setting stuff is a deep subject, and your SET command diving bell is located in Chapter 19.

- ✔ Refer to Chapter 16 for more information on subdirectories, such as the TEMP directory. There's also stuff in there about the _root directory_, if those two words have you scratching your head.

- ✔ Information on RAM drives is covered in Chapter 24.

Oh, DOSKey and its macros

A popular program to fire up in AUTOEXEC.BAT is DOSKey, DOS's command line editing tool and miracle worker. The typical command used to start DOSKey is as follows:

```
C:\>DOSKEY /INSERT
```

This command starts DOSKey in the *insert* editing mode, which makes it work more like a word processor.

After the DOSKEY command, you could put various DOSKey macros, if you're one of the rare folk who use them. They would look something like this:

```
DOSKEY D=DIR /O
DOSKEY M=MEM /C /P
DOSKEY H=DOSKEY /HISTORY
DOSKEY DEL=DEL $* /P
```

- ✔ The macro commands *must* come after the first command that starts DOSKey.
- ✔ Refer to Chapter 4 for more information on DOSKey and what it can do.
- ✔ Chapter 5 discusses DOSKey's macros.

File Management, Copying files to a RAM drive, and so on

The subject of "file management" or, what I prefer to call, *disk housekeeping* is covered in depth in Chapter 23. This section primarily refers to running special disk massaging programs such as DOS's DEFRAG and SMARTDrive, though there may be others equally capable.

File management also involves using the simple DOS file commands: COPY, MOVE, DEL, and REN. The only time I can think of using any of these in AUTOEXEC.BAT is to copy files to a RAM drive. For example, I use the following command in my AUTOEXEC.BAT file to copy all my batch files to RAM drive F:

```
C:\>XCOPY C:\BATCH\*.BAT F:
```

Batch files run faster from a RAM drive (and Chapter 24 contains this nifty knowledge nugget if you want to peruse the subject further).

Running the devious TSRs

TSRs are sneaky little programs that sit in memory, controlling something or offering a pop-up program, instead of quitting like normal programs do. These used to be the rage a few years back but have declined in popularity thanks to programs like Windows.

The most popular TSR of all-time was the SideKick handy pop-up program from Borland. Other TSRs include screen-saver programs, on-screen clocks, Quicken's BillMinder program (that tells you when to pay your nagging creditors), safe-erase disk utility programs, virus-checking programs, and a hoard of other programs that pop-up or hover over your screen at any given time or key press. Yup, AUTOEXEC.BAT is the place to start 'em.

- Refer to Chapter 11 for more information on TSRs or memory-resident programs.

- How did Windows defeat the TSR? By doing what's called *multitasking*. Windows has the ability to run multiple programs all at the same time; you don't have to quit one program to start working on another. That was the basic idea of the TSR pop-up. Windows does it much better, of course.

- There is a definite pecking order for TSRs. For example, Borland's SideKick insists on being the last TSR you start. Others may have problems coming first, last, before, or after other programs. Yes, this is one of those reasons why DOS is a pain.

Running special start-up programs, menu systems, Windows, or whatever else you want to do first

The last thing in your AUTOEXEC.BAT file should be the otherwise first command you would type at the DOS prompt. For example, if you always type MENU to start your menu system when the computer first starts, why not stick MENU in as the last item in AUTOEXEC.BAT?

```
MENU
```

Another very useful thing to do in AUTOEXEC.BAT is to make backup copies of both your AUTOEXEC.BAT and CONFIG.SYS files. Here are two commands to do that:

```
COPY C:\AUTOEXEC.BAT C:\TEMP
COPY C:\CONFIG.SYS C:\TEMP
```

The first command copies the AUTOEXEC.BAT file to the C:\TEMP directory. The second command does the same thing, but with the CONFIG.SYS file. This handy trick will preserve your start-up files should you accidentally erase them (which, I don't know about you, seems to happen a lot around here).

- RAM drives are covered in Chapter 24.

- Refer to Chapter 13 for more information on the XCOPY command.

Another popular command to end AUTOEXEC.BAT is WIN, the command that starts Windows:

```
WIN
```

Again, the idea here is that whatever you normally type at the DOS prompt after the computer starts is better put into the AUTOEXEC.BAT file. If you always start WordPerfect, put WP at the end of AUTOEXEC.BAT to run that program.

✔ Conversely, if your computer always starts a menu program or Windows and you typically quit it to return to the DOS prompt, you can always edit that command out. For example, remove the WIN from the end of AUTOEXEC.BAT, and you start your day at the DOS prompt. In Chapter 9, refer to the section, "Removing a Command from AUTOEXEC.BAT" for more information.

✔ Philosophically, it can be extracted that typing WIN at the DOS prompt is a type of gambling, much akin to muttering *Baby needs a new pair of shoes* whilst playing dice. I mean, "Win what?" Unfortunately, the payoff of this gamble is usually the Windows program, which may or may not be the win-result desired.

Part II
More Stuff

The 5th Wave   By Rich Tennant

In this part...

The theme of *More DOS For Dummies* is that you get more of the stuff you liked so much in *DOS For Dummies*. And for you, this is such a deal — or "value," which seems to be the marketing term *du jour*. The purpose of this section is to give you the stuff you want *more* of: primary information on files, disks, subdirectories, and the whole of DOS's ugly core. It's all in this part of the book, the section called, plainly, *More Stuff*.

Chapter 11

More on . . .
Files

● ●

In This Chapter

▶ Discerning the various types of files

▶ Naming your files

▶ Renaming your files

▶ Using wildcards

● ●

*D*on't you hate those computer books that claim a file is like "a file folder in a filing cabinet"? It just isn't true. Instead, files are containers. They're things in which information is stored in your computer, specifically on one of your wildly spinning disk drives. If you need a mental picture, think of your disk drive as this nicely waxed, black marble floor. A file is a salt shaker someone knocked over on the floor. The salt — some still in the shaker, some spilled on the marble floor — is your precious data. Now go get a broom and clean it all up.

Seriously, a file is a storage unit. It's the *thing* DOS uses to store information on a disk. The strange part is that files come in many different types and hold many different types of information. This chapter unscrews the lid on the subject and peers inside for a closer look.

The Tenor of Files

Central to everything done on your PC is the file. It's most important. Files hold all the stuff you have on your computer; from the programs you run to the documents you create — everything is stored on disk in a *file*. That's the classical definition, the one that, were this a textbook, would definitely be on the final.

The problems with files are many. It's as if medical science had evolved to the state where all your inner organs were referred to as *guts* and left at that. If that were the case, something like the following conversation might take place while you were under sedation:

FIRST SURGEON:	What's this thing?
SECOND SURGEON:	It's a gut!
FIRST SURGEON:	Where does it go?
SECOND SURGEON:	In there! With the other guts!

It's just that bad under DOS, primarily because DOS only lets you name your files using tiny, often cryptic names. Telling what's in a file by looking at the name can be challenge. The following sections mull over what's in a file and discuss how a file's contents are divvied up into various categories.

Who knows what evil lurks in the hearts of files?

Know ye a file not by its name! As far as DOS is concerned, a filename is only a handy, albeit brief title that you make up. The name has absolutely nothing to do with what's in the file or which program created the file or whether or not it's a file or a program or anything.

Don't get on the phone to the Kevorkian Institute just yet! Things aren't *that* dismal. Generally speaking, DOS deals with several different types of files. These aren't official categories, though you'll probably hear their names bandied about in magazines and by other users.

Text files: These are files that contain readable words. The typical text file is named README.TXT. It contains information someone wants you to read. (And note that the TXT filename extension isn't a rule; it's just a helpful hint that you have a text file.)

After text files, all other files contain gobbledygook. They may be important or serve a specific function, but they're definitely not text files, not suitable for human reading.

Program files: These files contain instructions for the computer, but they look just like gobbledygook.

Document files: Don't confuse these files with text files. Document files are produced by word processors. They contain text but may also contain formatting codes and other information that leads to massive gobbledygook.

Data files: This is the final, everything-else-goes-here category. What I call a data file can be just about anything. When in doubt, call it a data file.

✔ Refer to the later section "Peering into text files" for more information on text files.

✔ Refer to "Program files generally end in COM, EXE, or BAT" later in this chapter for information on program files.

Peering into files with special voyeuristic software

DOS may be stupid, but some special programs can actually peer into a file and tell you what it contains and even which program produced the file. These special programs are called *viewers*. They show a file's contents *in context —* just as the file would look if you viewed it in the program that created it. Yes, these programs are a boon to those of us who sloppily name our files.

Viewer programs (or *utilities*) are included with popular software packages like the Norton Utilities and PC Tools. XTree has one too, I believe. The best was the old Magellan program, which I highly recommend (if you can find it). Figure 11-1 shows Magellan looking at a graphics file — something you couldn't tell from looking at the filename alone.

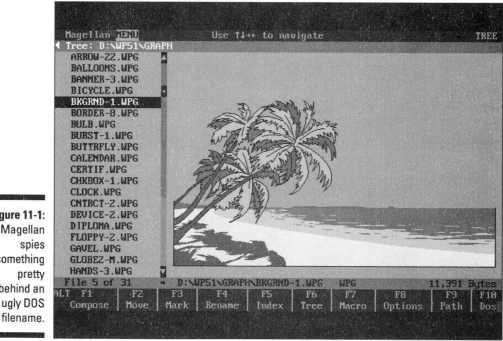

Figure 11-1: Magellan spies something pretty behind an ugly DOS filename.

✔ A viewer is a special program — a utility — that lets you see a file's contents the way they're supposed to look.

✔ When a file can't be displayed in context (the viewer doesn't know what's in it or the file has no context), then it's displayed in *hex dump* format. Hex dump format is ugly (see Figure 11-2).

✔ If you have a version of DOS that comes with the DOS Shell program, you can peer into a file to see its guts. Just highlight the filename and press the F9 key to peer into the heart of any file. The DOS Shell viewer is unsophisticated: It only shows plain text files or the infamous hex dump (see "Nerdy information on the obnoxious hex dump" nearby).

Peering into text files

The one thing that makes text files unique is that you can read them without the aid of a viewer program or a degree in programming science. DOS's TYPE command was built with this purpose in mind.

The AUTOEXEC.BAT file is a text file, containing readable commands (though it's not light or happy reading). You can use the TYPE command to display that file on the screen:

```
C:\>TYPE C:\AUTOEXEC.BAT
```

Figure 11-2:
The ugly hex dump format, used when the viewer doesn't know what the heck's going on.

MS-DOS Shell — COMMAND.COM					
Display View Help					
To view file's content use PgUp or PgDn or ↑ or ↓.					
00C0D0	99035245	4D060401	109A0443	4F505903	ŏ.REM....Ü.COPY.
00C0E0	E63D7C99	05504155	5345066D	1F149A04	µ=¦ŏ.PAUSE.m..ü.
00C0F0	44415445	02E73492	99045449	4D450250	DATE.т4Åŏ.TIME.P
00C100	35F49903	56455202	DA22FE99	03564F4C	5┌ŏ.VER.┌"■ŏ.VOL
00C110	03DE2106	9A024344	039A2A70	99054348	.▌!.Ü.CD.Ü╬pŏ.CH
00C120	44495203	9A2A7099	024D4403	052BC099	DIR.Ü╬pŏ.MD..+Ŭ
00C130	054D4B44	49520305	2BC09902	52440379	.MKDIR..+Ŭ.RD.y
00C140	2BE09905	524D4449	5203792B	E0990542	+αŏ.RMDIR.y+αŏ.B
00C150	5245414B	02DF3C66	99065645	52494659	REAK.■<fŏ.VERIFY
00C160	02223D02	9A035345	5406FA27	EC990650	."=.Ü.SET..'αŏ.P
00C170	524F4D50	5406E027	CC990450	41544802	ROMPT.α'¦ŏ.PATH.
00C180	4224C499	04455849	54003C27	BC990443	B$-ŏ.EXIT.<'⌐ŏ.C
00C190	54545903	8E258E99	04454348	4F06A53C	TTY.Å¿Åŏ.ECHO.Ñ<
00C1A0	189A0447	4F544F06	350D1E9A	05534849	.Ü.GOTO.5..Ü.SHI
00C1B0	465402BA	0C249A02	49460669	0B289A03	FT.║.$Ü.IF.i.(Ü.
00C1C0	464F5206	FE0F389A	03434C53	00EE2478	FOR.■.8Ü.CLS.€$x
00C1D0	99085452	55454E41	4D4503BA	26429A08	ŏ.TRUENAME.║&BÜ.
00C1E0	4C4F4144	48494748	02B86746	9A024C48	LOADHIGH.┐gFÜ.LH
00C1F0	02B86746	9A002E43	4F4D2E45	58452E42	.┐gFÜ..COM.EXE.B
00C200	41542D59	3F564241	50575248	53764441	AT-Y?VBAPWRHSⱱDA
◄┘=PageDown Esc=Cancel F9=Hex/ASCII					12:40p

TECHNICAL STUFF

Nerdy information on the obnoxious hex dump

The hex dump is really a programmer's tool, something mere mortals such as you or I need not bother with. Yet it's a common way nontext files are displayed on certain programs (such as the *friendly* DOS Shell).

The *hex* in hex dump is short for *hexadecimal,* a counting system that uses 16 numbers. (Decimal, the counting system humans use, has only 10 numbers.) The *dump* part means *to display without enthusiasm.* So, the hex dump display is just a list of numbers organized in rows and columns

that represents the contents of a file. The numbers are actually the values of the various bytes stored in the files.

Most hex dump formats also list what the contents would be in English. This usually happens in the far right-hand column, where characters are displayed instead of numbers. Occasionally, you can read bits of text in there, such as the DOS commands secretly encoded in Figure 11-2, which is a hex dump of the COMMAND.COM program file.

A better command to use for reading text files is the MORE command. For example, you could use the following command to see the contents of a README.TXT file:

```
C:\>MORE < README.TXT
```

First type **MORE**, then a space, and then a less-than sign, <. Then type another space and the name of the file you want to view, such as README.TXT above.

The advantage to the MORE command is that it automatically pauses after each screen of information is displayed. A — More — prompt appears, and you can press the Enter key to see the next screen.

- ✔ If you try either the TYPE or MORE command to view a file, and lo, it looks severely ugly on the screen, then what you have is not a text file.

- ✔ The MORE command is really a DOS filter. Information on how it's used, as well as what the < doodad means, is covered in Chapter 20.

- ✔ Text files don't have a de facto DOS extension (because DOS doesn't really care about filenames, and *de facto* is, in reality, a Latin expression). However, many people put the TXT extension on text files. Some text files may end in DOC, though that's usually reserved for word processing documents. Any file ending in BAT is a DOS batch file, which also contains readable text. CONFIG.SYS is also a text file, but it contains configuration commands.

✔ Text files are usually created using a text editor, which is a word proces-
sor-like program minus the fancy features. DOS comes with a text editor
called the DOS Editor, which is run using the EDIT command. In older
versions of DOS you use the EDLIN text editor to create or modify text
files.

✔ You can use any text editor to edit any text file, no matter which program
you used to create it.

✔ So what good is a text file? Primarily, text files are used to exchange
information between two incompatible programs or even two incompatible computers (such as the PC and the Mac). The text file provides a
common format between many applications. So you could create a
document in WordPerfect, save it as a text file (DOS text), and then put it
on a disk and give it to someone who has Microsoft Word, and he or she
can read the file.

Program files generally end in COM, EXE, or BAT

DOS is ignorant of all filenames except for these three filename extensions:
COM, EXE, and BAT. To DOS, these extensions identify program files — files
that contain instructions that tell the computer what to do.

✔ COM and EXE files contain computer code or instructions for the microprocessor directly.

✔ BAT files contain DOS commands and special batch file programming
instructions. These are text files, but DOS runs the commands listed inside
of a batch file.

How all this works depends on what you type at the DOS prompt. For example,
suppose that you type

```
C:\>BOVINE
```

DOS swallows that and tries to decide whether it's an *internal command* (like
COPY, REN, or DEL) or the name of a program file on disk. Failing to find
BOVINE as an internal command, DOS looks on the disk for a file named
BOVINE.COM or BOVINE.EXE or even BOVINE.BAT. If DOS finds such a file, it
runs that program. If DOS doesn't find the program, you see the Bad command
or file name error message.

- ✔ If you're running Windows, files ending in PIF are also considered programs. However, the PIF files merely run a COM, EXE, or BAT file in a way that makes Windows grin with glee.

- ✔ The nerdier crowd also declares, incorrectly, that files ending in SYS or BIN can also be considered programs. Wrong-o, geek-o. A SYS file (such as a device driver, explained in Chapter 7) is merely a gussied-up COM file. Ha! And BIN files can't run like other programs. DOS expects to see COM, EXE, or BAT, and nuthin' else.

- ✔ The world's largest bovine is the all-white Italian Chianinas, which can weigh up to 3,500 pounds. No beef!

The TSR is a special and strange program but (fortunately) not as popular as in days gone by

A special type of DOS program is the TSR. This program looks like a normal, mild-mannered COM or EXE file. What makes it different is that unlike the normal, mild-mannered COM or EXE file, a TSR program doesn't really quit. No, it stays low and lurks in memory. There, the TSR does its work silently or waits until called upon. Sneaky, sneaky.

The purpose of the TSR was to give DOS users access to special programs at any time. For example, if you were running the popular SideKick TSR program, you could use it any time by pressing the Ctrl and Alt keys together. In a spreadsheet? Just press Ctrl-Alt and up popped SideKick to do your bidding.

As you can guess, TSRs grew in popularity with DOS users. They wanted instant access to several programs, which was possible but eventually led to problems. Basically, the TSRs all fought with each other and punched up the computer instead. The end result was that PCs crashed or wouldn't work. You get the idea.

Today, TSRs are still used, although the pop-up variety (à la SideKick) isn't as popular. Your computer's mouse is controlled by a TSR. DOSKey is a TSR (see Chapter 4). They work just fine, providing you with fancy ways of doing things, and they're not as obnoxious as in days of old.

- ✔ Another term for *TSR* is *memory-resident program*. That's because the programs stay in memory instead of quitting like normal programs. I prefer the memory-resident term over TSR, though the marketing dorks in the computer industry have thrust TSR unwillingly down everyone's throat.

✔ And what is a TSR exactly? It stands for *Terminate and Stay Resident*. That's the name of the programmer's instruction that tells the program to go low and hide in memory. Programmer's called them TSRs once too often, and one day — unfortunately for us all — a marketing person was standing way too close.

✔ TSRs are installed in your AUTOEXEC.BAT file. Refer to Chapter 10 for information.

Boring information on the SETVER command

Right after DOS version 3.3 appeared, a really stupid thing happened. In the computer industry, this stupid thing has come to be known as DOS version 4. Later, it was called DOS 4.01, but it was still stupid.

The problem with DOS 4 was that it did a lot of wacky things that fouled up a lot of DOS programs, particularly the useful ones like the Norton Utilities. DOS 4 was bad, bad, *bad*. So, a lot of software developers decided to protect their software from DOS 4 (which few people ever used, as if that surprises you).

One of the developers' protection schemes was called *version awareness*. This worked by having the program first say *hello* to DOS and politely ask which version of DOS it was. If the version was anything greater than DOS 3.3, the program would refuse to run. Good programs would say Un- known or unsupported DOS — *i.e. I refuse to run (and you'll be thankful for it)*.

Microsoft fixed DOS nicely for version 5 and again with DOS 6, testing these versions with everything well before unleashing them on the public. Yet some programs out there still refused to run on any DOS version later than 3.3. To fix this problem, the SETVER program was written. SETVER intercepts a program's polite *hello* and responds with a bogus DOS version number. So, when the program says, "Are you greater than DOS 3.3?" SETVER — even if it belongs to version DOS 6.2 — responds, "No, I *am* DOS version 3.3!"

Yeah, it lies.

The moral of the story is that many programs still require SETVER to be installed in your PC's CONFIG.SYS file. This makes those few overly cautious programs believe they're running under an older, *safer* version of DOS, which makes them happy. (Refer to Chapter 6 for more information on CONFIG.SYS.)

Where Are Files?

Obviously, files are stored in the computer. That's safe enough knowledge for everyone. If you want to get specific, you can say files are stored on the disk drive, just as music is stored on cassette tape or CD. If you want to get ugly, you can say that files are stored magnetically on the hard disk medium. No sense in getting ugly, though.

DOS's *raison d'être* is to organize files on your disk drives. That's the task for which DOS was built (and for which it received a big C- from Mr. Hudson, Bill Gates's 10th grade computer science teacher). We don't have to worry about how files are stored on disks — DOS does the job for us. But if the subject concerns you, here are a few idea satellites orbiting the files-on-disk planet:

- ✔ DOS saves files to disk and can fetch them back when called for.

- ✔ DOS recognizes files by the filenames you give them. The filename is usually dreamt up right before the file is saved or first stored on disk.

- ✔ Internally, DOS keeps track of files on disk by using something called the FAT. Basically, the FAT is a map of where files are put on disk and is typically very rotund.

- ✔ DOS can duplicate files using the COPY command.

- ✔ DOS can rename files (which changes only the file's name-label, not the contents) using the REN or RENAME commands.

- ✔ DOS can obliterate files by using the DEL or ERASE commands.

- ✔ Files can be moved about the disk (copying and then deleting the original) using the MOVE command (with DOS 6 or later).

- ✔ For organizational purposes, files are put into directories.

You use the DIR command to get information about files on disk. DIR lists the files, plus information on how big the files are (giving the size in *bytes*) and the date and time the files were last saved to disk. Other information is stored on disk about the files as well but it's really technical, and I'd rather chop a gross of onions while listening to Judy Collins than write about it here.

- ✔ Files are created in memory and then saved to disk. Refer to Chapter 22 for a discussion of how this works.

- ✔ Copying and moving files is covered in Chapter 13. Chapter 14 has information on deleting files. Oh, and don't forget Chapter 12, which discusses the DIR command.

- ✔ Files are stored on the disk. The disk itself is only the storage device.

- ✔ Raison d'être is French. It means raisins are art.

Naming Your Files

Properly naming your files is important for two reasons: first, because the name must somehow reflect upon the file's contents, and second, because DOS isn't the most flexible thing when it comes to naming files. Indeed, if DOS were in charge of naming children, we'd all be named *Bob*. Even the women.

The basic file-naming rules

The most important file-naming rule is that DOS only gives you from one to eight characters to name a file. So you can have itty bitty filenames of one letter (or number), or you use up the full eight and no more.

```
0
TO
PUT
MORE
STUFF
BEYOND
LIMITED
FILENAME
```

The eight characters can be either letters or numbers in any order. This is the only other rule worth memorizing: Use only letters of the alphabet or numbers (0 through 9) to name your files. Follow that short order and you'll never be greeted by any file-naming boo-boos, ever.

Before moving on, I need to dispel a rumor: Yes, filenames *can* start with a number. The following filenames are perfectly okay:

```
1
22
37
43
HIKE!
```

 ✔ Only use letters and numbers when naming your files.

 ✔ Being clever also counts when naming a file, but try to keep the filename descriptive of the file's contents.

- One major boo-boo most users commit is trying to put a space into a filename. Space is for astronauts, not filenames.

- Some of the most popular computer software has always had eight-character names: WORDSTAR, VISICALC, SIDEKICK, and so on. You don't always have to use the full eight. Quattro Pro and Quicken both use Q (actually Q.EXE) as their filenames.

- For the specific characters that you cannot include in a filename, refer to the upcoming section "Characters you cannot use in a filename."

- There's also a filename *extension*, a second part to the typical DOS filename, that you can use to name files. It's covered next.

A brief yet worthy discussion of the filename extension

Filenames actually have two parts. First comes the name. The name can be followed by a dot (or period) and then from one to three additional characters. That last part, after the period, is called the *extension*.

```
HOOTER.OWL
```

In the above filename, the OWL part is the extension. In this case, it's required or my editor would have changed the first part — the file's name — to something else.

Extensions are generally used in DOS to tell the file type, whether it's a program, text file, word processing document, spreadsheet, whatever. But keep in mind that this isn't a hard and fast rule. The only important filename extensions are as follows:

COM   Denotes a DOS program file

EXE   Denotes a DOS program file

BAT   Denotes a DOS batch program file

Aside from these three extensions, everything else is fair game. For example, WordPerfect may stick the DOC extension at the end of files that it saves to disk, but so does Microsoft Word.

- Some programs assign extensions to the files or documents they create, some don't. For example, 1-2-3 sticks WKS or WK2 or something to the end of the files you save; Word sticks on the DOC extension; dBASE does the DBF extension; and so on. In those cases, you don't need to type the extension when you save a file.

✔ Refer to "Peering into files with special voyeuristic software" for more information on how a file's name doesn't relate one iota to its contents.

✔ The extension can be from one to three characters long. So the following extensions (the last part of the filename) are all okay:

```
CHAPTER1.A
CHAPTER1.WP
CHAPTER1.DOC
```

✔ Extensions, like filenames, can contain letters and numbers. They cannot contain the characters listed in the section "Characters you cannot use in a filename" coming up in this chapter.

Being clever with the extension

Most of the time your programs automatically slap on a filename extension for you. This means that you only type the first part of the filename, and the program adds the extension. So you save your spreadsheet as

```
EMBEZZLE
```

and 1-2-3 saves it to disk as

```
EMBEZZLE.WK3
```

There is a reason for this: organization. When you tell the program to *load* a file from disk, it typically looks only for those files with that specific extension. So, although the disk may be littered with files of various types, some programs use their own extensions to separate the wheat from the chaff. This is why it's a good idea not to mess with the extensions automatically handed out by a program.

Some programs don't tack on extensions when they save files. In those cases, you're free to be clever and make up your own. For example, at my old office, we used to organize files by month. I would save all my word processing files in January with the JAN extension. The truly useful reason for this comes to play with DOS wildcards (covered later in this chapter).

Characters you cannot use in a filename

As long as you stick by the "only letters and numbers" file-naming rules, you never have to worry about memorizing the following list of characters that you cannot use in a filename:

```
.  "  /  \  [  ]  :  *  |  < >  +  =  ;  ,  ?
```

Add to this list the "space" character. Also, note that you can use the period in a filename but only to separate the first name part from the latter extension part. The rest of the preceding motley crew have special meanings to DOS, which I don't need to dwell on here.

Changing your mind and renaming your file

DOS lets you rename any file by using the REN or RENAME commands (which both do the same thing, though REN is easier to type). You must still obey the file-naming rules and such, but you can change the name:

```
C:\>REN CAREBEAR.UGH BARNEY.UGH
```

In the preceding, the file named CAREBEAR.UGH is renamed to BARNEY.UGH.

- ✔ Always follow the file-naming rules, covered in the previous section "The basic file- naming rules," when renaming a file.

- ✔ Renaming a file changes only its name, not the contents.

- ✔ Rename a file if you were stupid when you first named it and then all of the sudden came up with a better, more clever name.

- ✔ It is unwise to rename any file's extension to COM, EXE, or BAT. Likewise, don't rename any file ending in COM, EXE, or BAT.

Untamed and Wildcards

Wildcards are special jots and tittles that allow you to work with files in groups instead of one at a time. That way you can copy, move, or delete a whole range of files with one command — wreak havoc on a global scale instead of having to torture each file individually! Yes, wildcards are another one of those computer timesaving devices that actually work — provided that you can put up with their close-to-cryptic nature.

TECHNICAL STUFF

Avoidable information on those other characters you can use in a filename

Some characters that DOS lets you use to name a file can come in handy from time to time. One of them is the underline character. You can use that instead of a space in a filename if you like:

GET_OUT.NOW

The exclamation point is also allowable in a filename:

HELP!

And the dollar sign is utterly permissible:

FINANCE$

The gist of the wildcard thing

DOS uses two wildcard characters:

- ✔ The ? (question mark) is set equal to any single character in a filename.
- ✔ The * (asterisk) is set equal to any glob of characters in a filename.
- ✔ A common variation of the * wildcard is the *.* (*star-dot-star,* which is really *asterisk-dot-asterisk*). It equals all files in a directory.

The following are examples of how you can use these wildcards:

```
C:\>DIR DOS*.*
```

The preceding DIR command displays all those files that have DOS as their first three letters. The asterisks mean that the rest of the filename and the whole extension could be anything. (Anything matches the asterisk.)

```
C:\>COPY CHAP??.DOC A:
```

The preceding COPY command copies all the files named CHAP — and then any two characters — with the extension DOC to the floppy disk in drive A. The CHAP??.DOC matches filenames such as CHAP01.DOC, CHAP02.DOC, on up to CHAP28.DOC, the spine-tingling conclusion.

```
C:\>MOVE *.JAN C:\MONTHS\BACKUP
```

The preceding MOVE command moves all the files with the JAN extension to the directory \MONTHS\BACKUP on drive C. The asterisk matches any filename, of any length. But it must have the JAN extension to be moved.

Information on using wildcards with the DIR command can be found in Chapter 12; using wildcards with the COPY and MOVE commands is in Chapter 13; and Chapter 14 covers using wildcards when deleting files. Alas, there is no information in this book on the game *Crazy Eights*.

Wildcards and renaming files

One tricky aspect of using wildcards comes with the RENAME command. This is tricky because wildcards can really foul up REN and mess up files on disk. You must be careful.

Generally speaking, only use REN with wildcards to rename a file's extension. For example,

```
C:\>REN *.BAK *.OLD
```

This command renames all files on disk that have the BAK extension with the OLD extension instead. That's about the best and only example worth mentioning for using REN with wildcards.

✔ The REN command? The RENAME command? Same thing.

✔ Additional information on using the REN command can be found in the section "Changing your mind and renaming your file" earlier in this chapter.

Chapter 12

More on . . . the DIR Command

The DIR command is possibly the most popular DOS command. Not the most favorite, just the one used most often. The reason is that DIR tells you what's on disk. It does this by listing files by name, size, date, and emotional state. Yet, I'd bet there are a few things about the DIR command you didn't know. This isn't trivial stuff, like DIR spied for France during the first World War. No, this is useful information, and it's all here, all glued into this chapter. Plus you'll find some fun stuff you may not have known and information on using DOS's interesting and bizarre ATTRIB command.

What the DIR Command Tells You

The DIR command bursts forth with lots of information, most of which you can cheerfully ignore. Figure 12-1 lists what could be considered typical DIR command spew. Table 12-1 describes these items.

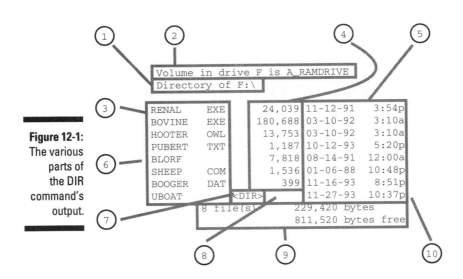

Figure 12-1:
The various
parts of
the DIR
command's
output.

Table 12-1   Important Stuff the DIR Command Tells You

Number	What It Could Possibly Mean
1	Tells you which disk drive and subdirectory you're looking at
2	Ignore this stuff. It refers to the disk's volume label. Refer to Chapter 15 for more information.
3	Filenames in the current directory. See how the DIR command uses spaces to separate the filename from the extension? This is just for lining-up purposes; don't type the spaces in to name a file. (Commas appear in big numbers only when you have MS-DOS 6.2 or later. Earlier versions of DOS display numbers chunky style.)
4	Sizes for each of the files. This column displays a file's size in *bytes.* Each byte is equal to one character, so the file PUBERT.TXT is 1,187 bytes or characters long — about one full screen of text or a double-spaced typewritten page.
5	Dates and times for the files. A file's date and time tell you when the file was last saved to disk. For example, the file RENAL.EXE was saved to disk at 3:54 p.m. on November 12, 1991. Most DOS gurus use the date to figure out which version of a file is the most recent. If a file has <DIR> instead of a size in bytes, then it's really a subdirectory. *See item 7.*
6	The BLORF file, my favorite made-up filename.
7	The <DIR> thing, which earmarks a subdirectory. Yes, the DIR command identifies subdirectories along with files. Refer to Chapter 16 for more information on subdirectories.
8	Where our love has gone.

Number	What It Could Possibly Mean
9	Ignore this stuff. It's just summary information. It tells you how many files the DIR command listed, their total size in bytes, and the number of bytes left on the disk drive. Versions of DOS prior to 5.0 displayed only the *bytes free* value.
10	A little *p* (means p.m. as opposed to *a* for a.m.)

The DIR command only displays information about the *current directory*. This concept is mulled over in Chapter 16. There are three bits of information the DIR command displays about your files:

✔ The filename and extension (Item 3 in Figure 12-1)

✔ The size of the file in bytes (Item 4 in Figure 12-1)

✔ The date and time the file was last saved to disk (Item 5 in Figure 12-1)

Using Wildcards with the DIR Command

Normally, the DIR command displays all the files on disk or in the current directory. However, you can direct DIR to display only certain files by using DOS's wildcards. For example,

```
C:\>DIR *.COM
```

In this DIR command, the asterisk tells DOS to match all filenames, no matter what, as long as they have that COM extension.

```
C:\>DIR W*.*
```

This wildcard directs DIR to display only those files that start with the letter W.

```
C:\>DIR CHAP??.DOC
```

This DIR command tells DOS to display files that have CHAP as their first four letters, then any two letters (represented by two question mark wildcards), and then the DOC extension.

```
C:\>DIR *.*
```

The preceding command is redundant. The *.* represents all the files, which DIR displays normally, all by itself, without any options.

✔ You can use the wildcard *. (asterisk, period) to find any subdirectories in the current directory:

```
C:\>DIR *.
```

Because subdirectories don't usually have extensions, the *. wildcard matches all "files" without any extensions, which includes subdirectories. (Also see the /A option, covered later in this chapter.)

✔ Wildcards are touched upon briefly during the closing moments of Chapter 11.

✔ Additional DIR command options are listed in the following sections.

Options Clinging to the Butt End of the DIR Command

There are a bunch of options you can type after the DIR command. The ugly DOS format looks something like this:

```
C:\>DIR [filename] [options]
```

There's no pressing need to dive any further into that format here. But all the options you can type at the tail end of the DIR command are listed in Table 12-2 for your eyeballing convenience. The tiny sections that follow detail how the more useful options alter the DIR command's behavior.

Table 12-2 All the Dang-Doogle DIR Command Options

Optional Doohickey	What It Does to the DIR Command's Output
/P	Pauses the display after each screen of files
/W	Displays only filenames, five across
/A	Displays only files with certain matching *attributes*
/O	Sorts the files by name, date, size, color, smell, and so on
/S	Displays files in any subdirectories as well
/B	The bare, or "nekkid," display; includes filenames only
/L	Displays filenames using chic lowercase letters
/C	Displays compression ratio on DoubleSpace-compressed drives

The wide, filename-only command is DIR /W

Use the /W option when you only want to see filenames and none of that other junk. This command is ideal for listings that would otherwise scroll off the screen or when the file size and date information cause your eyes to cross:

```
C:\>DIR /W
```

The following shows how my sample directory looks when listed by the DIR /W command:

```
Volume in drive F is A_RAMDRIVE
 Directory of F:\
RENAL.EXE    BOVINE.EXE    HOOTER.OWL   PUBERT.TXT   BLORF
SHEEP.COM    BOOGER.DAT    [UBOAT]
        8 file(s)        229,420 bytes
                         811,520 bytes free
```

> ✔ Yes, you can mix or match this option with any other DIR command option. To see a wide directory listing of lowercase filenames, type **DIR /W /L**.

> ✔ If you use the DIR command's /O option with /W, the filenames appear in sorted order; however, they appear across the screen, not in columns.

> ✔ When you use the /W option, subdirectory names are presented in square brackets — [UBOAT] in the preceding, for example.

The pausing command is DIR /P

More times than not, the files the DIR command lists scroll wildly off your screen. If you're quick, you can use the Ctrl-S key combination, as described in Chapter 2. Or if you're smart, you can remember to use the /P option with the DIR command:

```
C:\>DIR /P
```

This command directs DOS to *pause* after each screen full of files. You see the following message:

```
Press any key to continue . . .
```

Press the Enter key and the DIR command continues. If you have DOS 5 or later, the next line says something like

```
(continuing C:\DOS)
```

This message reminds you which directory you're viewing; in the preceding, it's C:\DOS. (Chapter 16 has more information on directories.)

- *Any key* = the Enter key.

- Some versions of DOS display the message Strike any key to continue. I suppose that *strike* means "to press with vigor." Or it could imply that you must picket any particular key to get managerial DOS to yield to your demands. But most likely it probably means to (gently) press the Enter key.

- Yes, you can mix or match this option with any other DIR command option. To see lowercase filenames one screen at a time, type **DIR /P /L**.

The chic lowercase command is DIR /L

The chic /L switch forces DIR to display filenames in lowercase letters. This should be called the e.e. cummings switch. Though it truly looks cool — nay, *chic* — there's nothing much else going on with the /L switch. The following shows what the sample directory looks like:

```
Volume in drive F is A_RAMDRIVE
Directory of F:\
renal    exe       24,039 11-12-91   3:54p
bovine   exe      180,688 03-10-92   3:10a
hooter   owl       13,753 03-10-92   3:10a
pubert   txt        1,187 10-12-93   5:20p
blorf               7,818 08-14-91  12:00a
sheep    com        1,536 01-06-88  10:48p
booger   dat          399 11-16-93   8:51p
uboat        <DIR>         11-27-93  10:37p
        8 file(s)      229,420 bytes
                       811,520 bytes free
```

Yes, you can mix or match this option with any other DIR command option. To see only filenames in lowercase, type **DIR /B /L**.

The bare nekkid command is DIR /B

The *B* in the DIR command's /B option must mean brief. When it is specified, DOS tells the DIR command to list only files — no other nonsense:

```
C:\>DIR /B
```

The sample directory, displayed with the /B option, is shown in the following:

```
RENAL.EXE
BOVINE.EXE
HOOTER.OWL
PUBERT.TXT
BLORF
SHEEP.COM
BOOGER.DAT
UBOAT
```

✔ Unlike the /W option, the /B option doesn't enclose subdirectory names in brackets. Instead, subdirectory names appear just like other files.

✔ Yes, you can mix or match this option with any other DIR command option — except for the /W command. To see a sorted list of brief filenames, type **DIR /B /O**. To see them a page at a time, type **DIR /B /O /P** (the DIR-BOP command).

The sorted directory output command is DIR /O

The DIR command's /O option allows you to see your files sorted alphabetically:

```
C:\>DIR /O
```

This command displays the files in alphabetical order. First come any subdirectories (also sorted in alphabetical order) followed by the rest of the files. The following shows the sample directory in sorted fashion:

```
Volume in drive F is A_RAMDRIVE
Directory of F:\
UBOAT        <DIR>          11-27-93  10:37p
BLORF               7,818  08-14-91  12:00a
BOOGER   DAT          399  11-16-93   8:51p
BOVINE   EXE      180,688  03-10-92   3:10a
HOOTER   OWL       13,753  03-10-92   3:10a
PUBERT   TXT        1,187  10-12-93   5:20p
RENAL    EXE       24,039  11-12-91   3:54p
SHEEP    COM        1,536  01-06-88  10:48p
         8 file(s)      229,420 bytes
                        811,520 bytes free
```

There are actually about 12 ways to sort files with the /O switch. These involve following /O with another letter to sort the files in a particular order:

To sort files in reverse alphabetical order, use

```
C:\>DIR /O-N
```

To sort files by size, from smallest to largest, use

```
C:\>DIR /OS
```

To sort files by size, largest to smallest, use

```
C:\>DIR /O-S
```

To sort files by date and time, oldest first, use

```
C:\>DIR /OD
```

To sort files and list the most recently created ones first, use

```
C:\>DIR /O-D
```

✔ I use the preceding command to find files that have been recently created or updated. (Actually, I add the /P switch as well, seeing as how my directories are kinda long.)

 ✔ There are other options you can type with the /O switch. For the latest list, type **DIR /?** at the DOS prompt if you have DOS 5 or later. And if you have an earlier version of DOS, well then, the /O switch just doesn't work. So there!

 ✔ Yes, you can mix or match this option with any other DIR command option. (Do you get the idea I'm copying and pasting this check mark item throughout this chapter? It's probably true.)

The all-or-nothing command is DIR /A

Files have these sneaky things attached to them called *attributes*. Attributes are covered in the section "File Attributes and Good Taste" later in this chapter. Using the DIR command's /A option, you can view files by their attribute types. Normally, this is a nerdy thing to do and not really necessary. But this chapter's running a few pages short, so I'll talk about it anyway.

Whiny information for those pre-DOS 5 users

Before DOS 5 added the /O switch, the only way to sort the DIR command's output was by using DOS's SORT command. Well, it isn't really a command. It's actually a *filter*, which is a special and potentially confusing command covered in this book's Chapter 20. Regardless, here are a few handy ways to sort the DIR command, using an arcane version of DOS.

To display a sorted directory listing, alphabetically A to Z, type the following:

```
C:\>DIR | SORT
```

That's DIR, a space, the pipe or vertical bar character, then another space, and the word SORT. This sorts the DIR command's output, but it also sorts other information. Just ignore the last part of the display. If you need to pause the listing after each screen of text, use the following goofy command:

```
C:\>DIR | SORT | MORE
```

That's the same command, but with an extra pipe at the end plus the word MORE. Please use this command and not DIR /P | SORT.

To sort files by their size, from smallest to largest, use this command:

```
C:\>DIR | SORT /+14
```

That's the same filename-sorting command, but you add a space, a slash, a plus sign, and then the number 14. To see the files sorted from largest to smallest, type the following:

```
C:\>DIR | SORT /+14 /R
```

Again, this is the same command, but with the /R option added.

By the way, these commands also work with later versions of DOS (still, the DIR command's /O switch is much handier).

```
C:\>DIR C:\ /A
```

This DIR command directs DOS to display all the files in the root directory of drive C. Type this command, and you see some files you don't normally see: MSDOS.SYS, IO.SYS, and so on. These are *hidden* or *system* files that DOS uses to start. They're protected by special file attributes, things that make the files invisible to the normal DIR command. With the /A switch you override that protection.

- ✔ It's important to note that you shouldn't mess with the secret files displayed by the DIR /A command.

- ✔ One useful variant of the /A switch is /AD. This allows you to view only the subdirectories in the current directory:

```
C:\>DIR /AD
```

After you type the preceding command and press Enter, DOS displays only the subdirectories of the current directory.

- ✔ Yes, you can mix or match this option with any other DIR command option. Refer to the previous sections for examples.

"Golly, I like that option and want to use it always"

Say you suddenly grow fond of using the DIR command's /O switch and, even more, the chic /L switch. So every time you use the DIR command, you always find yourself typing

```
C:\>DIR /O /L
```

That's kind of a pain, but the output is worth it. Still, computers *are* supposed to save you time. And surprisingly, DOS does have a solution for you. It's called the *I-want-to-use-that-DIR-command-option-all-the-time option*. It works like this:

1. Find out which DIR command option(s) you like and want to use all the time.

2. Use the SET command to create the DIRCMD environment variable. (I know, complex-sounding, but bear with me.)

   For example, you would type the following to permanently attach /O and /L to the DIR command:

```
C:\>SET DIRCMD=/O /L
```

That's the **SET** command, a space, then **DIRCMD**, the directory command environment variable. That's followed immediately by an equal sign and then the DIR command options you want. In the preceding, **/O** and **/L** are specified. Press Enter to lock this change in memory. From this point on, the DIR command automatically *assumes* the /O and /L options. Aren't computers the best?

✔ Would you like to make the SET DIRCMD options a permanent part of your PC? Turn to Chapter 10 to discover how to tuck that command into your PC's AUTOEXEC.BAT file.

✔ Refer to Chapter 19 for more information on the SET command and DOS's environment.

Finding a File

The DIR command displays files on disk. And when you use it with a specific filename, DIR displays information about that file and that file only. For example,

```
C:\>DIR PUBERT.TXT
```

When directed to find the file PUBERT.TXT, the DIR command makes the following report:

```
Volume in drive F is MS-RAMDRIVE
 Directory of F:\
PUBERT    TXT         1,187 10-12-93    5:20p
        1 file(s)          1,187 bytes
                         812,544 bytes free
```

Yeah, even though there may be other files on disk, the DIR command efficiently scopes out the one file, PUBERT.TXT, and only displays information about it.

If the file didn't exist, the DIR command would pop back with the following:

```
Volume in drive F is MS-RAMDRIVE
 Directory of F:\
File not found
```

The `File not found` error message means that PUBERT.TXT (or whatever) isn't to be found. However, the file may be lurking somewhere else on the drive, quite possibly in a subdirectory. Using the DIR command's /S option, you can scope it out. That's covered in the next section.

Likewise, if you use wildcards with the DIR command, only those files that match will appear. Refer to the section "Using Wildcards with the DIR Command" earlier in this very chapter.

The amazing /S option (briefly)

Normally, the DIR command only displays files in the current directory. With the /S option specified, the DIR command also lists files in any subdirectories of the current directory. Normally, listing subdirectory files is wholly unnecessary; the number of files displayed is immense. Even so, try the following command:

```
C:\>DIR C:\ /S
```

This command tells DOS to display all the files in the root directory of drive C. But the /S switch tells the DIR command to list files in any subdirectories as well. Because C:\ is the main directory from which all subdirectories branch out in a tree-like manner, this means the command displays *all* the files on the entire dang-doodle disk.

If the output boggles you, press Ctrl-C to stop it. Or if you really want to see all your files, try this command:

```
C:\>DIR C:\ /S /P
```

The /P option pauses the display after each screen full of text.

The find-any-file DIR command

No one in his right mind uses the DIR command's /S option; the information displayed is just too overwhelming. However, when it is coupled with the DIR command's ability to find information about specific files (such as PUBERT.TXT two sections back), you can use the /S switch to locate any file on disk. Here's how it works:

1. Think of the filename you want to find. Be as specific as possible.

2. Plug the filename into the *filename* spot in the following DIR command:

```
C:\>DIR C:\filename /S
```

That's the **DIR** command, a space, then **C**, colon, backslash, and the full name of the file you want to find. Then comes another space and **/S**. So if you want to find PUBERT.TXT, you'd type the following:

```
C:\>DIR C:\PUBERT.TXT /S
```

The DIR command starts hunting for the file in the root directory of drive C. If it's not found, no error message is displayed. Instead, thanks to the /S option, DIR keeps looking through every subdirectory on the drive.

3. If the file is found, you see a message like the following:

```
Directory of C:\LOST\FILES
PUBERT   TXT         1,187 10-12-93   5:20p
        1 file(s)          1,187 bytes
                      56,812,544 bytes free
```

The `Directory of C:\LOST\FILES` tells you where the file is located — in which directory. (Refer to Chapter 16 for information on getting at the file.) If the file is found in more than one spot, additional messages like this one appear. (You might want to add the /P, pause, option to the command as well.)

If the file isn't found, you see the traditional `File not found` message displayed. Oh well.

If the file isn't found, consider looking on another hard drive. For example,

```
C:\>DIR D:\filename /S
```

This command looks for *filename* on drive D. Change the D to an E to look for the file on drive E (providing you have drive E).

All about the .. and . Things

Two things always pop up and bug DOS users. Perhaps you may have seen this couple in the DIR command's output:

```
.            <DIR>       11-11-93  1:08a
..           <DIR>       11-11-93  1:08a
```

You try rubbing them out. You try buffing them out. But you just can't get rid of them, right? What *are* those two things?

Finding a file the easiest way possible

All this information on using DIR/S to find a file is really kinda lame. The best file-finding tool you have is available in the MSD program that comes with DOS 6 or later or Windows. Type **MSD** at the DOS prompt, and then press Alt-F to get at the File menu and press Enter to activate the Find File command. A box appears, similar to the following. This is the ultimate Find File command, hidden in the MSD program (see below).

In the Search for box, type the name of the file you're looking for. Press the Tab key when you're done. (You can use wildcards if you need to.)

In the Start from box, press the Delete key. This removes the directory name stored there.

Press the Tab key until the cursor is blinking under Include sub-dirs. Press the spacebar to put an X in the check box. Press the Tab key again until it's blinking under Search all drives. Press the spacebar to put an X into the check box.

Press the Enter key to start the search. In a few moments, a screen appears with all the found files listed. The files will be displayed by pathname, so refer to Chapter 16 if you need to know more about pathnames.

Press Esc and then F3 to exit from the MSD program.

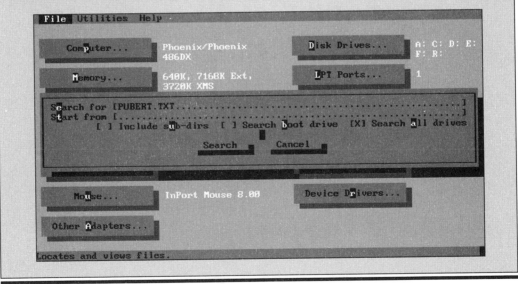

Actually, the dot and dot-dot files (as they're called) are really DOS wildcards. They represent subdirectories, not files, on your PC. They're listed by the DIR command for every subdirectory on your hard drive.

✔ The single dot is a shorthand for the *current directory*.

✔ The double dot is a shorthand for the *parent directory*.

Try this command:

```
C:\>DIR .
```

The single dot here isn't the dot that separates a filename from its extension; it's the current directory. Indeed, the dot is the same as *.* (star-dot-star).

To see files in the parent directory, type this command:

```
C:\>DIR ..
```

The double dots represent the parent directory.

✔ The *parent directory* is the directory "just above" the current directory. Or you could say that the current directory is a subdirectory of the parent. Or you could just flip up to Chapter 16 and chew the fat on the whole directory nonsense.

✔ Be careful with the . (current directory) abbreviation. The following command

```
C:\>DEL .
```

is the same as DEL *.* (delete everything). It will delete all the files in the current directory. Beware!

✔ Refer to Chapter 11 for more information on DOS's wildcards (though the . and .. things aren't covered there).

✔ The . also works in the root directory, when it's the current directory. But you cannot use .. in the root directory because the root directory has no parent directory. (If you try, you'll get an Invalid directory error.)

File Attributes and Good Taste

DOS knows lots of information about the files you store on disk, but it only tells you a little smidgen of that information. By using the DIR command, you can get a file's name, its size in bytes, and the date and time it was last saved to disk. Big deal! There's lots more cryptic information DOS knows about the file — stuff it selfishly won't tell you unless you know about a little jewel called the ATTRIB command.

Normally, there's no reason anyone should care about the ATTRIB command. It controls a file's *attributes*, which are neither here nor there as far as using a computer is concerned. But if you're willing to get a wee bit technical, you can actually twiddle the attributes yourself, using the ATTRIB command. This command can let you do at least a couple of interesting (or maybe even — dare we say it? — *useful*) things with your files.

Once upon a time, there were four li'l attributes . . .

The ATTRIB command is used to control four attributes DOS assigns to files. These I've listed in Table 12-3, following the Standard Computer Book Author Table-Making Rules set forth by the Geneva Convention.

Table 12-3	File Attributes You Need Not Concern Yourself With	
Attribute	**Name**	**Purpose in Life**
A	Archive	Gets flipped on only when a file is modified
H	Hidden	Hides files
R	Read-only	Makes it darn hard to delete a file
S	System	None whatsoever

Yes, there's no need to memorize these attributes. The next two sections describe how to manipulate the two most useful, H and R. Aside from that, this is all padding, designed to add value to the book.

✔ Attributes are switched on or off. When a file has an attribute, that attribute is *on*. So if the HERNIA.RIP file has the R attribute, the R attribute is on for that file. (Some nerds may say *set* instead of on and *reset* instead of off.)

✔ The A attribute is only attached to files that have been modified since the last backup. When you back up files, the BACKUP command (or third-party backup program) removes the A attribute from all files. Only those files modified after the backup will then have their A attribute on. This is what allows the BACKUP command to back up only modified files. Technical stuff. No need to worry about it.

✔ The H attribute makes files *invisible* or hidden. The files won't be listed by the DIR command, and the COPY, DEL, MOVE, or any other DOS command that uses wildcards will not mess with the file.

✔ Leave it to the French to put the *pain* into bread.

✔ The R attribute makes a file read-only. You can view, examine, maybe even poke a read-only file, but you cannot change or delete it. This is a great way to protect files from being accidentally cut off at the knees.

✔ The S attribute earmarks DOS's special system files. That's about it.

✔ To see which attributes are assigned files on your disk, use the ATTRIB command. Just type **ATTRIB** and press Enter. Like the DIR command, it lists files. Unlike the DIR command, it lists only the filenames along with A, H, R, or S for any attributes stuck on the files.

Locking on read-only protection

Read-only protection means that a file cannot be modified or deleted. This is a handy BandAid to apply to files you want to keep around and unaltered.

For example, suppose that you want to slap on read-only protection to your COMMAND.COM file — a good idea for everyone. Type the following:

```
C:\>ATTRIB +R C:\COMMAND.COM
```

Type **ATTRIB**, a space, **R**, a plus sign, another space, and then the filename of the file you want to protect: **C**, colon, backslash, **COMMAND**, period, **COM**. Doing so prevents any program from modifying or deleting COMMAND.COM. To protect other files, substitute their full pathname for C:\COMMAND.COM.

✔ If you try to mess with a read-only protected file, you'll get an Access denied error.

✔ To check for read-only protected files in the current directory, use the following command:

```
C:\>DIR /AR
```

That's the **DIR** command, a space, then **/A** and **R**. This displays only the read-only files. If none are found, you'll get the File not found message.

✔ To remove read-only protection, you must use the ATTRIB command again. Type the following:

```
C:\>ATTRIB -R filename
```

This is almost identical to the command you used to attach read-only protection. The only difference is the minus sign instead of the plus sign. Also, substitute the name of the file you want to unprotect in place of *filename*.

✔ BandAid is a registered trademark of the Johnson & Johnson company.

Hiding files (but don't get too excited about it)

Hiding files is more cute than useful. A hidden file cannot be seen by the DIR command and is ignored by all other commands that use *.* (the all-files wildcard). There are several weak-points to this type of "secret" command, which I'll tell later, as an anti-climax.

To hide a file, you use the ATTRIB command. For example, to hide the file JIMMYH.DOC, you would type the following:

```
C:\>ATTRIB +H JIMMYH.DOC
```

That's **ATTRIB**, a space, a plus sign, then an **H**. That means "Add the hidden attribute." Then comes another space and the name of the file you want to hide, **JIMMYH.DOC** in the preceding.

After hiding a file, type the DIR command. You won't see it listed anywhere.

And now . . . the bad news:

- ✔ Hey. You know about hiding files, and so does everyone else. Only the severely DOS sleepy don't know about it.

- ✔ You can easily unhide files using the ATTRIB -H command.

- ✔ Anyone who knows the exact filename can still access the file.

- ✔ You can see hidden files in any directory using the DIR /AH command.

- ✔ You can also use the ATTRIB command by itself to scope out hidden files. (Alas. I hope I didn't pop your balloon too loudly.)

- ✔ You cannot copy, delete, move, or rename hidden files by using wildcards.

   This command deletes every file — except for the hidden (and read-only) ones:

   ```
   C:\>DEL *.*
   ```

   You can, however, delete a hidden file if you know its filename and specify it exactly.

- ✔ You can also hide subdirectories by using the ATTRIB +H command (though I wouldn't have the foggiest idea why you'd want to).

Don't mess with the System attribute

The final attribute the ATTRIB command lets you twist is S, the *System* attribute. Don't mess with it!

Only two files on disk have the System attribute, the secret (and also hidden) files IO.SYS and MSDOS.SYS. Don't use the ATTRIB command to remove the S attribute from those two files. Don't use ATTRIB to give the S attribute to any other files. There. Enough said.

- ✔ Sometimes, compressed disk drive software, such as Stacker or DoubleSpace, uses the S attribute.

- ✔ Okay, so the logical question arises, "If they don't want us to mess with it, then why let the ATTRIB command do it in the first place?" The answer is that DOS gurus may want to use it when modifying the system files. Because that's something no one less than Einstein or Mr. Spock would worry about, let's leave it at that and call it a day.

Chapter 13

More on . . .
Copying and Moving Files

● ●

In This Chapter

▶ Copying a file and renaming it

▶ Duplicating files

▶ Using wildcards with the COPY command

▶ The super-dooper XCOPY command

▶ A really moving command

▶ Verification information

● ●

Copying files is something you do often in DOS, usually with ease and minus the bother of having to deal with the Xerox repairperson. Still, copying has a lot of negative connotations to it. There's the *copy-catter, dirty ratter*. Then there's the snooty *It's not an original, merely a cheesy copy* (though the affluent are loath to use the word *cheesy*). And of course, there's the whole ethical debacle with cloning and human embryos, which I can't get into here because my managing editor won't let me use the word *zygote* in a computer book.

Unlike the ethical dilemma over copying, DOS's COPY command, fortunately, has few negative connotations to it. It's a common DOS command. Simple. Used often. No messy grout or toxic cleanup involved. Yet I hope to open your eyes about a few COPY command basics in this chapter and wax nerdly on the XCOPY command — and maybe kiss up to the new DOS 6 MOVE command as well.

✔ If you have MS-DOS 6.2, then the COPY command warns you before it overwrites any file already on disk. You're prompted with an `Overwrite (Yes/No/All)` message; press Y to overwrite the existing file, N to skip. (Older versions of DOS callously overwrite files with no warning whatsoever.)

Whence Cometh and Thither Goest Thy Files?

The COPY command, which creates exact duplicates of the original, is used to duplicate files. This allows you to take a file from your office, copy it to a floppy disk, take it home, copy it to your home computer's hard drive, and pretend you're working on it at home.

- ✔ COPY is a command that's used with any computer operating system, not just DOS. You need that command to make duplicates of your files.

- ✔ In UNIX, the COPY command is named CP. That keeps with UNIX's tradition of cryptic commands and goes well with lazy UNIX typists.

A keen look at source and destination

Understanding the COPY command means that you need to know the concept of *source* and *destination* — that is, where the file you're copying is and where are you copying it to.

```
C:\>COPY ZYGOTE A:
```

This COPY command takes the file named ZYGOTE and copies it to the floppy disk in drive A. What DOS calls the *source* is the file ZYGOTE; the *destination* — where the file is being copied — is drive A.

```
C:\>COPY ZYGOTE C:\TEMP
```

In this example, the COPY command copies the ZYGOTE file to the TEMP directory on drive C. The source is the file ZYGOTE, and the destination is C:\TEMP. Yes, the destination can be either a disk drive or subdirectory.

```
C:\>COPY C:\RG\ZYGOTE D:\FRO
```

In the preceding, pathnames are used for both the source and destination. The COPY command takes the file ZYGOTE in the RG directory on drive C and then copies the file to the FRO directory on drive D. The source is C:\RG\ZYGOTE, and the destination is D:\FRO.

- ✔ The *source* is fancy nerd talk for the file you're copying or duplicating.

- ✔ The *destination* is fancy nerd talk for where you're placing the copy, such as on a floppy disk, hard drive, and so forth.

✔ Refer to Chapter 16 for the full details on pathnames and subdirectories.

✔ *Whence* means "from what place" and *thither* means "to that place." So, in a way, aren't you glad they use *source* and *destination* instead?

✔ Copies of computer files are identical to the originals. So unlike art, where copies are cheap and tawdry, computer files can be duplicated all day long without a trace of evidence.

Copying a file from the current directory (or "I just assumed you were here")

The COPY command makes a lot of assumptions. For example,

```
C:\>COPY NASTY.DOC A:
```

This command copies the file NASTY.DOC to drive A. It's assumed that NASTY.DOC is in the current directory. (And it's also assumed that a formatted floppy disk is in drive A.) If NASTY isn't in the current directory, DOS will bellow `File not found.` You'd need to specify the directory if that were the case:

```
C:\>COPY C:\UGLY\NASTY.DOC A:
```

In this example, the file NASTY.DOC is located in the UGLY directory on drive C.

✔ If you were going to be copying a lot of files and wanted to save time, you would change to the source directory (C:\UGLY in the preceding). In that case, typing the COPY NASTY.DOC A: command would work.

✔ By the way, this current directory assumption is a great argument to display the *path* in the DOS prompt. For example,

```
C:\NASTY>
```

This prompt tells you that the C:\UGLY directory is the current directory. Refer to Chapter 3 for more information on this type of DOS prompt.

✔ Refer to Chapter 16 for more information on what a *current directory* is.

Copying a file to the current directory (or "I just assumed you were coming here")

A strange aspect of the COPY command is its ability to assume the destination (the place to which you're copying files). For example,

```
C:\>COPY A:\HORRID.DBF
```

This command looks incomplete — but there goes DOS making assumptions again. It assumes that the file HORRID.DBF on drive A is the source and that the *current directory* is the destination.

For example, if the current directory were C:\AWFUL, then the file HORRID.DBF would be copied to that directory from drive A automatically. This is the same thing as the following command:

```
C:\>COPY A:\HORRID.DBF C:\AWFUL
```

However, if your prompt is set properly, you could see the current directory anyway:

```
C:\AWFUL>COPY A:\HORRID.DBF
```

In this example, the prompt tells you that C:\AWFUL is the current directory — the missing piece of the COPY command and what DOS assumes you mean as the destination.

✔ Mostly this current directory assumption is used when copying groups of files. For example, if you want to copy all the document files (*.DOC) from drive A to the hard drive, you would type

```
C:\THITHER>COPY A:*.DOC
```

This is generally easier to type than the following (which also works):

```
C:\THITHER>COPY A:*.DOC C:\THITHER
```

✔ The COPY command assumes that you mean the current directory as the destination when a destination isn't specified.

✔ You cannot use this variation of the COPY command to duplicate a file in the current directory. For example, suppose GAMETE is a file in the current directory:

```
C:\>COPY GAMETE
```

> This results in a `File cannot be copied onto itself` error. This is actually one of those rare moments when DOS is both smart and honest.

Blowing the COPY Command Way Out of Proportion

Most of the COPY command basics are fairly simple. Source. Destinations. Assumptions. Okay. The following sections mull over a few of the more eccentric aspects of the COPY command. Hopefully, there will be something useful in it for you.

Copying a file and renaming it

The COPY command takes a file and makes a duplicate:

```
C:\>COPY TAXSCAM.XLS A:
```

This command takes the file TAXSCAM.XLS and copies it to drive A. Here's what appears on the screen:

```
1 file(s) copied
```

That means there is now a duplicate file, TAXSCAM.XLS, on drive A.

The horrors of the COPY command, Part I: Concatenation

The COPY command has many more options than any mere mortal need worry about. One of the most bizarre is something called *concatenation*, which comes from the early Latin word for *shoving together with vigor*. Using concatenation, you can glue two or more text files together to create a larger text file. For example,

```
C:\>COPY GAMETE_X+GAMETE_Y ZYGOTE
```

This command takes the text file GAMETE_X and glues GAMETE_Y to the end of it. The resulting file is copied to a new file on disk, ZYGOTE.

Why this trick is inane: Because very few files on disk are text files. The trick really fouls up your files if you try it with anything else.

If you want to give the duplicate a new name, you must specify the new name as part of the COPY command's destination:

```
C:\>COPY TAXSCAM.XLS A:HONESTAX.XLS
```

In the preceding, the file TAXSCAM.XLS is copied to drive A. On drive A, DOS gives the file the name HONESTAX.XLS. Both files have the same contents, but the duplicate has a new name.

This renaming trick works best when you copy single files. When you work with wildcards, treat the COPY command more like the RENAME command (see Chapter 11). For example,

```
C:\>COPY *.DOC *.BAK
```

This COPY command copies all the DOC files from the current directory to drive A and renames each with the BAK extension.

Duplicating files with the COPY command

By its nature, the COPY command duplicates files; the duplicates just have the same name as the original (unless you rename them, as discussed in the preceding section). You can use COPY as a duplicator specifically to make backup copies of files without copying them anywhere:

```
C:\>COPY *.DOC *.BAK
```

The preceding command copies all the files with the DOC extension to new files with a BAK (backup) extension. This makes duplicates, or backups, of the DOC files.

The horrors of the COPY command, Part II: Weird and strange COPY command options you don't need to know

The COPY command has two optional switches: /A and /B. In the twisted way these things come to be, /A means text file and /B means not-a-text file. (Okay nerds: /A means ASCII and /B means binary. Big deal.)

You can place these two options after a file to force the COPY command to copy them. I know, sounds bizarre. But they're really used with concatenation and other left-field COPY command options that normal people don't bother with.

As another example, suppose that you want to keep each revision of a nasty letter you are writing. You want to track the revisions so that you can dramatically show your children how your mood calms down after venting on the computer. After writing the first document file, you decide to duplicate the file and start over:

```
C:\>COPY LETTER.DOC PEEVED.DOC
```

This command duplicates the file LETTER.DOC to a new file named PEEVED.DOC. At this point, you continue editing LETTER.DOC, using your word processor.

After saving LETTER.DOC to disk again, you decide to make another duplicate:

```
C:\>COPY LETTER.DOC ANGRY.DOC
```

The file ANGRY.DOC represents the second, toned-down version of the original file. So you edit LETTER.DOC again, and finally, it's calm enough to send. But on disk you have PEEVED.DOC and ANGRY.DOC, two duplicate files of earlier versions of the same letter.

Wildcards and the COPY command

Wildcards and the COPY command were made for each other. Rumor has it the wildcard guy programmer and the copy command gal programmer were "seeing" each other way back in the early days of Microsoft. Anyway, the following are examples of how you can use wildcards with the COPY command:

```
C:\>COPY *.* A:
```

This command copies all the files in the current directory (the *.* wildcard) to the floppy disk on drive A. The COPY command lists each file's name as it's copied. So you may see something like the following after you press Enter:

```
RENAL.EXE
BOVINE.EXE
HOOTER.OWL
PUBERT.TXT
BLORF
SHEEP.COM
BOOGER.DAT
        7 file(s) copied
```

The opposite of the COPY *.* A: command is one that copies all the files from drive A to the current directory:

```
C:\>COPY A:*.*
```

There is no need to specify the current directory; DOS assumes that's what you mean with the COPY command. See "Copying a file from the current directory (or 'I just assumed you were coming here')" earlier in this chapter.

```
C:\>COPY *.BAT C:\TEMP
```

The preceding command copies all the files with the BAT extension (batch file programs) from the current directory to the TEMP directory on drive C.

The horrors of the COPY command, Part III ("The Final Chapter"): Intensely strange by-products of toxic COPY command waste

DOS slaps the date and time on a file whenever you save it to disk. This can readily be seen by using any DIR command. In a strange twist of fate, you can use the COPY command to reset any file's date and time to today and right now. Here is the format:

```
C:\>COPY /B filename+,,
```

Just replace *filename* in the preceding with the name of the file whose date and time you want to change to right now. That's the COPY command, a space, /B, another space, the name of the file you want to update, a plus sign, and then two commas. Strange and possibly useful.

By the way, if you have MS-DOS 6.2, go ahead and answer Y (for Yes) to the Overwrite (Yes/No/All) prompt. DOS must overwrite the file as it updates the date and time.

By the way again: If you don't want the date and time set to "today, right now," use the DATE and TIME commands to set the date and time to whatever you want. Then use the COPY /B +,, whatever, command to change the date and time. Remember to change the date and time back to right now with the DATE and TIME commands when you're done.

By the way one last time: Do not use wildcards with this command! Wildcards will delete files instead of updating them. Sad, but true.

```
C:\>COPY CHAP??.DOC *.BAK
```

This COPY command copies files with the first four letters CHAP followed by any two characters (denoted by the two question mark wildcards) and having the DOC extension. The files are actually duplicated, each given the BAK extension and living in the current directory.

- ✔ The lowdown on wildcards is offered in Chapter 11.
- ✔ Current directory nonsense is unfolded in Chapter 16.
- ✔ Eventually, the wildcard guy programmer and the COPY command gal programmer got married. They've since moved over to the Windows programming group and have had one child — a boy, Dr. Watson.

COPY CON (is not the International Impersonator's Convention)

A strange variation on the copy command is COPY CON, which doesn't really copy a file — it copies a DOS *device*. Actually, it copies from a DOS device, the keyboard, to a file that you name on disk. The following tutorial shows you the ropes:

1. Type the COPY CON command followed by the name of a file you want to create. It should be a new file on disk; you cannot edit files, using COPY CON.

    For this example, type the following:

    ```
    C:\>COPY CON HANDSOME
    ```

    Press Enter.

2. The cursor waits.

    The cursor just sits and blinks. What's happening is that the COPY command is running. It's waiting for you to type in a file, using the keyboard — the CON device, according to DOS. (You're copying a file from CON to HANDSOME.)

3. Type something clever, like

    ```
    OH, YOU'RE JUST SUCH A HANDSOME DEVIL!
    ```

    Use the Backspace key to back up and erase. There is no word processor-like editing here, just raw text.

4. Press Enter to complete the line of text.

    Type more text if you like; repeat steps 3 and 4. There is no word-wrap feature with COPY CON. And if you type more than 127 characters, the computer beeps madly at you.

5. When you're done, press Ctrl-Z.

    Press and hold the Ctrl key, press Z, and then release both keys. This produces the ^Z character on the screen:

    ```
    ^Z
    ```

    Pressing Ctrl-Z tells the COPY command that the file is done. You need to press the Enter key to explain that to DOS:

6. Press the Enter key.

    ```
    1 file(s) copied
    ```

7. Use the DIR command to see whether the file HANDSOME appears on disk. You can use the TYPE command to view its contents:

    ```
    C:\>TYPE HANDSOME
    ```

✔ Here's another way to view the file:

```
C:\>COPY HANDSOME CON
```

This copies the file HANDSOME to DOS's CON device, which is the screen (as well as the keyboard). It works just like the TYPE command, but computer nerds prefer it, thanks to its cryptic aspect.

✔ DOS has many devices: The screen and keyboard (CON), the printer (PRN), and others that aren't worth mentioning. You can use the COPY command with just about any of them because DOS treats its devices just like files. Refer to Chapter 20 for the details.

✔ The Ctrl-Z character is used to end a "file" typed from the keyboard. (You can also press the F6 key.) You must press the Enter key after you type Ctrl-Z for DOS to hear it.

✔ To print a file, you COPY it to DOS's printer device, PRN. For example,

```
C:\>COPY HANDSOME PRN
```

This command copies the text file HANDSOME to the printer. Make sure your printer is on and ready to go before you type this command! Also, only copy text files to the printer; other files may make your printer puke.

Looking at two groups of files in the DOS Shell

One good way to copy files from one place to another on your computer is to use a file manager or shell program. Not only does the shell program show you files in a DIR command-like format, but you can view both source and destination directories at once. The popular XTree program was designed with this purpose in mind, as is PC Tools' PC Shell. The DOS Shell program that comes with most versions of DOS also lets you see files in two places at once (see Figure 13-1).

You must select the Dual File Lists command from the DOS Shell's View menu to see two lists of files, as shown in Figure 13-1. Then you can use the mouse to highlight files in one file list and drag-copy them over to the other list. Using the DOS Shell is an ideal way to work with files. It saves you from the randomness and "in-the-dark" aspect of copying at the DOS prompt.

- ✔ To select files in the DOS Shell, hold the Ctrl key as you click on the files, using the mouse.

- ✔ You can copy files in the DOS Shell by holding the Ctrl key and using the mouse to drag the files to their new destination.

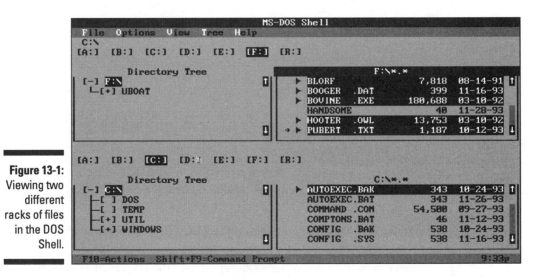

Figure 13-1: Viewing two different racks of files in the DOS Shell.

The XCOPY Command

An all-purpose super version of the COPY command is the XCOPY command, available with all DOS versions 3.2 hence. Essentially, the XCOPY command does the same, exact thing as the COPY command. In fact, you can substitute XCOPY for COPY and never really notice the difference, except that XCOPY is a bit faster when copying groups of files.

What XCOPY has going for it is the ability to copy groups of files quicker than the dull old COPY command, and it has many nerd-pleasing options and gewgaws that I'm not going to wade through here. Instead, my advice remains:

Whenever copying a group of files, use the XCOPY *command instead of* COPY.

For example,

```
C:\>XCOPY A:*.*
```

This command copies all the files from the floppy disk in drive A to the current directory. Unlike the COPY command, which reads in the files one at a time, XCOPY reads them in all at once. After pressing Enter, you see the following message:

```
Reading source file(s)...
```

This message means that XCOPY is gathering up all the files from the source, drive A in this case, and reading them into memory. When it's done, it copies the files in one quick burst to the hard drive:

```
RENAL.EXE
BOVINE.EXE
HOOTER.OWL
PUBERT.TXT
BLORF
SHEEP.COM
BOOGER.DAT
        7 file(s) copied
```

✔ The chief advantage of XCOPY over COPY is that it's faster when copying groups of files.

✔ You can just use XCOPY instead of the COPY command if you like.

✔ XCOPY's other advantage over the COPY command is that it sports a variety of options and other jobbies that sate the cryptic lusts of DOS nerds.

✔ Someone, somewhere, once claimed that the XCOPY command can be used as a substitute for the BACKUP command. While it's true that XCOPY does share some techy options with BACKUP, it is not a substitute.

✔ If you want to use the XCOPY command instead of COPY and you're using
the DOSKey program, you can create a COPY macro:

```
C:\>DOSKEY COPY=XCOPY $*
```

This DOSKey macro substitutes the XCOPY command for DOS's COPY
command. Refer to Chapter 5 for more information on DOSKey macros and
what all that means.

The MOVE Command

DOS 6 finally introduced a MOVE command into DOS's vocabulary. Before then,
Microsoft simply made the comment "Hey, moving files is the same as copying
them and then deleting the originals. So why would anyone need a MOVE
command?" They'd then grunt, huff, shrug, and go work on making Windows
run slower. In the mean time, DOS users would use the COPY and then DEL
commands as a poor substitute for a vital MOVE command. Since MS-DOS 6.0,
that's no longer the case.

Alas, if you don't yet have DOS 6 or later, you're stuck with copying files and
then deleting the originals to substitute for the legitimate DOS MOVE command.

Moving a file (to tears)

Moving a file works just like copying a file. Indeed, just type **MOVE** instead of
COPY and you're in bidness:

```
C:\>MOVE MOLDY A:
```

The preceding MOVE command copies the file MOLDY to drive A. Then the
original file MOLDY is deleted. The following message is displayed after this
happens:

```
c:\oldy\moldy => a:\moldy [ok]
```

The message lists the file moved by its full pathname, then a => something, and
then the full pathname of the file's final resting place. The words [ok] mean —
and I'm assuming this — that everything went okay. (The message always
appears in lowercase.)

✔ The MOVE command deletes the original file! If you want to make a duplicate, use the COPY command instead.

✔ Unlike the COPY command, you must always supply a source and destination for the files to be moved. Refer to the section "Copying a file to the current directory (or 'I just assumed you were coming here')" earlier in this chapter.

✔ If you do want a shortcut for the assumption, try the following:

```
C:\>COPY A:*.NEW
```

This COPY command copies the files *.NEW from drive A to the current directory. The following MOVE command moves the same files:

```
C:\>MOVE A:*.NEW .
```

See the extra dot (or period) at the end of the command? It's **MOVE**, a space, then **A:*.NEW** (the files you want to move), then another space and a period. The period represents the current directory, the destination. (Refer to Chapter 12 for more information on the . and .. things.)

✔ Like the COPY command, the MOVE command does assume that you're copying files from the current directory unless otherwise specified. (Chapter 16 is the current directory definition chapter.)

✔ Information on *full pathnames* is uncovered in Chapter 16.

Wildcards and the MOVE command

You can use wildcards with the MOVE command just as you can with the COPY command. It works the same way, except that the original files are deleted (and you must specify a destination). Refer to the section "Wildcards and the COPY command" earlier in this chapter for the details.

A special, multiple file MOVE command-only trick

Coming late in the game, Microsoft was able to make the MOVE command a lot smarter than any other DOS command. In the caveman days of DOS (before Bill Gates could grow a full beard, which is not to say whether he can or can't today), here is how you'd move three files to a floppy disk:

```
C:\HOUSES\PIG> COPY STRAW A:
        1 file(s) copied

C:\HOUSES\PIG> COPY TWIG A:
        1 file(s) copied

C:\HOUSES\PIG> COPY BRICK A:
        1 file(s) copied

C:\HOUSES\PIG> DEL STRAW

C:\HOUSES\PIG> DEL TWIG

C:\HOUSES\PIG> DEL BRICK
```

Three COPY commands are required to make duplicates of the three files, and then three DEL commands are required to delete the originals. And the computer is supposed to be a time-saver, right?

With the MOVE command, the innocent user may be tempted to type the following:

```
C:\HOUSES\PIG> MOVE STRAW A:
c:\houses\pig\straw => a:\straw [ok]

C:\HOUSES\PIG> MOVE TWIG A:
c:\houses\pig\twig => a:\twig [ok]

C:\HOUSES\PIG> MOVE BRICK A:
c:\houses\pig\brick => a:\brick [ok]
```

Ah-ha! But you, gentle reader, can do the following:

```
C:\HOUSES\PIG> MOVE STRAW,TWIG,BRICK A:
c:\houses\pig\straw => a:\straw [ok]
c:\houses\pig\twig => a:\twig [ok]
c:\houses\pig\brick => a:\brick [ok]
```

That's the MOVE command, which you know. Then come the files to move, *each separated by a comma*. Then come a space and the destination, drive A. By listing multiple files separated by commas, you can move a whole barnyard of files with a single MOVE command. Such ease. Such elegance. Who'da thought this could come from Microsoft?

Moving and renaming (the witness-protection program)

Renaming a file you're moving works just like copying a file and renaming it. For example,

```
C:\>COPY ITCH A:SCRATCH
```

The preceding COPY command makes a duplicate of the file ITCH on drive A, renaming the copy SCRATCH. You can move ITCH to drive A and name it SCRATCH as well:

```
C:\>MOVE ITCH A:SCRATCH
c:\skin\itch => a:\scratch [ok]
```

The MOVE command explains what it's done after the file is moved. (But remember that the original was deleted.)

> ✔ In a way, the MOVE command can work like the RENAME command. To wit,
>
> ```
> C:\>MOVE MONKEYW FOCUS
> ```
>
> The MOVE command moved a file — but only in the current directory. Because a source or destination was not specified, all that happened was that the file was renamed. (Seems like a lot of effort, no?)
>
> ✔ You can find more information on copying and renaming a file earlier in this chapter. See the section "Copying a file and renaming it."

Renaming directories (or the MOVE command's moonlighting job)

You can't use the MOVE command to move a subdirectory. (That's actually a technique called *pruning and grafting*, and DOS don't do it at all.) But you can use the MOVE command to rename a subdirectory. For example,

```
C:\>MOVE MOHAMMED MOUNTAIN
```

This MOVE command doesn't move anything. It merely renames the subdirectory named MOHAMMED to MOUNTAIN. The MOVE command's output reflects this:

```
c:\mohammed => c:\mountain [ok]
```

> ✔ If you try to use the MOVE command to move a subdirectory, you see the nefarious `Unable to open source` error message.

> ✔ Refer to Chapter 16 for more information on moving your subdirectories.

Verily I Say unto You, VERIFY

DOS has an often-neglected command with an earnest-sounding name, VERIFY. What it does is activate double-checking on all DOS's file copying activities. This sounds grand, but few people bother with it, which I'll get into shortly.

To switch the VERIFY command on, type the following at the DOS prompt:

```
C:\>VERIFY ON
```

Type **VERIFY**, a space, and then **ON**. Press Enter.

Nothing happens! Yet, DOS has switched on its double-checking verification. To prove it, type the VERIFY command by itself at the prompt:

```
C:\> VERIFY
VERIFY is on
```

Now DOS double-checks information each time it copies a file.

Most people don't switch on the VERIFY command for a few reasons. The one given most often is that, with VERIFY on, your computer takes longer to access the disk drives. Although this is true, on today's fast computers with still faster hard drives, the slowdown isn't noticeable.

The real reason you don't need to bother with the VERIFY command is that today's disks are much more reliable than the disks of DOS's early days. Back then, an unreliable floppy disk spelled certain doom. The VERIFY command saved you from any peril. Today, it's just not necessary.

To switch off the VERIFY command, type **VERIFY OFF** at the DOS prompt. You can type VERIFY again, by itself, to ensure that it's off.

✔ By all means, if you feel more comfortable with VERIFY ON, type it in and run your computer that way. Stick the command in your system's AUTOEXEC.BAT file for everyday activation. Refer to Chapter 10.

✔ How does DOS double-check, and why doesn't it do that all the time anyway? Normally, DOS reads information from disk, stores it in memory, and then writes it back to disk. That's how files are copied. When VERIFY is on, DOS reads from disk, stores it in memory, writes it back to disk — and then reads in exactly what it wrote, comparing it with what's in memory. If there's a difference, DOS rewrites the information again and then rechecks it. Because today's disks are highly reliable, this type of redundant checking isn't really necessary.

Chapter 14

More on . . .
Deleting and Undeleting Files

- -

In This Chapter

▶ Deleting files

▶ Deleting millions and millions of files

▶ Undeleting files

▶ Undeleting files without the pain

▶ Undeleting files, guaranteed

- -

"*W*hat ho, John! Looks like you've been out in the woods. Nice jacket and hat. And, hey, looka that gun. Been huntin'?" No, John's merely been deleting files — a common thing done on computers. Unfortunately, John didn't need to use his gun. The simple DEL command would have worked just fine. No bullets. No loud noise. And it wouldn't have alarmed the neighbors.

This chapter is about deleting files. Delete them one by one or in vast numbers. And to be balanced, this chapter also covers undeleting files. That's something Bambi's mother would have liked.

Deleting a File

When a file's time has come to pass, it can be killed quite easily in the hands of the DEL command:

```
C:\>DEL DOORNAIL.DOC
```

The preceding command deletes the file DOORNAIL.DOC from disk, rending it bye-bye.

- ✔ There is no message, no confirmation, no evil grin that lets you know the file is gone. To wit,

```
C:\SECRET\STUFF> DEL AFTRLIFE.DOC
C:\SECRET\STUFF>
```

In this sequence, the file AFTRLIFE.DOC — which describes exactly what happens to you after you die — has been deleted by the DEL command. There is no feedback. No warning. Nothing.

- ✔ A variant of the DEL command is ERASE. Both do the same thing:

```
C:\>ERASE MEMORY.DAT
```

This command erases the file MEMORY.DAT.

- ✔ Delete a file and you didn't mean to? Don't panic! DOS has an UNDELETE command to BandAid that boo-boo right quick. The latter part of this chapter has all the details.

- ✔ Unlike the REN command (which has a longer form — RENAME), there is no long version of the DEL command: no DELETE command as such.

- ✔ You must always follow DEL with the name of the file you want to delete. Include the entire name, with the extension if you want to avoid the dreaded `File not found` error.

- ✔ The DEL command assumes that the file you're zapping is in the current directory. If not, you must specify a drive letter or pathname to the file. Refer to Chapter 16 for more information on pathnames.

Don't bother reading this if you know why it's necessary to delete files

Some people may be disinclined to use the DEL command, fearful that they may erase something important. Personally, I *like* that attitude and share it with many DOS users. A good rule of thumb is *If you don't know what the heck it is, don't mess with it.*

This rule is gospel, even for techno-weenies. Programs get complex and require more than a single COM or EXE file to run. It's just bad computing to go in and delete any huge file because it's taking up space. The file may be important.

TECHNICAL STUFF

Unnecessary trivia on why there is an ERASE command

Most DOS users type the DEL command when they want to delete files. The ERASE command does the same thing, but it's not as popular. So why is it there in the first place?

The answer is — as with most ugly things about the computer — tradition. DOS was introduced in the early '80s when another microcomputer operating system, CP/M, was popular. (They were called *microcomputers* before they came to be known as PCs.) DOS tried really hard to look and act like CP/M because that's what people were used to at the time. What things did DOS borrow from CP/M?

✔ The ugly C> prompt was a CP/M idea.

✔ Drive letters A through Z was a CP/M idea.

✔ Eight-character filenames was a CP/M idea.

✔ Ctrl-P (print output) was an original CP/M idea.

✔ WordStar was a bad CP/M idea that still shows up today. The DOS editor uses WordStar key commands.

✔ The DIR, TYPE, ERA (ERASE), and REN commands were CP/M ideas.

So to make the DOS world comfortable to CP/M converts, Microsoft elected to borrow several CP/M concepts. The ERASE command was one of them, stolen from the ERA command and probably added at the last minute when too many old fogey CP/M users complained about typing DEL.

Incidentally (and this is really unrequired reading), Microsoft's earlier operating system attempt for Tandy, TRSDOS (*triss*-DOS) used the DIR, COPY, CLS, and other future DOS commands. The command to delete files? It was KILL. I like that. Vicious. Deadly. Why couldn't DOS have a KILL command?

And now, the big *but*: But it's okay to delete any file you create. Now, you just don't want to randomly do it. Instead, you need to remove unwanted or temporary files or anything else that's hanging around and, although it seemed useful at the time, is no longer needed. Chapter 23 of this book covers the topic of cleaning up files, which I call *disk housekeeping*. Refer to that chapter to quell your nerves about obliterating files.

A potentially safer way to delete files (just add a little P)

If you find yourself becoming too comfortable with deleting files (meaning that you're deleting things you don't want to), there is hope. You can add the special slash-P option to the DEL command. This option forces DEL to ask a question before it wipes anything out.

```
C:\>DEL UNCLEJOE /P
```

This command would delete the file UNCLEJOE without mercy if it weren't for the extra space and slash-P, which causes the DEL command to pause, reflect, and display the following message:

```
C:\FAMILY\MOMSSIDE\UNCLEJOE,   Delete (Y/N)?
```

DOS displays the file's full *pathname*, then a comma, and then the question Delete, followed by Y for Yes and N for No. Press Y to get rid of UNCLEJOE; press N to keep him.

- ✔ You can follow any DEL command with a /P to force DOS to ask politely before it deletes files. The /P must always come last.

- ✔ The /P thing also works with the ERASE command. (Both DEL and ERASE are the same thing, after all.)

- ✔ When you use the DEL command with wildcards, /P causes DOS to stop and prompt yes-or-no for each file. (Refer to the next section for information on deleting files with wildcards.)

- ✔ You can press the Ctrl-C key to break out of a monotonous stretch of pressing Y or N when deleting a slew of files.

Let's create the DEL DOSKey macro (only for those interested)

If you're fond of the /P option, you can make it a permanent part of the DEL command by creating a DEL DOSKey macro. The following command will do it:

```
C:\>DOSKEY DEL=DEL *$ /P
```

Type **DOSKEY**, a space, and then the name of the macro, **DEL**. Type an equal sign and then the macro's commands: **DEL**, a space, asterisk, dollar sign, a space, then **/P**.

The *$ thing tells DOS to put any options, filenames, whatever, right in that spot when the macro runs. This means that any DEL command you type at the DOS prompt will be translated into a DOSKey macro that always adds the /P switch.

Refer to Chapter 5 for more information on DOSKey's macros.

Deleting a Group of Files

If a file is a weed, the DEL command can yank it quite smartly. When you're faced with a field of weeds, the DEL command can instantly become your DOS weed-whacker, mowing them all down with one deft keystroke. You can do this by using wildcards with the DEL command.

Killing off backup files seems to be a popular pastime:

```
C:\>DEL *.BAK
```

The preceding command deletes all the files with the BAK extension in the current directory.

```
C:\>DEL FIG*.*
```

When followed with FIG*.*, the DEL command deletes any file starting with FIG and ending in anything.

Wildcards are discussed in Chapter 11, in the section "Untamed and Wildcards."

The deadly DEL commands of peril!

And now, the most deadly DEL command of them all:

```
C:\>DEL *.*
```

When followed by the *everything* wildcard — *.* (star-dot-star) — the DEL command deletes all the files in the current directory. The DEL command warns you when you do this:

```
All files in directory will be deleted!
Are you sure (Y/N)?
```

Whew! Be thankful you don't have an early version of DOS; there was no warning. Now, you should pause and read the message. Don't be too quick to press Y! If you don't want to delete the files, press N and Enter and mull it over. Press Y and Enter and all the files are gone!

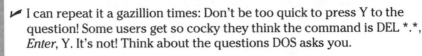

- ✔ Older versions of DOS display variations on the `All files will be deleted` message. Particularly, some versions only ask `Are you sure?`, which DOS users formerly assumed was a question posed on an antiperspirant commercial.

- ✔ If you use the /P switch with the DEL command, the `All files will be deleted` warning does not appear. Instead, DOS displays the name of every file to be killed along with the yes-or-no prompt.

- ✔ I can repeat it a gazillion times: Don't be too quick to press Y to the question! Some users get so cocky they think the command is DEL *.*, *Enter*, Y. It's not! Think about the questions DOS asks you.

- ✔ Okay. Whine not. If you do accidentally delete an entire directory of files or you just want a select few of them back, information on using the handy (and lifesaving) UNDELETE command is offered in the section "Undeleting Files with the Aptly Named UNDELETE Command" just a few column inches from this very spot.

Variations you probably didn't know (or want to know) about

You may think that the DEL *.* command is nasty enough. But no! There are other ways to delete all the files in a directory or on a disk using DOS's often haphazard abbreviations. There are two of them.

1. The sinister single-dot!

Beware of the following:

```
C:\>DEL .
```

The dot is an arcane DOS abbreviation. It represents the current directory or, with the DEL command at least, all the files in the current directory. Yes, this is the same as the DEL *.* command.

There doesn't need to be a space between the DEL command and the dot (DEL .). This can be particularly frightening for absolute beginners who feel the urge to end all DOS commands with a period.

2. The ominous subdirectory name!

DOS names subdirectories like files, and you may, one day, accidentally type a subdirectory name after the DEL command. To wit,

```
C:\>DEL UBOAT
```

Because UBOAT is a subdirectory name, you'll see the following message:

```
All files in directory will be deleted!
Are you sure (Y/N)?
```

This message appears because DOS has assumed that by typing in a directory name you want to kill off all the files in that directory. The solution is to press N (for No) and double-check your filename.

> ✔ If you really want to delete all the files in a subdirectory, you can use the directory name, if you like, or you can use the dot.

> ✔ To delete a subdirectory, you need to use the RD or RMDIR commands. These are covered in Chapter 16.

Undeleting Files with the Aptly Named UNDELETE Command

Well, there's good news for little Joey. The townspeople may have deleted the SHANE file, but the handy UNDELETE command can bring him back.

The UNDELETE command is really cinchy to use. You just type UNDELETE instead of DEL to recover a freshly deleted file. For example,

```
C:\>DEL MERCY.SAX
```

This command deletes the file MERCY.SAX from disk. Poof. It's gone. And you're probably glad. It was eating up 180K of disk space. You never used it. Indeed, you feel *good* about deleting it. That is, until your boss mutters something about that MERCY.SAX file and how proud he is of you for keeping it around.

To recover the file, and your job, substitute the UNDELETE command for DEL:

```
UNDELETE MERCY.SAX
```

Type **UNDELETE**, a space, and then the name of the file you deleted and want back. In this example, that was the MERCY.SAX file. Press Enter and DOS begins its recovery work.

Unlike deleting a file, undeleting involves a lot of on-screen text. The initial barrage is displayed in the following, which is how it would look should you undelete the file MERCY.SAX.

```
UNDELETE - A delete protection facility
Copyright (C) 1987-1993 Central Point Software, Inc.
All rights reserved


Directory C:\FORGIVE
File Specifications: MERCY.SAX

    Delete Sentry control file not found.

    Deletion-tracking file not found.


    MS-DOS directory contains    1 deleted files.
    Of those,    1 files may be recovered.

Using the MS-DOS directory method.


     ?ERCY   SAX    180668  3-10-92  ...A  Undelete (Y/N)?
```

To continue recovery, press Y. DOS then poses the following question:

```
Please type the first character for ?ERCY    .SAX:
```

DOS knows almost everything about the file, save for the first character in the filename (don't ask me why). Type **M** — or whatever the first letter may be — and then you see

```
File successfully undeleted.
```

You're back in business.

> ✔ The sooner you use the UNDELETE command after deleting a file or group of files, the better. It's not really a time-sensitive thing; you could wait weeks. But the more you use your computer, saving and deleting other files on the hard drive, the harder it is for the UNDELETE command to recover your files.

✔ When the UNDELETE command cannot recover your file, a lamentable message appears on the screen. You may just see that DOS has found 0 `deleted files` and `No entries found`. Sometimes there may be the following message displayed:

```
Starting cluster is unavailable. This file cannot be recovered
with the UNDELETE command.  Press any key to continue.
```

Try as hard as it can, DOS cannot undelete the file.

✔ You may see subtly different output from that shown in this section; DOS has updated the UNDELETE command several times, and there are other variations on UNDELETE, as the following sections illustrate.

✔ Alas, the UNDELETE command is only available with DOS 5 and later. Users of earlier DOS versions can either upgrade (which I recommend) or buy a third-party disk utility that can undelete files just as well as or better than DOS.

✔ Delete files with wildcards? UNDELETE can use wildcards too! So you can type

```
C:\>UNDELETE *.*
```

to recover an entire directory you may have accidentally sent off to roam the disk underworld. The recovery instructions work the same as outlined in this section, though you have to slug it through for each file, typing the first letter as you go.

To quickly recover a file without typing in the first character of its name, tack on the /ALL option to the UNDELETE command:

```
C:\>UNDELETE SHANE.GUY /ALL
```

This command recovers the deleted file SHANE.GUY automatically. DOS names the file #HANE.GUY because DOS is dumb and doesn't know the file's first characters. (You can use the REN command to rename it back to SHANE.GUY.)

This tip also works with wildcards:

```
C:\>UNDELETE *.BAK /ALL
```

In the preceding, all the deleted files ending in the BAK extension are recovered. The files will be named #-something because DOS doesn't remember the first filename character.

Trolling for deleted files

Sometimes you may return to work in a haze, remembering vaguely that you deleted some important file or another but not knowing exactly which one. This can prove frustrating if you want to use the UNDELETE command followed by a filename.

Ah-ha! The truth is that you don't have to use UNDELETE with a filename at all. If you don't — if you just type **UNDELETE** and press the Enter key — DOS trolls the current directory for dead and missing files, showing them to you with the aloofness of Quincy the Coroner.

```
C:\>UNDELETE
```

This command, all by its lonesome, causes DOS to scan the current directory for dead files that can be undeleted. You see the initial spasm of information, similar to that shown earlier. Then DOS prompts you to undelete each file that can possibly be recovered:

```
?0Z0    5678  4-01-94  ...A  Undelete (Y/N)?
```

Press Y and then answer the `Please type the first character` question with the file's true first character, and DOS recovers it.

> ✔ DOS displays the `No entries found` message if there are no files worth recovering. Sometimes the message may be more terse, but the end result is that you can't yank any files back to life.

Super UNDELETE

It's perfectly okay to get minorly miffed by the UNDELETE command's apparent stupidity at recovering files. Specifically, why must you type the first letter of the filename? Being a computer, wouldn't it just *know*? The answer is "Only if you tell it ahead of time."

To make the UNDELETE command automatically know about a file's first character and to make recovery a bit smoother, you can employ the Super UNDELETE command. This involves a bit of effort on your behalf, but it makes recovery a lot nicer.

Setting up Super UNDELETE involves sticking the following command into your PC's AUTOEXEC.BAT file:

```
UNDELETE /TC
```

That's **UNDELETE** — the UNDELETE command — followed by a space and then **/T** and a **C**. You can place this command anywhere in your PC's AUTOEXEC.BAT file.

You must save AUTOEXEC.BAT back to disk, quit your editor, and then reset your PC before the new command takes effect.

What happens? Nothing new, really. You see some extra text displayed when the computer starts and AUTOEXEC.BAT runs. The message tells you that UNDELETE is *loaded* and that the `Delete Protection Method is Delete Tracking`. Smile and nod when you see the message.

After installation, you'll notice the Super UNDELETE command's presence when you recover your deleted files. Nothing about the UNDELETE command changes, other than some extra text displayed. The big advantage is that DOS automatically knows the first character of the filename, and you don't have to type it. Such convenience! Just press Y for Yes when DOS asks if you want to undelete the file and — zap! — it's back to life.

✔ This trick is called *deletion tracking*. Try saying that with a mouth full of granola.

✔ The sole advantage of this trick is that you no longer have to type the first character in a deleted file's name. Otherwise, all the rules about using the UNDELETE command remain the same. Using this trick does not guarantee that your files can be recovered!

✔ If you have more than one hard drive, you need to activate the Super UNDELETE feature for each of your hard drives. It works like this: First, after the UNDELETE command, specify one /T option for each of your hard drives. Second, put the drive letter right after the /T. So if you have hard drives C, D, and E, you'd use the following command:

```
C:\>UNDELETE /TC /TD /TE
```

✔ More information on updating AUTOEXEC.BAT is offered in Chapter 10.

✔ This variation on the UNDELETE command is only available with DOS 6 and later.

Super Dooper UNDELETE

The Super UNDELETE command, described in the preceding section, is a boon if you dislike typing the first character of a filename. Other than that, the UNDELETE command doesn't change one iota. Now, the Super Dooper UNDELETE command does offer you some interesting features — including the guarantee of recovering just about any file — even weeks after you deleted it.

Like the Super UNDELETE feature, you must activate Super Dooper UNDELETE in your PC's AUTOEXEC.BAT file. Here is the command to do it:

```
C:\>UNDELETE /S
```

That's **UNDELETE** and then a space, and finally **/S**.

Stick this command into your PC's AUTOEXEC.BAT file. Save AUTOEXEC.BAT to disk and then reset your PC to lock the change into place.

You may see some new text displayed when the computer starts, but other than that, there's nothing new.

The bonus to using the Super Dooper UNDELETE comes when you use the UNDELETE command to recover deleted files. With Super Dooper UNDELETE installed, you never — well, barely ever — encounter a message that says the file cannot be recovered.

Although the Super Dooper UNDELETE command may sound grand, there are a few drawbacks. Secretly, you should know that Super Dooper UNDELETE works by not deleting files at all! Instead, it copies them to a secret location on disk, where they sit and wait. After a given amount of time, DOS deletes them. But up until that point, you can undelete any file — which the Super Dooper UNDELETE command merely copies from the secret location on disk to the file's original location.

The drawback to this approach is that the Super Dooper UNDELETE command uses a lot of disk space. Deleting a lot of files takes up disk space (because the files are moved, not deleted). This means that, if you're deleting files to save disk space, you're working against yourself. So my advice is to only use this variation of the UNDELETE command if you have an awful lot of disk space in the first place.

> ✔ The Super Dooper UNDELETE command does not affect the way the UNDELETE command works as described in this chapter. Oh, you may see some additional text displayed on the screen. Aside from that, everything works as advertised.

✔ This command is only available with DOS 6 and later.

✔ You cannot use both the Super UNDELETE and Super Dooper UNDELETE commands in AUTOEXEC.BAT. If you try, DOS ignores Super UNDELETE and uses Super Dooper UNDELETE instead.

✔ Personally, I recommend Super UNDELETE.

✔ Okay, no more kidding around: Super Dooper UNDELETE is officially called the *Delete Sentry* method of file UNDELETE protection. Whoop-dee-doo.

✔ To see which type of UNDELETE command you have installed, type the following at the DOS prompt:

```
C:\>UNDELETE /STATUS
```

✔ That's the **UNDELETE** command followed by a space, a slash, then the word **STATUS**. You'll see one of the following messages displayed:

　　• For normal UNDELETE:

```
Undelete not loaded
```

　　• For Super UNDELETE:

```
Deletion Protection Method is Delete Tracking
```

　　• For Super Dooper UNDELETE:

```
Deletion Protection Method is Delete Sentry
```

　　• For DOS 5 UNDELETE:

```
Invalid parameter specifications
```

Chapter 15

More on . . .
Disks and Drives

• •

In This Chapter

▶ Discovering drive letters A to Z

▶ Frightening information on phantom drives!

▶ Logging without offending owls

▶ Formatting drives from A to Z

▶ Making a boot disk

▶ Everything you want to know about disk labels

• •

For me, disks and drives are the best parts about computers. Most hardware remains hidden away inside or only shows a cold exterior — but disks, you can play with. Floppy disks look spiffy. They're a symbol of status. A few years ago only hopeless social basket-case nerds would walk around with a floppy disk. Today, businessmen wear them in their shirt pockets as a badge of pride. It says, "Hey, not only am I not afraid of this thing, but I can walk around with it in my pocket — risking social embarrassment — and know that I'm comfortable with technology."

Disks — all types of disks — are cool, from the old 8-inch floppies to the new 3½-inch disks that look like things Mr. Spock would shuffle on Star Trek (which were called *tapes*, by the way). Hard drives are also cool, even though they spin out of sight. This chapter covers them all, from A to Z (so to speak).

The ABC's of Drive Letters

What could be more basic than the disk drive letters? Disk drives, first to last, are named after letters of the alphabet, A through Z. Simple enough. In fact, it's even the same in Greek. No alpha to omega, the drive letters are still A through Z. (I gleaned this information from the Greek language version of *DOS For Dummies* — "ΤΟ DOS ΓΙΑ ΤΕΜΠΕΛΗΔΕΣ," in case you're curious.)

With a total disregard for logic and facing certain ridicule from the nerd priesthood for diving into what they consider a shallow subject, I will boldly type onward and discuss all sorts of stuff about disk drive letters. I believe you'll find this stuff of value, even though family-people don't discuss it often at the dinner table.

The logic behind naming your hard drive C instead of A

In the beginning there was . . . the tape drive! Seriously, the lowest-priced IBM PC first sold (for $1,565, no monitor, 16K RAM) lacked disk drives. Instead, you could use a tape recorder to load and save files. Were people really nuts back then, or what?

Actually, no one ever bought the tape-only PC. People instead settled for one or two floppy drives. The first drive was named A and the second one B — conveniently, the first two letters of the alphabet.

When the first hard drive PC was introduced, the hard drive was given letter C. C was used because people could already have two floppy drives (A and B) and then add a hard drive, which would then become C. Also, many programs assumed drives A and B to be floppy drives, and they'd probably pop an embolism if they encountered a hard drive. Any additional hard drives added to the PC were given letters D, E, F, and so on, on up through Z.

Yet, even if you had only one floppy drive (A), the hard drive was always drive C. The reason is that DOS lets you use drive B as a *phantom drive* (see the next section). With a phantom drive, you can work like you have two floppies, even though you only have one. Also, it helps that DOS consistently counts on drive C to be a hard drive.

- There is no logic in the computer industry.
- The old Radio Shack TRS-80 computer named its disk drives after numbers. But the first drive was drive zero (0) and the second drive was drive one (1).
- DOS can only handle 26 drives total, from A to Z.
- Above and beyond drive C, the drive letters could stand for anything. They could be more hard drives, more floppy drives, RAM drives, network drives, CD-ROM drives, and other strange types of devices that work like disk drives. Only letters A and B are reserved for use by floppy drives.

Yes, you have a B floppy drive, whether you like it or not

Who knows what evil lurks in the heart of drive B? . . . The phantom drive letter does! This isn't anything scary or strange. Instead, the phantom drive B can be highly useful on a one-disk system (though it's rarely necessary).

The following tutorial only works on a PC with one-floppy drive. (Everyone else can try it, but it's really unimpressive.)

Your PC only has one floppy drive, which you've come to know and love as drive A. But it also has a drive B that it can keep track of, using the old phantom drive trick. Try this:

1. Grab two floppy disks. It doesn't matter what they are, just as long as they have something on them and you can stick them into your PC's A drive. (Don't use blank disks.)

2. Log to drive A. Type the following:

```
C:\>A:
```

That's **A** and a colon. Press Enter. This *logs* you to drive A. You'll probably see an A in your DOS prompt. Good. You're on — or logged to or using — drive A.

3. Use the DIR command to look at the directory of drive A:

```
C:\>DIR
```

Type **DIR** and press Enter. You'll see a list of files scroll up the screen. Okey-doke.

4. Log to drive B. Don't shake your head and mutter "You're a fool! I have no drive B! I'm skipping up to the next section." Instead, type the following:

```
C:\>B:
```

That's **B** and a colon. Press Enter.

You see the following message displayed:

```
Insert diskette for drive B:
and press any key when ready
```

The message may read differently on your PC. (If you have a fancy DOS prompt, it may even look quite ugly.)

5. Remove the first floppy disk from drive A and replace it with the second disk. That disk is actually being put into the phantom drive B.

6. Press the Enter key.

   After you've switched diskettes, the new diskette is the one "in drive B" and your drive A is now acting like a drive B. Secretly, DOS is keeping track of everything (which amazes me to no end).

7. Use the DIR command to look at the directory of the now drive B:

```
C:\>DIR
```

   Type **DIR** and press Enter. Note how the first line reads Volume in drive B is ....

8. Find a small file on the disk and copy it to drive A. For example, on my disk the file CRUD.DOC is only 1,245 bytes long. I'll copy it to the disk in drive A with the following:

```
C:\>COPY CRUD.DOC A:
```

   This is the traditional COPY command, copying a file from the phantom drive B to drive A. Normally, you'd go nuts figuring this out right now, but bear with me. Type a similar COPY command on your computer to copy a small file to drive A. When you're done, press the Enter key.

   You see the following message:

```
Insert diskette for drive A: and press any key when ready
```

9. Do it; switch diskettes. When that's done, press the Enter key. DOS sniffs out drive A again and then asks you to reinsert the diskette for drive B. Do that and press Enter. Then switch disks again when asked, pressing Enter again. This goes on for a while. (Just follow the directions on-screen.)

10. Eventually, you'll be back on drive B. Type **A:** (A and a colon) to finally log back to drive A. The exercise is over.

✔ Now that you've gone through it, aren't you glad you don't live in the days of floppy drives?

✔ If you really need to copy a file from one disk to another, copy it to the hard drive first. Then switch floppy disks and copy the file back to the new disk.

✔ The tutorial has you copy a small file. If you copy larger files, you may have to swap diskettes back and forth a few times, quite possibly forever.

✔ Refer to the section "Easy logging (for those afeared of flannel) or "Change my disk drive, please!" for more information about logging, or changing, disk drives.

- If you already have a floppy drive B, you cannot use the phantom drive (you don't need to). Typing **B:** to log to drive B simply lets you use the disk in the B drive.

- Another term for the phantom drive is *logical drive*. The *physical drive* is the device itself, floppy drive A. However, physical drive A can magically become logical drive B when the phantom deems it so.

Easy logging (for those afeared of flannel) or "Change my disk drive, please!"

DOS only pays attention to one drive at a time. So although you look at everything as "on disk," DOS only sees what's on *this disk* and ignores every other disk. There are two ways to get it to pay attention to another disk.

The first way is to *log* to another disk. This action switches DOS's narrow attention to that particular disk. To log to another disk, you type the disk drive's letter, followed by a colon:

```
A:\>C:
```

That's actually a command. It's telling DOS to pay attention to drive C. "Here DOS, use drive C." The word *log* is most accurate, though it's a bit nerdy.

```
C:\>A:
```

The preceding command logs the computer to drive A. You enter this command when you want the computer to only pay attention to stuff on that drive.

The second way to get DOS to see something on another disk is to force it to pay attention by inserting the disk drive's letter, plus that special colon, into the command. This is how you get commands like

```
C:\>COPY A:\STUFF C:
```

The preceding command tells the computer to look on drive A for the file STUFF. (The backslash also tells DOS to look in a specific directory; more on that in Chapter 16.) This command also tells the computer to copy the file to drive C. This is arm-twisting DOS into paying attention to specific drives and not just assuming this-or-that (which it does all too well anyway).

✔ The drive DOS is using, or logged to, is also called the *current drive*.

✔ In addition to paying attention to only the current drive, DOS also only sees files in the *current directory*. Refer to Chapter 16 to iron out this wrinkly quandary.

✔ DOS only pays attention to files and programs in the current directory. The way around this is to use the PATH command to tell DOS where else you want it to look for files. This information is offered in Chapter 22.

✔ Why the colon? Because A is a legitimate filename. If you type A and press Enter, DOS actually looks for a program named A.COM or A.EXE or even A.BAT and tries to run it. You must tack on the colon to let DOS know you're talking about a disk drive and not a single-letter filename.

✔ Microsoft really hates the term *logging*. I learned this when writing the *MS-DOS 6.2 Upgrade For Dummies*. They prefer to say *changing*. But grammatically, a rugged verb like *log* or *logging* is needed. After all, you don't really *change* to drive A. That sounds wacky. Instead, when you understand what *log* means, it makes sense to *log to drive A*.

Formatting Section

You can't use a disk until it's been formatted. This is a strange concept. After all, you use a blank videotape to record a TV program without formatting it. Cassette tape? Hey, just load it in and press Play-Record. No formatting is necessary. But disks are different.

Unless you buy your diskettes pre-formatted (which is a real time-saver), you need to use DOS's FORMAT command. This command prepares disks for use by the computer. This is a basic part of using the computer, and the following sections briefly go into the primary formatting commands you need to know.

✔ Far more detailed information on formatting is offered in *DOS For Dummies*.

✔ If you do buy pre-formatted diskettes, make sure they're pre-formatted for IBM PC-compatible or DOS computers.

✔ Always buy the highest capacity disks for your disk drives. Don't mess with low capacity, and don't bother with those devices that claim to magically turn a low-capacity disk into a high-capacity disk.

Formatting a disk in drive A

The FORMAT command used most often in DOS is the following:

```
C:\>FORMAT A:
```

This command directs DOS to format, or prepare for sudden use, a diskette languishing in your PC's A drive.

Most of the full, gory formatting details are offered in the original *DOS For Dummies*. If I repeat them here, the computer press reviewers will trash this book as "re-hash." So instead, I'm offering the following observations on the FORMAT command. This is the kind of knowledge-enhancing stuff you only find in a *More* book:

✔ The FORMAT command always prompts you to insert a diskette and press Enter to begin formatting. Most people already have the disk in the drive, however.

✔ Full disks produce the error message `Insufficient space for the MIRROR image file` with DOS 6 and later. DOS always safe-formats its disks, allowing you to easily recover them with the UNFORMAT command. If the disk is full, however, this can't be done and that's what the error message is all about.

✔ From DOS 5 onward, DOS verifies any disk it's reformatting. This is just a polite message: `Verifying 1.44M`.

✔ A percentage indicator lets you know how much of the disk has been formatted. For example:

```
28 percent completed.
```

Older versions of DOS didn't display anything. Instead, you had to sit and watch a blank screen, praying the computer wasn't "hung" or anything.

✔ When the formatting is done, the `Format complete` message appears. But — ah-ha! — it's not done. You're asked to enter a volume label, disk statistics appear, and then you're asked whether you want to format another disk. In a way, this message is as evil as the dentist who mutters "Almost done" or the energetic scout leader who urges "Just a little farther." It's all lies!

✔ You don't have to type a volume label — nope, not at all. Just press the Enter key when asked. The last section in this chapter mulls over volume labels in depth.

✔ Nothing known to man uses the Volume Serial number. You can heave that — and other information displayed when disk formatting is done — into the mental trash can.

✔ Always format disks as soon as you buy a box and take them home.

✔ If you see a `Bad or unusable Track 0` type of error, you can try reformatting it as described in the section "Formatting deliberately" later in this chapter. If that doesn't work, toss the disk out. No sense in risking any important data on such a disk.

Formatting a low-capacity disk in drive A

You only need to do this if you're working with someone who uses only low-capacity disks. Otherwise, don't bother.

To create a low-capacity 5¼-inch disk in drive A, type the following:

```
C:\>FORMAT A: /F:360
```

That's the standard disk formatting command for drive A, plus a space, slash-F, a colon, and then the number 360. This command tells FORMAT to create a 360K disk in drive A.

To create a 720K diskette in a high-capacity 3½-inch drive, type this command:

```
C:\>FORMAT A: /F:720
```

Type the command you would use normally to format a diskette in drive A, but add a space, slash-F, colon, and then 720. This directs the FORMAT command to create a 720K disk in drive A.

To create a 1.4MB diskette in an extended-density 2.8MB 3½-inch drive, use the following command:

```
C:\>FORMAT A: /F:1440
```

This is the same FORMAT command, but with a slash-F, colon, and 1440. Only use this command if you have an extended-density drive and need to format 1.4MB diskettes for your pals who don't have such a keen device.

For older versions of DOS, use the following command to format a low-capacity 5¼-inch disk in drive A:

```
FORMAT A: /4
```

The following FORMAT command creates a 720K diskette in a 1.4MB drive for older versions of DOS:

```
FORMAT A: /N:9 /T:80
```

That's the slash-N, colon, 9 and slash-T, colon, 80 options, which tell the FORMAT command to spin out a 720K disk.

Formatting quickly

If you have a disk that's already formatted and you just want to reformat it, use the following command:

```
C:\>FORMAT A: /Q
```

Type **FORMAT**, a space, **A** and a colon to format a disk in drive A, another space, and finally a **/Q**. The slash-Q stands for Quick and — surprise! — this is the Quick formatting command; it even says so right on the screen. Press Enter to format the disk.

 ✔ The /Q option only works with DOS versions 5 and later. If you're using an earlier version of DOS, you must slug it through every time you format.

 ✔ When you format quickly, DOS does not verify the disk. So if the disk is shaky — or quite old — there may be an error that FORMAT /Q won't detect. My advice is to use FORMAT /Q only on newer diskettes.

Formatting deliberately

To deliberately erase everything on a disk — utterly reformat it and start over— you tack the /U (slash-U) option onto the FORMAT command. The U in this case stands for *unconditional*.

```
C:\>FORMAT A: /U
```

In the preceding. the FORMAT command is used to format a diskette in drive A unconditionally. The /U on the end sees to that. DOS rubs out the entire diskette and starts over on a clean slate — without mercy or thought for any data on the disk — so be careful with this one.

 ✔ The /U option only works with DOS versions 5 and later.

 ✔ You may want to try using the FORMAT command with the /U option when DOS gives you a `Bad or unusable Track 0` error.

 ✔ You would think that the FORMAT command always wipes out a disk's contents. But no! Normally, it just *verifies* that a disk can hold information. When you specify the /U option, FORMAT overwrites every square inch on the disk with new, blank information. It's not just mowing the lawn, it's sowing salt into the ground. Nasty, nasty.

All about the Format Another? question

No matter what, when DOS is done formatting a disk, it poses the following question:

```
Format another (Y/N)?
```

Press Y to format another disk or N to return to the cozy DOS prompt. But keep the following message in mind when you press Y:

> *The same FORMAT command will be used to format each additional disk.*

So if you start by typing **FORMAT A: /S** to create a boot floppy, when you answer Y to Format another(Y/N), DOS makes another boot floppy. If you type **FORMAT A: /F:360** to make a low-capacity 5¼-inch diskette, DOS will make another low-capacity 360K diskette.

The moral of the story is, if you want to format another diskette — but make that one different from the first one — you should press N for No and then type the new FORMAT command at the next DOS prompt.

Creating a Boot Disk

A boot disk is any disk you use to start your computer. Not every disk has the honor. Only disks that have the core DOS start-up files, as discussed in Chapter 1, can be boot disks.

On a PC, boot disks can be either a hard drive or a floppy disk. Most computers have drive C as their boot disk, and DOS automatically appears each time you start your computer. But it's also possible to transform a floppy disk into a boot disk and start your computer with it instead. Here are the reasons why you'd want that to happen:

- ✔ You live in the early 1980s and can't afford a hard drive, so you always start your PC with DOS on a floppy disk — a boot disk.
- ✔ You live in the early 1990s and, though you have a hard drive, it's broken and your PC won't start!

Seriously, there is no other reason to have a boot disk floppy than if your hard disk won't start. Unfortunately, that happens. When it does, you can create a boot disk, as described in the following tutorial.

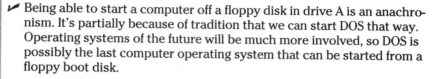

✔ You cannot start your PC with the boot disk in drive B. The computer only looks to drive A for a boot disk; then it looks to the hard drive C.

✔ Being able to start a computer off a floppy disk in drive A is an anachronism. It's partially because of tradition that we can start DOS that way. Operating systems of the future will be much more involved, so DOS is possibly the last computer operating system that can be started from a floppy boot disk.

✔ Doesn't it seem that when you microwave water for tea it gets colder faster than when you boil the water in a kettle?

The make-a-boot-disk tutorial

Follow these steps to make yourself a boot disk. I'll assume your computer is on and ready to go, the DOS prompt glows patiently on the screen, and your fingers are a-twitchin' over the keyboard.

1. Remove any floppy disk you may already have in drive A.

2. Get a new or unformatted floppy disk.

   Make sure the disk is the same size as your PC's drive A — a 3½-inch disk for 3½-inch drive or a 5¼-inch disk for a 5¼-inch drive. Also make sure the disk is the proper capacity for the floppy drive; if you have a high-capacity drive, get a high-capacity disk.

3. Put the floppy disk into drive A. The 3½-inch disks go in only one way; don't force 'em. The 5¼-inch disks go in label-up, oblong hole first. Remember to close the drive door latch for a 5¼-inch disk.

4. At the DOS prompt, type the following FORMAT command:

   ```
   C:\>FORMAT A: /S
   ```

   That's **FORMAT**, a space, **A** and a colon (meaning drive A), another space, and then **/S**. Double-check. Press Enter.

5. The computer responds with the following message:

   ```
   Insert new diskette for drive A:
   and press ENTER when ready
   ```

   You may see a subtly different message. Whatever. Press the Enter key because you're already ready.

6. Other information is displayed. For instance,

   ```
   Checking existing disk format
   Saving UNFORMAT information.
   Verifying 1.44M
   ```

DOS is just being careful here, though a side effect of this is that you may see the following:

```
Drive A error. Insufficient space for the MIRROR image file.
There was an error creating the format recovery file.
This disk cannot be unformatted.
Proceed with Format (Y/N)?
```

Press Y to format the disk. (The error message is unimportant when creating a boot disk.)

7. Time passes slowly.

A percentage ticker may indicate how much of your diskette is being formatted or *verified*. This is what's known in programmer circles as *busy messages*. They display something — anything — on the screen to let you know the computer is working and not stuck. Of course, if your floppy drive is as loud as mine, you'll actually *hear* the formatting as it takes place.

Another boo-boo you may see is the following:

```
WARNING: This disk cannot be unformatted if system
files are transferred.
Proceed with system transfer anyway (Y/N) ?
```

Just press Y. (It bugs me that DOS does this, because it's normally so casual about reformatting disks.)

8. Finally, you see the message

```
System transferred
```

This means the disk has magically become a boot disk. You can now start your computer with it, but first a few more questions are in order.

9. You can enter a volume label if you like:

```
Volume label (11 characters, ENTER for none)?
```

Just press the Enter key for now.

10. And then, swallow hard for the statistics lesson.

```
    1,457,664 bytes total disk space
      198,656 bytes used by system
    1,259,008 bytes available on disk


         512 bytes in each allocation unit.
       2,459 allocation units available on disk

Volume Serial Number is 205F-15DF
```

(You can ignore this stuff. Indeed, the number of bytes you see will differ, depending on the disk's size. The serial number is always different.)

11. One more question:

```
Format another (Y/N)?
```

Press N here; you do not need to make another boot disk. You'll be returned to the cheery DOS prompt.

The boot disk is now ready to rumble, the rumbling being described in the next section. Promptly remove the disk from the drive and stick a label on it. Write *Boot Disk* on the label — use a felt-tip pen or write softly. Keep the disk in a handy place in case you ever need to use it.

✔ Information on the volume label thing is found in the section "A Section on the Volume Label Thing" in this chapter.

Testing the boot disk

You don't need to make sure the boot disk works, but if you're the doubting type, you can always test it out. Here are the steps:

1. Put your boot floppy disk into drive A. Close the drive door latch if your drive A is a 5¼-inch drive.

2. Reset your computer. Press Ctrl-Alt-Delete or whack your PC's reset button.

3. DOS starts from drive A.

DOS starts much more slowly from drive A than from drive C, which just dramatically shows you how much spiffier hard drives are.

OK. You've seen it work. Now remove the boot floppy disk from drive A and put it back where you found it. Reset your PC again to start it properly from the hard drive.

- ✔ Because there isn't a CONFIG.SYS or AUTOEXEC.BAT file on the floppy boot disk, your computer starts with a "naked" DOS. Don't expect your mouse to work or programs like Windows to run; they need the commands in CONFIG.SYS or AUTOEXEC.BAT to function properly.

- ✔ The fastest way to reset is to press Ctrl-Alt-Delete. When you press your computer's reset button, it does a bunch of memory tests and such, which make it take longer to reset.

A few choice words on the SYS command

It's possible to make any disk a boot disk by using the SYS command instead of FORMAT with the /S option. Using the SYS command is the preferred way to make boot disks, especially hard drives that you don't want to erase with the FORMAT command.

For example, if you wanted to make any old floppy disk a boot disk, put it in drive A and type the following at the DOS prompt:

```
C:\>SYS A:
```

That's **SYS**, the SYS command, a space, and then **A** and a colon. Press Enter and DOS responds with

```
System transferred
```

Voilá! The disk in drive A is now a boot disk.

- ✔ Most of the time you can use the SYS command on any disk. However, if the disk is full, you see the error message No room for system on target diskette. This is why I recommend using FORMAT /S because it creates a new diskette, solely designed for the purpose of starting your computer.

- ✔ Sometimes you'll be shocked by the following message:

```
No system on default drive
```

This can drive you nuts; where did it go? You have two ways to solve the problem: First, log back to drive C and try it again. Second, type the following variation of the SYS command:

```
C:\>SYS C: A:
```

Type **SYS**, a space, the **C** and colon for drive C, and then **A** and colon for drive A, where you're making the boot disk. Essentially, you're copying the boot files from drive C to drive A with this command. (Which is what the SYS command does anyway but is occasionally too stupid to figure out.)

✔ SYS is pronounced *sis* as in *sister* or *system*; SYS does not rhyme with *ice*.

✔ Only drive C needs to be a boot disk. Don't bother using the SYS command on any hard drive other than C.

✔ If a disk is already a boot disk, there is no need to run the SYS command on that disk. (If your computer starts just fine now, don't mess with the SYS command.)

A Section on the Volume Label Thing

I had a nightmare the other night. My old boss, in the form a crow, came down from his perch holding a disk in his beak. Enthused, he told me in his coffee-tainted breath, "You know, Dan, it would be great if that darn DOS LABEL command would actually write something on the disk's label. What do you think of that? I mean, isn't Microsoft stupid for not programming that in? You use the LABEL command and you still have to write on the disk label. I tell you what, why don't you research the LABEL command for me and write up something on it. I mean, this thing has got to be useful, right?" I awoke in a cold sweat as he flew away, and then I hurriedly wrote the following.

What the heck is a volume label?

A disk's volume label is a joke. It's an optional name DOS attaches to a disk when the disk is formatted. I assume you could use it to identify the disk, but other than that it's really rather silly.

You'll see a disk's volume label displayed in the following places:

✔ Duh, the LABEL command displays a disk's volume label.

✔ The first line in the DIR command's output contains it.

✔ When you use the VOL command, it appears.

✔ The FORMAT command asks for it, so in a way you could say that it displays the volume label.

✔ The TREE command proudly proclaims a disk's volume label.

✔ The forbidden FDISK program refers to a hard disk's volume label.

✔ When you use a file manager, the volume label appears by the disk drive letter.

✔ Disk utility programs may mention volume labels.

Other than those situations, the volume label is a fairly useless thing — DOS's appendix, if it were a human being.

✔ You can create labels when you use the FORMAT command to format the disk. You can also create, change, or delete labels by using the LABEL command. This is described in the section "The sillier LABEL command" at the end of this chapter.

✔ See Chapter 12 for more information on the DIR command.

✔ Volume labels are always displayed in uppercase. I know: Whoop-dee-doo.

✔ The FORMAT command uses the volume label when confirming that you want to reformat a hard drive. Because I don't think anyone in his right mind would ever do that, there's no point in marching through the procedure here.

✔ The volume label has nothing to do with the sticky label you may peel and put on a disk. Actually, that label is more important than the volume label. Always label your disks and write on the label what the disk contains — not everything, just the general idea: Home work, Stuff for Sue, Games, Virus-infected dirty movie for Tom, and so on.

✔ The volume label is actually a *file* on disk! The file has no size or location or contents. It's just a name stored on disk like a file. This is why the volume label can only be 11 characters long.

The silly VOL command

The VOL command lives and breathes to display a disk's volume label and serial number. It dies for this.

```
C:\>VOL
```

You can type the VOL command alone, as done in the preceding, or you can follow the command with a space and drive letter (plus colon) if you want to see the volume label for another disk drive:

```
C:\>VOL F:
```

The output looks like this:

```
Volume in drive C is TOO LOUD
Volume Serial Number is 1234-ABCD
```

✔ When it's not followed by anything, the VOL command displays the volume label for the current drive.

✔ If a disk drive doesn't have a label, then you see `Volume in drive X has no label` displayed.

✔ Earlier versions of DOS, plus some third-party disk formatting programs, didn't stick serial numbers on disk. In those cases, the serial number information is not displayed.

✔ The VOL command is one of a pair of nutty DOS commands, the other being VER. VER and VOL. Sounds like a Norwegian comedy team from the '40s.

The sillier LABEL command

Even if you don't slap a label on a disk when it's formatted, or if you goof up, you can change a disk's label using the LABEL command. Here are the LABEL command's duties:

1. Add a label to a disk.

2. Change a disk's label.

3. Remove a disk's label.

Completely silly and useless information on labeling your disks

As a person with an odd sense of humor, I'm always on the lookout for silly things to do on a computer — like practical jokes I'd play on Mr. Spock. One of the best and most tempting things is a disk's volume label. No matter what, DOS always displays a volume label in the following manner:

`Volume in drive X is blah-blah`

This leads to a great chance for punnage. To wit, what is the volume? Consider the following names I've given my various disks and how the VOL command's output appears:

```
Volume in drive C is TOO LOUD
Volume in drive D is TOO SOFT
Volume in drive E is JUST RIGHT
Volume in drive C is HEAVY
Volume in drive D is AFRAID
Volume in drive C is TOO SMALL
Volume in drive D is TOO HOT
Volume in drive F is SMELLY
Volume in drive C is TIRED
```

In all cases, you type the LABEL command at the DOS prompt:

```
C:\>LABEL
```

Type **LABEL** and press Enter. DOS spits up the following:

```
Volume in drive C is MISSING
Volume Serial Number is FACE-B0B0
Volume label (11 characters, ENTER for none)?
```

Type in a new label at the prompt. Only type 11 characters, no more. Be creative, but you can't use specific characters (listed by a check mark, below). Press Enter to add or change the label. Or just don't type anything and press the Enter key by itself to remove the volume label.

If you press Enter without typing anything, you delete the old volume label. DOS will wonder `Delete current volume label?` Press Y to zap it, N to give up.

> ✔ To change the label on another disk drive, follow the LABEL command with that drive's letter and a colon. For example, to change the label on drive A, type
>
> ```
> C:\>LABEL A:
> ```
>
> ✔ Following are forbidden characters you cannot stick into a volume label:
>
> , " & ( ) * + . / : ; < = > ? [\ ] ^ |
>
> You can, however, stick a space in the volume label.

> ✔ You can prelabel your disks by using the FORMAT command. Just type in the label when asked. Or you can use the /V option to specify the label before you format:
>
> ```
> C:\>FORMAT A: /V:WORKDISK
> ```
>
> The preceding command formats a disk in drive A and then automatically gives it the WORKDISK label.
>
> ```
> C:\>FORMAT A: /V:"WORK DISK"
> ```
>
> This command formats a disk in drive A and gives it the WORK DISK label with a space between *work* and *disk*. You can do this if you put the label name in double quotes, as done in the preceding.

Chapter 16

More on . . . Subdirectories

● ●

In This Chapter

▶ Understanding directory terminology

▶ Using the TREE command

▶ Getting around with the CD command

▶ Naming subdirectories

▶ Managing directories

● ●

*N*othing will pop your cap quicker than messing with subdirectories. The terms! The concepts! The backslash-mess! It's a hassle. Unfortunately, subdirectories are an important part of life on a DOS computer. You *need* them. It's all about organization and making sure your computer's files never get as cluttered as your computer's desk. This chapter discusses all the details, giving you a nice mental image and showing you a few subdirectory and related-stuff tricks.

Directory Nomenclature

Directories are storage places on disk — almost like disks within disks. You store files and programs into directories and then use the various directories to keep the files all organized.

The reason we have directories is that hard drives can store thousands and thousands of files. If we just put them all on the disk, without putting them in directories, it would be disastrous: The DIR command would take weeks to display all the files. You'd quickly run out of filenames. And Charlton Heston would drive his Jeep over the rubble, rip off his aviator glasses and mutter, "Oh. My. God." over and over.

✔ You create directories using the MD command, as described in this chapter's section "Creating and naming directories."

✔ Every disk has one main directory, the root directory, discussed in the next section.

✔ You can find the subject of organizing your hard drive by using subdirectories in Chapter 22.

The root directory (Or BDOD)

Every disk has one main directory. It's called the *root directory* because, in a funny way, any other directories on the disk *branch out* from this directory. Oh, har har. Maybe it was Arbor Day when the boys in the lab thunk that one up.

In DOS, the root directory has a symbol. It's the backslash character, which looks like this:

```
\
```

Yeah, that's actually the *name* of the root directory. It appears in various pathnames as the first item after the drive letter (and colon), indicating the disk's main directory.

✔ The FORMAT command creates the root directory on every DOS disk. They all have 'em. It's the main, big cheese directory.

✔ Some ersatz cool users call it *the root*.

✔ You can find the backslash character over the Enter key on most computer keyboards; sometimes it's just next to the Backspace key. The backslash points north-northwest and south-southeast. The forward slash (/) is found under the question mark key. They're *not* the same thing.

✔ DOS also uses the backslash character to separate directories in a pathname. (Pathnames are discussed later in this chapter.)

✔ The root directory is an exclusive storage place for special types of files. Only those that absolutely must be in the root directory live there: COMMAND.COM, CONFIG.SYS, AUTOEXEC.BAT, DBLSPACE.BIN, and a handful of others. Everything else should be sluffed off to its own subdirectory, which is covered in Chapter 22.

✔ There is one of those annoying DOS limitations on the root directory: it can only hold so many files. On a floppy disk, that's about 112 files. On a hard drive, you can put maybe 512 files in the root. After that — no matter how much free space is left — you'll get a `disk full` error message. This is yet another argument for putting files and such in subdirectories.

✔ BDOD = Big Directory On Disk.

What's a subdirectory and what's a directory?

This is cinchy: A directory is a noun and a subdirectory is a preposition. Okay! Okay! No English grammar lessons here. (Besides, they're both nouns.) Actually, both terms refer to the same thing, which should really be called a *directory*. Subs are for sandwiches.

The term *subdirectory* is typically used to refer to a directory in the current directory. The techy crowd calls a subdirectory a *child directory*. For example (and you can refer to Figure 16-1 here), you could say that directory C:\GAMES is a subdirectory of the root directory. But GAMES is not a subdirectory itself; only when referenced from another directory does it become a subdirectory.

✒ Yeah, this is more a question for semanticists to debate than anything worth wasting gray matter on here.

✒ Nerds refer to a subdirectory as a *child* directory. So C:\GAMES would be a child directory of the root directory (see Figure 16-1). In that instance, the root directory would be the *parent* directory of GAMES. (No, smart guy, GAMES is not the grandparent of the SHHH! directory.)

✒ This ties in nicely with the . (dot) and .. (dot-dot) things in a directory listing (refer to Chapter 12): The single dot represents the current directory and the double dots represent the parent directory.

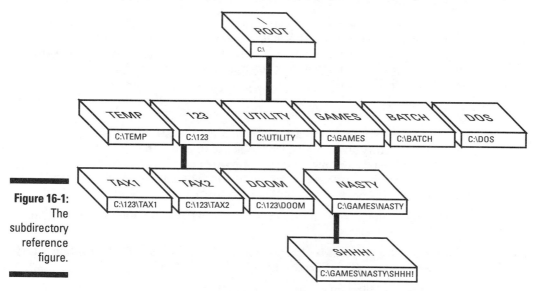

Figure 16-1:
The subdirectory reference figure.

What's a path/pathname?

A pathname is a longer version of a filename. In addition to naming a file, it also pinpoints the file's location. Pathnames generally include a file's disk drive as well as in which subdirectory the file lives.

The following is a sample pathname:

```
C:\123\TAX1
```

This path refers to the subdirectory named TAX1 in the directory 123 on drive C. Here's how it breaks down:

C: Drive C

C:\   The root directory

C:\123   The 123 directory, a subdirectory of the root

C:\123\TAX1   The tax1 directory, a subdirectory of 123

This pathname pinpoints a file's location on disk:

```
C:\DOS\DEFRAG.EXE
```

The pathname pinpoints the location of the file DEFRAG.EXE, which is on drive C in the DOS subdirectory. This is how you would reference that file if you were logged to another disk drive or in another subdirectory on this disk, or if you were paid by the hour and it took you longer to say "C:\DOS\DEFRAG.EXE" than just "DEFRAG.EXE."

- You use backslashes to separate directory names.

- I'm using Figure 16-1 as a subdirectory map illustration. Your disk's subdirectory structure doesn't look like that, but the figure gives you a graphical feel for how the directories are organized and how the pathnames look. Refer to the section on "The mighty TREE command" later in this chapter for another directory structure view.

- A pathname doesn't have to end with a filename. It shouldn't end with a backslash, either.

- The drive letter and colon are optional if you're referring to a subdirectory or filename on the current drive.

- The TAX1 directory is the one shown to the IRS.

What is the current directory?

The current directory is the directory on disk you happen to be using. DOS can only use one directory — and can only immediately access files in that directory — at a time. After all, there can be hundreds of directories on a disk. DOS isn't God, y' know.

You can see the pathname for the current directory, using the CD command. Just type **CD** at the DOS prompt and press Enter:

```
C:\>CD
C:\>GAMES
```

In the preceding, the CD command tells the boss that you're using the GAMES directory again. Tsk, tsk.

✔ People who get paid by the word may call it the *currently logged directory*.

✔ More information on the CD command is offered later in this chapter. See the section "Getting around with the CD Command."

✔ CD = Current Directory.

✔ Nothing is more refreshing to the ears of long distance dialers than the sound of the AT&T bong.

The Mighty TREE Command

Figure 16-1 illustrates one way of looking at a directory tree structure. Another way is to use the TREE command that comes with DOS. That way you can see graphically what your hard drive looks like. Using the TREE command is easy:

```
C:\>TREE
```

Type **TREE** and press Enter. You see something like the following, which is the TREE command's output for one of my office computers. Rather than display a traditional tree-like tree, the TREE command lists directories and their subdirectories in the order they were created, top to bottom:

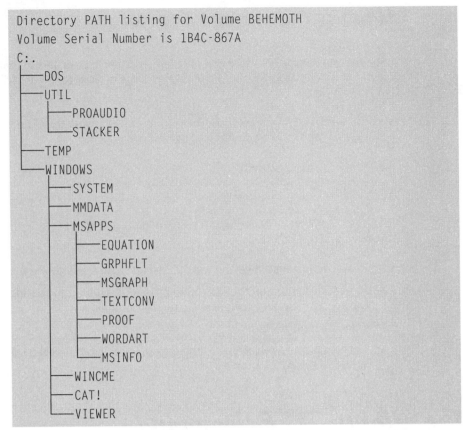

```
Directory PATH listing for Volume BEHEMOTH
Volume Serial Number is 1B4C-867A
C:.
├───DOS
├───UTIL
│   ├───PROAUDIO
│   └───STACKER
├───TEMP
└───WINDOWS
    ├───SYSTEM
    ├───MMDATA
    ├───MSAPPS
    │   ├───EQUATION
    │   ├───GRPHFLT
    │   ├───MSGRAPH
    │   ├───TEXTCONV
    │   ├───PROOF
    │   ├───WORDART
    │   └───MSINFO
    ├───WINCME
    ├───CAT!
    └───VIEWER
```

✔ The TREE command is a great one to type on a new computer, one you haven't worked on before. Doing so will show you exactly how the hard drive is organized.

✔ To print the TREE command's output, make sure your printer is on and ready to print. Then type the following command:

```
C:\>TREE > PRN
```

That's **TREE**, a space, a greater-than thing (>), another space, and then **PRN**. Press Enter, and DOS prints a copy of your hard drive's tree structure.

✔ If your printer can't display the graphical characters (in other words, your output sucks), try the following command instead:

```
C:\>TREE /A > PRN
```

That's the **TREE** command, a space, then /A, and the rest. The slash-A tells DOS to display the TREE command's output using simple characters (ASCII characters) instead of line-drawing characters.

✔ Another TREE command option is /F. This command tells DOS not only to display directories in your hard drive's tree structure, but to also list the files in those directories:

```
C:\>TREE /F
```

This command's output can be quite lengthy (which is an understatement on some hard drives).

✔ If you turn your head sideways to the right, the TREE command's output kinda looks like one of those windswept trees on Aruba.

✔ You can also view your tree structure in the DOS Shell program. Most file manager shells graphically display a disk's tree structure.

✔ See if you can find the cat stuck in the tree in the example tree structure given earlier.

Getting around with the CD Command

Just as DOS can only use one disk at a time, it only pays attention to one subdirectory at a time. That subdirectory is the *current directory*. When you use any DOS commands, it automatically assumes you're referring to files only in the current directory. Other directories — even if they're on the same drive — DOS couldn't care less about.

Paying attention to another directory

In order to make DOS pay attention to other files in other directories, you have two options. First, you can specify those files' full pathnames. For example,

```
C:\>COPY C:\TEMP\OLDNEWS A:
```

This command copies the file OLDNEWS from the TEMP directory on drive C to drive A. This is an example of using a full pathname to tell DOS specifically which file you mean. If the TEMP directory isn't the current directory, DOS would never have found the file.

The second way to make DOS pay attention is to use the CD command to change directories. Because most files in a subdirectory are related, folks don't bother with the full pathname option and vie for using the CD command instead.

To change to another directory, type **CD** followed by the name of the new directory you want DOS to find:

```
C:\>CD \WP60
```

In the preceding, DOS changes its focus to the WP60 directory.

Generally speaking, specify the full pathname of the directory you want to change to (the drive letter is unnecessary):

```
C:\>CD \DOS
```

This command focuses DOS's attention to files stored in the DOS directory.

- ✔ DOS aficionados pronounce it *see-dee*.

- ✔ Like many DOS commands, the CD command has a longer version no one uses: CHDIR. Both mean the same thing: change directories.

- ✔ Unless you specify a full pathname, DOS assumes you mean files in the current directory for all its commands: DIR, COPY, REN, DEL, MOVE, ATTRIB, LEAK, and so on.

- ✔ The CD command only changes directories on the current drive. So if you're on drive D in the UNDERH2O directory and you want to change to C:\GAMES, you must log to drive C and then change to the GAMES directory. That takes two DOS commands:

```
C:\>C:
C:\>CD \GAMES
```

- ✔ Sometimes I goof up and say "log to this or that directory" as opposed to "change to this or that directory." Both are fine; you can use *change* or *log* when referring to directories. But when changing disk drives, it's more proper to say "log to" as opposed to "change to this drive." I vent on this at length in Chapter 15.

- ✔ Did you know that Al Gore's "Reinventing Government" handbook was printed on expensive paper that cannot be recycled? This book is printed on and from recyclable paper, thank you.

CD, all by itself and lonely

If you type the CD command by itself, DOS displays the current directory:

```
C:\>CD
```

Just type **CD** and press Enter. DOS responds with the current directory in the form of a pathname:

```
C:\DOS
```

- ✔ This is the only way to tell "where you are" on a disk, unless . . .
- ✔ If you use the PROMPT command's $P dollar-sign thing, you'll always know the current directory because it appears as part of the DOS prompt. Refer to Chapter 3 for more information.
- ✔ To see the current directory on another drive, follow the CD command with that drive letter:

  ```
  C:\>CD D:
  ```

  The preceding command tells DOS to display the current directory for drive D. DOS responds accordingly:

  ```
  D:\
  ```

  Oh. Looks like drive D is using the root directory. Party on, drive D.

- ✔ Checking out the current directory on another drive is a good trick to use when working with files between two drives. For example,

  ```
  C:\>DEL D:*.*
  ```

  In this command, you're assuming that all the files on drive D will be deleted — but is drive D logged to the proper directory? Better check with the CD command, lest you zap some files you didn't plan on.

Some CD command tricks 'n' stuff

Here are some common CD command variations and shortcuts you may find useful:

```
C:\>CD \
```

The preceding command changes directories to the root directory of the current drive. This is a popular spot to visit — but don't visit it when you don't need to.

Many DOS users "climb the tree" when changing directories. For example, (look at Figure 16-1), if you're going from the C:\GAMES\NASTY directory to the C:\123\DOOM directory, you *do not* have to type the following:

```
C:\>CD \
C:\>CD \123\DOOM
```

Only the second command is necessary. DOS doesn't have to climb up one directory branch and then down another.

The following CD command is a great shortcut:

```
C:\>CD ..
```

Type two dots after the CD command to change to the *parent* directory of the current directory. This uses the handy dot-dot abbreviation for the parent directory you see in the DIR command's output — and it's a handy shortcut.

Consider Figure 16-1. Suppose that you're buried in the SHHH! directory and want to change to the NASTY directory. Unknowing DOS users would use the following CD command:

```
C:\>CD \GAMES\NASTY
```

That gets you to the NASTY directory, but CD .. does it just as well and takes less time to type.

Another common CD command *faux pas* is specifying a full pathname when you don't have to. Leaning back on the Figure 16-1 crutch, consider that you're using the 123 directory and want to log to the TAX1 subdirectory. Some DOS users may be inclined to type the following:

```
C:\>CD \123\TAX1
```

This command works, and it gets you there, but it requires too much typing. Because TAX1 is a subdirectory of the 123 directory — and you're in that directory — you only need to type the following:

```
C:\>CD TAX1
```

A full pathname is never required when logging to a subdirectory.

Likewise (and going back to the figure), suppose you're in the GAMES directory and you want to change to the SHHH! directory. The following command does the trick:

```
C:\>CD NASTY\SHHH!
```

Again, only a partial pathname was used; NASTY is a subdirectory of the current directory, and SHHH! lives under it.

- ✔ *Faux pas* is French and means *false step* or *blunder*. It's pronounced *fo-pa*, which is how someone from Oklahoma would say "for my father."

- ✔ Most of my in-laws are from Oklahoma, so I have nothing personal against the state — or the musical. (Ever get that *"I'm Just a Girl Who Can't Say No"* song stuck in your head?)

Doing Things with Subdirectories

Subdirectories are often treated like files, which is sad because they deserve more respect. For example, subdirectories are named like files and they appear in the DIR command's output just like files (but with the ⟨DIR⟩ thing). Yet, aside from that, there are few file-like things you really can do with subdirectories.

Unlike files, subdirectories aren't often copied, moved, renamed, or deleted. Generally, subdirectories stay in place and hold files until your hard drive becomes full, someone accidentally erases everything, or the computer blows up. Before that happens, you may be inclined to do something with a subdirectory, either individually or including the whole subdirectory branch. The following sections outline the do's and donuts.

Creating and naming directories

You create directories by using the MD command, which stands for *make directory*. Before making a new directory, follow these steps:

1. Think of what the directory will contain and dream up a name accordingly.

   For example, batch files go in a BATCH directory. You'd put your poetry in a directory named POETRY. Tax stuff may go in the TAXSTUFF directory.

You get the idea. Of course, you're limited to file-naming conventions, so it has to be eight characters or less.

2. Change to the new directory's parent directory.

   For example, if you're creating a new subdirectory in the GAMES directory, change to that directory. If you're making a new directory off the root, change there. (This isn't a requirement, it just makes the operation easier.)

3. Make sure there isn't a file in the directory that has the same name as the one you've chosen.

   For example, if you have a file named NORTON in the root directory and you try to create a directory named NORTON, you get an `Unable to create directory` error.

4. To make the directory, type the **MD** command followed by the new directory's name:

```
C:\>MD JUNK
```

   The preceding command creates the directory JUNK in the current directory. (JUNK will be a subdirectory of the current directory.)

5. There is no feedback, but you can use the DIR command to confirm that the directory was created. Or you can visit it by using the CD command.

✔ Subdirectories use the same DOS naming conventions that files use. You can use only letters and numbers, and the subdirectory name can be from one to eight characters long. For the complete list of file naming do's and don'ts, refer to Chapter 11.

✔ Though subdirectories can have extensions, few people give them one. Even so, don't let a subdirectory with an extension toss you a loop.

✔ The MD command has a longer version that does the same thing: MKDIR. Don't bother.

✔ You can rename a directory by using DOS 6's MOVE command. The section "Yes, it's possible to rename directories" later in this chapter has the details.

✔ You can destroy directories by using the RD command. Refer to the section "Subdirectories aren't deleted; they're removed with the RD command."

Let's-all-make-a-TEMP-directory tutorial

I recommend that everyone have a TEMP directory, perched right off the root directory. Use this directory to store temporary or junk files.

1. Log to drive C. Type

```
C:\>C:
```

That's **C** and a colon. Press Enter.

2. Change to the root directory with the CD command:

```
C:\>CD \
```

That's **CD**, a space, and then a backslash, representing the root directory.

3. Now you're ready to make a TEMP directory. Type the following command at the DOS prompt:

```
C:\>MD TEMP
```

That's **MD**, a space, and then the name of the directory you're creating, **TEMP** in this case. Press Enter.

DOS won't have any feedback to offer, but the directory has been created. To see it, use the following DIR command:

```
C:\>DIR TEMP
```

You see the TEMP directory listed on the screen. Visit it with the CD command if you like (though it's empty now).

✔ For more information on the TEMP directory as well as the all-important SET TEMP=C:\TEMP command in AUTOEXEC.BAT, refer to Chapter 10.

✔ If you get a `Directory already exists` error, well then, by golly, you already have a TEMP directory on drive C. Sho-nuf.

Yes, it's possible to rename directories

Suppose one night you're in a hurry (or drunk) and you name a subdirectory something inappropriate. Or, more likely, the subdirectory's purpose changes over time and you want to give it a new name to reflect its contents. Prior to DOS 6, you'd be out of luck; there was no way to rename a directory. But with DOS 6, you can rename directories, using the unlikely MOVE command.

When you use the MOVE command with a subdirectory name instead of a file name, the MOVE command works just like the REN command. Type the old subdirectory name and then the new name, following proper file-naming rules, of course:

```
C:\>MOVE BADFILES OKFILES
```

In the preceding, the subdirectory named BADFILES is renamed OKFILES.

```
C:\>MOVE D:\GRAPHICS\UGLY INSPIRED
```

In the preceding, the directory UGLY on drive D is renamed INSPIRED. This usually happens when the person who created the graphics in that directory has access to your PC.

- ✔ More information on naming files, including file-naming rules, is found in Chapter 11.
- ✔ Using the MOVE command to actually move files is covered in Chapter 13.
- ✔ Alas, you cannot move a subdirectory using any single command in DOS. Instead, follow the steps outlined in the next section.

Moving a subdirectory branch

There are those days when you just get frustrated and want to rearrange your house, your life, or your hard drive. When that day comes, pray your hard drive is already in order. Rearranging a directory structure is a mess and time consuming. There is no single DOS command to do it. But it can be done. Bear with me.

As an example (refer to Figure 16-1), suppose you're moving the DOOM subdirectory from the 123 directory to the BATCH directory. So what was once

```
C:\123\DOOM
```

will become

```
C:\BATCH\DOOM
```

Briefly, here are the steps that do it:

Ho! I recommend backing up your hard drive before you try this. Good idea.

1. First, you must copy the subdirectory to the new location. This is done with the following variation of the XCOPY command:

```
C:\>XCOPY C:\123\DOOM C:\BATCH\DOOM
```

Type **XCOPY**, a space, then the original subdirectory's pathname, another space, and then the final destination pathname. Make sure that the destination pathname includes the new subdirectory name. In the preceding, both pathnames end in DOOM.

2. DOS asks the following:

```
Does DOOM specify a file name
or directory name on the target?
(F = file, D = directory)?
```

DOS is wanting to know whether you want to create a new directory or not. (The "not" means that all the files will be copied to a single file named DOOM — which isn't what you want.)

3. Press D for *directory*.

The files are copied and the new directory is created.

A move is a copy-delete operation; after the files are copied, the originals must be deleted.

4. *Carefully* type the following DOS command:

```
C:\>DELTREE C:\123\MOVED
```

This deletes the subdirectory named MOVED and all the files it once contained. *Please be careful with the* DELTREE *command!* Double-check that you've followed it with the name of a directory you want to utterly delete. There is no "undo" for this command!

✔ Substitute your directory name — and the proper source and destination pathnames — in the preceding steps to move any subdirectory on your hard drive.

✔ Need I mention this is a scary thing? Be careful! Also remember that other programs may expect the files you moved to be in the old spot on disk. You may have to update CONFIG.SYS, AUTOEXEC.BAT, and other program files if you moved some vital stuff. (You'll discover this as you use your PC.)

✔ To move a directory — and all its subdirectories and their files as well (which is the true definition of a "subdirectory branch") — you need to add the slash-S option to the XCOPY command in step 1:

```
C:\>XCOPY C:\123\DOOM C:\BATCH\DOOM /S
```

Just type the source and destination pathnames; then tack on a space and slash-S. All the other steps remain the same.

- ✔ More information on removing subdirectories is offered in the next section.

- ✔ Information on the deadly DELTREE command is presented gingerly in the section titled "Deleting a subdirectory branch (or The true killer-diller DELTREE command)" later in this chapter.

- ✔ When you do move a subdirectory, be aware how it affects other parts of the computer. For example, if CONFIG.SYS was looking for a device driver in a subdirectory you just moved, it won't be able to find it the next time the computer starts. The same holds true for batch files that expect files to be in a certain spot.

- ✔ File management disk utilities are the best tools for "pruning and grafting" parts of your subdirectory. One of the best is XTree, though other file managers are capable of this act as well. (The XTree people send me free software, so I mention them outright.)

Subdirectories aren't deleted; they're removed with the RD command

When you tire of a directory, you can delete it by using the RD command, which stands for *remove directory*. You can do this only under the following circumstances:

- ✔ There cannot be any files or subdirectories still living in the directory. (If so, delete them first.)

- ✔ The directory you're deleting cannot be the current directory (which is like blowing up the vault while you're still in it).

- ✔ You cannot delete the root directory. (Many have tried; most have died.)

Given all that, it's cinchy to zap a directory to kingdom come. Just type the **RD** command followed by the directory's name:

```
C:\>RD \123\TAX2
```

In the preceding, the TAX2 directory is zapped from the disk. (Some clever user must have deleted all its files first.)

✔ There is no way to undelete a directory.

✔ The RD command has a longer version, RMDIR. Both do the same thing. No one bothers with RMDIR, however.

✔ If you "absolutely swear on a stack of DOS manuals" that you deleted all the files but still see a `directory not empty` error, then there are probably some hidden or read-only files (or subdirectories) that you haven't gotten rid of. Refer to Chapter 11 for information on using the ATTRIB command to scope out stubborn files.

✔ A spiffier way to delete a directory is with the DELTREE command, covered next.

Deleting a subdirectory branch (or The true killer-diller DELTREE command)

The DELTREE command is a DOS 6 only thing — and a deadly thing at that. It is even more perilous than the slithering, saliva-dripping mouth of a cave-dwelling, Dorito-famished proto-nerd. Essentially, DELTREE is a super DEL command — and an unforgiving one at that.

DELTREE works like the DEL command. But you type **DELTREE** and follow it with the name of a subdirectory:

```
C:\>DELTREE GAMES
```

In the preceding, the DELTREE command wounds — nay, slays — the directory GAMES. It deletes all the files in that directory, and then it removes the directory itself. Before that dramatic moment, you'll be offered fair warning:

```
Delete directory "GAMES" and all its subdirectories? [yn]
```

Press Y and press the Enter key and . . .

```
Deleting GAMES...
```

It's gone!

✔ There is no undo for the DELTREE command. DOS cannot resuscitate deleted subdirectories or their files.

✔ Not only did DELTREE remove the GAMES directory and all its files, but judging from Figure 16-1, it also deleted the NASTY directory and all its files and the SHHH! directory and all its files as well. Vicious.

✔ The [yn] thing translates as "You can type the Y or N keys here. I assume you gather that Y stands for Yes and N stands for No."

Building a tree house on a subdirectory branch

This isn't recommended. And if you try, please don't hammer nails into the tree (which the tree finds painful). Instead, use ropes or metal brackets to tie support beams to the tree. Then hammer away into the support beams.

- ✔ Some tree-sensitive parents actually put the tree house on poles next to the tree.

- ✔ Please inform your son(s) that it's not politically correct to have a boys-only tree house. Indeed, this may constitute sexual harassment and potentially thwart their future political ambitions.

Part III
Batch Files 'n' Stuff

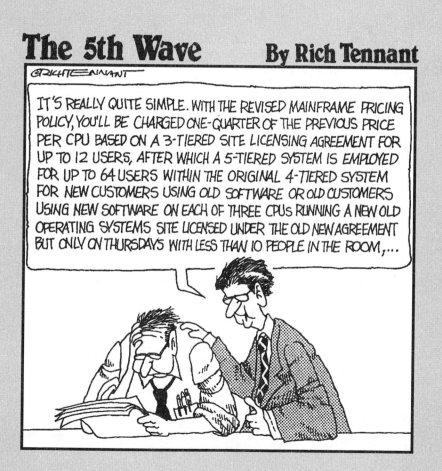

The 5th Wave — By Rich Tennant

IT'S REALLY QUITE SIMPLE. WITH THE REVISED MAINFRAME PRICING POLICY, YOU'LL BE CHARGED ONE-QUARTER OF THE PREVIOUS PRICE PER CPU BASED ON A 3-TIERED SITE LICENSING AGREEMENT FOR UP TO 12 USERS, AFTER WHICH A 5-TIERED SYSTEM IS EMPLOYED FOR UP TO 64 USERS WITHIN THE ORIGINAL 4-TIERED SYSTEM FOR NEW CUSTOMERS USING OLD SOFTWARE OR OLD CUSTOMERS USING NEW SOFTWARE ON EACH OF THREE CPUs RUNNING A NEW OLD OPERATING SYSTEMS SITE LICENSED UNDER THE OLD NEW AGREEMENT BUT ONLY ON THURSDAYS WITH LESS THAN 10 PEOPLE IN THE ROOM,...

In this part...

The two things *DOS For Dummies* readers requested *more* of were more cartoons (done) and information on batch files. Normally considered "intermediate to advanced" material, batch files do have a certain charm. They're really programs, but anyone can write them. They make using the computer easier. And they're fun to tinker with. This section covers all that, introduces you (from a distance) to DOS's batch file programming language, and generally has fun with some zany topics related directly or not to batch files.

Chapter 17
Batch File Basics

* *

In This Chapter

▶ Discovering the practical reason for batch files

▶ Understanding the basic batch file

▶ Canceling a batch file

▶ Playing around with batch files

▶ Typing in batch files from books and magazines

▶ Unraveling the @ECHO OFF mystery

* *

DOS's batch files are appealing for a number of reasons: They're easy (and admittedly fun) to create. *Anyone* can create them. And, most importantly, they serve a somewhat vital purpose in making your computer easier to work with.

Be careful not to let yourself go nuts with batch files, however. There is a limit to what they can do. Often times, batch file beginners get carried away and work on a project that's better done by true programming languages like BASIC or the C language. As long as you stick by the guidelines and other suggestions offered in this chapter, you should keep your sanity.

✔ That sanity thing is not a promise, by the way.

✔ DOS comes with its own programming language, QBasic. I often get asked to recommend a book for learning that BASIC programming language. Here 'tis: *Learn BASIC Now* from Microsoft Press.

The Real Reason for Batch Files

The absolute "this is why they did it" reason for batch files is offered in the box "The Paleolithic reason behind batch files, which you don't need to read," which isn't important. Instead, the reason *you* want to have batch files is to *execute commands in a batch*. This means instead of typing the following commands:

```
C:\>C:
C:\>CD \WP60
C:\>WP
```

you would just type **RUNWP**, the name of a batch file, and DOS would automatically type those commands for you.

- ✓ A batch file is nothing more than a collection of DOS commands, each listed one after another, in a text file.

- ✓ All batch files end in the BAT filename extension. Because DOS recognizes this as a type of program, all batch files are programs.

- ✓ Batch files can also contain special programming commands that make them behave like a real programming language. These commands are listed in Chapter 18.

Where to shove your batch files (or Creating the C:\BATCH directory)

If you haven't yet been there, then know that Chapter 22 of this book covers the subject of hard disk organization. The theme is that all files belong somewhere on your hard drive. Batch files are no different. They should go in their own specific directory, preferably a BATCH directory you create specifically for them.

The best spot for a batch file directory is right off the root directory on drive C. The following DOS command creates a BATCH directory right at that spot:

```
C:\>MD C:\BATCH
```

That's **MD**, the make-directory command, a space, then **C**, colon, backslash, **BATCH**. This creates the subdirectory BATCH on drive C. When you create any batch file, place it into that subdirectory for safekeeping.

- Information on directories and the MD command is offered in Chapter 16.

- It's just the best idea to put all your batch files into a BATCH directory or a similar directory set up for that purpose. Create all your new batch files there as well. Avoid the temptation to strew them around the hard drive, and for heaven's sake, don't clutter the root directory with batch files (other than AUTOEXEC.BAT).

- Wise computer users put the BATCH directory on DOS's search path. Doing this is covered in Chapter 22. 'Tis a wise thing.

- Also see Chapter 22 for more information on hard disk organization.

- See Chapter 16 for detailed information on subdirectories and stuff like that. Figure 16-1 in that chapter illustrates how a BATCH subdirectory would look on disk — graphically speaking, of course.

- Another interesting thing worth considering is copying your batch files to a RAM drive after the computer starts. Doing this is covered in Chapter 10 on AUTOEXEC.BAT; RAM drives themselves are given the once-over in Chapter 24.

What to do with your batch files

With batch files, you can easily run all the programs on your PC. For example, most of the time you may find yourself typing the following commands to start the Quattro Pro spreadsheet:

```
C:\>C:
C:\>CD \QUATTRO
C:\>Q
```

First, you log to drive C, and then you change to Quattro's directory, and then you type the command to start Quattro. Three commands are required. Three times you must type something in. Three times there is a possibility for error.

Proving that computers can save you time are batch files. Because a batch file is a collection of DOS commands, you can just stack those three commands into a batch file. Name it Q.BAT. That way, running Quattro Pro is as easy as typing the name of the batch file (Q); the computer does the rest of the work.

- Making this happen means you must create batch files to run all your programs. That sounds like a pain, but most batch file contents are as simple as the three lines shown above to run Quattro Pro.

- You must also put all these batch files into a single directory, such as the BATCH directory mentioned in the previous section. Then you place that directory on DOS's search path, using the PATH command as discussed in Chapter 22.

✔ An example of creating a simple, program-running batch file is provided in the next section.

✔ Sometimes your guru — yes, the nice person you rely upon for PC advice — will claim that you can run your applications without batch files simply by using the DOS search path or the PATH command. This is a solution, but not the best one. Running programs with batch files is much better than having a long PATH command. Chapter 22 does a lot of finger-wagging on this particular subject, if you're interested.

The create-your-own-program-running-batch-file tutorial

The following tutorial will help you create a batch file to run any program on your hard drive:

1. Start by creating the BATCH subdirectory as described in the section "Where to shove your batch files (or Creating the C:\BATCH directory)," up front in this chapter.

2. Review the commands you use to start the program — all the commands.

   For example, to run WordPerfect, you probably type three commands:

   ```
   C:\>C:
   ```

   First, you log to drive C by typing **C:**.

   ```
   C:\>CD \WP60
   ```

   Then you change to the WordPerfect directory using the **CD** command followed by the directory name (**WP60** in the preceding, although it may be WP51 if you haven't yet upgraded).

   ```
   C:\>WP
   ```

   Finally, you type **WP** to run WordPerfect.

   • You don't need to type these commands; though doing it "for real" may help you remember how they go.

   • The first command, logging to drive C, is most important. If you're already on drive C, you may not need to type this when you run WordPerfect. However, sometimes you do (when you're not on drive C to start). To cover all the bases, include the C: command in the batch file.

   • These three steps — log to a drive, change to a directory, run a program — are almost universal for any program.

3. Use a text editor to create the batch file. For example, you can use the DOS Editor. Start it by typing the **EDIT** command at the prompt and follow it with the name of the batch file you want to create:

```
C:\>EDIT WP.BAT
```

In the preceding, you start the DOS Editor by typing the **EDIT** command. That's followed by a space and then **WP.BAT**, the name of the batch file to start WordPerfect.

- It's a good idea to name the batch files something simple. Naming the WordPerfect batch file WP make sense because you always type WP to start WordPerfect. Name other batch files you create similarly: Q for Quicken; 123 for Lotus 1-2-3; FOX for FoxPro; and so on.

- Remember that all batch files end in the BAT extension.

- Yes, it's okay to name a batch file the same thing as the program name. Chapter 22 describes how all this works.

4. The Editor starts, giving you a blank screen for editing.

5. Type the traditional first line in the batch file. Type in the following:

```
@ECHO OFF
```

That's the @ character (above the number 2 key), then the word **ECHO**, a space, and then the word **OFF**. Press the Enter key to end this line and start the next.

6. The next few lines are the same commands you use to start your program. In the case of this WordPerfect example, they'd be

```
C:
CD \WP60
WP
```

Press Enter after each line.

7. Review everything, double-checking all the stuff you've typed. Figure 17-1 shows how the sample WP.BAT file would look in the DOS Editor.

8. Save the batch file to disk. In the Editor, you select the **S**ave command from the **F**ile menu. Use your mouse or press Alt-F and then S.

If you haven't yet given the file a name, do so now (as you're saving it to disk). Name the file according to the suggestions mentioned earlier in this tutorial.

9. Quit the text editor. Select the E**x**it command from the **F**ile menu in the DOS Editor. (You can use your mouse, or you can press Alt-F, X using the keyboard.)

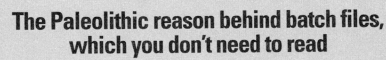

```
 ile   dit   earch   ptions                                      elp
                              WP.BAT
@ECHO OFF                                                            ↑
C:
CD \WP61
WP




                                                                    ↓
←                                                                   →
MS-DOS Editor  <F1=Help>  Press ALT to activate menus    │  C   00005:001
```

Figure 17-1:
This is how
the WP.BAT
sample
batch file
looks in the
DOS Editor.

10. Test the batch file! Type its name at the DOS prompt:

    ```
    C:\>WP
    ```

    Like any other DOS program, you only need to type the first part. In the
    preceding, WP was typed to run the sample file, WP.BAT. Cross your fingers.

11. If everything works, you can create more batch files to run more programs.
    But before doing that, I'd recommend reviewing Chapter 22 on hard disk
    organization to get a feel for what this is all about.

The Paleolithic reason behind batch files, which you don't need to read

Batch files were actually a last-minute deal, dreamt up near the end of development on DOS 1.0. IBM told Microsoft that they wanted some way to test the new PC over and over. They needed a way to have the computer self-run a set of commands again and again to see how well the computer performs. Microsoft responded by creating batch files.

What batch files do is run commands in a *batch*, one after the other. Microsoft didn't really think much of that ability and only created a handful of programming commands to control how the batch file worked (these are all listed in Chapter 18).

Through the years, Microsoft has added only a few commands to the batch file language. The CALL command came about in 1987 with DOS 3.3, as did the @ thing. The CHOICE command was added in 1993 with MS-DOS 6. Yet regardless of its limitations, batch files are still a popular toy for DOS tinkerers to fiddle with.

What nerds do with batch files

Batch files can get quite monstrous. I'd list some doozies here if this book weren't 100 pages longer than promised and two weeks past due. Because batch files hold DOS commands, computer zanies often use them to completely automate some mundane processes.

About the most complex thing that can be done with batch files is to create a DOS menu system. That's something that appears on the screen and presents a list of options: word processing, financial stuff, games, and so on. These appear on the screen, and you then punch in a number to run that program. That's impressive, and it can be done with batch files, but it's a lot of work. Many third-party programs do the job much better and

easier. In particular, I'm fond of the program Direct Access from Fifth Generation Systems.

Other batch file tasks are more geek-o-centric. Batch files can be written to find programs on disk, to scan for files needing backup, to produce a job log of activities on your PC, to format disks without erasing programs, and to replace DOS commands with "safer" versions.

By the way, if you're interested in such batch files, magazines usually showcase the best. *DOS Resource Guide* lists dozens of enthralling batch file programs each month. And *PC/Computing*'s latter pages offer some intriguing batch files. This is definitely hard core nerd stuff. *Caveat lector.*

✔ To run WordPerfect, all you need to do is run the WP.BAT file, or whichever batch file you've created for whichever program.

✔ If you want to have WordPerfect (or whatever) load a document when it starts, you need to change the last line in the batch file as follows:

```
WP %1
```

Type **WP** (the program you're running), then a space, a percent sign, and the number one. This tells the batch file to read in the first *command line parameter* and tell your program about it. (Refer to Chapter 18 for more information on command line parameters.)

✔ Batch file run amok? Press Ctrl-C to cancel it. Press Y to answer Yes to the Terminate batch job? message.

✔ If you see a sea of Invalid directory errors, then you have a typo in your batch file. Press Ctrl-C to cancel it. Then edit the batch file and check the CD command.

✔ Why all the Invalid directory errors over and over? Because DOS doesn't change directories, and then it runs the final command in the batch file. If that final command is the same as the batch file's name (WP in the example), then the batch file runs over and over. It's computing run amok! Press Ctrl-C and Y to cancel; then edit your work.

- ✔ If the batch file doesn't run for any other reason, edit it and review the commands one by one. Make sure you start with a drive letter change (such as C:) as the first command after @ECHO OFF. Then check that CD command.

- ✔ `Bad command or file name` error? You probably have an antique version of DOS, prior to version 3.3. Older versions of DOS didn't understand the @ECHO OFF command. The solution is to edit that line and remove the @ symbol.

The Gist of Batch Files

Wow! Programs you can write, using simple tools you may find lying about your disk drive. Could it be that easy? Yes. Providing you follow some of the rules and suggestions mentioned in the following sections.

Batch file rules

Here are the rules and such for DOS's batch files:

- ✔ A batch file must be a text file.

- ✔ The batch file filename must end with the BAT extension.

- ✔ The batch file must contain DOS commands, batch file programming commands, or a combination of both.

- ✔ Commands in a batch file are run from top to bottom.

- ✔ Each line in a batch file can be no more than 128 characters long.

- ✔ Blank lines in a batch file are okay.

- ✔ The DOSKey, Ctrl-T ¶-thing does not work in a batch file.

- ✔ DOSKey macros do work in batch files.

- ✔ In MS-DOS 6.2, the COPY, XCOPY, and MOVE commands do not warn you before they overwrite existing files with the same name.

- ✔ If the batch file is not a text file, DOS may not run it or may just decide to throw up all over the screen. To ensure that the batch file is a text file, only use a text editor, such as the DOS Editor, to create the batch file.

- ✔ If you use a word processor to create your batch files, be sure to save them to disk as unformatted DOS text, plain text, or ASCII files. Also, try to turn off the word wrap feature if possible. In some word processors, you can do this by setting the right margin to 14 inches (or higher).

- Batch files with strange things in them produce `Bad command or file name` errors when they run. (This is the same error you get when you type goofy at the DOS prompt.)

- Commands in batch files run from the top down. An exception to this is when you use the GOTO batch file command to change the order in which the commands are run. (See Chapter 18 for more information on the GOTO command.)

- A blank line in a batch file is the same as just pressing the Enter key at the DOS prompt. No damage done. (You can also indent lines in a batch file.)

- Using the Ctrl-T multiple commands at a DOS prompt thing is pointless in a batch file. Instead, just type each of the commands on a line by itself inside the batch file.

- Nope, DOSKey macros don't work in batch files. If you've written a DOSKey macro as a substitute for the DEL command (see Chapter 14), then remember that only the "real" DEL command will work in your batch files.

Batch files aren't the peppiest things around

Some users go bananas over batch files and dream up all sorts of interesting things for them to do. One thing they discover along the way — something no one else will tell you beforehand — is the following:

Batch files are slow!

Batch files run slowly because . . . (and you don't need to read this) . . . DOS types in each line, one at a time. To do that, DOS opens the batch file, reads the line, and then closes the batch file. It does this repeatedly, accessing the disk way too much for each line in the batch file. For short batch files, you actually feel DOS is working fast because the commands fly by faster than you can type. Long stuff? Hey, call me back next Christmas.

Cramming commands into a batch file

There are three ways to copy commands into a batch file. The first is just to remember what the commands are. But if your brain is as good as mine, you'll probably try the second way: Write the commands down. If that seems a bit much for a computer, then you can use the ultimately spiffy way: Use DOSKey's History command.

The following tutorial outlines how to use DOSKey to "remember" commands for a batch file.

1. Start up DOSKey if you haven't already. Instructions are offered in Chapter 4.

2. Press the Alt-F7 key combination (press and hold the Alt key and tap the F7 key, and then release both keys). This clears DOSKey's command history. You're starting with a new slate, and DOSKey will remember each of the commands you type.

3. Start typing the commands you want to place into a batch file. For example,

```
C:
CD \123
123
```

The preceding starts the program you want to run, Lotus 1-2-3. That's okay.

4. Quit the program right away and return to the DOS prompt.

5. Type the following command to create your batch file:

```
C:\>DOSKEY /HISTORY > C:\BATCH\123.BAT
```

That's **DOSKEY**, a space, then slash-**HISTORY**, another space, the greater-than symbol, another space, and then the full pathname of the batch file you want to create. In the preceding, I typed C:\BATCH\123.BAT to create a batch file for running Lotus 1-2-3 in the C:\BATCH directory. Type a batch file named appropriately. (Be sure to end it with the BAT filename extension.)

6. Edit the batch file using a text editor. For example, if you were using the DOS Editor, you would type the following:

```
C:\>EDIT C:\BATCH\123.BAT
```

The EDIT command starts the DOS Editor. That's followed by a space and then the pathname of the file you're editing. In the preceding, the sample file is 123.BAT in the C:\BATCH directory.

7. What you see in the text editor will look something like this:

```
C:
CD \123
123
DOSKEY /HISTORY > C:\BATCH\123.BAT
```

The first three lines are your batch file — the commands you wanted to record. The last line is unnecessary and will be deleted in step 9.

8. Add the following command to the top of your batch file. Move the cursor to the top of the file if necessary (press Ctrl-Home in the DOS Editor):

```
@ECHO OFF
```

Type the preceding line — the @ symbol, **ECHO**, a space, and then **OFF** — and press Enter. This should appear on a line by itself as the very first thing in your batch file.

9. Press the down-arrow key until the last line — the DOSKey command — is highlighted. Then delete that line. In the DOS Editor, the key command is Ctrl-Y to delete a line of text.

10. Your batch file should now look something like this:

```
@ECHO OFF
C:
CD \123
123
```

11. Save the batch file to disk. Select the **S**ave command from the **F**ile menu in the DOS Editor; use the mouse or press Alt-F, S.

12. Quit the Editor. Select E**x**it from the **F**ile menu in the DOS Editor (press Alt-F, X or use the mouse).

13. Test the batch file. It will probably work as advertised because the commands were "recorded" before you wrote the file.

✔ You can use this nifty trick to create any batch file.

✔ If there are extra commands or boo-boos, you can do one of two things. You can start over (press Alt-F7 as described in step 2), or you can just edit out the bad commands when you edit the file.

✔ More information on using the > character (I/O redirection) is offered in Chapter 20.

✔ More information on the miraculous DOSKey is provided in Chapter 4.

✔ Information on pathnames is covered in Chapter 16.

✔ Refer to the section "Where to shove your batch files (or Creating the C:\BATCH directory)" earlier in this chapter for information on the BATCH directory.

✔ I admired the way she spoke Russian. Especially her ability to make a double glottal stop and the charming manner in which she produced a bilabial fricative.

Canceling a Batch File Run Amok

DOS's universal cancel key is Ctrl-C. Okay, you can also use Ctrl-Break, but the Break key isn't a key by itself. It's on the front of another key, possibly the Print Screen key on your keyboard. Anyway, for canceling a batch file that's gone batty, you press Ctrl-C.

When you press Ctrl-C to halt a batch file, DOS displays the following message:

```
Terminate batch job (Y/N)?
```

DOS has stopped the batch file. The screen stops dancing. The orchestra takes a breather. If you press Y, the batch file ungracefully ends, and you'll be deposited at the next DOS prompt. If you press N, the batch file continues.

- Press Ctrl-C (Control-C) to cancel any batch file.

- Because you typed Ctrl-C to cancel the batch file, my advice is to always press Y for Yes to the `Terminate batch job` message.

- If you press N to continue the batch file, then it may not work properly. Pressing Ctrl-C actually cancels a command inside the batch file, interrupting the batch file's flow. If you press N, the batch file *may* continue okay, but don't count on it. Some batch files may foul up and not behave properly.

- If you just want to pause a batch file, press the Pause key on your keyboard or press Ctrl-S to pause. Press the Enter key to continue.

- Some keyboards (okay, Tandy 1000 keyboards) have a Hold key instead of Pause. Press the Hold key once to pause, press it again to continue.

- Before DOS displays the `Terminate batch job` message, you may see a ^C on the screen. That's the character produced by pressing Ctrl-C. Indeed, nerds often pronounce the ^ as *control*, as in "You have no self-^."

- I've never liked the words *terminate* and *job* in the same sentence.

Typing Tips for Batch Files You May Find in Other Books and Magazines

Though they aren't as popular as they used to be, quite a few magazines and several books often list batch files you can type in. These batch files usually serve some purpose, either proving a shortcut or demonstrating some interesting batch file trick. Whatever. Batch file zanies abound.

If you're ever faced with such a batch file listing, then follow these brief rules for typing it in:

✔ Some magazines list line numbers with the batch file. Don't type them in! The line numbers are for reference purposes — such as "In line 462, this batch file folds up and dies."

✔ Always double-check what you type. If the batch file doesn't run, it was probably a typo on your behalf.

✔ Don't discount mistakes! Magazines often misprint and books aren't 100-percent accurate all the time. If you think you've found a mistake, type it in anyway and check to see whether the batch file works. If not, then iron out the mistake on your own or write an angry letter to the editor.

✔ Save the batch files you type in their own special directory or your own BATCH directory.

✔ Some batch files may rely upon utilities you don't have, such as the popular ASK.COM program (used before DOS introduced the CHOICE batch file command). These programs are typically made using the DEBUG utility that comes with DOS. This is technical stuff, not covered in this book.

The Reason behind @ECHO OFF (If You Really Want to Know)

Batch files allow DOS to automatically type commands for you at the DOS prompt. They do exactly that and the results look the same as if you typed the commands yourself — that is, they look ugly. It's very un-program-like. Therefore, to make the batch files run silently and not display too much junk on the screen, the ECHO OFF command is used.

The following sections describe the ins and outs of ECHO OFF. This is entirely optional reading, but you may find it amusing. To assist you in the joy of discovery, you can type in the batch file listed in the following. Create that batch file using your text editor and save it to disk as SILLY.BAT.

```
VOL
VER
ECHO ALL DONE!
```

✔ This whole section is just one big, fun tutorial. That probably means my editor will be mad because I'm spending time dinking on this when I could be writing more important stuff, like Chapter 18. (Bah!)

✔ The SILLY.BAT file contains three lines, three DOS commands: the VOL command, the VER command, and then the ECHO command.

✔ Boy, I hope you created your SILLY.BAT file in your general-purpose batch file directory. If not, use the MOVE command to put it there now; refer to the section "Where to shove your batch files (or Creating the C:\BATCH directory)" earlier in this chapter for more information.

✔ The ECHO command is used to display information on the screen. It's covered in Chapter 18.

✔ Did I hear an echo?

✔ Did I hear an echo?

Running a batch file (like SILLY.BAT) without @ECHO OFF

Here is what happens when you type **SILLY** at the DOS prompt to run the SILLY.BAT program:

```
C:\BATCH>SILLY
C:\BATCH>VOL
 Volume in drive C is MANIC
C:\BATCH>VER
MS-DOS Version 6.20
C:\BATCH>ECHO ALL DONE!
ALL DONE!
C:\BATCH>
```

True-to-form, the batch file automatically types the commands for you at the DOS prompt. Unfortunately, this isn't the way you see most batch files work. Indeed, it's quite "junky." This is why you use the @ECHO OFF command at the start of the batch file. It prevents the commands in the batch file from being displayed, but it still allows the commands to display their output.

✔ The spacing of the output on your screen may be a bit different from that shown in the preceding. You'll find a lot of "air" (blank lines) between the commands on your screen.

✔ Batch file zanies often delete the ECHO OFF from the start of their batch files on purpose. This allows them to see the batch file run and helps them pinpoint errors and other flubs. But when they're done, they stick the @ECHO OFF right back in there.

The whole ECHO ON/ECHO OFF deal

The ECHO command is used to display information when a batch file runs. For example,

```
ECHO This is boring.
```

This command displays the message This is boring on the screen. (Type it in at the DOS prompt; it works there, too.)

The ECHO command is also used to control whether or not a batch file displays information as it runs. Two commands do this:

```
ECHO OFF
```

The preceding command tells DOS not to display the batch file as it runs. Commands in the batch file still display messages on the screen, but the batch file itself runs silently.

```
ECHO ON
```

This command tells DOS to display the batch file as it runs. No one uses ECHO ON, however, because people think the display is ugly with the echo on.

- ✔ The @ sign is used in front of the ECHO OFF command to start just about every batch file. What @ does is discussed in the next section.

- ✔ Using the ECHO command to display information in a batch file is covered in Chapter 18.

The logic and reasoning behind adding the @ECHO OFF thing

The @ thing is used in batch files to prevent a command from being displayed on the screen. Theoretically, you could start every line in a batch file with the @ thing to prevent it from being displayed.

If you're gutsy, edit the SILLY.BAT file and stick an @ at the start of each line. It should look like this when you're done:

```
@VOL
@VER
@ECHO ALL DONE!
```

Save the batch file to disk, exit your editor, and then run it. You'll notice that none of the commands (or the DOS prompts) are displayed when the batch file runs.

Instead of starting each line with an @ sign, batch file mavens start their batch files with the ECHO OFF command. That suppresses things from being displayed and doesn't junk-up the file with @ signs.

Feel free to edit SILLY.BAT again. Remove the excess @ signs and insert a new line at the top of the file. Type **ECHO OFF** and press Enter to make that the first line in the file. SILLY.BAT should look like this when you're done:

```
ECHO OFF
VOL
VER
ECHO ALL DONE!
```

Save the now-modified SILLY.BAT batch file to disk and quit the editor. Run SILLY.BAT again to see how quiet it looks.

Unfortunately, the first ECHO OFF command is still displayed on-screen. This is because the batch file echoes commands until ECHO OFF tells it not to. The solution is to suppress that one line from being displayed, stifling it with an @ sign. To do that, edit SILLY.BAT one more time, this time sticking an @ sign before ECHO OFF. (Yes, creating the @ECHO OFF thing.)

Save SILLY.BAT back to disk one last time, leave your editor, and then run SILLY.BAT at the DOS prompt. You'll only see the output from the commands as opposed to the whole darn thing.

✔ I certainly hope this lesson sates your desire for knowing why there's an @ECHO OFF at the start of each batch file.

✔ See how easy it is for computers to get cryptic? Something like @VOL would have made you queasy a few days back.

✔ Before DOS 3.3, there was no @ thing. All batch files started with the tell-tale message:

```
ECHO OFF
```

Of course, from that point forward, nothing else was displayed.

✔ Because early batch files started with ECHO OFF displayed, many early batch file programmers followed it with a CLS command to clear the screen. If you run a batch file that clears the screen when it starts, it was probably run by some old fogey batch file programmer who's just used to doing things that way.

Chapter 18

Batch File Command Roundup (or "Yikes! Where Did I See That Before?")

· ·

In This Chapter

▶ Looking at (but not touching) the batch file commands

▶ Discovering other symbols and doodads in batch files

· ·

This is not a book on batch file programming. Really, such books exist, and they're chock full of interesting things you can do with batch files. Uh-huh. Rather than run that by you here (and make this book even longer), I've written this chapter as a "Reference for the rest of us." If you've gone though Chapter 17 and that piqued your interest in batch files, then turn here for more information. Otherwise, use this chapter as a reference for those times when you stumble upon something in a batch file and want to know, really, what the heck it does.

The Basic Nine Batch File Commands

The number of commands you can use in a batch file is limitless. Any DOS command, program name, utility, or whatever you type at the DOS prompt can appear in a batch file. However, for batch file *programming*, DOS supplies nine commands to carry out basic programming language chores. These are listed in Table 18-1, which I'm required to show you.

Table 18-1	DOS's Nine Batch File Commands
Command	**Purpose in Life**
CALL	Allows one batch file to run another batch file as a command
CHOICE	Prompts the user (that's you) to press Y or N or one of a listed group of keys
ECHO	Displays text on the screen
FOR	Repeats a command for a given number of times
GOTO	Branches or *loops* inside the batch file
IF	Makes decisions (albeit poor ones)
PAUSE	Displays the `Press any key to continue` message
REM	Allows you to shove comments into batch files
SHIFT	Fiddles with options typed at the DOS prompt

✔ Sheesh. Don't bother memorizing this table.

✔ The sections that follow detail each batch file command as much as I deem necessary. DOS's HELP command gurgles forth more information, if you truly lust after it.

✔ The commands are listed in the following sections in alphabetical order. This will prove a boon to those readers familiar with the alphabet — yet another value-packed feature of this book.

✔ You can type nearly all of the batch file commands at the DOS prompt. Sometimes this is useful, most times not.

✔ The SET command is very popular in batch files, though it's not a batch file command per se. Refer to Chapter 19 for more information on SET.

The CALL command

Batch files can contain anything you type at the DOS prompt. However, if a batch file contains the name of another batch file, then the second batch file just takes over; the remainder of the first batch file is never processed. To fix this problem, they dreamt up the CALL command.

What CALL does is allow one batch file to run another batch file — to *call* it — and then pick up where it left off when the second batch file is done. Here's what it would look like:

```
CALL FILEFIXR
```

Suppose FILEFIXR is the name of another batch file. The preceding CALL command tells DOS to run that batch file program. When it's done, control returns to the current batch file, starting with the next line.

> ✔ The CALL command may also be used in a batch file to run some stubborn DOS programs. For example, an old version of WordStar used to thomp any batch file that ran it. The solution was to CALL WORDSTAR, which allowed the batch file to keep running after WordStar was done.

> ✔ No, the CALL command does not produce the Wrong number error message.

The CHOICE command

This command allows you to type in the answer to a yes-no or multiple choice question. The answer is then fed back to the batch file for examination.

A typical CHOICE command may look like this:

```
CHOICE Is it okay if I reformat the hard drive
```

This displays the following message on the screen:

```
Is it okay if I reformat the hard drive [Y/N]?
```

DOS then sits and waits for you to peck Y or N.

> ✔ The CHOICE command is only available with DOS 6.

> ✔ Typically, you'll find an IF ERRORLEVEL command after the CHOICE command in a batch file. The IF ERRORLEVEL command is used to examine which key was pressed, Y or N or whatever. See "The IF command (and its ugly cousins)" later in this chapter.

> ✔ The CHOICE command has many options and variations, all of which are cheerfully listed in the on-line help (type **HELP CHOICE** at the DOS prompt). This is truly a command for batch file zanies.

The ECHO command

ECHO is the most versatile and popular of all the batch file commands. It's used two ways: first, to display information and second, to control whether a batch file displays its commands as it runs.

In its most basic form, the ECHO command displays text. To wit,

```
ECHO I'd be having a good day...
ECHO ...if I weren't a computer
```

The preceding two lines display two messages on the screen for you to read and enjoy. This works both in a batch file and at the DOS prompt.

In its second incarnation, the ECHO command tells DOS whether or not to display a batch file as it runs. This happens automatically unless you turn off the display with the ECHO OFF command:

```
ECHO OFF
```

You can switch on the echoing of commands with the ECHO ON command:

```
ECHO ON
```

To see whether the echo is on or off (like, duh, you can't tell by looking at the screen), you type the ECHO command by itself:

```
ECHO
```

DOS displays a message, either `ECHO is on` or `ECHO is off`, depending on whether echo is on or off.

✔ You cannot use the ECHO command to display the single word *off* or *on*. That's because ECHO OFF and ECHO ON are really ECHO commands. Funky, but them are the rules.

✔ To display a blank line, follow the O in ECHO with a period:

```
ECHO.
```

This command displays a blank line. If you forget the period, then DOS displays either `ECHO is on` or `ECHO is off`. If you put a space before the period, then DOS displays the period.

✔ Annoy your friends with the following:

```
ECHO ^G
```

Type **ECHO**, a space, then Ctrl-G (press and hold the Ctrl key and press a G; then release both keys). That puts a ^G thing on the screen. Press Enter and your computer beeps in an impolite manner.

✔ I've been playing with DOS for almost 10 years now and have yet to see the
ECHO ON command used. (Okay, some batch file zanies use it to get the
bugs out of their batch files.)

✔ If you type **ECHO OFF** at the DOS prompt, the prompt disappears! Type
ECHO ON to switch it back on again.

The FOR command

One of the strangest batch file commands is the FOR command. It allows you to
repeat a specific DOS command a given number of times. For example, type the
following at the DOS prompt:

```
C:\>FOR %A IN (1 2 3 4 5) DO ECHO I'M CRAZY!
```

Carefully type in the preceding command. Type **FOR**, a space, a percent sign, **A**,
a space, the word **IN**, another space, and then the numbers 1 through 5 in
parentheses (with a space between the numbers, as shown). Follow the parenthesis with another space, and the words **DO ECHO I'M CRAZY!**. Press Enter.

DOS types the ECHO command five times. Yes, the computer is crazy.

Here is another, more realistic example:

```
C:\>FOR %C IN (*.COM *.EXE *.BAT) DO DIR %C
```

Carefully type in the preceding command at the DOS prompt. Double-check
what you type. Press Enter, and DOS types the DIR command three times,
listing all COM, EXE, and then BAT files.

What the FOR command does is to repeat a DOS command a certain number of
times. The format is complex and involved, but the good news is that it doesn't
affect any other part of a batch file.

✔ When the FOR command is used in a batch file, two percent signs appear.
The two examples in this section would look like this in a batch file:

```
FOR %%A IN (1 2 3 4 5) DO ECHO I'M CRAZY!
FOR %%C IN (*.COM *.EXE *.BAT) DO DIR %%C
```

✔ The FOR command uses its own *variable*, which appears as the second
thing on the line (after FOR). The variable starts with a percent sign and
has a letter of the alphabet as its second character.

✔ After the variable, come the word *IN* and then a set of parentheses. Inside the parentheses is a group of items, separated by spaces. The items are usually filenames, though they could be anything (as long as they're separated by spaces). The FOR command supposedly does something with those items.

✔ After the parenthesis, comes the word *DO* and then a DOS command.

✔ If you forget any part of the FOR command, DOS coughs up a `Syntax error` message.

✔ No, the FOR command does not have a companion BECAUSE command.

The GOTO command

It's the GOTO command that makes batch files behave similarly to real programming languages. What it provides is the ability to *loop*, or run a segment of a batch file over and over. Also, the GOTO command can be used to hop, skip, and jump around parts of a batch file.

GOTO works in conjunction with another point in the batch file, called a *label*. The label is any line in the batch file that starts with a colon. For example,

```
GOTO HOME
```

The preceding command tells the batch file to stop what it's doing and immediately look for the line that looks like this:

```
:HOME
```

In this example, you have the HOME label. After the GOTO HOME command, DOS picks up with the command right after :HOME.

✔ Yeah, this is all fairly technical stuff. If you're looking at a batch file and see a GOTO command, just let your eyes wander and find its matching label. Keep reading from that point on.

✔ There can be many GOTO commands in a batch file. Each must be followed by a label name and that label should live somewhere else in the batch file.

✔ Label lines, or any lines starting with a colon, are ignored by DOS when the batch file runs.

✔ GOTO is pronounced "go to" — the two words spoken separately. Do not fall into the trap of saying gotto, which is like *grotto* without the *R*.

The IF command (and its ugly cousins)

One of the most complex batch file commands is IF. It carries out an important decision-making role in a batch file. (Decision-making is a big slice of the PC programming pie.) What the IF command basically says is, "If such-and-such is true, then go off and do this." For example,

> *If I would have bet against Buffalo, I would be a millionaire.*

In the preceding, the IF command examines the condition "betting against Buffalo." If that condition is true (and, unfortunately, it usually isn't), then the result happens, or "I would be a millionaire." Unfortunately, computer parlance is a bit more terse:

```
IF "%1"=="OFF" GOTO NETOFF
```

In this IF command, DOS compares the first command line parameter, %1, to the word **OFF**. If the first parameter is indeed the word **OFF**, then the batch file command GOTO NETOFF is executed. (I hope this presents a brief glimpse at why computing is often considered an anti-social hobby.)

There are actually three variations on the IF command, each of which are briefly described in the following:

✔ IF = = (comparing two things)

The IF command can check command line parameters or environment variables, using this format. The things being checked are usually put in double quotes ("), and there are lots of percent signs to boggle your mind.

✔ IF EXIST (testing to see whether a file exists)

You can use the IF command to see whether a file exists. IF EXIST is followed by the name of a file.

✔ IF ERRORLEVEL (checking how a program ran)

Most programs and quite a few DOS commands leave a little deposit slip in a mail box after they run. On the deposit slip is printed a number called the Errorlevel value. Using the IF ERRORLEVEL command, a batch file can see what the number is and misbehave accordingly.

The IF command is perhaps the most complex of all the batch file commands:

✔ When the IF command discovers something that's true, the rest of the command is executed. For example,

```
IF EXIST C:\COMMAND.COM ECHO HALLELUJAH!
```

If there is a file named C:\COMMAND.COM on disk, then the second half of the IF command works, and the message HALLELUJAH! is echoed to the screen.

✔ You can insert the word NOT before any of the things the IF command tests. For example,

```
IF NOT ==
IF NOT EXIST
IF NOT ERRORLEVEL
```

This allows the batch file programmer to see when things didn't happen.

✔ Refer to the section "The GOTO command" for information on that command, which often appears along with the IF command.

✔ Two equal signs are used when the IF command compares something to something else. If you forget one of the equal signs, DOS flashes a Syntax error message your way.

✔ Information on command line parameters is presented in the section titled "The Bizarre and Technical Nature of Command Line Parameters" later in this chapter.

✔ Information on environment variables is offered in Chapter 19.

✔ Q: Why did the post office raise the price of stamps?

A: To pay for all the storage.

The PAUSE command

Ah, the pause that refreshes. What is that anyway? Never mind. The PAUSE command is responsible for displaying the following message on-screen:

```
Press any key to continue . . .
```

Then the computer sits and hums while you find the "any" key.

They use this command in batch files to slow things down (stop them, actually) and allow you a chance to read the screen, breathe, go to the water cooler, and so on.

✔ Press the Enter key to continue. The Enter key is the "any" key.

✔ Sometimes the message may read Strike any key when ready. Same difference.

The REM command

The REM command allows you to insert comments into a batch file. Sometimes putting comments in a batch file is necessary; for example, when you're in school, the professor decides that he wants you to do it. In real life, it's rarely done.

Because DOS ignores everything after the REM command (plus a space), you can type anything. Here are some examples:

```
REM This batch file was written by Nigel Corothers
REM Ha! I really hate this computer! Ha!
REM I have no idea what the following command does
REM The person who runs this PC smells bad!
```

- ✔ You can also use the REM command to disable commands in a batch file. Just insert REM (and a space) before the command that you want DOS to ignore.

- ✔ You can also use the REM command in CONFIG.SYS for inserting commands and disabling commands. This is covered in Chapter 6.

- ✔ Lots of REM commands slow up your batch file, but not by that much. My advice is to avoid them if you can.

- ✔ Perhaps professors like REM commands in program files because they themselves don't really know what's going on. Same thing can be said of project managers at major software companies.

The SHIFT command

Batch files can examine special goodies called *command line parameters* and futz with them to no end. One way to futz with command line parameters is with the SHIFT command.

What the SHIFT command does is rearrange the command line parameters. The second one becomes the first, the third one the second, and so on. It's like everyone moves up one place in line. This is primarily used in batch files that work with GOTO loops and when examining any parameters after the ninth one.

- ✔ The SHIFT command shifts the command line parameters down one in value.

- ✔ The subject of command line parameters is covered in the section "The Bizarre and Technical Nature of Command Line Parameters."

- ✔ SHIFT serves no function when typed at the DOS prompt. Given that, you can walk up to an unsuspecting friend and say, "Hey, try this new command that gives you super Shift keys." And you type **SHIFT** and press Enter. Then say, "Do you notice anything different?" Unfortunately, most people say "No."

The Bizarre and Technical Nature of Command Line Parameters

Command line parameters. It's a 640K phrase that basically means "the stuff you type after a program name at the DOS prompt." DOS allows batch files to examine and manipulate those items, just as other programs can.

DOS lets batch files examine up to nine options typed after a batch file name at the DOS prompt. Figure 18-1 illustrates the concept.

Each parameter is given a secret symbol. The first is %1, the second %2, the third %3 on up to the ninth, which is %9. No matter what appears after the batch file name at the DOS prompt, those symbols represent it, in order.

Table 18-2 shows how the various items in Figure 18-1 line up. (Tables make things so much easier, and they're required by law.)

Figure 18-1:
How command line parameters fall into place.

Batch File Program Name   **Command Line Parameters**

```
                 %1     %2 %3  %4 %5  %6    %7  %8   %9
                 |      |  |   |  |   |     |   |    |
C:\> FINGER BRUISE WART SCAB CUT MOLE FESTER OOZE BLOAT AMPUTATE
```

Table 18-2   Percent Sign Thingies and the Parameters in Figure 18-1, Together at Last

%-Thing	Represents This Item
%1	BRUISE
%2	WART
%3	SCAB
%4	CUT
%5	MOLE
%6	FESTER
%7	OOZE
%8	BLOAT
%9	AMPUTATE

✔ You can use command line parameters to represent whatever was typed after the batch file name at any point inside the batch file. A common example is "passing along" a filename to a program. For example,

```
WP %1
```

In this, the batch file passes along the name of a document file to WordPerfect. Supposedly, the document filename was typed after the command that started the batch file.

✔ They may be called *command line parameters, command line options,* or *replaceable parameters.* It's all the same thing.

✔ You can also use command line parameters with the IF command in comparison tests:

```
IF "%1"=="NO" ECHO OKAY, I WON'T
```

✔ DOSKey's macros use a concept similar to command line parameters. They're called *replaceable parameters,* and the $1 through $9 dollar-sign things are used to represent them. Refer to Chapter 5 for more droll details.

Other Weird Stuff You May See in a Batch File

Oh, things float around in batch files like flotsam in a dirty fish tank. Strange, eerie things that you may wonder about. I'll try to explain the most unusual ones in the following sections. Please keep in mind that this is a look-only thing. There are batch file programming books that are far more specific than I'll ever get into here.

✔ Okay, if you're curious: I wrote a book on batch file programming and am quite fond of it. The current rendition is called *Batch Files and Beyond,* and it's available from McGraw-Hill/Windcrest books all over the place. End of plug.

The %something% floater

DOS's environment variables appear in batch files cloaked in percent signs. For example,

```
ECHO %PATH%
```

This command tells DOS to display the contents of the environment variable PATH. When the batch file runs, DOS *expands* the %-something-% (PATH, in the preceding) into whatever that variable means.

- ✔ Refer to Chapter 19 for more information on environment variables.
- ✔ The environment variable has percent signs on both sides. If there is a percent sign on only one side, then it's something else — some other floater.

The %%-letter cryptogram

Double percent signs followed by single letters are used in the FOR batch file command. These appear only on that line and nowhere else. Refer to the FOR command earlier in this chapter.

The %1 cryptogram

Any time you see a percent sign followed by a number, you're looking at a command line parameter. These are covered in the section titled "The Bizarre and Technical Nature of Command Line Parameters" amidst this chapter.

The : (colon) something

Any line that starts with a colon in a batch file is a *label*. It's used by a GOTO command elsewhere in the batch file. Some batch file programmers use the colon to start a line that contains comments. Hey, DOS isn't fussy about some things.

The %% hieroglyph

Two percent signs are required in a batch file when it references a filename or command that contains only one percent sign in real life. For example, suppose the following is the name of a file that exists on your hard drive:

```
SEVEN%
```

If this filename were to be referred to in a batch file, the percent sign would be doubled:

```
SEVEN%%
```

This is because batch files "eat" percent signs, using them for many purposes. If you have just one percent sign, then DOS won't see it. That's why the %%, doubled-up percent signs, appear in batch files.

The mysterious blotchy-looking @ something

The @ (at sign) character may appear in batch files as the first character on a line. What that does is tell DOS not to display that command as the batch file runs. The command's output is displayed, but not the command itself or the DOS prompt.

The most common occurrence of the @-thing is on the first line of most modern batch files:

```
@ECHO OFF
```

The ECHO OFF command turns off a batch file's annoying tendency to display itself as it runs. The @ in there also prevents the ECHO OFF from being displayed.

✔ Some batch file programs just stick an @-thing at the start of every line in their batch file. This is the same as having @ECHO OFF at the start of the batch file, so I suppose they're just making things cryptic on purpose.

✔ The male giraffe has the longest tail of any land mammal.

Chapter 19

Respecting the Environment

- -

In This Chapter

▶ Understanding the environment

▶ Using the SET command

▶ Creating environment variables

▶ Destroying environment variables

▶ Using environment variables

- -

*T*his chapter has nothing to do with cutting down trees, dumping oil, or owls, smelts, snails, cockroaches, or fungi on the endangered species list. Instead, it deals with the plight of a small thimbleful of memory DOS uses as a scratch pad of sorts. That memory is called the *environment,* and DOS uses it to remember things, just as we humans use a scratch pad to keep track of appointments, jot down notes, and scratch an itch.

The 5th Wave   By Rich Tennant

UNDER PRESSURE TO INCREASE PRODUCTIVITY, THE SYSTEMS MANAGER AT MONDO CORP. READS THAT COMPUTER CHIPS RUN FASTER AT COLDER TEMPERATURES...

OK, BOB, THE PRINTER'S ON LINE!

Fifty Brief Words on DOS's Environment

Deep inside your PC's memory, you'll find DOS's hall closet. There DOS stores a bunch of information — stuff it needs to know, but also stuff that you can change now or in the future. The closet is called the *environment,* and inside are DOS's *environment variables.*

- ✔ You use the SET command to peer into DOS's hall closet — the environment.

- ✔ The SET command is also used to put items — variables — into the environment and to take them out.

- ✔ The environment variables are used by DOS to configure parts of itself. For example, information used by the PROMPT command is stored in the environment, as is DOS's search path (created by the PATH command) and other goodies.

- ✔ Other programs may use the environment, storing their own variables there. This is usually described in the program's manual or mentioned when the program is installed.

- ✔ The environment has enough space to store, oh, about 256 characters of text (256 bytes of information). If you want to make it larger so that you can store more stuff, you need to use the SHELL configuration command in CONFIG.SYS and specify COMMAND.COM's /E switch, followed by a colon and the larger closet size you want. For example,

```
SHELL=C:\COMMAND.COM /E:1024 /P
```

This command in CONFIG.SYS sets aside 1,024 characters for the environment. Check out Chapter 8 for more information on the SHELL configuration command.

The SET Command (Your Key to DOS's Environment Closet)

The SET command is yet another DOS command that does many different things, depending on how you type it. Its general purpose is to futz with the environment. Using SET, you can look into the environment or add, change, or delete a variable.

- ✔ The SET command is typically used in AUTOEXEC.BAT to set up various variables as the computer starts. Refer to Chapter 10 for more information on what else can be done in your PC's AUTOEXEC.BAT file.

> ✔ In DOS 6, you can also use the SET command in your PC's CONFIG.SYS file. It works the same way as in AUTOEXEC.BAT or at the DOS prompt. Most people opt to keep SET in AUTOEXEC.BAT, however.

> ✔ No, the SET command is nothing you ever *must* mess with. Only if you hear or read something about environment variables should you bother with it.

Using the SET command to peer into the environment

When typed by itself at the DOS prompt, the SET command displays everything in DOS's closet — the whole dang doodle environment.

```
C:\>SET
```

Typing **SET** and pressing Enter produces output similar to the following:

```
COMSPEC=C:\COMMAND.COM
PROMPT=$P$G
PATH=C:\DOS;C:\WINDOWS
TEMP=C:\TEMP
```

This means there are four items in this PC's environment. The four items are COMSPEC, PROMPT, PATH, and TEMP.

> ✔ You may see more or fewer variables displayed by the SET command on your PC.

> ✔ At the least, DOS's environment will contain the COMSPEC and PATH variables.

Ugly rumors about the COMSPEC variable

In days gone by, the rule used to be that, if you use the SHELL configuration command in CONFIG.SYS, you must also set the location of COMMAND.COM by setting the COMSPEC variable in AUTOEXEC.BAT. Ugh. This was complex and involved yet required if you had DOS 3.3 or earlier. It went like this:

```
SET COMSPEC=C:\COMMAND.COM
```

The COMSPEC variable is what tells DOS where to find COMMAND.COM (and it avoids the ugly `Cannot find command/system halted` error). If you have DOS 5 or later, however, there's no need to do this; the SHELL configuration command just got a lot smarter.

Reading what you see in the environment (or "That environment variable format")

All variables you find in DOS's environment-closet have the following format:

```
NAME=WHATEVER
```

First comes the variable name, which is one of the items DOS stores in the environment. That's followed by an equal sign. Then comes the variable's contents or whatever the variable represents. The contents vary, which is why it's called a variable.

- ✓ The environment variable name can be any length, though shorter, more descriptive names are used over longer ones.
- ✓ The variable names are always shown in ALL CAPS in the environment.
- ✓ The variable's contents look just as they did when created: uppercase, lowercase, or mixed case.
- ✓ Variable names should contain only letters and numbers.
- ✓ The variable's contents can contain just about anything (but don't push your luck).

Using the SET command to create a variable

You can create any variable you like by using the SET command. DOS diligently places it into the environment. You follow SET with the variable name, an equal sign, and then what it represents. To wit,

```
SET DIRCMD=/L
```

Type **SET**, a space, then **DIRCMD**, an equal sign, and then a slash-L. Press Enter to create the DIRCMD variable. There is no feedback, although you can type the SET command again (by itself) to confirm that DIRCMD lives in DOS's environment closet.

- ✓ You use the DIRCMD variable with the DIR command to preset options. The /L option means the DIR command displays filenames in lowercase all the time. Type the DIR command at the next DOS prompt to confirm this. (Refer to Chapter 12 for more information on the DIR command.)
- ✓ The DIRCMD variable is only available with DOS 5 and later.
- ✓ You typically use the SET command in AUTOEXEC.BAT to create variables for use by DOS and your programs.

- ✔ Of course, the idea is to create variables that DOS or some other program can use. Variables unto themselves just clutter the environment closet.

- ✔ Never pad the equal sign with spaces! Type the variable name, then the equal sign, and then the variable's contents. The contents can have spaces in it, but no spaces on either side of the equal sign, please.

  WRONG:

  ```
  SET BLAH = UGH ARGH!
  ```

  CORRECT:

  ```
  SET BLAH=UGH ARGH!
  ```

- ✔ If a variable with the same name already exists, the SET command replaces it. As you would expect, there is no warning when this happens.

- ✔ The complete list of environment variables DOS uses and understands is presented in Table 19-1.

- ✔ The environment is only so big. If DOS can't stuff anything else into its environment closet, an `Out of environment space` error message appears. You need to modify the SHELL configuration command in your PC's CONFIG.SYS to give the environment more space. Refer to Chapter 8.

Using the SET command to utterly destroy a variable

What SET giveth, SET can also taketh away. To destroy a variable, you merely set it equal to nothing. I give you the following:

```
SET DIRCMD=
```

This command is **SET**, a space, then a variable name (**DIRCMD** in this case), then an equal sign and . . . nothing! Press Enter to delete the DIRCMD variable.

- ✔ You can confirm that the variable is gone by typing the SET command by itself at the DOS prompt.

- ✔ Using SET to destroy a variable's contents also removes that variable from the environment. You need to re-create that variable with another SET command when it's needed again.

- ✔ You should use the PATH and PROMPT commands to set those variables (though you can use the SET command if you're feeling particularly nerdy about it). Refer to the section "Mysteries about the PATH and PROMPT variables" later in this chapter.

Environment Variables to Make You Loopy

DOS peers into the environment quite often. And I'm sad to report that most of the time it's sorely disappointed. Sure, there are times DOS actually finds something it can use in the environment. But most of the environment variables it could use go ignored. This is actually a happy thing for us — one of those rare occasions where ignoring the problem doesn't make it worse. However, there are a few environment variables worth noting.

TEMP: The most popular variable

The only environment variable you'll ever need to worry about setting up in AUTOEXEC.BAT is TEMP. That variable tells DOS where to store temporary files it may create.

I recommend setting the TEMP variable equal to a C:\TEMP subdirectory, such as the one discussed in Chapter 16. The following SET command does the job:

```
SET TEMP=C:\TEMP
```

First comes the **SET** command, a space, and then the **TEMP** variable. That's followed closely by an equal sign and then the place where DOS can store temporary files. In the preceding, that's the TEMP directory on drive C.

- ✔ You can set the TEMP variable at the DOS prompt, although most users stick that command in their AUTOEXEC.BAT files.

- ✔ You don't have to set TEMP equal to a TEMP directory. For example,

  ```
  SET TEMP=D:
  ```

  In the preceding, drive D is probably a RAM drive. Or how about this:

  ```
  SET TEMP=C:\MISC\JUNK
  ```

  In this, the temporary files directory is set equal to C:\MISC\JUNK.

- ✔ Windows also uses the TEMP variable to discover where it should stuff temporary files.

- ✔ If you specify a RAM drive as the location for your temporary files, make sure its big enough! About 500K is the minimum size I'd suggest for a temporary file RAM drive.

- ✔ If you don't specify the TEMP variable, DOS shoves its temporary files into the root directory.

> ✔ DOS creates temporary files when you use the pipe (|) and with some of DOS's filter commands. (Filters are discussed in Chapter 20.) The temporary files are usually quite small, named funkily, and quietly deleted by DOS when it's done with them. (Windows uses the TEMP directory to store all sorts of junk, some of which it may delete when it's done.)

Mysteries about the PATH and PROMPT variables

When you create a fancy prompt or set up a DOS search path, the PROMPT and PATH commands secretly place that information into DOS's environment. They do this automatically, without bothering with the SET command. For example,

```
PROMPT ($P)
```

The preceding PROMPT command sets DOS's command prompt to look something like this:

```
(C:\BATCH)
```

Nifty, no? The same command also places the following into DOS's environment:

```
PROMPT=($P)
```

The PATH command does the same thing with its list of subdirectories:

```
PATH C:\DOS;C:\WINDOWS
```

This PATH command places the following information into the environment:

```
PATH=C:\DOS;C:\WINDOWS
```

> ✔ Yes, you can use the SET command instead of the PATH or PROMPT commands. (In DOS 6, this is how you would set the search path or DOS prompt in CONFIG.SYS instead of AUTOEXEC.BAT.)
>
> ✔ The following two commands do the same thing in DOS:
>
> ```
> PROMPT ($P)
> SET PROMPT=($P)
> ```

Ditto for these two:

```
PATH C:\DOS;C:\WINDOWS
SET PATH=C:\DOS;C:\WINDOWS
```

Most people opt to use the PATH or PROMPT commands alone because the format is uncomplicated.

✔ The PROMPT command is covered in Chapter 3; the PATH command is covered in Chapter 22.

✔ The PATH command that deletes the search path (PATH ;) places the following item into the environment:

```
PATH=
```

This is just DOS's way of knowing it can't look too far for any programs to run.

Other variables you may see lurking about

Oh, I remember the good old days — back when DOS only had three environment variables: COMSPEC, PATH, and PROMPT. Them days are gone, gone, gone. DOS 5 added an army of new variables, and then DOS 6 added even more. Everything is listed in Table 19-1 for your referencing pleasures.

Table 19-1	DOS's Full Armada of Environment Variables
Variable Name	**What It Represents**
APPEND	The APPEND command's search path
COMSPEC	COMMAND.COM's location on disk
CONFIG	The configuration selected from multiple configuration CONFIG.SYS file
COPYCMD	Whether or not COPY, MOVE, or XCOPY overwrites files already on disk
DIRCMD	Options for the DIR command
DOSSHELL	The location of the DOS Shell program's DOSSHELL.INI file
MSDOSDATA	The location of MSBackup and MSAV's configuration files
PATH	DOS's search path (a list of subdirectories)
PROMPT	The commands to set up the DOS prompt
TEMP	A disk drive/directory for storing DOS and Windows temporary files

✔ No one in his right mind needs to use all these variables.

✔ Typically, you set the PATH and PROMPT variables by using the PATH and PROMPT commands. See Chapter 3 for information on the PROMPT command; Chapter 22 covers the PATH command.

✔ Of course, this list does not include any variables used by any third-party programs.

✔ The DIRCMD variable is covered in Chapter 12 on the DIR command.

✔ The COPYCMD variable is only available with MS-DOS version 6.2.

✔ I've also seen the WINDIR variable, which is set by Windows when a DOS program runs. WINDIR usually contains the location of the Windows main subdirectory on disk.

✔ Computer Book Writer's Guild Book of Rules, Section 31, Subsection 9, Paragraph 1a: "All book authors shall make liberal use of tables to display information. Advanced and intermediate-level books shall further explain the table in a diatribe consuming no less than three (3) typewritten pages. Beginner-level books and books aimed at humans need not bother with such nonsense."

Eye-crossing stuff on when environment variables crop up in batch files

Batch files can use environment variables, but only when they're hugged by percent signs. For example,

```
ECHO %PATH%
```

This command tells DOS to display the contents of the PATH variable. On either side of the variable name are percent signs. When the batch file runs, DOS stumbles over the percent signs and translates the environment variable from the ugly-looking %PATH% something into that variable's contents:

```
ECHO C:\DOS;C:\WINDOWS
```

In the preceding, the %PATH% variable has been expanded in the batch file to equal the variable's contents. The contents will be displayed by the ECHO command.

Environment variables also crop up with the strange IF command:

```
IF "%TEMP%"=="C:\TEMP" ECHO Thank
   you for following orders
```

The preceding IF command compares the contents of the TEMP variable with C:\TEMP. If they're equal, then the message is displayed. (This is complex batch file programming stuff; don't let it spin your head like an emetic Linda Blair.)

Chapter 20

Being Clever with I/O Redirection and Filters

*T*iny things are secretive and cryptic. James Bond's coolest gadgets (aside from his cars) were the tiny ones: the tie clip that injected a knock-out drug; the swizzle-stick blow gun; the combination nail clipper/radio communicator/ homing beacon/fax machine; the martini olive spy camera; and the disarming glance. The same rule holds true with DOS and its tiniest gadgets.

The most cryptic aspect of DOS is perhaps the general topic of I/O redirection. It's not that understanding this stuff is difficult. It's that the symbols used to accomplish the feat are mysterious: the greater-than (>), less-than (<), and enigmatic pipe (|) characters. These are all relatively easy to handle, providing you skim through the sections in this chapter (and take a few kind words of advice from agent Q).

The whole topic of I/O, devices, redirection, pipes, and filters leans a bit to the advanced side of the technometer. If the subject makes you queasy, feel free to skip this chapter. (I'm not trying to force anyone into becoming a computer nerd.)

I/O! I/O! It's Off to Work We Go

I/O is computer slang for input and output, which is really what computers are all about: You type something and that's input. What the computer displays is output. I could make an analogy here to a baby, but the conventions of polite behavior prevent it (especially the output part).

With DOS, input and output aren't really tied down to the keyboard and screen. For example, in addition to displaying information on the screen, DOS can also send stuff to the printer or, if you're warm to the idea, send output to a file on disk. This is called *redirecting output,* and it is the subject of a major hunk of this chapter.

- ✔ I/O is pronounced "I owe."

- ✔ Input is information that goes into the computer. Output is the stuff the computer produces.

- ✔ Normally, DOS expects input from the keyboard. Output goes to the screen.

- ✔ What's unique about DOS's input and output is that it's not tied down to any particular part — or *device* — attached to the computer. DOS can get its input from a number of places other than the keyboard and can send its output to places other than the screen.

- ✔ The good part of all this is that you control where the input comes from and where the output goes. The bad part is that you need to know about DOS's device names and some cryptic input/output symbols to carry out the job.

- ✔ You may have heard of the nerd acronym *GIGO.* It stands for *Garbage In, Garbage Out.* What it means is that when given nonsense, the computer produces nonsense. In other words, the computer isn't smart by itself — you can't shove a lump of coal into a disk drive and expect the PC to spit out a diamond.

Just your standard I/O

DOS thirsts for input and it provokes an urge to output. But whence cometh thine input? Why, from the standard input device, the keyboard. Output? It goes churning out the standard output device, the screen.

- ✔ The *standard input device* is the keyboard. DOS naturally expects all its input to come from the keyboard unless told otherwise.

- ✔ The *standard output device* is the screen. DOS likes to send its output to the screen unless told otherwise.

- ✔ Together, the screen and keyboard are what DOS calls the *console device*, or CON for short. (Refer to the next section for more on the console.)

- ✔ A *device* is something DOS can either receive input from or send output to. DOS has a lot of devices it can use for I/O, some of which are listed in Table 20-1.

- ✔ On a human, the standard input device would probably be the eyeballs or maybe some combination of eyeballs and ears. The standard output device is the mouth (no doubt about that).

What the heck is the console?

The console, or CON, is DOS's standard I/O device. It's made up of the keyboard and screen. The keyboard is the standard input, and the screen is the standard output. Together, they make beautiful I/O.

- ✔ Yeah, even though the screen and keyboard could be considered *two* devices, DOS thinks of them as one console, which is called the CON device.

- ✔ They probably call it the *console* because that's what computers were called in the prehistoric days. Actually, the *computer* was a bunch of refrigerator-sized boxes sitting in another room or another building. You sat down at a console — a screen and keyboard — and chatted with the computer via a wire or network hose.

- ✔ Another term for console is *terminal*. Yeah, I like console better too.

- ✔ CON is actually a prefix that means *against*. It's the opposite of the PRO prefix that means *in favor of*. (So, does that mean that *congress* is the opposite of *progress*?)

DOS's Daffy Devices (or Other I's and O's for Those Who Wants to Knows)

Input and output wouldn't be an issue if they were limited to the keyboard and screen. Instead, DOS has a gaggle of devices it can use as alternatives to the screen and keyboard for input and output. These are all conveniently listed in Table 20-1.

Table 20-1	The Short List of Devices		
Device Name	*What It Is*	*Can It I?*	*Can It O?*
AUX	First serial port	Yes	Yes
CON	Screen and keyboard	Yes	Yes
PRN	Printer	No	Yes
NUL	Nothing!	Yes	Yes
A: – Z:	Disk drives	Oh yes	Oh yes

- ✔ The CON device used for input is the keyboard. This is also known as the *standard input* device. That means DOS naturally looks for input from the keyboard, or CON device.

- ✔ The CON device used for output is the screen, which is known as the *standard output* device. DOS naturally sends its output to the screen.

- ✔ The AUX device is also called the standard auxiliary device. It's pronounced "ox." Normally, AUX is your PC's first serial port (also called the *com port* or COM1). Using AUX with I/O redirection is kind of complex and not covered in this book.

- ✔ The PRN device is also called the standard printer device. It's pronounced "prin," although many people say "printer." If you have more than one printer on your PC, PRN is the first printer (also known as LPT1).

- ✔ Though PRN, AUX, and NUL are called standard devices, they're not as big on the whoop-dee-doo factor as the CON device.

- ✔ The AUX, CON, and PRN devices are called DOS's *character devices*. The disk drive devices are called *block devices*. I bring this up out of my sheer lust for triviality.

- ✔ DOS has more devices than those listed in Table 20-1. Oh, there are the LPT1, LPT2, and LPT3 devices and then COM1, COM2, COM3, and COM4. The items listed in Table 20-1 will get you by for now. Buy a serious and frowning computer book if you want to know more about the others.

Daffy Devices and That Crazy COPY Command

The COPY command does more than just copy files: It actually copies information from one DOS device to another. Normally, that information is stored in a file, and the file lives on a disk-drive device. But that doesn't always need to be the case.

In an I/O kinda way, the COPY command works like this:

```
C:\>COPY input output
```

The COPY command reads input from a device and tosses it up as output to another device. So you can substitute just about any of DOS's input devices for the *input* in the preceding command; same for *output* and DOS's output devices. (Refer to Table 20-1 for a list of input and output devices.)

✔ You must copy from an input device to an output device.

✔ A common variation of this is the COPY CON "command," which some DOS gurus use to quickly create text files. Refer to Chapter 13 for more information on COPY CON.

✔ Other variations — some of them useful, even — are listed in the sections that follow.

Printing a file with the COPY command

The following COPY command copies a file from DOS's disk device (drive C) to the printer device (PRN). Make sure your printer is on and ready to print before typing this command:

```
C:\>COPY AUTOEXEC.BAT PRN
```

That's **COPY**, a space, the name of the file you want to print, and then the destination device, the printer or **PRN**.

To see something you've printed on your laser printer, press its *Eject* or *Form feed* button.

DOS's typewriter

The following command is often called DOS's typewriter:

```
C:\>COPY CON PRN
```

That's the **COPY** command, a space, the **CON** device, another space, and the **PRN** device. This command tells DOS to copy information from the console (the keyboard) to the printer.

After you type the command and press Enter, DOS sits and waits for you to type. Type anything:

```
It was a dark and stormy night.
```

Use the Backspace key to erase and press Enter at the end of each line. (Your printer may not print when you press Enter. That's okay.)

After you type the last line, press Ctrl-Z — that is, press and hold down the Ctrl key and press the letter Z. This produces the ^Z character thing on the screen. That's the end-of-file marker and it tells DOS and the COPY command that you're done typing. Press Enter. Your magnificent work will appear on your printer.

Laser printers may not print anything until you've typed a whole page. To see part of a page, press the printer's *Eject* or *Form feed* button.

Copying a file to the console

Any file on disk can be copied to the CON device:

```
C:\>COPY SCAM CON
```

On normal observation, this looks like a COPY duplicating command. But no: The COPY command copies the file named SCAM to the CON device, which in this case is the screen.

The following command produces the same output:

```
C:\>TYPE SCAM
```

✔ Normally, the TYPE command is used to display a file on the screen.

✔ Files are about the only thing you'll copy to the console device. You cannot do a COPY PRN CON command because the printer is not an input device (see Table 20-1).

Redirecting Output (or Let's Play Mailman)

Normally, DOS sends its output to the screen — the standard output device. Text merrily marches there, happy to know that it will soon be appreciated by an eager user. (A-hem.) However, that doesn't always have to be the case.

By using *output redirection*, you can send DOS's output to any of its output-friendly devices: the printer, the mysterious NUL device, or to a file on disk. This all happens using that li'l greater-than symbol (>).

- ✔ The output redirection symbol is > (the greater-than character).
- ✔ Normally, DOS sends all its output to the screen, which is the output half of its console device (see earlier Table 20-1).
- ✔ Output redirection to disk always creates text files. Yes, this is one of those rare instances when text files have a big role to play. Refer to Chapter 11 for more information on text files.

You can output only to one of DOS's output-happy devices (see Table 20-1) or to a file on disk.

Sending things that go to the screen somewhere else

To get comfy with the idea of redirected output, you must accept the notion that DOS automatically sends information to the screen. It does this every time a command runs and displays something. It's *standard output*. But by using the > output redirection symbol, you can tell DOS to send its output to another place, either to another device or a file on disk. It works like this:

THE > POLICEMAN: Wait up! Where do you think *you're* going?

INNOCENT TEXT: Why, I'm going to the screen. That's where I always go.

THE > POLICEMAN: Not today. I'm sending you off to the PRN device. Move along.

INNOCENT TEXT: Oh, bother.

To make the text go somewhere other than the screen, you follow the DOS command with the > output redirection symbol and then with a device name or filename.

Type in the following DOS command:

```
C:\>ECHO This is a fine way to create a file
```

Diligently, DOS displays your message on the screen using the ECHO command (covered in Chapter 18).

Now try this variation:

```
C:\>ECHO This is a fine way to create a file > AFILE
```

Just press the F3 key, a space, the greater-than symbol, another space, and then type **AFILE**. Press Enter.

This time, DOS doesn't display anything. Instead, the output that would normally have gone to the screen was redirected to a file named AFILE on disk. (Use the TYPE AFILE command to display your file. Cool.)

✔ You can redirect output to any DOS device that's output-happy (which means all of them) or to a filename on disk.

✔ When you redirect output to a file, DOS creates that file on disk. If the file already exists, it's overwritten. There is no warning, not even with "passenger-side airbag" MS-DOS 6.2.

✔ You can use > PRN after any DOS command to print that command's output. However, if you just want to print what DOS displays on the screen, then use the Ctrl-P trick (as discussed in Chapter 2).

✔ The "eject a page" command uses output redirection:

```
C:\>ECHO ^L > PRN
```

The preceding ECHO command sends the Ctrl-L character out to the PRN device, the printer. On most printers, Ctrl-L is a command that means *eject a page right now!* Type **ECHO**, a space, Ctrl-L (don't type ^ and then L), another space, greater-than, a space, and then **PRN**.

✔ Although you can redirect the output of DOS commands, few of your programs care about it. Most applications manipulate your computer's hardware directly, bypassing DOS and its devices. The moral of the story is *Don't expect to redirect WordPerfect's output and have it work.*

You cannot redirect the output of a batch file . . . unless you use the following format:

```
C:\>COMMAND /C UGLY.BAT > PRN
```

The batch file in question is UGLY.BAT, and its output is redirected to the printer, the PRN device. This works with any batch file: Just type **COMMAND**, a space, slash, C, and another space before the batch file name. You can then redirect the batch file's output as you would any other DOS command.

✔ My car only has a passenger-side airbag when I drive my mother-in-law around. Ba-Boom!

Printing a text file (Oh, let me count the ways...)

DOS has more ways to print a text file than you can believe. Here they are.

You can use the COPY command to copy the text file to the PRN device:

```
C:\>COPY CONFIG.SYS PRN
```

You can use the TYPE command and redirect its output to the PRN device:

```
C:\>TYPE XMASLIST.TXT > PRN
```

You can use the DOS Editor to print the file. (Load the file into the Editor and then select Print from the File menu.)

> ✔ Information on using the COPY command to copy a file to the PRN device is covered earlier in this chapter. See the section "Printing a file with the COPY command."

> ✔ Redirecting output to the printer is covered in "Sending things that go to the screen somewhere else," earlier in this chapter.

Redirecting output to the NUL device

DOS's NUL device is a strange little booger. It toils not, neither does it spin. When you output to the NUL device, the output goes nowhere. Input from the NUL device is just about as filling: It's nothing.

So what good is it? Because it swallows up output, batch file programmers use the NUL device with output redirection to "silently" run DOS commands that would otherwise display bothersome information on the screen. For example,

```
C:\>COPY *.* A: > NUL
```

The preceding COPY command would display the names of each file it copied as it copied and then the final Zillion file(s) copied message. It *would* do that were it not for the output's being redirected to the NUL device. Because of that > NUL thing there, the command has no output.

> ✔ NUL is pronounced "null," which rhymes with *dull* (and *numskull,* sort of).

> ✔ The > NUL must be the last item on each line you want to suppress.

▶ Refer to Chapter 17 for additional information on batch files.

▶ Although it's true that the ECHO OFF command stops the batch file from displaying commands, only by redirecting output to the NUL device can you make them totally shut up.

Appending with the >> Thing

When you want to redirect output to a file without destroying that file, you need the double-greater-than symbol, >>. This symbol tells DOS to redirect *and append* its output to a file on disk instead of wiping it out. This is so much nicer than the > thing.

For an example, you can use the ECHO command:

```
C:\>ECHO And then everyone died > GAN.TXT
```

The preceding command sends its output to a file named GAN.TXT (*GAN* being the *Great American Novel*). The file is created by output redirection.

Now try this command:

```
C:\>ECHO Except Bud, who survived >> GAN.TXT
```

The preceding command sends its output to the *end* of the file named GAN.TXT. The file isn't overwritten with new text. Instead, the text is stuck to the end of the first file. This happens because two greater-thans were used, producing output redirection with append.

After the final command, the GAN.TXT file contains the following text:

```
And then everyone died
Except Bud, who survived
```

There. You're all set up for the sequel.

▶ *Append* means to add to the end of something. For example: "Cindy eats lots of candy, which her body then appends to her butt."

▶ The append >> thing is used only when redirecting output to a file. There is no point, really, in appending to the printer or CON device.

 ✔ If someone wanted to see a copy of your CONFIG.SYS and AUTOEXEC.BAT files, you could send these to them in one file:

```
C:\>TYPE CONFIG.SYS > BOTH.TXT
C:\>TYPE AUTOEXEC.BAT >> BOTH.TXT
```

The first command sticks CONFIG.SYS into a file named BOTH.TXT. The second command appends AUTOEXEC.BAT to that file.

 ✔ There is no input-redirection-append command, no <<. Come to think of it, I wouldn't know why one was needed either.

Redirecting Input (Just Too Darn Weird to Deal With)

Redirecting DOS's output is fun and potentially profitable. The little > doodoodle is a busy guy. But redirecting input is strange and must be treated with care. This is because output can be spilled just about anywhere. But input is how you talk to the computer. If you mess up input redirection, then the computer sits around, deaf as a post, and *nothing* you type at the keyboard is heard.

 ✔ The input redirection symbol is the less-than character (<).

 ✔ DOS normally expects input to come from the keyboard, which it calls the standard input device.

 ✔ By using the < symbol, you can tell DOS to get its input from another device or a file on disk.

 ✔ A list of DOS devices is provided in Table 20-1. Only those devices that are input-happy can be used with input redirection.

A scary explanation of why input redirection is dangerous

Your control over DOS depends on the keyboard. When you redirect input, you're telling DOS to ignore the keyboard. This is similar to saying the following to a bus driver: "Okay, just ignore that red light up there and keep your eyes on this photo of Fabio."

The problem with input redirection is that you must be sure whatever is supplying input will be smart enough to eventually let the keyboard have control again. For example,

```
C:\>FORMAT < FDATA
```

The preceding FORMAT command uses the text in the file FDATA for standard input instead of the keyboard. If so, then the FDATA file should contain all the keystrokes required by the FORMAT command. If that file is missing something, the screen says

```
Format another (Y/N)?
```

and DOS waits an eternity for either a Y or N to come from the FDATA file.

- ✔ If you ever do mess with input redirection and suddenly notice that the computer is going nowhere, you must reset. Pressing Ctrl-C doesn't work because DOS is ignoring the keyboard. Only pressing Ctrl-Alt-Delete or whacking the reset button gives you control again.

- ✔ Input redirection is popular with the MORE command, as described in the next section.

- ✔ Occasionally, you may see input redirection used in books or magazines. It may appear in a batch file that must automatically type commands for DOS's DEBUG program. For example,

  ```
  C:\>DEBUG < ASK.DAT
  ```

  The text in the preceding file ASK.DAT is being fed into DOS's DEBUG program. Hopefully, ASK.DAT contains the command to quit DEBUG. If not, DOS waits and waits for that command, ignoring the keyboard the entire time.

The most common use for input redirection (not scary)

A nifty way to view a text file on disk is to use the MORE filter (discussed later in this chapter). The first format for this command is as follows:

```
C:\>TYPE ENDLESS.TXT | MORE
```

Here, the MORE filter is used with DOS's pipe character (the whys and hows of this are covered in the next section — basically, output from the TYPE ENDLESS.TXT command is fed into the MORE filter using the pipe).

A more popular command that does exactly the same thing is

```
C:\>MORE < ENDLESS.TXT
```

In this case, the MORE filter is used like a DOS program. It receives input from the ENDLESS.TXT text file on disk. This works because the text file tells DOS "Okay, I'm done now," and control returns to the keyboard.

> ✔ Input redirection also works with the MORE filter because it pays attention to the keyboard when it displays its – *More* – prompt. It stops when it sees a Ctrl-C.
>
> ✔ A filter is a special type of DOS program you can read about in just a few pages.

Plumbing Output with the Pipe

The most cryptic of DOS's tiny I/O commands is the *pipe,* which is represented by the | character. Some folks call it a *vertical bar*, but I personally think that's an elevator that serves drinks. No, call it a pipe because what it does is more like plumbing anyhow.

What the pipe does is take the output of a DOS command and force that output into a second DOS command. So the pipe takes output and converts it to input. Strange, but it is useful.

> ✔ The pipe usually appears between two DOS commands. The first command must produce output. That output is then squirted into the second command as input. Refer to the following section for a real-live demonstration.
>
> ✔ Fortunately, few DOS commands rely on the pipe.
>
> ✔ Is it called the pipe? Is it a vertical bar? Is it a lowercase I? Whatever, this book calls it a pipe — as in "Stick that in your | and smoke it."

A slow, careful demonstration of how the pipe works

To see how the pipe works, you need a DOS command that expects input and one that produces output. The following ECHO command is used to display a blank line:

```
C:\>ECHO.
```

Type **ECHO** and then a period. There is no space between the *O* and the period. Press Enter to see the infamous blank line. (Impressive, no?)

The TIME command displays text but also requires input. Type the following:

```
C:\>TIME
```

Type **TIME** and press Enter. DOS displays the current time and then asks for the a new time:

```
Current time is  9:44:27.45p
Enter new time:
```

I'll take for granted that what you see displayed on your screen is the proper time. Press Enter. (Oh, you can type in a new time if you feel like it.)

And now a quick mental review:

- ✔ The ECHO. command produces standard output, sending a blank line to the screen.
- ✔ The TIME command also uses standard output but waits for standard input.

The idea behind the pipe is to send ECHO's output to the TIME command as input; ECHO will provide TIME's input.

You might innocently assume the following would work:

```
C:\>TIME < ECHO.
```

This looks like it would work — the ECHO command would supply standard input for the TIME command. Alas, it just ain't so. When DOS sees the preceding command, it looks for a file on disk named ECHO to provide standard input to the TIME command. What you really need is the pipe.

Type in the following command:

```
C:\>ECHO. | TIME
```

That's **ECHO** and a period, then a space, the pipe, another space, and then the **TIME** command. Mull this over before pressing the Enter key: ECHO. produces output which is then *piped* over to the TIME command as input. Press Enter.

```
Current time is  9:48:38.57p
Enter new time:
```

The time is displayed, but there's no waiting at the Enter new time prompt. Thanks to the pipe, the ECHO. command pressed Enter there for you.

🖙 Wow! Thank goodness that's over.

🖙 Please refer to "Just your standard I/O" earlier in this chapter for an explanation of DOS's standard input and output.

Using the pipe command with filters

Most often, the pipe thingy is used with DOS's filters. This is why the filters were made: so that they could modify the output of a DOS command. The only way to get a command's output into the filter is with the pipe. Here's an example:

```
C:\>DIR | SORT
```

In the preceding, the DIR command sends its output through the SORT filter. The SORT filter massages the output (okay, sorts it alphabetically) and then displays the result — a sorted directory listing. That's what the pipe lives and breathes for. Filters are covered right next.

Filters to Clean Out Your PC's Brain

A filter is a special type of DOS program. What it does is modify the output of a DOS command — massage it, give it a trim, press its trousers. That sounds like fun, and it would be useful perhaps to Mr. Spock or some closet-dwelling UNIX nerd. For the rest of us, though, filters are just a curious aspect of DOS, one we really don't need to mess with.

🖙 Filters modify output from a DOS command, using the pipe (|).

🖙 DOS comes with three filters: FIND, MORE, and SORT. These are covered in the sections that follow.

🖙 Smokers will appreciate DOS's CHARCOAL filter. (Yes, this is a joke.)

🖙 Information on using the pipe is covered in the section "Plumbing Output with the Pipe," earlier in this chapter.

🖙 Actually, filters only modify standard input and produce standard output. However, you can use the pipe to squirt a command's standard output into standard input for a filter. *Sigh.* I know this is obtuse, but so is the entire subject for the rest of this chapter.

MORE! MORE! MORE filter!

The MORE filter is used to display a – More – prompt at the bottom of the screen and wait for a key to be pressed. It does this after a full screen of text has been displayed. For example,

```
C:\>TYPE SPEECH | MORE
```

The preceding TYPE command displays a file, SPEECH. But that output is piped into the MORE filter. MORE displays the text as well, but at every screen, it pauses and displays the – More – prompt and waits for a key to be pressed.

- The MORE filter can be used after any DOS command and a pipe:

  ```
  C:\>MEM /C | MORE
  ```

  Here, the MORE filter pauses the long output of the MEM /C command, allowing you time to see what it says.

- In a way, you can say that the MORE filter is used to "slow down" quickly displayed DOS commands.

- The MORE filter is often used with input redirection to display a file a screen at a time:

  ```
  C:\>MORE < SPEECH
  ```

  This works because the MORE filter works with standard input and output. In the preceding command, the input is supplied from the SPEECH file. When a pipe is used, input comes from a DOS command's output.

Sorting out the SORT filter

The SORT filter has all sorts [sic] of options and doodads for sorting information. You can sort alphabetically, forwards, and backwards (and in Chinese you can actually sort sidewise and diagonally). When used by itself, the SORT filter sorts information alphabetically:

```
C:\>TYPE WORDS.TXT | SORT
```

The preceding TYPE command displays the file WORDS.TXT. That output is then sent to the SORT filter, which displays a sorted result.

```
C:\>TYPE WORDS.TXT | SORT > WORDLIST.TXT
```

The preceding command does the same thing, but now the sorted output is sent to a file on disk, WORDLIST.TXT. That file will contain the same information as WORDS.TXT, but it will be alphabetically sorted.

- ✔ I have no disrespect for the Chinese language, which, as any good University Boy can tell you, cannot be alphabetically sorted anyhow.
- ✔ As a trivial point, when Wally Wang and I were first working on the *Illustrated Computer Dictionary For Dummies*, we created a list of words in a text file named WORDS.TXT. I typed the second command previous to create our final word list file, which contained all the definitions included in the final book.
- ✔ Wally Wang is Chinese.
- ✔ Refer to the DOS manual or the on-line HELP command for more information about the SORT command. Prepare to be overwhelmed.

Because a filter works with standard input, try the following command:

```
C:\>SORT
```

Just type **SORT** at the DOS prompt and press Enter. DOS is waiting for you to type a "file" to sort. Using your keyboard, type in the following items:

```
VODKA
GIN
WHISKEY
SCOTCH
```

Press Ctrl-Z and then press Enter to end the "file." Having its standard input, the SORT filter then displays the sorted result on the screen (the standard output).

Finding with the almost useful FIND filter

The FIND filter is probably the most useless of DOS's filters. Actually, some new users assume that it's a file-finding command. Surprise! It's not. What the FIND filter does is locate text in a text file or in a DOS command's output. It's involved and complex, and I really don't feel like showing an example, but I will.

```
C:\>TYPE NAUGHTY.TXT | FIND "UNDIES"
```

The preceding TYPE command displays the text file NAUGHTY.TXT. The output is piped into the FIND filter, which is told to look for the word *UNDIES*. If that word is found, the FIND command displays that line of text from the NAUGHTY.TXT file. For example,

```
SHE WAS SHOCKED TO FIND UNCLE CEDRIC WEARING HER UNDIES."
```

✔ The FIND command can actually find text in files without using the pipe. You only really need the pipe when searching for text in a DOS command's output.

✔ Yes, the full boring details on the FIND command — should you want them — can be found in your DOS manual or by typing **HELP FIND** at the DOS prompt.

✔ Refer to Chapter 11 for a nifty way to find lost files.

"Who's the joker who put the BBDBAMEL and BBDBAMFB files in my directory?"

To make its filters work, DOS sometimes creates temporary files on disk. These files can have bizarre names, like BBDBAMEL and BBDBAMFB. They'll drive you nuts if you don't know why they were created or what they do.

✔ The temporary files may not be named exactly BBDBAMEL or BBDBAMFB, but that's close enough.

✔ DOS's temporary files usually have a size of zero (0) bytes. In fact, you usually see them when you run the DIR command through the SORT filter (see earlier in this chapter).

✔ Refer to Chapter 19 for information on creating the TEMP environment variable. That tells DOS where to put any temporary files it creates.

Chapter 21

The Colorful and Lively World of ANSI

In This Chapter

▶ Using ANSI commands at the DOS prompt
▶ Making colors appear on-screen
▶ Spicing up your batch files
▶ Messing with the keyboard's mind

Since Version 2, DOS has come with a device driver called ANSI.SYS. Most DOS users installed it and never knew what it did; they never took advantage of ANSI.SYS. Yes, ANSI.SYS was sad and lonely. No one realized how ANSI.SYS can make the DOS prompt appear in color or how it can spruce up your batch files like Airwick spray can make your moldy bathroom smell like a pine forest. Yeah, ANSI.SYS can do amazing things, so I hope you'll find the examples in this chapter exciting, worthwhile, and of added value to the book.

✔ The ANSI.SYS driver gives you more control over your keyboard and screen by using ANSI commands, which can be included in a text file, batch file, or used with the PROMPT command.

✔ ANSI.SYS is the name of a device driver; ANSI refers to the commands that splash color on-screen, control the cursor, and mess with the keyboard's mind. The commands themselves are known as *escape sequences*.

✔ Before you can use ANSI.SYS, it must be installed in your PC's CONFIG.SYS file. This task is covered at the end of Chapter 7, in the section, "Adding a device driver to CONFIG.SYS (an Example to Follow)."

✔ This book doesn't claim to tell you *everything* about DOS. No, that's the topic of drier, thicker, and pricier books on DOS. So, although I describe a few of the ANSI commands in this chapter, you'll have to look elsewhere for the complete list. If you have DOS 6, you can type **HELP ANSI.SYS** at the DOS prompt. For DOS 5 and earlier versions, refer to the DOS manual.

How ANSI.SYS Works (Briefly)

The ANSI.SYS device driver subtly modifies the way DOS deals with the screen and keyboard. DOS waits for you to enter an ANSI command (an escape sequence) on-screen, and the ANSI.SYS driver does whatever the command tells it to do.

All ANSI commands have the following format (more or less):

```
←[n;nL
```

This command line is officially known as the *ANSI Escape Sequence*. First comes the Escape character, which is shown in the preceding as a left-pointing arrow (←). That's followed by a left bracket. This is how all ANSI commands start: ←[. Then come numbers, sometimes with a semicolon (;) between them, and then a letter of the alphabet ends the whole thing. Ugly. Obtuse. Hey, it's ANSI.

✔ Before you can use ANSI.SYS, it must be installed in your PC's CONFIG.SYS file. This is covered at the end of Chapter 7, see the section "Adding a device driver to CONFIG.SYS (an Example to Follow)."

✔ Yes, it *is* weird: ANSI commands must be *displayed* on-screen for them to work. You cannot type an ANSI command at the DOS prompt.

✔ ANSI commands are used as part of the PROMPT command, in batch files by using the ECHO command, and in text files displayed on-screen.

✔ The Escape character appears as a left-pointing arrow (←) in this chapter. Refer to the sidebar, "The exasperating Escape key and Escape character," for information on how you can produce that character at the DOS prompt in a text file.

✔ ANSI.SYS does not affect your applications. It only modifies text that DOS displays or affects the keyboard for DOS programs. Anything else, forget it!

✔ ANSI is an acronym for the American National Standards Institute. They sit around and dream up standards for computers, which the computer industry then promptly ignores.

ANSI, Live at the DOS Prompt

The easiest way to mess with ANSI is by using the PROMPT command. This ease is thanks to the $E dollar-sign thing, which lets you stick the all-important Escape character into a PROMPT command.

By sticking ANSI commands into the DOS prompt, you can make a fancy DOS prompt, including color and other magic. The following sections dwell on changing the prompt using ANSI commands.

 ✔ The full thrust of the PROMPT command is covered in Chapter 3.

 ✔ Who would have thought the PROMPT command could have "full thrust"?

Using the $E thing in a PROMPT command

To include an ANSI command inside a DOS prompt, you need to use the ANSI Escape Sequence, which is introduced in the section "How ANSI.SYS Works (Briefly)" earlier in this chapter. Here it is in case you don't want to flip back a page:

```
←[n;nL
```

In the PROMPT command, the $E thing is used to represent the Escape character (← in the preceeding). Here is how the ANSI Escape Sequence looks in a PROMPT command:

```
$E[n;nL
```

TIP

The exasperating Escape key and Escape character

All ANSI commands start with the Escape character, which this book shows as a left-pointing arrow, ←. That's the same character that would be produced by pressing the Esc key on your keyboard. Unfortunately, it doesn't work that way.

At the DOS prompt, pressing the Esc key erases the command line and lets you start over. In text editors, pressing Esc cancels a command or doesn't do anything. So the idea is to somehow get the Escape character into an ANSI command without angering any programs.

One solution is to use the PROMPT command. One of the PROMPT command's dollar-sign thingies is $E, which represents the Escape character. That makes it easy to stick ANSI commands in the DOS prompt. (Refer to Chapter 3 for more information on the prompt; see Table 3-1 for the $E thing.)

The only other solution is to use a text editor that allows you to type in special characters such as Escape. The DOS Editor lets you do this in a secret fashion, as will other good text editors. First you must press Ctrl-P, which is the *prefix* command. After you press Ctrl-P, the Editor closes its eyes and inserts the next character you type while ignoring what that key does in real life. If you press Escape, you'll insert the very same Esc character into your text, which appears as a left-pointing arrow (←) on-screen.

To show how this works, type the following PROMPT command. This changes the DOS prompt by making it bright white on a blue background:

```
C:\>PROMPT $E[1;37;44m$P$G
```

Type **PROMPT**, a space, the **$E** thing, a left bracket, the number **1**, a semicolon, the number **37**, another semicolon, the number **44**, and a lowercase **m**. Next come **$P** and **$G**, which are two prompt command things you can look up in Chapter 3 if you're curious. Press Enter, and the next prompt is in color.

✔ Type the CLS command to clear the screen and change the entire screen to bright white on blue text.

✔ The PROMPT command really has two parts. First comes the ANSI command to set the color:

```
←[1;37;44m
```

Then come the commands to set the prompt to the current directory ($P) plus a greater-than sign ($G).

Here are the details on these ANSI commands and codes:

←[	The ANSI Escape Sequence that tells DOS "Here's an ANSI command!"
1	Displays text as **bold.**
;	Separates numbers.
37	Sets the foreground color to white.
;	Separates numbers.
44	Sets the background color to blue
m	Tells ANSI that the command changes colors on the screen.

✔ If you like the color but prefer another type of prompt, just replace the PG part of the prompt command with your own favorite variation.

✔ If you'd prefer another color, see the following section.

✔ If your prompt looks like this,

```
←[1;37;44mC:\DOS>
```

then you probably don't have the ANSI.SYS device driver installed in your PC's CONFIG.SYS file. Refer to the end of Chapter 7 for how it's done.

✔ If your prompt looks like this (or similar):

```
:\>
```

then you probably mistyped the ANSI command. Re-read the preceeding instructions. Remember that there must be a lowercase *m* after the command.

Making colorful prompts

Adding color to the DOS prompt is one of ANSI's favorite tricks. The following are some sample PROMPT commands you can type to change the screen's colors.

This prompt sets the screen colors to bright yellow on red:

```
C:\>PROMPT $E[1;33;41m$P$G
```

Enter this PROMPT command to see a cool light-green-on-blue background:

```
C:\>PROMPT $E[32;46m$P$G
```

The following prompt produces annoying, blinking red text:

```
C:\>PROMPT $E[5;31;40m$P$G
```

Finally, this PROMPT command returns the screen to normal:

```
C:\>PROMPT $E[0m$P$G
```

- Type **CLS** to clear the screen and rid yourself of blinking red text.

- Follow the lowercase *m* with the dollar-sign commands you prefer to create your own DOS prompt. This section uses the standard PG things.

- The format for the ANSI color command goes like this:

```
C:\>PROMPT $E[code;code;codem$P$G
```

The ANSI Escape Sequence for setting the screen colors starts with the ←[and ends with a lowercase *m*. Between are various *code* numbers that tell DOS how to paint the screen. More than one code number can be used, but stick a semicolon between them.

- Tables 21-1 and 21-2 list the various code values and how they change colors on-screen.

- The ANSI character attribute code for underline text (Code 4 in Table 21-2) works only on monochrome monitors. This means about 95 percent of us will never see it.

Table 21-1			**ANSI Color Values**
Code	*Foreground Color*	*Code*	*Background Color*
30	Black	40	Black
31	Red	41	Red
32	Green	42	Green
33	Yellow	43	Yellow
34	Blue	44	Blue
35	Magenta	45	Magenta
36	Cyan	46	Cyan
37	White	47	White

Table 21-2	**ANSI Character Attribute Values**
Code	*Effect*
0	Back to normal!
1	Bold text
4	Underline text
5	Annoying blinking text
7	Reverse video text
8	Invisible text

Big and disastrous prompts (optional reading)

ANSI commands aren't all about color. They can also move the cursor to various points on-screen and erase parts of the screen. DOS gurus and twisted nerd types use these variations to create gargantuan and ugly DOS prompts. Bear with me through the following examples.

The following prompt displays the greater-than symbol for input, hops up to the top row on-screen to display the current directory, only to hop back down to the greater-than symbol and wait for input. Looks cool. Is complex:

```
C:\>PROMPT $G$E[s$E[1;1H$P$E[u
```

First, type **PROMPT** and a space. Then type the following tidbits as outlined below:

$G	PROMPT command displays the greater-than symbol.
$E[s	ANSI command "saves" the cursor's position.
$E[1;1H	ANSI command moves the cursor to the first row and first column (1;1) on-screen.
$P	PROMPT command displays the current directory.
$E[u	ANSI command restores the cursor's position (moves the cursor back to where $E[s saved it). Yoikles! This is complex. Looks ugly, too. But it creates a funky prompt.

Press Enter after double-checking everything. (Be sure that you type these commands exactly as shown, using the same lowercase and uppercase letters. These commands are case sensitive.) Examine the resulting prompt. Type a few DOS commands to get a feel for how it works.

The following PROMPT command is another variation on this complex DOS prompt. It uses *even more* ANSI commands. (Type this command all on one line.)

```
PROMPT $G$E[s$E[1;1H$E[7m$E[K$P  $D @ $T$H$H$H$H$H$H $V$E[0m$E[u
```

Start by typing **PROMPT** and then a space. The rest of the commands are listed below:

$G	PROMPT command displays the greater-than symbol.
$E[s	ANSI command "saves" the cursor's position.
$E[1;1H	ANSI command moves the cursor to the first row and first column (1;1) on-screen.
$E[7m	ANSI command activates "inverse" text.
$E[K	ANSI command erases a line of text on-screen. (After the previous ANSI command, the effect here is that the top line appears in inverse text.)
$P	PROMPT command displays the current directory, followed by two spaces.
$D	PROMPT command displays the current date, followed by a space, an @ sign, and another space.
$T	PROMPT command displays the current time.
$H (x6)	Type six $H (backspace) commands and then a space.

$V — PROMPT command displays the DOS name and version number.

$E[0m — ANSI command resets the text to "normal."

$E[u — ANSI command restores the cursor's position (move the cursor back to where $E[s saved it).

Jeepers, that's a long and potentially bogus prompt. The effect is kind of neat, but it's a bit much.

✔ Thank goodness you can stick a command like that in AUTOEXEC.BAT and never have to type it again.

✔ The ANSI command to move the cursor on-screen is

```
←[row;col H
```

First comes ←[and then the row and column where you want to stick the cursor, with each value separated by a semicolon. The last letter is an uppercase *H*. The upper-left corner of the screen is row 1, column 1. On most screens the lower-right corner of the screen is row 25, column 80.

✔ The ←[K ANSI command erases a line of text on-screen. In the last, ugly PROMPT command in this section, a color ANSI command appears first (←[7m). That way, the screen is erased with the color's "inverse," which is what code 7 represents.

✔ By the way, the ANSI code to erase the entire screen is ←[2J. I don't know why I'm bringing this up.

Batch Files and ANSI Commands

Outside of the DOS prompt, ANSI commands appear most often in batch files. They're used to spice things up, add some color, or pull some other ANSI stunts and impress maybe a handful of PC users at the most.

You can use ANSI commands and batch files in two ways. The first is to display the required text — the *escape sequence* — by using the ECHO command. The second method, useful for those times when you have a ton of commands to type, is to shove them all into a text file and then use the TYPE command to display everything. Both of these tricks work in a batch file.

✔ To insert an Escape character into the DOS Editor, press Ctrl-P and then press the Esc key. That sticks a ← into your text, which is the Escape character.

> ✔ The basic ins and outs of batch files are covered in Chapter 17. Using ANSI in a batch file is considered an "advanced" trick, but I'm showing it to you here anyway.

ECHOing the ANSI commands

Because the ECHO command displays text on-screen, and ANSI commands must be displayed to work, they are the ideal couple. To see how everything works, you can play with the following tutorial:

1. Start by changing to your batch subdirectory, the place where you store your PC's batch files.

   Refer to Chapter 17 for more information on this directory if you haven't yet been there.

2. Fire up the DOS Editor with the following command:

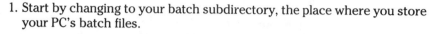

```
C:\>EDIT WARNING.BAT
```

   Type **EDIT**, a space, and then the name of this text batch file, **WARNING.BAT**.

3. In the Editor, type the following three echo commands:

```
@ECHO OFF
ECHO I'm about to format the hard drive
ECHO ←[5;31m!! Warning !!←[0m
```

   The first command is the traditional @ECHO OFF, which starts each DOS batch file. The second ECHO command just displays text, but the third ECHO command has some ANSI tricks in it.

   In the Editor, press Ctrl-P and then the Esc key to produce the Escape character. It appears as a left-pointing arrow (←) on-screen.

   The first ANSI command is ←[5;31m. This changes the screen color to garish blinking red text! The second ANSI command, ←[0m, changes the text back to normal.

4. Save the WARNING.BAT file to disk.

   In the Editor, select the **S**ave command from the **F**ile menu; press Alt-F, S.

5. Quit the Editor.

   Select E**x**it from the **F**ile menu, or press Alt-F, X.

6. Test-run the batch file.

Type **WARNING** at the DOS prompt:

```
C:\>WARNING
```

You see the text displayed as you typed it, although the second line is colored red and flashing.

7. Finish the batch file . . . if you dare! You're on your own for this one.

✔ The color codes you can use in the ANSI color escape sequence are listed in Tables 21-1 and 21-2.

✔ You can put more than one ANSI escape sequence after an ECHO command. The object is to avoid having four or five ECHO commands in a row for four or five ANSI sequences. Instead, just put 'em all on one line with one ECHO command.

✔ Another trick you can use to display multiple ANSI commands is to type them all into a text file. Then, from your batch file, use the TYPE command to display the text file and "run" the various ANSI commands.

✔ No, you cannot use the ECHO command at the DOS prompt to display ANSI commands; there's no way to type the Escape characters.

ANSI keyboard commands (only for the daring)

Aside from controlling the screen, ANSI commands also can mess with the keyboard. The commands alter the function of various keys, so when you press one key, another letter or maybe a whole sentence appears. I suppose this is useful to some people.

There are two problems with using ANSI keyboard commands. The first is that only DOS can understand and use them. Your applications programs access the keyboard directly and happily ignore any changes ANSI makes.

The second problem is that it's a very complex thing to do. For example, the following ANSI sequence is used in a batch file's ECHO command to reassign the output of the Ctrl-F1 key combination in DOS:

```
ECHO ←[0;94;"The Ctrl-F1 key"p
```

The ECHO command is followed by Escape, left bracket, zero, semicolon, 94. That's the code for the Ctrl-F1 key. It's followed by another semicolon and then text in double quotes, "The Ctrl-F1 key". The command ends with a lowercase *p*.

When a batch file runs this command . . . nothing happens! The command appears, and then ANSI swallows it. After that, any time the Ctrl-F1 key is pressed, DOS displays the message The Ctrl-F1 key. Big deal.

✔ I shouldn't be too hard on this trick. There actually would be some usefulness to having specific keys behave a certain way. Unfortunately, it's just too clumsy to use ANSI commands for this. Other solutions are available, including some third-party utilities that can do wonders with the keyboard. One such utility, once sold as a companion to SideKick, is Borland's SuperKey program. I don't know if it's still available, but it once did a marvelous job giving the keyboard a once-over.

✔ The Ctrl-F1 key is code 0;94 according to ANSI.SYS. When that key is pressed, ANSI displays the text The Ctrl-F1 key. This is fine because the Ctrl-F1 key doesn't normally do anything in DOS.

✔ All the secret key codes for your PC's keyboard are listed in the DOS manual or in DOS 6's on-line help. Type **HELP ANSI.SYS** at the DOS prompt, and then keep pressing the PgDn key until you see all the codes.

✔ Please don't let the secret key codes fall into the hands of former Soviet agents. Thank you.

Part IV
Keeping Your Stuff Organized

The 5th Wave　　　　　　**By Rich Tennant**

"When he said he was going to 'tame that wild beast,' I thought he was talking about his cock-a-poo."

In this part...

Organization is such a chore, but the payoffs can be great. I remember growing up and helping my mother spray the weeds. She must have exuded tons of the sticky stuff all over our property, squelching the existence of pesky weeds for over a decade. The result? She never sees any weeds any more. Okay, and nothing else grows on the land, either. And my niece was born with a third eye. All that aside (and getting back to the subject), if you're diligent about something, such as organizing your hard drive, the payoff will be a smoothly run system and maybe some sanity for yourself (if not an extra appendage).

Chapter 22
Taming the Wild Hard Disk Territory

● ●

In This Chapter

▶ Discovering the joys of hard disk management

▶ Keeping the root directory "clean"

▶ Using the PATH command

▶ Setting up DOS's search path

▶ Understanding the PATH command

▶ Organizing your files

● ●

*F*ace it, if DOS were your mother, she'd be riding you constantly about what a messy hard drive you keep. "Look at those files! What have you been doing here? Did a tornado strike while I was out? How can you *live* like this?" So you'd hang your head and make a lot of mumbled promises and then get back to playing games while she bustled out of view.

Seriously, organizing a disk drive is an important task and one I'd say just about everyone neglects. Put it off no more! This chapter shows you the basics of organizing your files. You'll need to keep the root directory clean, set up a proper DOS search path, and organize your files into subdirectories. It's all here. Read it now or regret it later.

The Basics of Hard Disk Management

Boy, how about *hard disk management* for a real turn-off term? It has *hard,* it has *disk,* it has *management.* All it needs is *government,* and no one would bother. Technicalities aside, hard disk management is really the ongoing process of organizing your hard drive. That's it. There are three general rules:

Keep the root directory clear of clutter.

Organize your programs and files into subdirectories.

Maintain order.

✔ The first two rules are covered in this chapter. Maintaining order is the topic in Chapter 23.

✔ I made these "rules" up. The DOS manual contains no serious information about organizing your hard drive. The reason is that the organization is up to you. That's nice, but it also leads to creeping clutter if you don't obey these three rules.

✔ There is no need to feign a German accent to maintain order, though pounding your fist on the table helps.

Keeping the root directory clean

There should only be a few files in your hard drive's root directory. My rule of thumb is that you should type **DIR ** and be able to see all the files and subdirectories listed on one screen. In fact, the output from that command on my DOS 5 PC is shown in Figure 22-1.

```
[C:\] DIR C:\
 Volume in drive C is TOO LOUD
 Volume Serial Number is 2E1D-07F1
 Directory of C:\
DOS          <DIR>     07-02-92   7:13p
LANTASTI NET <DIR>     07-02-92   7:35p
TEMP         <DIR>     07-03-92   8:03a
UTIL         <DIR>     07-02-92   8:20p
COMM         <DIR>     07-02-92   9:53a
WINDOWS      <DIR>     07-04-92   5:15p
AUTOEXEC BAT     1571  07-30-93   9:56a
COMMAND  COM    47845  04-09-91   5:00a
NEW-WARE LOG     1052  11-20-93   3:34p
SYCONFIG TXT       63  08-31-92   4:18p
CONFIG   SYS      464  12-27-92   9:58p
        13 file(s)       50995 bytes
                     155873280 bytes free
```

Figure 22-1:
The DIR command should list less than a screen of files in the root directory.

There should only be two types of files in the root directory: those that absolutely must be there and subdirectories. You should move everything else into a proper subdirectory somewhere else on the hard drive.

✔ The root directory is the main directory on your hard drive. See Chapter 16 for more information and details.

✔ Table 22-1 lists files that are okay to have in the root directory or that must be there.

✔ The TREEINFO file is placed on disk by one of Peter Norton's file management programs. Other, similar programs may place files like this in the root. They're like roaches: you can't get rid of them, so don't even try.

✔ There are also various hidden files stuffed into the root directory. Don't delete them ever! Refer to Chapter 11 for information on the ATTRIB command; some of the hidden files are mentioned in Chapter 1.

✔ Aside from being cluttered, another reason to keep files out of the root directory is that it can only hold so many. The typical hard drive only has room for 512 files in the root directory. Add any more and you get a Disk full error — despite megabytes of available space on the disk. This is why you need subdirectories for storing your files.

✔ What is the absolute minimum number of files that can live in the root directory? One! Only CONFIG.SYS needs to be in the root directory; you can use the SHELL configuration command and stick COMMAND.COM in a subdirectory (though I don't recommend it). And it's possible to live without AUTOEXEC.BAT, but then again, that is the little nerd guy icon over there and I'm just flapping my lips over here.

Table 22-1   Files That Usually Must Live in the Root Directory

Filename	*Purpose in Life*
AUTOEXEC.BAT	Special start-up file (Chapters 1 and 9)
COMMAND.COM	DOS's command interpreter (Chapter 1)
CONFIG.SYS	DOS's main configuration file (Chapters 1 and 6)
DBLSPACE.BIN	The program that runs DoubleSpace with DOS 6
MIRROR.*	Files used by DOS 5's MIRROR utility
TREEINFO.*	Files used by a file manager (Norton's in this case)
WINA20.386	A Windows 3.0 device driver

Moving files out of the root directory

If your root directory is a mess, then you need to put the files that don't belong there somewhere else. For example, Windows may have installed its HIMEM.SYS file in your root directory. It doesn't *need* to be there (see Table 22-1), so you can move it elsewhere.

The following steps show you how to move a file from the root directory to another, more appropriate place on your hard drive. The file HIMEM.SYS is used as an example:

1. Decide on a better place for the file.

   For example, if you're moving a HIMEM.SYS file that Windows installed, why not stick it in the Windows own directory? Other files may have their own place as well. Batch files in the root directory? Copy them to the BATCH directory. DOS files? Copy them to your DOS directory. For files that you don't know where they go, copy them to a TEMP directory for now.

2. Copy the file to that better place:

   ```
   C:\>COPY HIMEM.SYS C:\WINDOWS
   ```

   Type **COPY**, a space, the name of the file you're copying (HIMEM.SYS in the preceding), another space, and then the directory where you want to put it. In the preceding, that's the Windows subdirectory, C:\WINDOWS. Press Enter.

   ```
   1 file(s) copied
   ```

3. Delete the file that was lounging in the root directory:

   ```
   C:\>DEL HIMEM.SYS
   ```

   Type the **DEL** command, a space, and then the filename.

4. Repeat steps 1 through 3 for each misplaced file in the root directory.

   ✔ HIMEM.SYS is a device driver, possibly mentioned in your PC's CONFIG.SYS file. If you move it, remember to update CONFIG.SYS to include the file's new, full pathname. (Refer to Chapter 7 for more information on CONFIG.SYS and device drivers.)

   ✔ If the file isn't in Table 22-1, you should move it from the root directory. If you're nervous about doing this, have your guru do it for you or ask which files you should keep and which you can move.

   ✔ Sometimes you can just delete files lingering in the root directory. For example, report files from DOS's ScanDisk or Anti-Virus programs can go bye-bye after you've typed them out; MSAV.RPT can be deleted; SCANDISK.LOG can go. If you don't find these files offensive, move them to the TEMP subdirectory.

   ✔ You might want to print a copy of the root directory out on hard copy so that you can check off each file as it's moved. To do so, use the following command:

   ```
   C:\>DIR C:\ > PRN
   ```

Type the **DIR** command, a space, **C:** (the root directory), another space, a greater-than sign, another space, and then **PRN**. Make sure your printer is on and ready to print. Press Enter.

✔ If you have DOS 6, you can combine steps 2 and 3 into one MOVE command:

```
C:\>MOVE HIMEM.SYS C:\WINDOWS
```

That does the whole job. (Aren't you glad you upgraded?)

✔ Information on creating the BATCH directory is covered in "Where to shove your batch files" in Chapter 17. Creating the TEMP directory is covered in Chapter 16, in the section "Let's all make a TEMP directory tutorial."

Beating a Path to DOS's Door

DOS tries very hard not to display the dreaded `Bad command or file name` error message. In its desperation to please you, DOS will look almost everywhere for a command to match what you've typed at the DOS prompt.

First, DOS looks inward, reflecting a moment to see whether what you typed isn't really a DOS command — something simple like COPY, REN, or DIR. If that's not the case, dejected but still motivated, DOS looks elsewhere.

Second, DOS looks for matching program names in the current directory. If you typed ZIPPY, DOS will look for a file named ZIPPY.COM, ZIPPY.EXE, or ZIPPY.BAT in the current directory. If the file wasn't found, DOS doesn't give up just yet.

Finally, DOS looks to its *search path*. That's a list of subdirectories stored in DOS's environment. DOS looks for a COM, EXE, or BAT file in each of the subdirectories listed on the search path. Only then — after all that looking — does DOS give up the ghost and display the infamous `Bad command or file name` error message.

✔ The search path is one instance where DOS doesn't focus its attention on just the current directory.

✔ The search path is created by the PATH command, covered in the next section.

✔ DOS uses the search path only to find programs to run. Commands that deal with files — COPY, DEL, MOVE, and so on — still see files in the current directory only (unless you specify a full pathname).

✔ Refer to Chapter 19 for more information on DOS's environment — its storage closet for a whole lotta junk.

A look at your search path

To view which directories you have on your PC's path, type the PATH command by itself:

```
C:\>PATH
```

Type **PATH** and press Enter. You'll see something like the following displayed:

```
PATH=C:\DOS;C:\BATCH;C:\WINDOWS
```

There are three subdirectories on the preceding DOS search path:

    C:\DOS

    C:\BATCH

    C:\WINDOWS

Each directory is separated by a semicolon (;) character.

On your screen, you'll probably see a different list of subdirectories, with different names and such.

   ✔ In addition to displaying directories on the path, the PATH command also sets DOS's search path.

   ✔ The search path is saved in DOS's environment in the PATH variable. Refer to Chapter 19 for more information on the environment.

Setting up your own PATH command

You use the PATH command to create DOS's search path. That's a list of directories in which DOS looks for programs to run. The idea is to list subdirectories that contain programs you want to run. For example,

```
C:\>PATH C:\DOS
```

The preceding PATH command puts the C:\DOS subdirectory on the path. That means you can type the name of a DOS program, and DOS will find that program no matter which disk drive you're logged to or which subdirectory you're using. DOS will always be able to hunt down files in that one directory.

Setting up a PATH command on your PC means you first have to know where your programs are located. For example,

```
C:\>PATH C:\DOS;C:\123;C:\WP60
```

This PATH command lists three directories: C:\DOS, for all the DOS programs and such; C:\123, which contains Lotus 1-2-3; and C:\WP60, which contains WordPerfect.

- ✔ When a directory is listed on the search path, DOS can find programs in that directory from any other disk drive or subdirectory on your PC.

- ✔ When you create a PATH command, type **PATH**, a space, and then list each directory's full pathname. Use a semicolon to separate more than one directory.

- ✔ The PATH command is usually placed in AUTOEXEC.BAT. Typically, it appears quite early in that file, setting the search path up for other programs that may be run in AUTOEXEC.BAT. See Chapter 10 for more details.

- ✔ You can change the path at any time by typing a new PATH command at the DOS prompt. When you do this, however, the old search path is erased and replaced with the new list of subdirectories you just typed. For example,

```
C:\>PATH C:\WINDOWS;C:\DOS
```

The preceding PATH command changes DOS's search path to look in just the C:\WINDOWS and C:\DOS directories. Whatever was on the old path is forgotten.

- ✔ You can list as many directories in a PATH command as there is room for. (DOS only allows you to type 127 characters at the prompt, so that means you can type up to 122 characters for your various directory names.)

- ✔ I recommend against packing up the PATH command with too many directories. The next section offers a detailed explanation why.

"Hey! Why not just put everything on the path?"

The idea behind DOS's search path is to list directories that contain the names of programs you run. That way you'd never have to change to any directory to run a program; you could type any program name, and DOS would be able to find it for you. Isn't that the kind of convenience computers are all about? Well, not really.

Consider the following monster:

```
PATH C:\DOS;C:\QMODEM;C:\GAMES;C:\Q;C:\WP; C:\QPRO;C:\PRODIGY
```

This search path lists seven directories DOS will look in for programs:

Directory	Type of Stuff Inside
C:\DOS	DOS programs
C:\QMODEM	QModem communications program
C:\GAMES	Games to play
C:\Q	Quicken
C:\WP	WordPerfect
C:\QPRO	Quattro Pro
C:\PRODIGY	Prodigy

This sounds ideal. Obviously, it's neat to type **PRODIGY** anywhere and have DOS find and run Prodigy for you. However, such a long path slows down your PC. I give you the following reasons:

- DOS looks in each directory on the path every time you type a program name at the prompt. If you type **PRODIGY**, DOS looks in the current directory and then in seven more directories before it finds that program.

- If you make a typo, DOS looks through the current directory and every directory on the path for your typo as a file to run. It may take a while before you eventually see the Bad command or file name error — not a long time, but long enough to frustrate you.

- Most of the directories on the search path contain only one program name. Just one! Is it worth it to put the C:\123 directory on the path when all you do is run 123.EXE in that directory?

- The better path is one that contains maybe two or three directories max. Heck, my own PC's search path has only *one* directory listed. How'd I do that? By the miracle of batch files, which is what you can read about in the section titled "How batch files fit into the picture" later in this chapter.

- The path example in this section is mild. I've seen search paths with a dozen or more directories on them.

✔ "But it's not my fault!" Having a long search path may actually be due to some installation programs instead of anything you did. You must keep an eye out for programs that modify the PATH command in AUTOEXEC.BAT. When that happens, you need to reedit the PATH command and patch up the situation by writing a batch file, as described in the following section.

How batch files fit into the picture

The ideal path for your PC need only contain two directories:

```
PATH C:\DOS;C:\BATCH
```

DOS's directory should go on the search path. That way you have access to all DOS's programs and utilities. Next, you should put a BATCH subdirectory on the path, the directory that contains all your PC's batch files.

This shortened search path works, providing you have a lot of batch files that run other programs on your PC. (Batch files were discussed in Chapter 17.)

For example, instead of putting WordPerfect's directory (C:\WP60) on the path, you can create a WP.BAT batch file in the BATCH directory. That batch file runs WordPerfect. A similar batch file, 123.BAT, could be created to run Lotus 1-2-3. Already you have two batch files in the BATCH directory; that means you can remove C:\123 and C:\WP60 from the PATH command.

✔ For more information on writing batch files to run your PC's programs, turn to Chapter 17.

✔ To create the BATCH subdirectory, refer to Chapter 16.

✔ If you have a UTIL or UTILITY directory, one that contains a bunch of handy disk utilities, put that on the search path as well:

```
PATH=C:\DOS;C:\BATCH;C:\UTIL
```

✔ Having an ideal path and organizing your programs and files into subdirectories go hand in hand. Refer to the section "On the Proper Use of Subdirectories" later in this chapter to get a grip on things.

✔ One handy thing about the path and batch files: if you need a longer path, you can set one up with a path command in your batch file. For example,

```
PATH C:\TC\BIN;E:\TASM;C:\DOS;C:\UTIL
```

Forbidden secrets on the author's path on his very own system

Here is the path command I use in my PC's AUTOEXEC.BAT file:

```
PATH=F:\
```

That's it. Everything worth running on my computer is stored on drive F in the root directory. I know — I said never to put anything in the root directory. But because drive F is a RAM drive on my PC, it's okay.

Drive F is created using a DEVICE=C:\DOS \RAMDRIVE.SYS command in my PC's CONFIG.SYS file. (See Chapter 24 for more information on RAM drives.) In AUTOEXEC.BAT, a COPY command then copies all my PC's batch files to RAM drive F. Then I set the path to drive F, and I'm ready to go.

Essentially, every command on my computer has a corresponding batch file setup to run it. Most of the batch files are simple two-liners:

```
@ECHO OFF
C:\DOS\FORMAT
```

The preceding is the FORMAT.BAT program, which runs DOS's FORMAT command. For every DOS program, there is a batch file. For ever other program I run on my PC, a batch file exists. When the computer starts, the whole barrel is copied up to the RAM drive, and the RAM drive's letter is then used as my path.

The preceding PATH command appears in a batch file that runs Borland's C++ programming environment. After C++ is done, the batch file changes the path back to normal:

```
PATH C:\DOS;C:\UTIL
```

On the Proper Use of Subdirectories

Subdirectories were introduced in DOS 2.0 for the sake of organization. IBM had announced the PC/XT, which came with a whopping 10MB hard drive. They desperately needed subdirectories to organize the potential hundreds of files that would be put on that mammoth drive.

Ha! Your hard drive today probably stores many times over what the original PC's hard drive held. The need for subdirectories to organize your stuff is as great as your hard drive is massive.

- Chapter 16 covers the subject of directories and subdirectories. Refer there for a refresher before reading the following sections.

- Every DOS disk starts with a root directory. Refer to the section "Keeping the root directory clean" at the very start of this chapter.

- No more wire hangers, ever!

Organizing your hard drive

There are many ways to organize a hard drive. Rather than list them all and let you choose one, I'll describe the best one, which works for just about everyone. Here are the steps:

1. Create general-purpose directories.

2. Have each of your applications in its own directory.

3. Make data directories under your applications' directories.

That's really all you need. True, it can get more complex. But not for now.

- Hopefully, most of this stuff will already be done for you.

- Organizing your hard drive is up to you. It's an active thing! You must constantly keep an eye on how your files live on disk, making sure it keeps with your organizational scheme.

- Beware of installation programs that innocently suggest where to install themselves! *You* should decide where programs go. (Of course, if you have no idea, the installation program's suggestion is probably okay.)

Making the general subdirectories

Organization usually works this way: Each application on your hard drive has its own directory. DOS is in C:\DOS; WordPerfect is in C:\WP60; Prodigy is in C:\PRODIGY; and so on. But there's also a need for *general directories*. These are subdirectories into which you put a variety of related programs.

A good example is the DOS directory. When DOS 5 or DOS 6 was installed on your PC, it placed itself into the C:\DOS directory. That's where DOS's SETUP program copied all DOS's files, utilities, and other programs. They all live in C:\DOS (unless you told the SETUP program to put them elsewhere).

Another example is the BATCH batch file subdirectory discussed in this chapter (and in Chapters 16 and 17). Into that directory you should place all your PC's batch files plus any other related files.

Finally, there's the TEMP directory, also discussed in this book (see Chapter 16). It's used for . . . anything! Temporary files, junk files, stuff you don't know about but don't want to delete — anything.

✔ The idea behind a general-purpose directory is to store files that are related but that may be mislaid elsewhere on the disk. For example, I've run into several installation programs that put a batch file into the root directory. Obviously, batch files go into the BATCH directory on my PC, so I have to move them.

✔ If you need them, create other general-purpose directories on your PC. Consider the following, for example:

- Make a GAMES directory and install all your PC's games into that directory. If you play a lot of games, put that directory on the path.

- Make a UTIL directory and install various PC utilities into it. Although I have separate directories on my computer for the Norton Utilities and PC Tools, my general-purpose utility directory contains lots of little things I've picked up at user groups or downloaded from CompuServe or local BBSs.

- Make a GRAPHICS directory for your graphics files. I download GIF picture files from CompuServe and GEnie and save them in a graphics directory.

You can create any of these general-purpose directories right off the root directory. Read Chapter 16's "Creating and Naming Directories" section for more information.

✔ Refer to the section "Moving files out of the root directory" earlier in this chapter if, somehow, your copy of DOS was installed in your PC's root directory. (Yuck! Get it outta there, quick!)

Creating all-important data directories

One of the worst sins most of us commit is to just save a file anywhere. But it's so tempting, so convenient: You press Alt-S to save a file, type in a filename, and then count you're blessings that it's saved to disk. But where? Will you be able to find it again? You would, if you used *data directories*.

When a program is installed on your hard drive, it creates its own directory. Take WordPerfect 6.0's C:\WP60 directory (please!). Into C:\WP60, WordPerfect's Install program copies all the files and programs that make the bulk (literally) of WordPerfect.

Your very next step after installation should be to create data directories under the C:\WP60 directory. The data directory is where you put your files. For example,

```
C:\>MD \WP60\MISC
```

The preceding command creates a MISC subdirectory in the WP60 directory. When you save a whatnot file in WordPerfect, you can save it in that directory. More importantly, however, you should create *specific* data directories for your projects.

The following is a list of subdirectories you might create under the C:\WP60 directory:

Directory	Stuff It Might Include
C:\WP60\LETTERS	Letters you write
C:\WP60\NOVEL	That novel you promise to finish
C:\WP60\REPORTS	Reports and stuff for work
C:\WP60\XMAS	The Christmas letter and shopping lists
C:\WP60\EDITOR	Letters to the Editor you've written

The idea is to *organize*. If you write a letter to a relative, save it in the C:\WP60\LETTERS directory when you're done.

- You should take this approach with all your programs, not just WordPerfect. Make data directories for any application that creates files: Lotus 1-2-3, Quattro Pro, Word, MultiMate, Harvard Graphics, and so on.

- Each DOS program has a Save command. Use it to save your stuff in specific data directories. Don't be sloppy! Save every file to a place on disk where it belongs or where you can find it later.

- Most sophisticated programs, such as WordPerfect, let you change directories or even create new directories right in the program. If not, you have to make directories at the DOS prompt before you use your applications.

Creating topical subdirectory branches (or "Ode to my COMM directory")

When things get real hairy, you need to organize your programs into what I call *topical branches*. For example, I have about nine subdirectories that hold modem programs. These are all living under a topical COMM directory right off the root directory. Figure 22-2 shows how this looks, using the TREE command (I erased the other subdirectories from the figure to make COMM stand out).

```
C:.
 └── COMM
        ├── BOYAN
        ├── CSERVE
        ├── DOWNLOAD
        ├── GARBAGE
        ├── LAPLINK
        ├── MCI
        ├── PRODIGY
        ├── UPLOAD
        └── ZMODEM
```

Figure 22-2:
The topical COMM subdirectory, as seen by the TREE command.

I need a COMM directory on my computer because I have a lot of communications programs. It helps whenever I have something new to install. For example, I just installed a new version of Prodigy on my computer, and I stuffed it in my COMM directory. Prodigy's installation program really wanted to put it into a C:\PRODIGY directory, but I told it to go to C:\COMM\PRODIGY instead.

✔ You can apply this same type of trick to anything you have a lot of on your PC. For example, consider a topical GRAPHICS directory if you have a lot of graphics programs; put the programs in their own subdirectories in the GRAPHICS directory, and then create other directories to hold graphical images and such.

✔ If you use this approach, you must be on your toes when an installation program suggests where it wants to put a new program.

✔ If you like this approach but your subdirectories aren't organized this way, take heart. Turn to Chapter 16 and devour the subject of grafting and pruning directories. See the section titled "Moving a subdirectory branch" for the details.

✔ Only for those who care, here is how the directories in my topical COMM branch work out:

BOYAN	Boyan is my DOS communications program, and it lives here.
CSERVE	CompuServe's WINCIM program is installed here.
DOWNLOAD	Any program that downloads files is told to deposit them in this directory.
GARBAGE	This is a general-purpose junk directory for stuff I'm fond of.
LAPLINK	LapLink is installed here (PC-laptop communications).
MCI	The program I use to access MCI Mail lives here.

PRODIGY	Prodigy lives here.
UPLOAD	Files awaiting upload are placed here (and programs are told to look for files to upload in this directory).
ZMODEM	Zmodem files are placed here.

✔ Ah, sweet organization. It can make you nuts. It certainly has done that to me.

Avoiding a bloated directory

Even if you're well-organized, subdirectories can get full. For example, I write a lot of letters to readers (and to the Editor and my congressman and others I pester). One day I noticed there were about 300 letters in my C:\WP60\LETTERS directory. I was a desperate man.

The solution was to create other directories for the files in the one bloated directory. You can do this with any large data directory. I created various subdirectories for different years. For example:

    C:\WP60\LETTERS\1991 (Letters written in 1991)

    C:\WP60\LETTERS\1992 (Letters written in 1992)

    C:\WP60\LETTERS\1993 (Letters written in 1993)

If you notice your graphics directory is bursting with graphical images, consider making subdirectories in it as well:

    C:\GRAPHICS\PEOPLE   (Images of people)

    C:\GRAPHICS\GIFS   (GIF files)

    C:\GRAPHICS\WILDLIFE (Images of animals)

    C:\GRAPHICS\CLIPART   (Clipart files)

    C:\GRAPHICS\VIDEO   (Video "movies")

Copy off the related files into subdirectories. This keeps the hard drive organized and avoids the clutter.

✔ Refer to the section "Moving files out of the root directory" earlier in this chapter for a rundown of how files are moved into subdirectories.

✔ You can have as many subdirectories as you want. DOS keeps track of everything.

✔ There really is nothing wrong with having a subdirectory with hundreds of files in it. Unlike the root directory, subdirectories can have any number of files.

✔ Okay. There is one *small* problem: Not only will files get lost in a bloated subdirectory, but the larger the directory gets, the longer it takes DOS to access its files. A good size to stay below is about 300 files. Anything more and DOS is putting in overtime that it doesn't really need.

✔ Actually, there is a limit on subdirectories: A pathname cannot be longer than 63 characters. This usually allows for subdirectories four or five levels deep — enough for any sane man or woman.

Chapter 23

Keeping House (or Playing House, Depending on Your Mood)

* *

In This Chapter

▶ Deleting excess files

▶ Preventing file disaster

▶ Optimizing your hard drive

* *

*O*rganization means nothing without upkeep (just look at the Pentagon). Even if you follow this book's organization suggestions in Chapter 22, you're going to need some routine disk housekeeping. This is not something that requires wearing an apron or talking like Shirley Booth (remember *Hazel?*). All you need to do is follow the few suggestions in this chapter, add a few throw pillows, some mirrors, and no one will ever call your hard drive "a dump" again.

▸ Use this chapter as a checklist of tasks that you should perform on a regular basis to keep your PC in tip-top form.

▸ Many of the items explained in this chapter are covered in greater detail in the latest edition of *DOS For Dummies*.

What Exactly Is Housekeeping?

Housekeeping is a friendly term that means to keep your PC's disk "house" in order. You need to do a few things on an occasional basis:

▸ Delete old files.

▸ Get rid of old programs you don't use any more.

▸ Keep things organized.

The 5th Wave

By Rich Tennant

INDUSTRY WATCHERS PREDICTED THAT IN THE NEAR FUTURE, MONDOTECH CORP. WILL UP THE ANTE IN THE **AT** CLONE MARKET BY INTRODUCING A PC THAT'S COMPATIBLE WITH BOTH IBM, APPLE, AND KIRBY VACUUM CLEANERS.

✔ Maintain your CONFIG.SYS and AUTOEXEC.BAT files.

✔ Protect your files.

✔ Optimize the disk.

✔ Every so often you should scour your disk for files you don't use any more. Delete them! If you're using a TEMP directory, check it every so often for junk you don't need any more.

✔ Disk utilities can help you find files you want to kill off. It's much easier to see a group of files in a disk manager, such as DOS Shell, than it is to keep using the DIR command.

✔ Don't delete anything you didn't create yourself! Housekeepers may occasionally kill off their employers, but that doesn't mean you need to get overzealous with the DEL command.

✔ Hazel never killed anyone, not even Mr. B.

✔ A great disk-scouring utility is Elite's Disk Sweep program. It works with both DOS and Windows.

✔ Don't delete old programs you don't use any more! Instead, copy them to a floppy disk for long-term storage. You can use your PC's backup program for this purpose. (It's technically called *archiving*.)

✔ Keep things organized! Constantly check files in your directories. If you need to further organize by creating more subdirectories, do it! Refer to Chapters 16 and 22.

✔ Protect your files! Refer to the section "Protecting Your Files from Potential Disaster."

✔ Disk optimization means that you run special software that makes certain your hard drive is working at 100-percent efficiency. Two programs that come with DOS do this quite well: the SMARTDrive disk cache and the disk optimization program DEFRAG. Both are covered later in this chapter.

Protecting Your Files from Potential Disaster

Your files — the very ones you worked so hard to create — require protection. Nothing evil *should* happen to your stuff. But to increase the chances of recovery if it does, I recommend three things: backing up your files regularly, checking your disk, and checking for computer viruses.

Backing up

Backing up your files creates a duplicate copy of everything. After you back up, for every file on your hard drive a twin exists on a backup disk or tape somewhere else. If anything happens to the file on the hard drive, you can quickly recover the duplicate from the backup disk (or tape).

Backing up makes so much sense, and yet often it takes a complete disk disaster for somebody to become religious about it. If you haven't been hit by a disk mishap, and you don't believe in backing up, then it's only a matter of time. Don't play the fool! Back up regularly. Here's what I suggest:

✔ Every day, back up the files you worked on that day.

✔ At the end of the week (or month), back up your whole hard drive.

Follow those two simple rules and you'll always be able to recover your files in case of a disk disaster.

✔ DOS comes with programs for backing up your files. Prior to DOS 6, the BACKUP command was used. DOS 6 comes with MSBACKUP, a more-professional backup program.

✔ To back up today's work, you have two options. The first is to do an *incremental* backup. That backs up all the changed files on your hard drive. The second is to back up your work directory only, but that only works if you're using a single work directory instead of files all over the hard drive.

The following BACKUP command does an incremental backup for drive C:

```
C:\>BACKUP C:\*.* A: /S /M
```

That's the **BACKUP** command, a space, **C**, colon, backslash, asterisk, period, asterisk, a space, **A**, and then a colon. That backs up all the files on drive C that have changed to floppy disks that you put in drive A. The two options are slash-S and slash-M.

✔ In the MSBACKUP program, available only with DOS 6, be sure to select Incremental from the Backup Type on the main backup screen.

✔ You should do a full hard disk backup at least once a week or once a month, depending on how much you use your computer and how often you do an incremental backup.

✔ The backup command to do a full hard drive backup is

```
C:\>BACKUP C:\*.* A: /S
```

That's the **BACKUP** command, a space, **C**, colon, backslash, asterisk, period, asterisk, a space, **A**, colon, a space, and then slash-**S**.

✔ With MSBACKUP, you can perform a full backup by selecting Full from the Backup Type menu.

✔ Remember to back up each of your hard drives if you have more than one. This requires using the old BACKUP command on each drive. In MSBACKUP, you can select all your hard drives at once for a heavy-duty *gang* backup.

Checking your disk (or scanning your disk)

Every so often — at least once or twice a month — you should check your hard drive for lost files or anything out of the ordinary. Prior to MS-DOS 6.2, this you did this with the CHKDSK command. With MS-DOS 6.2, you can use the spiffier SCANDISK command.

To use CHKDSK, type **CHKDSK** at the DOS prompt:

```
C:\>CHKDSK
```

Press Enter, and the program checks your disk. Most of the time, it reports only harmless disk statistics — something you could read over the phone to a computer-illiterate friend and completely impress him or her with.

To use SCANDISK, type **SCANDISK** at the DOS prompt:

```
C:\>SCANDISK
```

Press Enter, and SCANDISK checks your hard drive, scoping out interesting places that you never knew existed.

In either case, if CHKDSK or SCANDISK reports an error, you need to fix it. With SCANDISK, follow the instructions on-screen. With CHKDSK, you need to run the program again with the slash-F option, as in

```
C:\>CHKDSK /F
```

Press Y followed by Enter if you're asked to convert lost files into chains or clusters or something like that.

- ✔ Whenever CHKDSK or SCANDISK reports finding lost files, it saves them in the root directory with names like FILE0000.CHK, FILE0001.CHK, and on up. It's perfectly okay to delete these files — they generally contain hard drive junk.

- ✔ You can follow the CHKDSK or SCANDISK commands with a space and a drive letter (plus a colon) to check that drive in particular:

```
C:\>CHKDSK F:
C:\>SCANDISK F:
```

The preceding CHKDSK and SCANDISK commands give drive F the once-over.

- ✔ When SCANDISK asks `Do you want to perform a surface scan now?`, answer Yes: press Y and then Enter. The surface scan really puts the disk through the wringer and finds anything peculiar or out of the ordinary. You need to do a surface scan routinely (but only about once a month or so).

✔ What's *out of the ordinary?* A bear vacuuming. With your disk drive, potentially anything unknown that may be affecting the hard drive is out of the ordinary. Things such as cross-linked files, damaged directories, bits of Cheetoz on the drive, and so on. These things happen and only a disk-utility program like CHKDSK or SCANDISK can find them.

Virus bugaboo

We live in the sad age of evil computer programs. Some of them masquerade as useful, and others sneak into your computer and infect it by altering your programs or reformatting your hard drive in a blink. These types of files have come to be called *viruses*. Protecting your computer from them and getting rid of any infections is a top priority.

I don't mean to alarm you: Viruses are real but very rare. Your chances of getting one are reduced to nearly zero if you follow these suggestions:

✔ Never start your PC using a strange disk such as a free game or demo.

✔ Don't let others mess with your computer or use it to "test" things.

✔ Use virus-scanning software on your computer to ensure that it's free from infection.

You can buy virus-scanning software anywhere software is sold. Norton makes it, PC Tools does too — just about everyone does. DOS 6 comes with the Microsoft Anti-Virus program, which does a fair job of looking for and removing viruses. Any of these programs should be a part of your regular file-protection arsenal.

✔ If you don't have DOS 6 yet, you should get a virus-scanning/removal program at once!

✔ The virus scanner examines a disk or file for signs of a virus. If it finds a virus, the program either removes the virus or erases the infected file. The end result is that your PC is free from any infection or potential damage.

✔ Nothing beats that swell feeling you get after running a virus scanner and finding your PC is uninfected.

✔ The most popular way to get a virus is to try out "free" software. For example, lots of folks innocently (and *illegally*) give their friends games and other programs. These programs reside on boot disk floppies. When the unsuspecting person starts his or her PC from such a disk, it's instantly infected. So, two things are wrong here: using illegally copied software and distributing infected programs to your friends. The Romper Room Lady would not be pleased.

✔ More information on MSAV, the DOS 6 Anti-Virus program, can be found in the latest edition of *DOS For Dummies*.

Making Your Hard Drive Run Better

No voodoo you can do will make your disk run faster. Of course, a lot you can do without thinking about it will make your disk run *slower*. So the idea behind making your hard drive run better is to avoid what slows it down and keep it running as fast as you can.

Running SMARTDrive

SMARTDrive is a special program that uses your PC's memory to help improve the way the disk drive works. It does this by *magic*.

Actually, SMARTDrive sets up what's called a *disk cache* in memory. (See the next sidebar in this chapter for a technical description of what a disk cache is.) All you need to know is that the cache makes your hard drive run faster. You can use SMARTDrive by editing your AUTOEXEC.BAT file to include the following command:

```
SMARTDRV
```

Type **SMARTDRV**, which is DOS talk for SMARTDrive. If you haven't set a *search path* in AUTOEXEC.BAT (see Chapter 22), then specify the full pathname:

```
C:\DOS\SMARTDRV
```

SMARTDrive lives in your DOS subdirectory, shown here as C:\DOS\SMARTDRV.

You may not immediately notice the speed improvement that SMARTDrive has to offer. *Note:* In a weird twist, SMARTDrive improves disk performance the more you use your disk.

- You can only use SMARTDrive if you have a computer with *extended* memory. (Refer to Chapter 25 for more information on that type of memory.)
- SMARTDrive automatically consumes as much memory as it needs. The values it uses can be found in the DOS manual or in the DOS 6 HELP command (type **HELP SMARTDRV**).
- If you're using DOS 5, I recommend putting the following SMARTDrive command in AUTOEXEC.BAT:

```
SMARTDRV C
```

This command is the same as with DOS 6 except that you follow SMARTDRV with the letters of all your hard drives, such as C in the preceding. The technical reason for this particular command is that it disables SMARTDrive's *write-ahead cache*. Nontechnically speaking, it means you're better off typing the drive letters than not typing the drive letters.

✔ I'd rather have memory devoted to a disk cache like SMARTDrive than to a RAM drive. If memory is scarce, get rid of the RAM drive.

✔ Third-party disk caches are also available. They offer more features and are usually faster and more whiz-bang than SMARTDrive. I guess that's why SMARTDrive comes free with DOS.

✔ Cache is pronounced "cash." It's not cachet, pronounced "ka-shay." (The two things are quite different.)

✔ Refer to Chapter 10 for more information on placing SMARTDrive into AUTOEXEC.BAT.

✔ Play the new Data Wiz game, and you can win valuable prizes or disk cache!

If you really want an answer to the question "What is a disk cache?"

A *cache* is a storage place in memory. Its specific purpose is to speed things up. It does this to your disk drive by remembering the last few items that DOS read from disk. If you type **DIR** to see a list of files, the disk cache keeps all that information in memory. If you type **DIR** a second time, DOS normally goes through the efforts of reading in the same information all over again from the disk. But — *ah-ha!* — in steps the disk cache, which provides the information conveniently and quickly from memory.

Incidentally, several types of caches exist in PCs. SMARTDrive runs its own disk cache, but your PC's disk hardware may use another type of cache or may have a *cached controller.* A cached controller does the same thing as SMARTDrive's disk cache — they both cut down on disk access and make everything work faster.

Another type of cache is a *microprocessor cache,* which works in almost the same way: A program is stored in memory, and the microprocessor reads it from memory. But the microprocessor itself is much faster than memory. So a processor with an "on-board cache" can read programming instructions from memory faster just as a disk cache makes reading disks faster . . . yeah, it works something like that.

Running a disk optimizer

A disk optimizer is a program that looks at your hard drive, shakes its head in utter disgust at how DOS has sloppily placed files on it, and then proceeds to clean everything up. The idea here is to fight creeping *disk fragmentation,* a disease all hard drives are subject to but which can be cured.

Many programs (or *utilities*) can cure disk fragmentation. The job is called *defragmentation,* but because my word processor's spell checker doesn't recognize that word, I prefer to call it *disk optimization.* (Actually, the spell checker doesn't know *optimization* either.) If you have DOS 6, you can use the DEFRAG program to clean up a fragmented (or unoptimized) disk.

To run the DEFRAG program that comes with DOS 6, follow these steps:

1. Type **DEFRAG** at the DOS prompt:

   ```
   C:\>DEFRAG
   ```

   DEFRAG pops up on the screen. It's a happy, graphical, mouse-oriented program, yet still it is ugly because this is, after all, DOS.

2. Select a hard drive to optimize. Type the drive letter or use the mouse to select it from the list.

   DEFRAG looks over the drive, poking it and prodding it in various unmentionable ways.

3. After a while, DEFRAG offers you a suggestion. If it says No optimization necessary, you're done! Skip up to step 7. Otherwise, it suggests optimizing the disk.

4. Press Enter to optimize the disk. This may take a moment, but the display is interesting to watch and anyone walking by will naturally assume you're busy at the computer.

5. Da-DA-*DA!* It's done. (I hope that didn't scare you like it does me. I have these loud, thundering speakers attached to my computer, and that always startles me.) Press Enter. You have Finished condensing.

6. You can select another drive to optimize or quit the DEFRAG program at this time. If you want to optimize another drive, press Enter and skip back to step 2. Otherwise, press the Escape key to quit DEFRAG.

7. You're done. (This is the final step I had to write in case you didn't need to optimize your hard drive.)

I recommend that you reset your PC after you optimize your hard drive. Press Ctrl-Alt-Delete or punch the Reset button. Optimizing your disk rearranges files on the disk, which may goof up some strange DOS programs. To avoid any problems, your best bet is to start your computer again. That will straighten out anything goofy.

If you don't have DOS 6, you can use the disk optimizers that come with many of the popular third-party utilities: Norton has one, PC Tools has one — heck, everything comes with one, just about.

O, please tell me about disk fragmentation!

Disk fragmentation is a by-product of the way DOS stores files on disk. No, DOS isn't really sloppy—it's just trying to make the best of an ugly situation and being quick about it.

As you copy and create files on a hard drive and then delete them, you form various "holes." When you delete a 500K file, a 500K space appears on your disk. Sure, DOS stores other files in that space, but often nothing perfectly fits the 500K chunk left by the first file. So, to fill in the holes, DOS splits up or *fragments* files. That way, everything fits.

Fortunately, DOS keeps track of files that have been *fragmented*. It assembles all the pieces back in order when you load the file from disk. No problem. But assembling the pieces makes working with that file take longer. And the more

fragmented files that DOS has to deal with, the slower and slower your disk drive becomes.

What disk optimization software does is take the fragmented files and reassemble them, making everything fit on disk in one piece. Actually, the software does this in two ways: The first way is called *unfragment only* or the *fast* version, in which only the fragmented files are optimized and put on disk in one piece. The second way is the *full* or *slow* version, where all the files on disk are moved around by the disk optimizer, and any holes between them are filled in. The DOS DEFRAG program gives you a choice between these two methods. Specify the /F option for the full, slow version, or the /U for the fast, unfragment-only method.

Chapter 24

Worrying about Disks, RAM Drives, and All That

In This Chapter

▶ Dealing with multiple hard drives

▶ Understanding disk partitions

▶ Setting up a RAM drive

▶ Using a RAM drive with batch files

*O*ne day in ancient Greece, a mysterious man walked atop Mars Hill and posed the following rhetorical question: "What is drive D?" The Greek philosophers responded, calling out "It's a RAM drive!" and "It's a second hard drive!" and even "It's a CD-ROM drive!" The mysterious man shook his head. "No," he said, "it could be just about anything." So they threw small rocks at him and compared him to various animal smells.

DOS gives you drive letters A, B, and C for three definite things: two floppy drives and a hard drive. Beyond that, who really knows what the letters could stand for? This chapter looks into the situation by discussing multiple hard drives, disk partitioning, RAM drives, and a whole host of disk-related stuff.

✔ Nothing here is worth getting pelted with rocks over.

✔ Refer to Chapter 15 for general information on disks and disk drives. (This chapter is more . . . well, philosophical.)

Multiple Hard Drive Mania

Rare is the PC today that has only drive C as a hard drive. A lot of folks get a second hard drive or have their first drive *partitioned* into more hard drives. Oh, then there are RAM drives and CD-ROMs and other strange drives. DOS politely hands out letters to each of them, making everyone happy.

To scope out the disk drives on your PC, run the Microsoft Diagnostic program. Type **MSD** at the DOS prompt:

```
C:\>MSD
```

The MSD program examines your computer's guts and reports back what it finds. On the main screen, you see a panel that reads Disk Drives. Next to the panel are all your disk drive letters. Press D to select that panel and see more information about your disk drives.

What I see on my screen is shown in Figure 24-1. Most of the information is technical; ignore it. What's important to see is how the drive letters are assigned to various different types of drives: a floppy drive, a fixed disk (IBM-talk for a hard drive), a RAM disk, CD-ROM drive, and so on. This is perhaps the only way in DOS to get a grip on what type of drive you're using when you *log to drive F*.

  ✔ Fixed disk = hard drive. I suppose they call it a *fixed* disk because unless you suddenly transform into the Incredible Hulk, there's no way you can rip it out of the PC.

  ✔ MSD is available with Windows 3.0 and 3.1, and it also comes with DOS 6.

Figure 24-1: The MSD program describes your disk drives in long-winded detail.

```
 File  Utilities  Help
 ═══════════════════════════════ Disk Drives ═══════════════════
  Drive  Type                                Free Space  Total Size ↑
  ──────────────────────────────────────────────────────────────

   A:    Floppy Drive, 3.5" 1.44M
             80 Cylinders
   C:    Fixed Disk, CMOS Type 48              278M        324M
             1009 Cylinders, 12 Heads
             512 Bytes/Sector, 55 Sectors/Track
         CMOS Fixed Disk Parameters
             1023 Cylinders, 12 Heads
             55 Sectors/Track
   D:    Fixed Disk, CMOS Type 49    █         112K        201M
             985 Cylinders, 12 Heads
             512 Bytes/Sector, 35 Sectors/Track
         CMOS Fixed Disk Parameters
             1023 Cylinders, 12 Heads
             35 Sectors/Track
   E:    RAM Disk                              1018K       1018K ↓
             512 Bytes/Sector

                            ▄▄▄▄▄▄ OK ▄▄▄▄▄▄
 Disk Drives: Displays disk drive types and sizes.
```

Suggestions for organizing multiple hard drives

Having more than one hard drive is good because it means you have more room to store information on your computer. That's really the bottom line. Even so, having multiple hard drives brings up a few organizational points (but nothing for single hard drive users to sit, fidget, and get jealous over).

Drive C is always the hard drive that starts your computer. Because of that arrangement, DOS, Windows, and important files should live on drive C. What else can go there? Anything that fits. Remember, this is DOS and there are no rules, only suggestions.

If you like, you can designate other hard drives in your system for a specific purpose. I use drive D to hold word processing stuff. Someone else might elect to put graphics files on drive D. Maybe drive D holds games. If you're a programmer, drive D may have all your programming junk on it. Or maybe you use drive D for all your data files and just put program files on drive C. Whatever — there is no penalty for being creative.

- ✔ I guess the bottom line is not to let multiple hard drives bother you. Use them any way you please.

- ✔ Yes, you can and should put files on other hard drives into subdirectories. The same rules about the root directory apply to hard drives D, E, F, and on up to Z.

- ✔ Because you use only drive C to start the computer, you don't need COMMAND.COM, CONFIG.SYS, or AUTOEXEC.BAT on drives D, E, F, and so on.

- ✔ Don't forget about any extra drives you may have! If you just ran the MSD program as described in the preceding section and said "Hey! I didn't know I had a CMOS Type 49 hard drive D with 324MB of storage on it," well then, *use it!*

- ✔ Actually, having extra drive letters means you keep having to log to this or that drive to get things done. It's a bother.

- ✔ If you only have a C drive, don't fall prey to the lure of *partitioning* your hard drive so that you get a drive D, E, or whatever. This deadly subject is covered in the section "Why you don't need to repartition anything" later in this chapter.

The mystique of partitioning

Occasionally, you may stumble over the disk term *partitioning*. It means *to take one humongous disk drive and split it up into several smaller, more manageable disk drives.* The DOS FDISK command does this. Yes, the same FDISK command I've recommended not using throughout this book (and throughout *DOS For Dummies*).

Many people get all huffy over the subject of partitioning, but it's no big deal. In fact, it's really unnecessary. It *used* to be necessary. Back before DOS 4, DOS could only handle a hard drive that was 32MB in size — nothing bigger.

For example, if your PC had a 40MB hard drive, that hard drive had to be split into two separate drives — two *logical drives* — so DOS could use it. (This explains why so many PC/AT computers out there have a 32MB drive C and a puny 8MB drive D.)

Since DOS 4, though, you can shove a 4 gigabyte (4,096MB) hard drive into a PC and DOS will swallow it whole. Of course, organizing that sucker with subdirectories is a must. Aside from that, there is no need to bother with disk partitions or FDISK.

- *Partitioning* creates *partitions* on a hard drive.

- Since version 4, DOS can deal with huge hard drives. There is just no more need to partition, unless you want multiple drive letters for some twisted reason.

- The FDISK program carried out the partitioning action, splitting a disk drive up into smaller chunks. One 90MB drive I had was split evenly into three 30MB drives to deal with DOS 3.3. The three drives became C, D, and E on my computer.

- Another reason they give for partitioning a hard drive is to set aside part of its storage for another operating system. The DOS manual said that you may want to use 10MB for DOS and then 10MB for UNIX or OS/2 or something. Blech! Never happens.

- Do not use FDISK! In the process of partitioning, it erases everything on a hard drive. This command should only be used when installing a new hard drive, and then by someone who's familiar with how it works. Very dangerous.

An example of partitioning that you don't have to read

Consider that your spouse, who until now has considered your PC to be an intruding lover prying you away, decided to — on a whim — buy you a huge 600MB hard drive. The guru he or she hired to install the hard drive partitioned it into three *logical drives:* 200MB for drive C, 200MB for drive D, and the last 200MB for drive E.

The one hard drive is the *physical* disk drive. The three drive letters, C, D, and E are *logical* drives created on three disk partitions. Because drive C is used to start the computer, it's called the *boot*

partition. The other partitions are referred to as *extended DOS partitions.* This is neither here nor there as far as using a computer is concerned.

The guru copied all your stuff from your old 200MB hard drive C to the new drive C partition. Yet now you still have two new, unused, and totally empty 200MB drives on your computer: drives D and E. That's what it looks like from the outside. Inside, though, it's just one moby hard drive with three partitions. Buy your spouse flowers for this and for finally coming around.

Why you don't need to repartition anything

Occasionally, some users get a desire to "test everything out." This is often the case with partitioning a hard drive. Some users, whose boldness exceeds their wits, decide to back up the hard drive and *repartition* it. When I ask why, they claim it's for organizational purposes. Ugh.

Please use subdirectories to organize your files! That's what they're for!

No matter what argument you can come up with for repartitioning your hard drive, the answer is to use subdirectories to organize your files. Really, with today's versions of DOS, you don't need to break up large hard drives any more.

Mental agony over disk storage and RAM

I've received a lot of mail from *DOS For Dummies* readers posing the following question: How can you copy a 1.2MB file from one disk to another without running out of memory? The answer is that you can, and not to worry about it. Ah, but there are details. . . .

DOS can copy a file of any size — well, the limit is really something like four gigabytes or some huge value. Even though you'd be hard pressed to find a drive that could hold a file that huge, DOS can still copy it. That's because DOS only copies a

small amount of the file at once. Typically, DOS reads in 512 bytes of a file at a time and then writes it back out to disk. This happens quickly, and the end result is that DOS can copy any file on disk no matter how much memory your PC has — and without running out of memory.

If you want to think of it another way, imagine someone saying you could never eat your Thanksgiving dinner because you couldn't possibly put all the stuff on your plate into your mouth at once. Yes, DOS takes little bites and eats a lot.

Rambling about RAM Drives

One of the many things you can do in CONFIG.SYS is set up a RAM drive.
Provided that you have enough memory to justify it, RAM drives are wonderful
for storing temporary files, running batch files, or just experimenting.

- ✔ You create RAM drives using a device driver in your CONFIG.SYS file. In
  this section, the RAMDRIVE.SYS device driver is used as an example. Your
  version of DOS may call this device driver VDISK.SYS. Both drivers are the
  same.

- ✔ IBM, for some lurid reason, calls a RAM drive a *virtual disk*. Oh, I don't
  know, it could be Microsoft who dreamt that one up. Whatever. Virtual
  disk = RAM drive.

All about RAM drives

I'm a big RAM drive fan. All my computers have one. They come in handy.

A RAM drive is really a chunk of your computer's memory. A special program (a
device driver) takes that chunk of memory, gussies it up, and presents it to DOS
claiming "Psst! This is really a disk drive." Being gullible, DOS believes it,
assigns a drive letter to the chunk of memory, and then treats the RAM drive
just as it would any other disk drive. Believe it or not, that's how it works.

Here are the two main things to like about RAM drives:

- ✔ A RAM drive is the fastest drive you can have on your computer.

- ✔ Programs that rely heavily on disk access run quickly on a RAM drive.

And here are even more things to like:

- ✔ The device driver used to create the RAM drive is RAMDRIVE.SYS. It's
  installed in your CONFIG.SYS file.

- ✔ RAM drives are fast because they use electronic memory, which moves at
  the speed of light (and sometimes faster). The other disk drives in your
  computer are mechanical. They spin and whir and can never move as fast
  as the speed of light (according to my friend Albert Einstein).

- ✔ Because RAM drives are so fast, programs that access files on the RAM
  drive access them almost instantaneously.

- ✔ To take advantage of the RAM drive, you must either create files or copy files
  to it. Copying files can be done in your PC's AUTOEXEC.BAT file. See Chapter
  10. If you create a file on your RAM drive, be sure to copy it to the hard
  drive for permanent storage.

- ✔ My astrologer tells me that Aries is the best sign for a RAM drive.

Perils of a RAM drive

RAM drives aren't all fun and glory. They have the following drawbacks:

- ✔ RAM drives use precious memory.

- ✔ To run disk-intensive software on a RAM drive, you need a lot of memory.

- ✔ A RAM drive is erased every time the power goes off or you reset your computer.

The last item is the most important: RAM drives aren't permanent. When you turn off your PC, everything on the RAM drive goes *poof*. Even when you just reset, the RAM drive is instantly erased.

- ✔ Only bother with a RAM drive if you have *extended* memory in your computer. This is true for any PC that has over 1MB of RAM in it. But really, you need more than that to make a RAM drive truly useful.

- ✔ You can also create a RAM drive in *expanded* memory or in *conventional* memory. (See Chapter 25 for definitions of the various memory management terms.)

- ✔ Never create any new files on a RAM drive. If you do, immediately save them to the hard drive if you expect to keep them.

- ✔ Some laptop RAM drives *are* permanent, saving information when you turn off the computer. This is done through battery magic, and it's only available on a few laptop models. Don't get cocky with it.

- ✔ About the nerdiest thing I've ever done is configure Windows to run from a RAM drive. I did this on a 16MB computer. First, I created an 8MB RAM drive, and then I copied Windows vital core files to that drive. It took a while, but eventually I got it to work. The stupid part is (aside from wasting a lot of time — though I was under orders from an editor) that Windows *still* accessed the hard drive when it started. There was no way to avoid it. Alas. (Actually, I'm kinda *embarrassed* to admit to this.)

Steps to create your own, personal RAM drive

If you want to create a RAM drive, follow these steps:

1. Figure out how much RAM you want to forgo for the RAM drive. Memory in a PC is precious. (Use the MEM command as discussed in Chapter 25 to figure out how much memory your PC has.)

2. Decide which type of memory you want to use for the RAM drive: conventional memory (not recommended), expanded memory, or extended memory. I recommend extended memory.

3. Edit your PC's CONFIG.SYS, using the DOS Editor. Instructions for editing CONFIG.SYS are found in Chapter 6. You are adding the RAMDRIVE.SYS device driver.

   The command that loads RAMDRIVE.SYS can go just about anywhere in your CONFIG.SYS file. Putting it at the end is perfectly okay.

4. Type in the following command, filling in the blanks as described in the following:

```
DEVICE=C:\DOS\RAMDRIVE.SYS size /where
```

   That is, type **DEVICE**, an equal sign, then **C**, colon, backslash, **DOS**, backslash, **RAMDRIVE**, period, **SYS**, and a space. (I'm assuming that C:\DOS is your DOS directory — if not, specify the proper path in CONFIG.SYS.)

   After you type **SYS** and a space, type in the size of your RAM drive in kilobytes (K). For example, type **512** to create a 512K RAM drive; type **64** to create a 64K RAM drive; you get the idea.

   If you're putting the RAM drive in conventional memory, you're done. (By the way, I wouldn't recommend doing this. If you must, then make the RAM drive only 16K in size — any more, and you're using too much memory.)

   If you're putting the RAM drive in expanded memory, add a space and **/A** (slash-A).

   If you're putting the RAM drive in extended memory, add a space and **/E** (slash-E).

   The following command creates a 1,024K (one megabyte) RAM drive in extended memory:

```
DEVICE=C:\DOS\RAMDRIVE.SYS 1024 /E
```

5. Save your changes to CONFIG.SYS.

6. Quit the DOS Editor.

7. At the DOS prompt, reset your PC. When the computer starts, you'll see a new message displayed, informing you that a RAM drive has been created. It may look something like this:

```
Microsoft RAMDrive version 3.07 virtual disk E:
    Disk size: 1024k
    Sector size: 512 bytes
    Allocation unit: 1 sectors
    Directory entries: 64
```

Here, DOS is screaming that it's built a 1,024K RAM drive and given that drive the letter E. The rest of the information is just so much nonsense.

✔ To see how much memory you have in your PC, use the MEM command. Refer to Chapter 25.

✔ The RAMDRIVE.SYS device driver will be in your DOS subdirectory. For most of us, the path is C:\DOS\RAMDRIVE.SYS. Refer to Chapter 16 for more information on what a *path* is.

✔ You can't create a RAM drive that uses more memory than your PC has! It just doesn't work that way.

✔ If you have expanded memory, stick the RAM drive there. Add /A (slash-A) to the end of your RAMDRIVE.SYS command in CONFIG.SYS.

✔ Your PC's expanded-memory device driver must appear in CONFIG.SYS before the command that creates the RAM drive in expanded memory.

✔ If you have extended memory, stick the RAM drive there. Add /E (slash-E) to the end of the RAMDRIVE.SYS command in your CONFIG.SYS file.

The lure of creating multiple RAM drives

You can create as many RAM drives as you like, provided that you have enough memory for all of them. DOS builds each RAM drive in memory, assigning a new, higher drive letter to each. For example,

```
DEVICE=C:\DOS\RAMDRIVE.SYS 1024 /E
DEVICE=C:\DOS\RAMDRIVE.SYS 1024 /E
DEVICE=C:\DOS\RAMDRIVE.SYS 1024 /E
```

The preceding commands in CONFIG.SYS create three RAM drives in extended memory, each 1,024K (one megabyte) in size. If drive C is your *highest* letter hard drive, then the preceding commands create RAM drives D, E, and F.

There are only two issues to consider when creating multiple RAM drives: First, do you have enough RAM? And second, why bother? For example, why make three 1MB RAM drives when you can just make one big 3MB RAM drive? What's the point?

One possible argument is to create different RAM drives for different purposes. On my system, RAM drive F is used to hold all my batch files, small utilities, and other programs that I use all the time. RAM drive G is a *temp* RAM drive, used to hold junk files and "important" memos sent by my publisher — stuff I can get rid of easily by pressing the reset button.

Batch files and RAM drives

Batch files are disk-intensive programs. RAM drives are well suited to disk-intensive programs. Hey, it sounds like a match made on *Studs!* Bring out the contestants!

But seriously, although this book tells you (in Chapter 17) to put all your batch files in a BATCH directory, it's a good idea to copy them to a RAM drive for faster execution. This can be done in AUTOEXEC.BAT, as described in Chapter 10.

✔ Be sure to put your batch file RAM drive on the path (instead of the BATCH directory). See Chapter 22 for more information on the PATH command.

✔ Continue to create your batch files in the BATCH directory, but then copy them to the RAM drive when you're done.

✔ A batch file RAM drive doesn't need to be all that large, but it may need more room in its root directory. For example,

```
DEVICE=C:\DOS\RAMDRIVE.SYS 16 128 128 /E
```

The preceding command in CONFIG.SYS creates a 16K RAM drive. The sector size is set low, equal to 128 bytes. That's because RAM drives are typically 128 bytes or less in size. Setting a sector size of 128 optimizes disk access for the tiny files. The last number sets the number of files in the root directory to 128. If you didn't set that value, the drive would be full after 64 batch files; because most people have more than that, I set the number to 128.

✔ *Studs* is a TV show in the *Love Connection/Dating Game* genre. I used to watch it because it was on after *Star Trek* each weeknight.

✔ MARK.BAT is a typical southern California batch file: tanned, well groomed, *cyooot,* but not too bright. MARY RAMDRIVE is a perky blond surfer girl, tanned and partially plastic, looking for a man with a sense of humor but who is definitely taller than she is. *Oh goodness, I'm going to be sick. . . .*

Chapter 25

Messing with Memory Management

● ●

In This Chapter

▶ Looking at your PC's memory

▶ Using MemMaker to manage your memory

▶ Making DOS start a wee bit faster (but at a risk)

▶ Understanding memory management terminology

● ●

Memory management should really be a non-issue. Sadly, due to the hectic and haphazard way the PC evolved, it's just not. Memory management is big and ugly and stares you in the face like a 300 pound transvestite named Beaula who has her eyes on your friend and you're too drunk to stand up to her. It's ominous! It's scary! It's everywhere!

Fortunately, this chapter comes to your rescue with a few vital words of advice regarding memory management, plus a brief glossary of memory management terms, filenames, and what it all means.

A Quick Look at How Your PC Uses Memory

Looking at memory is boring. They're just chips: little, rectangular black bugs with metal legs. They look like Keebler Fudge Sticks on a diet. Boring things. Rows and rows of chips. Of course, that's not important. What is important is how your PC uses that memory and what you can do with it.

- ✔ The most important thing to remember is how much memory you have.
- ✔ Also important is knowing how much of what *type* of memory you have.

There are four types of memory in a PC

You would think the whole thing would be called *memory*. Alas, it just ain't so. Here are the four types of memory in a PC:

Conventional memory

Upper memory

Expanded memory

Extended memory

- ✔ Do not memorize this. In fact, if people anywhere are using this book as a textbook, they've given me their word that none of this will be on the final.
- ✔ Not every PC has every type of memory.
- ✔ Not every PC *needs* every type of memory.
- ✔ There is a glossary of sorts on memory terms at the end of this chapter. Refer there for definitions of each memory type.

MSD tries to show you what's up with memory

You can use the Microsoft Diagnostic program to get an accurate description of how your computer uses memory and how much of what type of memory you have. But don't get your hopes up and expect it all to suddenly make sense.

Start MSD by typing **MSD** at the DOS prompt:

```
C:\>MSD
```

Type **MSD** and press Enter. You see the main summary screen displayed (see Figure 25-1). Second down on the left is a box/button that says Memory with some cryptic numbers next to it. Press M to activate this box and the memory display.

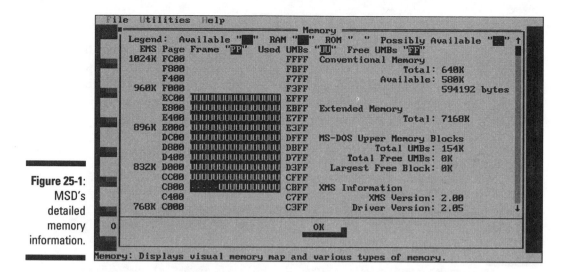

Figure 25-1:
MSD's
detailed
memory
information.

Figure 25-1 shows something similar to what you see on your screen. On the left is a memory map, which you can ignore. On the right are some summary statistics:

Conventional Memory: This tells you how much conventional memory you have, which will probably be 640K total. The second value tells you how much is *available* for use by your programs.

Extended Memory: This tells you how much extended memory lives in your PC.

Expanded Memory: Ditto here for expanded memory.

MS-DOS Upper Memory Blocks: Whatever these are, they're discussed on the screen as well.

Other stuff. I see something about XMS information plus some drivel about DMPI. Whatever. Amazing stuff.

- ✔ You can press the PgDn key to see the rest of this interesting display.

- ✔ Just nod at this information and go, "Hmmm, interesting." Then press the Escape key and then the F3 key to return to the DOS prompt.

- ✔ The MSD utility comes with Windows 3.0 or later or with DOS 6. If you don't have either, hey, you're screwed.

A brief look at the MEM command

The MEM command provides a brief summary of your PC's memory. Well, maybe not brief. But it is informative. Well, maybe not *really* informative. But it's interesting. Well . . . look at Figure 25-2 for a sample of what the MEM command's output looks like.

```
C:\> MEM

Memory Type        Total =    Used +    Free

Conventional        640K       58K      582K
Upper               155K      155K        0K
Reserved            384K      384K        0K
Extended (XMS)    7,013K    5,989K    1,024K

Total memory      8,192K    6,586K    1,606K

Total under 1 MB    795K      213K      582K

Largest executable program size      582K  (595,472 bytes)
Largest free upper memory block        0K       (0 bytes)
MS-DOS is resident in the high memory area.

C:\>
```

Figure 25-2:
The MEM command spews forth memory information.

The four types of memory are listed in the first column: Conventional, Upper, Extended, and Expanded. (You may not see all four; Figure 25-2 is missing Expanded.) The next column tells how much memory total you have for each of those. The final column tells how much memory is available or unused.

✔ For some reason, the MEM command splits upper memory into two parts: reserved and upper. Oh, but that part of memory is complex, so feel free to ignore the information.

✔ The MEM command only comes with DOS versions 4.0 and later.

✔ The output in Figure 25-2 is from a PC with MS-DOS 6.2 installed. Earlier versions of DOS won't have handy commas in the big numbers, and their output may be subtly different.

✔ If you have DOS 5, the MEM command's output will look something like this:

```
   655360 bytes total conventional memory
   655360 bytes available to MS-DOS
   594048 largest executable program size
 15663104 bytes total contiguous extended memory
        0 bytes available contiguous extended memory
  1048576 bytes available XMS memory
          MS-DOS resident in High Memory Area
```

Conventional memory is mentioned, as will be extended or expanded if they're available.

How to Not Go Wrong with DOS's Memory Management

Top on everyone's memory management wish list is "Never having to mess with it." The best way to do that is to have the computer mess with it, get it out of the way, and then let you get on with your work.

- ✔ DOS memory management only makes an impact on PCs with 386 or 486 (or Pentium) microprocessors. To see which type of microprocessor you have in your PC, run the MSD program; type **MSD** at the DOS prompt and look by the word Computer to see your microprocessor type. Press the F3 key to quit MSD.

- ✔ DOS's memory management will help you a tad if you have an 80286 computer. The old 8088 PCs? Weep bitterly, for there is no hope.

Run MemMaker and your worries will be over

While DOS 5 introduced memory management as a part of DOS, it took Microsoft until DOS 6 to provide a memory optimization utility, MemMaker, to make it all easy.

To optimize your PC's memory — nay, to make it all automatic and painless — type **MEMMAKER** at the DOS prompt:

```
C:\>MEMMAKER /BATCH2
```

In the preceding, **MEMMAKER** is typed, followed by a space and then slash-**BATCH2**. That runs the MemMaker program and optimizes your memory with your having to do little more than stare at the screen. After the dust settles, your memory will be fully managed. Thank you.

- ✔ MemMaker resets your computer a few times as it figures out what's going on. Don't be alarmed.

- ✔ Yes, it really is that easy.

- ✔ Run MemMaker after updating CONFIG.SYS or AUTOEXEC.BAT.

"But I don't have DOS 6!"

If you don't have DOS 6, what you need is a memory manager that has an optimization program like MemMaker. You can buy a third-party memory manager, such as 386MAX or QEMM/386. Or you can slug it out with DOS 5 and do everything manually.

- ✔ I feel both 386MAX and QEMM/386 are worthy memory managers. For ease of use, I recommend 386MAX. For the ability to tweak memory management, QEMM/386 is my choice.

- ✔ MemMaker is yet another reason to consider upgrading to the latest version of DOS.

What you're not to mess with (munge stuff)

MemMaker optimizes the way your PC uses memory by modifying your CONFIG.SYS and AUTOEXEC.BAT files. Don't mess with any of the changes!

What MemMaker does in CONFIG.SYS is change a few DEVICE configuration commands into DEVICEHIGH commands. In AUTOEXEC.BAT, the LOADHIGH command is occasionally shoved in front of a TSR or other DOS command or program. This is all touchy-not stuff.

- ✔ Cryptic items and hieroglyphs follow the DEVICEHIGH and LOADHIGH commands. Don't mess with 'em.

- ✔ Munge (*munj*) is a variation of the acronym MUNG. It stands for Mash Until No Good, and generally refers to fouling something up by making it overly complex.

How to make DOS start a wee bit faster (if you dare)

If you have MS-DOS 6.2 and wonder why DOS takes a little bit longer to get started, take heart; it's nothing you've done. Instead, it's the "new and improved" HIMEM.SYS memory management device driver. But don't delete that command from CONFIG.SYS just yet.

One of the improvements they made to HIMEM.SYS was to add a memory test. Never mind that your PC does a memory test when it starts (obviously Bill Gates doesn't trust it), HIMEM.SYS does one for you again! But I'm certain someone somewhere has received the following, dreaded message:

```
ERROR: HIMEM.SYS has detected
unreliable XMS memory at
address 00000000
```

```
For more information, type HELP
TESTMEM at the command prompt.

To continue starting your
computer, press ENTER.
```

How dreadful. But that's not my point here. If you want to switch off the error message, add the following option to the line in your PC's CONFIG.SYS file that starts the HIMEM.SYS device driver:

```
/TESTMEM:OFF
```

Type a slash, **TESTMEM**, a colon, and then **OFF**. This should be tacked on to the end of the line that reads something like `DEVICE= C:\DOS\HIMEM.SYS` in your **CONFIG.SYS** file. See Chapter 7 for more information on the **DEVICE** command.

Memory Terms and Filenames Explained

The following sections define and explain various words, acronyms, and memory management jargon you may encounter.

Conventional memory

This is DOS's main memory, where all of your programs run. It's pronounced *kon-ven-shun-al mem-o-ree*. Not only do your programs run in conventional memory, but they want — nay, *crave* — as much of it as possible. This is why memory management emerged as a topic in the first place; programs were running out of room in conventional memory.

- Conventional memory is limited to 640K. It can be less — but never more — than that.
- Most of the PCs sold today have 640K of conventional memory.
- Memory management makes more conventional memory available by moving some hoggy programs from there into upper memory.
- Conventional memory is also known as *main memory* or sometimes *DOS memory*.

DEVICEHIGH

This is a configuration command used like the DEVICE command in CONFIG.SYS. Pronounced *dee-vise-hi*, the DEVICEHIGH command loads device drivers into upper memory, not conventional memory. This makes more conventional memory available, which is nice because that's what most DOS programs want.

Don't mess with the DEVICEHIGH configuration command. The MemMaker program sticks it into your CONFIG.SYS file and sets all the right options. You shouldn't mess with it. No, not never.

DOS (configuration command)

This poorly named command is used in CONFIG.SYS to tell DOS where in memory it should live. There are two variations you may see:

```
DOS=HIGH
```

This command tells DOS to stick itself (oh, if you could only stop reading here, what a glorious command it would be) up into the high memory area. The result is quite a bit of memory savings, making more of that precious conventional memory available.

The other variation is

```
DOS=UMB
```

This tells DOS to work with UMBs, which are defined elsewhere in this chapter.

✔ The HIMEM.SYS device driver is required to be present in CONFIG.SYS before the DOS command will work. (HIMEM.SYS usually appears first, before the DOS command.)

✔ Sometimes both commands may appear on the same line, which is okay:

```
DOS=HIGH,UMB
```

✔ The DOS=UMB command is only one step. You also need to install the EMM386.EXE device driver and use the DEVICEHIGH and LOADHIGH commands to complete the picture. This is what MemMaker does automatically.

EMM386.EXE

This is DOS's expanded and upper memory device driver software. It's pronounced *ee-em-em-three-eighty-six-dot-ee-ecks-ee*. In its most common form, you'll see this device driver installed as follows:

```
DEVICE=C:\DOS\EMM386.EXE NOEMS
```

✔ Refer to Chapter 7 for information on the DEVICE command.

✔ You must use the HIMEM.SYS device driver in order for EMM386.EXE to work. Most users place the two commands in CONFIG.SYS one after the other, HIMEM.SYS first.

EMS

This acronym is pronounced *ee-em-ess*. It stands for *expanded memory specification,* which is a set of rules for using expanded memory in your computer. A device driver is installed in CONFIG.SYS to make sure that happens. It's called an *EMS* device driver, and typically it's named EMM.SYS.

✔ A longer version of this acronym is LIM EMS, which is also defined in this chapter.

✔ On 386, 486, and Pentium computers, the EMM386.EXE device driver is used to set up the EMS standard-thing in memory.

Expanded memory

This is special memory used by DOS programs that crave more memory, more than the puny 640K conventional memory has to offer. It's pronounced *ex-span-ded mem-o-ree.*

Expanded memory must be added to an old 8088 or 80286 computer with a special expansion card. Then special EMS software is required to make it all work. After that, DOS and a few programs can use the expanded memory.

On 386 and later microprocessors, expanded memory is created by using spare extended memory. This magic is accomplished with DOS 5 and later, using the EMM386.EXE device driver.

- Expanded memory used to be "it" as far as extra memory in a computer was concerned. Today, "it" is really extended memory.

- Expanded memory. Extended memory. They must have been a little short of the creativity juice that day in the lab. Otherwise, why name two different types of memory so similarly? If I had my way, expanded memory would be called *bonus memory*.

Expanded memory manager (EMM)

This is a piece of software, a device driver, that rules over expanded memory. I don't know how it's pronounced because it's not that popular of a term. (Oh, I could take a stab, but why bother?)

For 386 and later microprocessors, DOS's EMM386.EXE device driver provides expanded memory management. For other computers, you'll use the EMM.SYS program that came with your expanded memory hardware upgrade.

The expanded memory manager is what forces your computer to obey the rules and regulations of EMS.

Extended memory

This is memory in your 286 or higher computer that lives way up there, up beyond 1MB. So if you have 2MB of memory in your computer, 1MB of that is extended memory. If you have an 8MB computer, then you have 7MB of extended memory.

Extended memory is used by special advanced programs, such as Windows. These programs crave extended memory and want lots of it. In DOS, RAM drives and the SMARTDrive disk cache are created in extended memory, which subtracts from what Windows wants. This is why I recommend giving up as much extended memory as possible to Windows, which makes it happy (and no one really wants to anger Windows).

- More information on creating a RAM drive is offered in Chapter 23.
- Refer to Chapter 24 for information on the SMARTDrive disk cache.

Extended memory manager

This is a special device driver that controls all of extended memory, boldly proclaims the XMS standard, and indulges all programs to pay heed and obey. In DOS, that's done through the meek HIMEM.SYS device driver.

High Memory Area (HMA)

The HMA is a special part of extended memory used by DOS to store some interesting things, primarily itself. It's pronounced *atch-em-ay*. The HIMEM.SYS device driver creates this 64K chunk of memory from the first 64K of extended memory in your PC.

Normally, DOS uses the HMA to store itself and some of its programs. Windows also uses the HMA, elbowing DOS out of the way because Windows is greedy and has this personality thing where it thinks it's better than DOS.

DOS uses the HMA when directed to load "high" by the DOS configuration command in CONFIG.SYS.

HIMEM.SYS

This is DOS's chief memory management device driver program, loaded in the CONFIG.SYS file. It's pronounced *hi-mem-sis*. It's supposed to control high memory.

The HIMEM.SYS device driver has several duties. First, it establishes the XMS standard on your computer, controlling all of extended memory. Second, it creates a special area of memory called the HMA, the high memory area. Third, it elbows its way to the top of the memory management organizational chart and demands total obedience by all your PC's memory.

- ✔ Your PC must have at least 384K of extended memory for HIMEM.SYS to work.

- ✔ Refer to Chapter 7 for information on the DEVICE configuration command and how it's used to install HIMEM.SYS.

- ✔ The HIMEM.SYS device driver comes with DOS 5 and later, as well as Windows 3.0 and later. This brings up the interesting question. . .

- ✔ "Which HIMEM.SYS driver should I use?" Check the date on the file. If the one that came with Windows is more recent, use it. Otherwise, use the copy that comes with DOS.

LIM EMS

These two acronyms stand for *Lotus-Intel-Microsoft expanded memory specification*. It's pronounced letters-only. Basically, this is a standard that Lotus, Intel, and Microsoft thought up to add more memory to early PCs. In fact, I don't know of anyone who readily uses this term any more.

LOADHIGH (or LH)

This is a DOS command typically finding itself in AUTOEXEC.BAT. It's pronounced *load-high,* and it has a shorter version, LH. What it does is to load memory-resident programs (TSRs) into upper memory. Usually, MemMaker takes care of this, so you never need to bother with it.

- Don't ever mess with a LOADHIGH command in AUTOEXEC.BAT.
- What DEVICEHIGH is to CONFIG.SYS, LOADHIGH is to AUTOEXEC.BAT.

Shadowing (also ROM Shadowing)

"Something's been following my ROM for days!"

Shadowing is a technique in which the computer's ROM or BIOS is copied into memory. The trick makes things run faster, although it may cause some problems.

- Your PC may be capable of shadowing its BIOS or ROM. This is usually done through the hardware Setup program.
- DOS's memory management doesn't mind if BIOS shadowing is on. Other memory management products may ask you to switch it off, or they may provide their own, faster solutions.

Stealth

Pronounced *stealth*, this is a technology that third-party memory manager QEMM/386 uses to squeeze out more upper memory. I don't know how it works. I don't know if it works. I don't know if it's magic. But I think it does explain why I tend to forget things easily: I have too much stealth memory.

UMB

This acronym stands for *upper memory blocks*. It's pronounced *You-Em-Bee*. A UMB is a chunk of upper memory that can be used for storing a device driver or TSR. Memory management optimization programs, such as DOS's MemMaker, do this for you. Unfortunately, you'll still have to put up with the term UMB.

- UMBs is the plural of UMB.
- The DEVICEHIGH and LOADHIGH commands place programs into UMBs. MemMaker sets it all up.

> ✔ Third-party memory managers use their own commands to put programs into UMBs.

> ✔ The process of putting programs into UMBs is called *loading high*.

Upper memory

Upper memory is a portion of the PC's memory that lives just above conventional memory. When IBM designed the original IBM PC, they set this area of memory aside for future expansion.

Most of upper memory remains unused. What a memory manager will do is to "fill it up" with usable memory, which creates the famous *upper memory blocks* (UMBs). Device drivers and TSRs can be shoved up there, using memory management magic, or the DEVICEHIGH and LOADHIGH commands — governed, of course, by an optimizer like MemMaker.

> ✔ This type of memory may also be called *reserved memory, upper DOS memory,* or *high DOS memory.*

> ✔ Some of the things that are placed in upper memory include video memory, the video BIOS, the hard drive BIOS, the PC's BIOS, network BIOS, and BIOS-BIOS-BIOS. You get the idea.

XMS

This is an acronym pronounced *ecks-em-ess.* It sounds like a mood altering drug. Really, XMS stands for *extended memory specification.* Essentially, that's a list of rules and regulations for working with extended memory.

In order to make XMS happen on your computer, you need an XMS device driver program. With DOS, the program is named HIMEM.SYS. Third-party memory managers use their own device drivers.

> ✔ Occasionally, some dopey DOS program refers to extended memory as XMS memory. Same difference.

> ✔ No, XMS is not Christmas memory.

Part V
Shortcuts and Tips Galore

The 5th Wave   By Rich Tennant

IN A STROKE OF SELF-RELIANCE, RAY EXTENDS THE POWER ON HIS LAPTOP BY TAPPING INTO THE BATTERY ON HIS SLEEPING NEIGHBOR'S HEARING AID.

In this part...

This last section provides a fun way to end what's been a mostly technical book. The chapters here contain tips, warnings, plus a few trick-or-treats for the DOS fancier. Also, as a response to overwhelming reader desire, this book's final chapter provides the most unique conclusion to any computer book yet written.

Chapter 26
1100101 DOS Tips

In This Chapter

▶ Lots of DOS tips

▶ In no particular order

*N*o, this chapter really doesn't contain over one million DOS tips. I'm being sneaky. The actual number of tips crammed into this single chapter is more like 101 (one hundred and one). What I did was to pull off some nerd humor and write the number 101 in the binary counting system. All the ones and zeros in binary add up to 101. That's about all the tips I could think of in the time allowed, though I'm sure there are more. These are my favorite, presented in no particular order.

✔ Some are tips, some are warnings, some are suggestions.

✔ Most of the tips have references to the chapter in this book where the topic is discussed at length.

✔ There are definitely more tips than the 101 listed here. In fact, computer book author Kris Jamsa once did a book with 1,001 tips in it. No, that ain't binary.

1. After disks are formatted, label them.

Write on the label before you stick it on the disk. Describe the disk's contents or give the disk a name so that you can tell it from other disks lying around. (People apply the same logic to naming their children.) The label also lets you know that the disk is formatted.

2. All commands in CONFIG.SYS go on a line by themselves.

3. Always buy the highest capacity disks for your floppy drives.

4. Always check to make sure you're not in Windows or a menu program before you reset the PC.

A good way to tell whether you are is to type the EXIT command:

```
C:\>EXIT
```

If you're in Windows or running some type of menu program, typing **EXIT** quits the DOS program and returns you to Windows (or whatever). Only after you've quit Windows or a menu program should you reset your computer.

5. Always format your disks as soon as you take the box home (or to the office).

6. Always scan the README.TXT files that come with some programs.

README.TXT files usually contain up-to-date fixes to the manual, plus a list of hardware incompatibility problems.

7. Avoid booting your PC from an unknown diskette!

This is how viruses are spread. Refer to Chapter 23 for more information on viruses.

8. Back up before you attempt any major subdirectory pruning or grafting.

Yes, a full hard disk backup. Why? The only way you can undelete a subdirectory is to restore it from a recent backup.

9. Back up CONFIG.SYS and AUTOEXEC.BAT each time your computer starts.

You back up these files at start-up by putting the following two commands in AUTOEXEC.BAT:

```
COPY C:\AUTOEXEC.BAT C:\TEMP
COPY C:\CONFIG.SYS C:\TEMP
```

In the preceding, both files are copied to the C:\TEMP directory. If you accidentally delete either file, you need only copy them back to the root directory.

10. Back up today's work!

11. Be careful where you place DEVICE commands in CONFIG.SYS

Some device commands may have a pecking order. Refer to Chapter 7 for more information.

12. Beware of the DEL. command!

That's DEL followed by a period. The period is DOS shorthand for all files in the current directory. Yowser!

13. Change your password often!

DOS doesn't use passwords, but some programs do. First, *don't forget* your password. Second, change it so that no one else figures it out.

14. Check out the current directory on another disk drive before deleting files there.

Type the **CD** command followed by the drive letter:

```
C:\>CD D:
```

This command tells DOS to report the current directory for drive D. Make sure the directory is the one you assume it is.

15. Do not delete the COMMAND.COM file.

16. Don't be too quick to press the Y key!

17. Don't bother with a RAM drive if your PC is low on RAM or if you run Windows.

Even if you have a 4MB computer, that memory is better used by Windows than anything else.

18. Don't bother with disk compression unless you really, really have to.

Compressing your disk is really only a temporary solution. A better one is to buy a new, larger hard drive.

19. Don't delete the secret MSDOS.SYS or IO.SYS files.

20. Don't forget double dollar-sign ($$) thingies.

Dollar signs have special purposes with the PROMPT command and when you create DOSKey macros. Refer to Chapter 3 for more information on the PROMPT command; see Chapter 5 for DOSKey macros.

21. Don't forget the Ctrl-P print DOS command trick.

Pressing Ctrl-P once at the DOS prompt causes DOS to print everything as well as display it on-screen. Press Ctrl-P again to turn off this feature. See Chapter 2 for more info.

22. Don't forget the Ctrl-T multiple command DOSKey trick.

When DOSKey is loaded, you can type more than one command at any DOS prompt. Press Ctrl-T to separate the commands. That sticks a ¶ character — the command separator — on the screen.

23. Don't get carried away with batch files!

Instead, consider learning a real programming language, such as C or BASIC. DOS comes with a BASIC language program for free. It's called QBasic, and it's really rather nice.

24. Don't keep using the same disk for years.

This is a bad one: "But I've used this diskette as my backup disk for three years now. How come it won't work?" Duh! Sandpaper don't last forever, and neither do floppy disks.

25. Don't mess with any hidden files on your disk!

Okay, if you hid them yourself, then you can mess with 'em.

26. Don't use disk partitioning as a substitute for organizing files in subdirectories.

DOS uses subdirectories to organize files. Disk partitioning was dreamt up for other reasons. Besides, I don't recommend that anyone use the FDISK command (unless you're installing a *new* hard drive).

27. Drive slowly in icy weather.

Chains and snow tires will help you get started, but nothing makes you stop on a sheet of ice. (I wouldn't have known this if I still lived in Southern California.)

28. Eject a page from your laser printer.

Use the following command:

```
C:\>ECHO ^L > PRN
```

Type **ECHO**, a space, Ctrl-L, a space, a greater-than sign, a space, and then **PRN**. This sends the Ctrl-L character to the printer, which tells every laser printer to spit out a page. Refer to Chapter 20 for more information on I/O redirection and the > thing.

29. End AUTOEXEC.BAT with the first command you type every day.

"I always start my day by typing WP to run WordPerfect. Hey! If that command were the last thing in my computer's AUTOEXEC.BAT file, then I would start my day quicker!"

30. Find files quickly by using the MSD program.

MSD is the Microsoft Diagnostic program, included free with MS-DOS 6 and Windows. In the File menu, select the Find File command. Detailed instructions are offered in Chapter 12.

31. To make DOS 6 start a wee bit faster, add the SWITCHES=/F command to your CONFIG.SYS file.

The SWITCHES=/F command doesn't make DOS start any faster. It just skips the 2-second delay after the Starting MS-DOS message appears.

32. Have a TEMP directory for your temporary files.

33. Have someone else to blame. (Remember that it's probably never your own fault.)

34. If a disk won't format, toss it out!

I'm serious. Keeping a dead disk drawer is a waste of space.

35. If you have trouble remembering which drive is A and which is B, label them.

36. If you're in doubt as to which display or microprocessor you have, run the MSD utility to find out.

Type **MSD** and press Enter. If you have Windows or MS-DOS 6, the MSD (Microsoft Diagnostic) program runs. The main screen lists or describes most of your PC's basic components.

37. If you're using a word processor to edit CONFIG.SYS or AUTOEXEC.BAT, save the file in the plain text format.

Plain text format might also be called the DOS text format, unformatted, or ASCII text.

38. If you're using the SHELL configuration command in CONFIG.SYS, remember the /P switch.

It's the /P switch that tells COMMAND.COM to run the AUTOEXEC.BAT file.

39. Install DOSKey in the Insert Mode.

Use this command in your AUTOEXEC.BAT file:

```
DOSKEY /INSERT
```

Chapter 4 has more information on DOSKey.

40. Instead of pressing Ctrl-S to pause a long display, pipe the output through the MORE filter.

This works with any DOS command. Just add the following two items at the end of the command line:

| MORE

Type your command, the one that displays a few yards of text, then type a space, the pipe character (I), another space, and then **MORE**.

41. Keep a regular backup schedule.

Here is my schedule: Daily, I do a work backup. Weekly, I do a "new files" backup. Monthly, I back up the whole hard drive, all 600MB of it.

42. Keep a short path.

Refer to Chapter 22 for my moaning and groaning about long search paths.

43. Keep the root directory clean!

This means files that must live in the root directory are the only things that should be there (along with subdirectories).

44. Move excess files out of the root directory.

Any files other than those that must live in the root directory you can move elsewhere. Refer to Chapter 22.

45. Never change a file's S attribute.

You can do this with the ATTRIB command (or not, as the case might be).

46. Never delete any file that starts with DBLSPACE!

47. Occasionally run a disk-checking utility, such as DOS's SCANDISK.

Run your disk-checking utility about once a month. Do a surface scan every few months or so. See Chapter 23.

48. Occasionally run a disk optimizer, like DOS's DEFRAG.

Keep an eye on the optimizer's evaluation of your disk drive. If it says no optimization is necessary, then don't bother.

49. On a cold day, wear a hat.

Heat escapes rapidly from the head, no matter how much hair you have. So if you want to keep warm, wear a hat. Also, put a cap on baby, even in the summer (to shade her eyes).

50. Save files in a text format to share them with other PCs.

The text (or ASCII) format is a common file format for just about any program. If you save a WordPerfect file in text format, a Microsoft Word user can read that file. By doing this, you and your friends can share information without having the same program.

51. Only use letters and numbers when naming your files.

52. Only work on CONFIG.SYS or AUTOEXEC.BAT one command at a time.

Change the command, save the file to disk, and reset to test. If it works, you can work on another command. But avoid doing too much at once. That way, if something goes wrong, you know what caused it.

53. Organize your hard drive.

Chapter 22 has the details.

54. Place miscellaneous files into general-purpose subdirectories.

Again, turn to Chapter 22.

55. Press Ctrl-Alt-Delete to reset quickly.

Pressing the reset switch makes resetting the computer take longer than it would if you press Ctrl-Alt-Delete to reset. This is because the reset switch tells DOS to re-test its guts, and that takes longer.

56. Press the spacebar to skip over your PC's start-up memory tests.

This may not work on all computers, but when you're in a hurry, it does speed things up a tad.

57. Print the output of any DOS command by adding > PRN to the end.

Type the command and then add the following:

```
> PRN
```

Type a space, a greater-than sign, another space, and then **PRN**. Make sure your printer is on and ready to print before you press the Enter key.

58. Put all your batch files into a BATCH directory.

Not only should all your batch files live in the BATCH directory, they should be born there, too.

59. Put the PATH command first in AUTOEXEC.BAT.

This allows DOS to find programs to run in AUTOEXEC.BAT, without your having to type their full pathnames.

60. Run batch files from a RAM drive.

61. Run MemMaker after updating your CONFIG.SYS or AUTOEXEC.BAT files.

62. Run virus-scanning software, such as DOS's MSAV, on each new disk you use on your computer.

63. Set your CD-ROM drive to a specific drive letter.

You can do this by using the /R option after the MSCDEX.EXE command in your PC's AUTOEXEC.BAT file. Type slash-R, a colon, then the drive letter for your CD-ROM. That way, your CD-ROM always has the same letter, no matter how many other drives you add or remove from your PC. (See Chapter 10 for an example.)

64. Load MSCDEX before the SMARTDrive disk cache in AUTOEXEC.BAT.

If you do that in MS-DOS 6.2, SMARTDrive will cache the CD-ROM, making it work a bit faster.

65. Stick new commands at the end of CONFIG.SYS.

Generally speaking. Unless told otherwise.

66. Take care of your files!

Back up! Check the disk with the CHKDSK or SCANDISK commands! Check for viruses!

67. Take your spoon out of your iced tea before you drink it.

It could stab you in the eye.

68. The best way to view text files is to "edit" them in the DOS Editor.

You can use the PgUp and PgDn keys in the Editor, unlike the TYPE or MORE commands, to view different parts of the file. You can also use the Search command to locate specific bits of text.

69. The examples in DOS 6's HELP program often show you exactly what you're looking for.

Type **HELP**, a space, and then the name of the command or device driver you want help with. Press the Tab key until the cursor is under the word *Examples*. Press Enter to see some actually useful examples.

70. There are three ways to print a text file in DOS.

1) You can copy the file to the printer:

```
C:\>COPY BOVINE PRN
```

2) You can redirect output to the printer:

```
C:\>TYPE BOVINE > PRN
```

3) You can edit the file in the DOS Editor and then use the **Print** command in the **File** menu to print it.

71. To see a directory of directories, use DIR *. or DIR /AD

The DIR *. command works because directories usually lack extensions. Unfortunately, that doesn't guarantee each file you see is a directory. For DOS 5 and later, the following always works:

```
C:\>DIR /AD
```

72. Try not to put more than 300 files into any directory.

This isn't a rule — it's just that when you overload a directory with that many files, DOS has to work overtime to manage them all. Also, it probably means the files aren't organized. (Any application that breaks this rule is forgiven; your C:\WINDOWS directory and its ilk are exceptions here.)

73. Turn word wrap off when editing CONFIG.SYS or AUTOEXEC.BAT in a word processor.

Commands can't wrap in CONFIG.SYS or AUTOEXEC.BAT. Setting the right margin to 14 inches or so usually fixes this problem in most word processors. (Text editors? Don't worry!)

74. Type DIR /W to see a list of files by name only.

75. Type DIR > PRN to print a list of files.

Remember to have your printer on and ready to print before you type this command.

76. To quickly get a feel for the subdirectory structure on a new computer, type the TREE command.

77. Unless you have MS-DOS 6.2, the COPY, MOVE, and XCOPY commands overwrite existing files — with no warning.

With MS-DOS 6.2, these commands display a message:

```
Overwrite BOVINE.COW (Yes/No/All)?
```

Press Y to overwrite the file, N to skip, and A to overwrite everything (when you're using wildcards).

78. Upgrade your software when necessary.

Ignore the propaganda! You only need to upgrade when the new version offers some feature you *really* need. They'll keep you on their mailing list, don't worry.

79. Don't mess with any alterations a memory optimizer makes to your CONFIG.SYS or AUTOEXEC.BAT files!

80. Use >> to append redirected output.

Unlike the single greater-than character, >> sends output to a file on disk but doesn't overwrite that file. Instead, any new text is glued to the end of the file — appended, so to speak.

81. Use a RAM drive for temporary file storage.

Set the TEMP variable equal to your RAM drive as discussed in Chapter 19. The RAM drive should be a reasonable size for this, at least 500KB or thereabouts.

82. Use a RAM drive to store your batch files.

83. Use a screen dimmer or shut down your monitor.

The perils of phosphor burn-in are a bit overstated on today's color monitors. Still, turning off the monitor when you won't be using the computer or employing a screen dimmer program is a good idea.

84. Use Alt-F7 to erase DOSKEY's command history.

You only need to do this if you're worried that someone who knows DOSKey will use the F7 key (by itself) to see what commands you've been typing. You can also use it to clean out DOSKey's command history when you're creating batch files (as described in Chapter 17).

85. Use ANSI commands to add color to the DOS prompt.

See Chapter 21.

86. Use ATTRIB +R to protect files from accidental erasure.

See the end of Chapter 12.

87. Use AUTOEXEC.BAT to automatically type your PC's start-up commands.

See Chapter 10.

88. Use batch files to run your programs.

See Chapter 17 for detailed info about batch files. Chapter 22 mentions batch files a little bit.

89. Use DOSKey macros to disable dangerous DOS commands.

This is covered in Chapter 5.

90. Use DOSKey to make command line editing easier.

91. Use MemMaker to organize your PC's memory.

92. Use SMARTDrive to improve disk access.

93. Use the /TESTMEM:OFF option with HIMEM.SYS to disable its arduously long memory test.

Refer to Chapter 25 for more information.

94. Use the DEL /P command instead of DEL.

Refer to Chapter 14 for information on creating a safety delete DOSKey macro.

95. Use the DIR /P command to pause the display after each screen of files.

96. Use the DIRCMD environment variable to preset your favorite DIR command options.

To see an example of how to do this, refer to Chapter 12.

97. Use the F8 key to search and grab from DOSKEY's history.

Just type the start of any old DOS command — something you've used before. You only need to type the first part of the command and then press the F8 key. DOSKey scans its history and grabs the first matching command. If that's the command you want, press Enter or edit the command. If it's not the command you want, press F8, and DOSKey searches again.

98. Use the FORMAT /Q command to quickly reformat old diskettes.

Beware of using FORMAT /Q on diskettes that are too old! If you are using old disks, better use the straight FORMAT command. That command fully scans the disk for any defects.

99. Use the MORE < command to quickly view text files.

100. Use the REM command to disable commands in CONFIG.SYS and AUTOEXEC.BAT.

Chapters 6 and 9 provide you with examples.

101. Use XCOPY instead of COPY for copying large groups of files.

XCOPY is the "super copy" command. But aside from its large assortment of options, its best value comes from its speed when you copy a large number of files. See Chapter 13.

Chapter 27

Dirty Tricks (to Play on Your Friends)

· ·

In This Chapter

▶ Nasty things to do that annoy others

▶ Trivial arguments for DOS over Windows

· ·

*I*f DOS doesn't intimidate you any more, then you can use it to intimidate your friends! Oh, I don't mean to be nasty. But if you're willing to have a little fun, I'm not going to hold you back. This chapter contains a bunch of interesting things you can do to make DOS more lively, plus some other stuff I tossed in for humor purposes only.

> ✔ Disclaimer: The author and publisher take no responsibility for any side effects caused by eating this book's paper.

The Dirty Tricks

None of the items that follow do any serious damage to any PC. These are just funny things you can try — practical jokes to play on friends and get them flustered. There's only one request I make: After laughing, please show them what you've done and admit that you're a jerk. Thank you.

Abort, Retry, Fail? DOS prompt

Type in the following PROMPT command:

```
PROMPT $_Not ready reading drive $N$_Abort, Retry, Fail?
```

Type a dollar sign and an underline; then type in **Not ready reading drive**, a space, then a dollar sign, the letter **N**, another dollar sign, an underline, and finally **Abort, Retry, Fail?**. Press Enter.

This changes the DOS prompt to read like the dreaded error message:

```
Not ready reading drive C
Abort, Retry, Fail?
```

The $N in the prompt means it always displays the proper drive letter.

✔ Stick this command in a coworker's AUTOEXEC.BAT file. Refer to Chapter 9.

✔ More information on the PROMPT command can be found in Chapter 3.

The CLS prompt

The following command produces one highly annoying DOS prompt:

```
PROMPT $E[2J$P$G
```

Type the **PROMPT** command, a space, a dollar sign, the letter **E**, a left bracket, the number **2**, the letter **J**, a dollar sign, the letter **P**, a dollar sign, and then the letter **G**. Press Enter.

This PROMPT command always clears the screen before it displays the DOS prompt:

```
C:\DOS>
```

That way your target never sees any output or anything DOS displays.

✔ This prompt requires that the ANSI.SYS device driver be installed. Refer to Chapter 21 for more information on ANSI.SYS.

✔ It's the $E[2J part of the prompt command that clears the screen. The other commands (PG in the preceding) display the prompt.

Bogus hard disk formatting batch file

Nothing is more humorous than reformatting your hard drive — especially when DOS seems to take off and do it for no apparent reason.

Featured in Figure 27-1 is the YUCKS.BAT batch file, a DOS 6 batch file that simulates some heinous command reformatting your hard drive.

```
1.    @ECHO OFF
2.    CLS
3.    ECHO ^G
4.    VER
5.    ECHO ←[AHard Disk Format Program
6.    ECHO WARNING! You are about to format
7.    ECHO Your hard drive.
8.    ECHO.
9.    CHOICE Are you sure you want to do this /C:y /T:y,10
10.   ECHO Formatting: ←[s
11.   :LOOP
12.   ECHO ←[u.←[s
13.   DIR \ | SORT > NUL
14.   GOTO LOOP
```

Figure 27-1:
The
YUCKS.BAT
batch file.

Start your editor and type in the batch file commands illustrated in Figure 27-1. Don't type in the line numbers! They're for reference-purposes only. Table 27-1 describes how to type some of the more difficult lines.

Table 27-1	Help for Typing in the YUCKS.BAT Batch File
Line#	*Hint/Description*
3	Type **ECHO**, a space, then Ctrl-P, and then Ctrl-G. This inserts the Ctrl-G character (it makes the speaker beep) into the batch file. On your screen, it will look like a tiny dot.
5	After ECHO, type a space, then Ctrl-P, and then press the Esc key. This inserts the Escape character into the editor. (The Escape character looks like a left-pointing arrow: ←). After that, type a left bracket and then the capital letter *A* (it must be big *A*); then type the rest of the command.
8	Follow ECHO with a period. There is no space between the *O* and the period.

(continued)

Table 27-1 *(continued)*

Line#	Hint/Description
9	The CHOICE command ends with slash-C, colon, **Y**, a space, then slash-T, colon, **Y**, a comma, and then the number **10**.
10	After the colon, type a space, press Ctrl-P, Esc (to insert the Escape character), left bracket, and then a little *S* (it must be a little *S*).
11	Start this line with a colon and then type **LOOP**.
12	Type **ECHO**, a space, then the Escape character (Ctrl-P, Esc), a left bracket, and a little *U*. Type a period, then the Escape character again (Ctrl-P, Esc), a left bracket, and then a little *S*. It must be a little *U* and a little *S*.
13	Type **DIR** a space, backslash, a space, the pipe character (|), another space, **SORT**, a space, a greater-than character, then **NUL**.

Save the batch file to disk as YUCKS.BAT. When you type **YUCKS** at the DOS prompt, the screen clears, the speaker beeps, and you see something similar to the following:

```
MS-DOS Version 6.20
Hard Disk Format Program
WARNING! You are about to format
Your hard drive.
Are you sure your want to do this [Y]?
```

The user has only one option: to press Y. Any other key causes the computer be bleep horridly.

After 10 seconds, the Y is typed automatically. Then the "formatting" begins. It's only a screen display; however, line 13 in the batch file causes the display to pause briefly and creates some "disk activity" that sounds like formatting. (This is *truly* evil.)

To cancel the batch file (and stop them from screaming), press the Ctrl-Break key combination, and then press Y.

- ✔ This batch file requires two goodies to work: DOS 6 and the ANSI.SYS device driver. Refer to Chapter 21 for info on ANSI.SYS.

- ✔ The VER command in line 3 displays the current DOS version. This makes the innocent user suspect it's a real DOS program running.

- ✔ The ECHO ^G command makes the computer beep to draw attention to the screen. If you stick this command in AUTOEXEC.BAT, the user might not see it or pay attention.

Fun with do-nothing commands

Some of DOS's batch file commands (see Chapter 18) have a life only inside a batch file. Outside the batch file, at the DOS prompt, they don't do squat. Still, when you type them, an error message doesn't occur. This leaves ample room for jocularity:

- ✔ **The bogus SHIFT command**

  YOU: Have you seen the new Shift Key enhancement command?

  NF*: No.

  YOU: It's great! It comes with DOS. Type this in:

  ```
  C:\>SHIFT
  ```

  YOU: Tell me if you notice a difference in the Shift Keys after typing a while.

- ✔ **The bogus REM command**

  YOU: Whoa! Wait a second. Before you do anything on the computer, you should type the REM command:

  ```
  C:\>REM
  ```

  NF: What does that do?

  YOU: It makes DOS remember where you were should there be a system crash. Just type **REM** to make DOS remember. Then after a crash, type

  ```
  C:\>REM AGAIN
  ```

  YOU: DOS automatically restores your computer.

  NF: That's neat!

- ✔ **The bogus PAUSE command**

  YOU: Wait! Don't just get up from the computer. First type the PAUSE command:

  ```
  C:\> PAUSE
  Press any key to continue . . .
  ```

  NF: What does that do?

  YOU: It tells DOS to pause processing until you get back. That way the computer won't do anything — you know, erase files or whatnot — without your being here. When you come back, just press the Enter key.

  NF: How cool! I'm so glad I have a friend like you to show me these things.

*NF = Naïve friend.

Hey: Slavic keyboard!

Try this command:

```
KEYB SL,852,C:\DOS\KEYBOARD.SYS
```

This activates the Slovak keyboard, which makes DOS type like a computer in Slovakia (formerly of Czechoslovakia). The Z and Y keys are reversed. The number keys are replaced by diacriticals. It's strange and may not throw someone right away, but still it's kinda nasty.

> ✔ Put the command in a friend's AUTOEXEC.BAT for permanent keyboard fun!

The bogus prompt batch file

Creating a false DOS prompt requires building on disk a text file that looks like a DOS prompt. To do that, type the following command:

```
C:\>COPY CON BOGUS.DAT
```

This tells DOS to create a text file named BOGUS.DAT using the COPY command. On the next line, press the Enter key alone.

On the next line, type **C:\>** (which is what a prompt looks like), but after the greater-than sign, press Ctrl-Z. You see the following on your screen:

```
C:\>^Z
```

Press Enter. This ends the file and returns you to the DOS prompt.

Now add these two lines to the end of your victim's AUTOEXEC.BAT file:

```
TYPE BOGUS.DAT
COPY CON NUL
```

The first command displays the file BOGUS.DAT. (Be sure to specify a full pathname to that file.) The second command allows the user to type harmlessly on the screen.

The effect of this addition to AUTOEXEC.BAT will be the following:

```
C:\>DIR
DIR
HELP!
```

Unsuspecting friends will see what they think is a DOS prompt and type a command. Nothing happens! Nothing is displayed! They'll be certain they broke something.

- ✔ Typing Ctrl-Z or Ctrl-C stops the madness.
- ✔ You can find more information on pathnames in Chapter 16.
- ✔ Refer to Chapter 20 for information on COPY CON and the NUL device.

Arguments for DOS over Windows

Well, which is better? Is it DOS or is it Windows? Fact is, for right now, you *need* to know DOS to get anything out of Windows. That will probably still hold true, even when Windows runs "without DOS." You'll need to know about eight-letter filenames, subdirectories, the whole ugly knot of glue.

For your amusement, I've concocted the following arguments for DOS over Windows. If you can think of any more, please send them to me care of IDG Books, 155 Bovet Road, Suite 310, San Mateo, CA 94402. I'll include some of the choicest comments in an upcoming edition — and if I include your comments, I'll send an autographed copy your way *gratis*.

WINDOWS Windows displays information using cute icons and graphics

DOS Icons and graphics went out with the Ancient Egyptians. DOS is text, man, and text is what we read. Graphics are for couch potatoes!

WINDOWS Windows displays text in a variety of fun fonts.

DOS DOS displays text in the one font that's on everyone's printer. Can't argue with that.

WINDOWS Windows is fun, graphical, easy to learn and use.

DOS No, Windows is fun, graphical, easy to learn and use *and slow*.

WINDOWS Most new software runs under Windows.

DOS   The old software, which everyone already has, runs better under DOS. And it's cheaper. And it's generally faster.

WINDOWS   Windows lets you run several programs at the same time.

DOS   It only takes one dead program to stink up the house! If you want to run multiple programs in DOS, check out Software Carousel or DESQview. (The latter is a humdinger, in my opinion.)

WINDOWS   Windows has the File Manager.

DOS   DOS can do COPY *.DOC A: forty seconds faster than you can do it with the File Manager.

WINDOWS   Windows is pretty.

DOS   If computers were meant to be pretty, they'd sell software in Victoria's Secret.

WINDOWS   Windows is the future!

DOS   Until then, DOS is holding Windows's reins.

Chapter 28

The Last Chapter

● ●

In This Chapter

▶ A desperate situation

▶ Colonel Bean comes out of the closet

▶ A surprising deduction is made

▶ A last desperate chance is taken

▶ And the estate winds up in the hands of . . .

● ●

*T*his chapter is intended especially for those who, against the author's wishes, have read this book from front to back. Delicately scrawled upon the following pages is information intended just for you so that you may end your *More DOS For Dummies* reading adventure on a high note. (And I do sincerely thank you for reading the book from cover to cover.)

A Desperate Situation

It was quickly nearing the midnight hour — just twenty minutes to go before Uncle Cedric's will would be void. Lightning flashed! Thunder crashed! Aunt Velma lit up another cigar. The evil corporate lawyers from Greedex paced nervously, wringing their hands and licking what would have been their lips had they any.

Young Hank sat in the big, overstuffed chair, the parlor's focal point. Ahead of him, the computer. "C:\>," it said. Cold beads of sweat dotted Hank's forehead. His fingers poised over the computer keyboard:

```
C:\>
```

it said.

Finally, he broke down. "I just can't do it. I just can't do it, Aunty," he cried.

"You're a worthless putz," Velma said, drawing deep on her cigar and blowing the wicked-smelling blue smoke at the nearest lawyer.

Hank's elder sister, Ophelia, screwed up her face and screeched at Hank — albeit in an extremely lady-like manner — "I don't know why you don't get that thing." She paused, allowing time for her beady little eyes to bulge out of her head a few more microns. "You spend all day with *the computer.* You always talk about *the computer.* And now you sit there like a total dope." She breathed in and out dramatically for a few moments. Darren, her doting husband, came over and offered her a glass of water. One of the lawyers — the goofy one — made an awkward face like he was about to say something. But he didn't.

"I disown you," Ophelia squealed. "I disown you for now and forever." She tossed her pointy little nose up in the air.

Husband Darren consoled her. "Why, Ophelia, relax. We're all out of Valium, dear," he said. She looked at him desperately. Maybe he shouldn't have said it. Not the Valium part.

Colonel Bean Comes Out of the Closet

Hank looked desperately at Aunt Velma. She ignored him, concentrating instead on the numb, dizzy feeling the stogie was giving her. It made reality less cold and wet.

One of the lawyers, the tall grim one, noticed Hank's desperation. With only minutes to go, he could feel the entire estate slipping into his oily hands. Professional decorum prevented him from yipping like a love-sick mongrel.

Another click of the giant grandfather clock sliced through the silence. Then came an unpleasant sound. It was a ruffle. A stirring. The gentle playfulness of a cat frolicking through a garbage sack — or the sounds of a man gagged and bound and shoved into the closet.

Curious, Hank rose from the computer and walked cautiously toward the closet. The rustling intensified, accompanied by muted cries. Hank rushed forward and pulled open the closet door. There, inside the closet, bound and gagged but still smartly dressed in his old cavalry uniform — monocle in place, large white mustache unruffled — was Colonel Bean, Hank's PC Guru.

"Colonel Bean!" Hank exclaimed.

Ophelia's eyes bulged even more, the white part getting bigger and the dark iris growing smaller. If they bulged anymore, they'd surely pop out of her petite little head.

Colonel Bean's presence startled the lawyers, but Aunt Velma seemed unsurprised by it. She shrugged and said, "I thought it was the cat."

Although exhausted and sore, Colonel Bean was conscious and quite alert. Hank helped him remove the gag and untie his hands.

"Can I get you something?" Hank offered. He supported the Colonel with one arm as he led him over to the table.

"Oh," began the Colonel, "I could use a good back rub."

"No, I meant something to drink or something. Like that," Hank offered again. He sat Colonel Bean down in front of the computer.

"No, thanks," the Colonel said. He then noticed the computer. Then the time. Then the lawyers. Though stiff with pain, he quickly deduced what was going on. But was he too late?

The Deduction!

"Hank, have you been able to find Uncle Cedric's will in the computer?" the Colonel asked quickly. Hank shook his head.

"Typical incompetence," said Ophelia, in her snooty, sing-song voice. She tried to maintain composure, but her imminent breakdown was approaching. "Oh," she bellowed, beginning the breakdown that would take some seven precious minutes of the time they'd have left. "I just knew this would happen. I knew it. Aunty, we're going to lose the estate. Lose it all! All that work, all Uncle Cedric's hard work! It's going down the drain and into the hands of these filthy rat lawyers."

Darren tried again to console her. But, being inept and thinking about a football bet he'd made instead of the estate thing, he said, "Don't worry, sweetheart. We may lose the game, but we beat the point spread."

There was an awkward silence as everyone in the room tried to figure out what he meant.

Ophelia continued her bawling, muttering, and crying in such a lyric fashion that the melody itself conveyed her feelings without anyone understanding what she was saying. Then, finally, "Oh, and dear God, we'll probably have to fly home *coach*." She cried some more.

Ignoring her, Colonel Bean turned to the computer. "Hank, did you try searching for the file?"

"Yes, but I kept getting a `File not found` error."

"Did you use the file-finding command, as described in Chapter 12 of this book?"

Hank nodded.

Colonel Bean put a hand to his chin. "What if we don't know the filename?"

Hank had thought of that. "I used the TREE command, which was covered in Chapter 16, to scope out all the files on disk. None of them match anything close to what would be a will. Nothing. Nada. Zilch."

A Last, Desperate Chance!

Colonel Bean sat at the computer, fingers poised and occasionally twitching over the keyboard. His eyes lost focus on the screen. He tried to peer into the machine's bowels, its guts, its inner soul. Unfortunately, all he could think of were those cartoonish "Intel Inside" TV spots. Nothing helped.

Bubbling up from the silence, Hank heard Aunt Velma laughing. It was a deep, resonant laughter, gurgling in the phlegm-lined throat of an elderly cigar-chomping widow. She closed her eyes and enjoyed the laughter, marinating herself in the chaos, preparing for the feast the lawyers would have devouring the estate.

Colonel Bean cleared his throat. "Velma," he barked. "This is neither the time nor the situation for levity. If we don't find the will file, all this," he gestured to all that, "will be lost." Aunt Velma just laughed.

Huffy, but still able to speak, Ophelia quickly shrieked out the following command in about one eighth the time a sober person could say it, "Don't just sit there, do something!"

Hank nodded to Colonel Bean, who was still frustrated. "Do what?"

"Do anything," urged Hank. "Do whatever. Do something."

Colonel Bean typed

```
C:\>DIR
```

and pressed Enter. The root directory scrolled quickly up the computer screen. That was when it caught Hank's eye. Nothing anyone else would have seen. But Hank was well-read on computers and spied something out of the ordinary.

"Colonel Bean," Hank began, "check out the size on that CONFIG.SYS file."

Colonel Bean examined the DIR command's output. Puzzled, he said, "Wow, 16 thousand bytes is a bit much. Not even MemMaker increases the typical CONFIG.SYS by that much."

"Type it out," Hank urged.

"No, I'll use the MORE command. That will pause it after each screen full of information. We can read it that way." Colonel Bean typed

```
C:\>MORE < CONFIG.SYS
```

Much to their delight, tucked away inside the CONFIG.SYS file, was Uncle Cedric's will. He had cleverly written it into the CONFIG.SYS using various REM commands:

```
REM This is the will of Uncle Cedric Hollybaster
REM
REM I, Cedric Peanut Hollybaster, being of sound
REM mind and body, do affirm that this is my
REM final will and testament.
DEVICE=C:\DOS\HIMEM.SYS
REM I hereby will to my wife, dearest Velma
```

And the will went on from there.

And They All Lived . . .

The tall, greedy lawyer frowned. He waited patiently for the happy parties to settle down. Hank was pleased and slapped Colonel Bean just a little bit too hard on the back. Velma lit up another cigar. Ophelia passed out, and Darren went looking for water. The other lawyers would have wept, had they tear ducts.

The greedy lawyer said, "I guess you keep the estate." He frowned deeper and then tore up the possession papers he was holding in his long, cold, bony fingers. He added, "I will need a hard copy of that file by morning, thank you."

Hank smiled and nodded. Colonel Bean coughed. Velma closed her eyes, thankful that some of her good genes passed along to her nephew after all.

And they all lived happily every after. Except for the 15 minutes during which Hank, Colonel Bean, Ophelia, and Darren had to share the same Super Shuttle to the airport with the lawyers.

Index

• •

• *Symbols* •

• *A* •

• D •

• *E* •

• *F* •

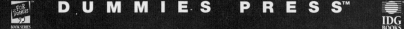

DUMMIES PRESS™

BOOK SERIES FROM IDG

IDG BOOKS WORLDWIDE

10/31/95

The Fun & Easy Way™ to learn about computers and more!

Windows® 3.11 For Dummies,® 3rd Edition
by Andy Rathbone
ISBN: 1-56884-370-4
$16.95 USA/
$22.95 Canada
SUPER STAR

Mutual Funds For Dummies™
by Eric Tyson
ISBN: 1-56884-226-0
$16.99 USA/
$22.99 Canada
SUPER STAR

DOS For Dummies,® 2nd Edition
by Dan Gookin
ISBN: 1-878058-75-4
$16.95 USA/
$22.95 Canada
SUPER STAR

The Internet For Dummies,® 2nd Edition
by John Levine & Carol Baroudi
ISBN: 1-56884-222-8
$19.99 USA/
$26.99 Canada

Personal Finance For Dummies™
by Eric Tyson
ISBN: 1-56884-150-7
$16.95 USA/
$22.95 Canada
SUPER STAR

PCs For Dummies,® 3rd Edition
by Dan Gookin & Andy Rathbone
ISBN: 1-56884-904-4
$16.99 USA/
$22.99 Canada

Macs® For Dummies,® 3rd Edition
by David Pogue
ISBN: 1-56884-239-2
$19.99 USA/
$26.99 Canada
SUPER STAR

The SAT® I For Dummies™
by Suzee Vlk
ISBN: 1-56884-213-9
$14.99 USA/
$20.99 Canada
SUPER STAR

Here's a complete listing of IDG Books' ...For Dummies® titles

Title	Author	ISBN	Price
DATABASE			
Access 2 For Dummies®	by Scott Palmer	ISBN: 1-56884-090-X	$19.95 USA/$26.95 Canada
Access Programming For Dummies®	by Rob Krumm	ISBN: 1-56884-091-8	$19.95 USA/$26.95 Canada
Approach 3 For Windows® For Dummies®	by Doug Lowe	ISBN: 1-56884-233-3	$19.99 USA/$26.99 Canada
dBASE For DOS For Dummies®	by Scott Palmer & Michael Stabler	ISBN: 1-56884-188-4	$19.95 USA/$26.95 Canada
dBASE For Windows® For Dummies®	by Scott Palmer	ISBN: 1-56884-179-5	$19.95 USA/$26.95 Canada
dBASE 5 For Windows® Programming For Dummies®	by Ted Coombs & Jason Coombs	ISBN: 1-56884-215-5	$19.99 USA/$26.99 Canada
FoxPro 2.6 For Windows® For Dummies®	by John Kaufeld	ISBN: 1-56884-187-6	$19.95 USA/$26.95 Canada
Paradox 5 For Windows® For Dummies®	by John Kaufeld	ISBN: 1-56884-185-X	$19.95 USA/$26.95 Canada
DESKTOP PUBLISHING/ILLUSTRATION/GRAPHICS			
CorelDRAW! 5 For Dummies®	by Deke McClelland	ISBN: 1-56884-157-4	$19.95 USA/$26.95 Canada
CorelDRAW! 5 For Dummies®	by Deke McClelland	ISBN: 1-56884-042-X	$19.95 USA/$26.95 Canada
Desktop Publishing & Design For Dummies®	by Roger C. Parker	ISBN: 1-56884-234-1	$19.99 USA/$26.99 Canada
Harvard Graphics 2 For Windows® For Dummies®	by Roger C. Parker	ISBN: 1-56884-092-6	$19.95 USA/$26.95 Canada
PageMaker 5 For Macs® For Dummies®	by Galen Gruman & Deke McClelland	ISBN: 1-56884-178-7	$19.95 USA/$26.95 Canada
PageMaker 5 For Windows® For Dummies®	by Deke McClelland & Galen Gruman	ISBN: 1-56884-160-4	$19.95 USA/$26.95 Canada
Photoshop 3 For Macs® For Dummies®	by Deke McClelland	ISBN: 1-56884-208-2	$19.99 USA/$26.99 Canada
QuarkXPress 3.3 For Dummies®	by Galen Gruman & Barbara Assadi	ISBN: 1-56884-217-1	$19.99 USA/$26.99 Canada
FINANCE/PERSONAL FINANCE/TEST TAKING REFERENCE			
Everyday Math For Dummies™	by Charles Seiter	ISBN: 1-56884-248-1	$14.99 USA/$22.99 Canada
Personal Finance For Dummies™ For Canadians	by Eric Tyson & Tony Martin	ISBN: 1-56884-378-X	$18.99 USA/$24.99 Canada
QuickBooks 3 For Dummies®	by Stephen L. Nelson	ISBN: 1-56884-227-9	$19.99 USA/$26.99 Canada
Quicken 8 For DOS For Dummies,® 2nd Edition	by Stephen L. Nelson	ISBN: 1-56884-210-4	$19.95 USA/$26.95 Canada
Quicken 5 For Macs® For Dummies®	by Stephen L. Nelson	ISBN: 1-56884-211-2	$19.95 USA/$26.95 Canada
Quicken 4 For Windows® For Dummies,® 2nd Edition	by Stephen L. Nelson	ISBN: 1-56884-209-0	$19.95 USA/$26.95 Canada
Taxes For Dummies,™ 1995 Edition	by Eric Tyson & David J. Silverman	ISBN: 1-56884-220-1	$14.99 USA/$20.99 Canada
The GMAT® For Dummies™	by Suzee Vlk, Series Editor	ISBN: 1-56884-376-3	$14.99 USA/$20.99 Canada
The GRE® For Dummies™	by Suzee Vlk, Series Editor	ISBN: 1-56884-375-5	$14.99 USA/$20.99 Canada
Time Management For Dummies™	by Jeffrey J. Mayer	ISBN: 1-56884-360-7	$16.99 USA/$22.99 Canada
TurboTax For Windows® For Dummies®	by Gail A. Helsel, CPA	ISBN: 1-56884-228-7	$19.99 USA/$26.99 Canada
GROUPWARE/INTEGRATED			
ClarisWorks For Macs® For Dummies®	by Frank Higgins	ISBN: 1-56884-363-1	$19.99 USA/$26.99 Canada
Lotus Notes For Dummies®	by Pat Freeland & Stephen Londergan	ISBN: 1-56884-212-0	$19.95 USA/$26.95 Canada
Microsoft® Office 4 For Windows® For Dummies®	by Roger C. Parker	ISBN: 1-56884-183-3	$19.95 USA/$26.95 Canada
Microsoft® Works 3 For Windows® For Dummies®	by David C. Kay	ISBN: 1-56884-214-7	$19.99 USA/$26.99 Canada
SmartSuite 3 For Dummies®	by Jan Weingarten & John Weingarten	ISBN: 1-56884-367-4	$19.99 USA/$26.99 Canada
INTERNET/COMMUNICATIONS/NETWORKING			
America Online® For Dummies,® 2nd Edition	by John Kaufeld	ISBN: 1-56884-933-8	$19.99 USA/$26.99 Canada
CompuServe For Dummies,® 2nd Edition	by Wallace Wang	ISBN: 1-56884-937-0	$19.99 USA/$26.99 Canada
Modems For Dummies,® 2nd Edition	by Tina Rathbone	ISBN: 1-56884-223-6	$19.99 USA/$26.99 Canada
MORE Internet For Dummies®	by John R. Levine & Margaret Levine Young	ISBN: 1-56884-164-7	$19.95 USA/$26.95 Canada
MORE Modems & On-line Services For Dummies®	by Tina Rathbone	ISBN: 1-56884-365-8	$19.99 USA/$26.99 Canada
Mosaic For Dummies,® Windows Edition	by David Angell & Brent Heslop	ISBN: 1-56884-242-2	$19.99 USA/$26.99 Canada
NetWare For Dummies,® 2nd Edition	by Ed Tittel, Deni Connor & Earl Follis	ISBN: 1-56884-369-0	$19.99 USA/$26.99 Canada
Networking For Dummies®	by Doug Lowe	ISBN: 1-56884-079-9	$19.95 USA/$26.95 Canada
PROCOMM PLUS 2 For Windows® For Dummies®	by Wallace Wang	ISBN: 1-56884-219-8	$19.99 USA/$26.99 Canada
TCP/IP For Dummies®	by Marshall Wilensky & Candace Leiden	ISBN: 1-56884-241-4	$19.99 USA/$26.99 Canada

Microsoft and Windows are registered trademarks of Microsoft Corporation. Mac is a registered trademark of Apple Computer. SAT is a registered trademark of the College Entrance Examination Board. GMAT is a registered trademark of the Graduate Management Admission Council. GRE is a registered trademark of the Educational Testing Service. America Online is a registered trademark of America Online, Inc. The "...For Dummies Book Series" logo, the IDG Books Worldwide logos, Dummies Press, and The Fun & Easy Way are trademarks, and ---- For Dummies and ... For Dummies are registered trademarks under exclusive license to IDG Books Worldwide, Inc., from International Data Group, Inc.

For scholastic requests & educational orders please call Educational Sales at 1. 800. 434. 2086

FOR MORE INFO OR TO ORDER, PLEASE CALL ▶ 800. 762. 2974

For volume discounts & special orders please call Tony Real, Special Sales, at 415. 655. 3048

The Internet For Macs® For Dummies® 2nd Edition	by Charles Seiter	ISBN: 1-56884-371-2	$19.99 USA/$26.99 Canada
The Internet For Macs® For Dummies® Starter Kit	by Charles Seiter	ISBN: 1-56884-244-9	$29.99 USA/$39.99 Canada
The Internet For Macs® For Dummies® Starter Kit Bestseller Edition	by Charles Seiter	ISBN: 1-56884-245-7	$39.99 USA/$54.99 Canada
The Internet For Windows® For Dummies® Starter Kit	by John R. Levine & Margaret Levine Young	ISBN: 1-56884-237-6	$34.99 USA/$44.99 Canada
The Internet For Windows® For Dummies® Starter Kit, Bestseller Edition	by John R. Levine & Margaret Levine Young	ISBN: 1-56884-246-5	$39.99 USA/$54.99 Canada

MACINTOSH

Mac® Programming For Dummies®	by Dan Parks Sydow	ISBN: 1-56884-173-6	$19.95 USA/$26.95 Canada
Macintosh® System 7.5 For Dummies®	by Bob LeVitus	ISBN: 1-56884-197-3	$19.95 USA/$26.95 Canada
MORE Macs® For Dummies®	by David Pogue	ISBN: 1-56884-087-X	$19.95 USA/$26.95 Canada
PageMaker 5 For Macs® For Dummies®	by Galen Gruman & Deke McClelland	ISBN: 1-56884-178-7	$19.95 USA/$26.95 Canada
QuarkXPress 3.3 For Dummies®	by Galen Gruman & Barbara Assadi	ISBN: 1-56884-217-1	$19.99 USA/$26.99 Canada
Upgrading and Fixing Macs® For Dummies®	by Kearney Rietmann & Frank Higgins	ISBN: 1-56884-189-2	$19.95 USA/$26.95 Canada

MULTIMEDIA

Multimedia & CD-ROMs For Dummies® 2nd Edition	by Andy Rathbone	ISBN: 1-56884-907-9	$19.99 USA/$26.99 Canada
Multimedia & CD-ROMs For Dummies® Interactive Multimedia Value Pack, 2nd Edition	by Andy Rathbone	ISBN: 1-56884-909-5	$29.99 USA/$39.99 Canada

OPERATING SYSTEMS:

DOS

MORE DOS For Dummies®	by Dan Gookin	ISBN: 1-56884-046-2	$19.95 USA/$26.95 Canada
OS/2® Warp For Dummies® 2nd Edition	by Andy Rathbone	ISBN: 1-56884-205-8	$19.99 USA/$26.99 Canada

UNIX

MORE UNIX® For Dummies®	by John R. Levine & Margaret Levine Young	ISBN: 1-56884-361-5	$19.99 USA/$26.99 Canada
UNIX® For Dummies®	by John R. Levine & Margaret Levine Young	ISBN: 1-878058-58-4	$19.95 USA/$26.95 Canada

WINDOWS

MORE Windows® For Dummies® 2nd Edition	by Andy Rathbone	ISBN: 1-56884-048-9	$19.95 USA/$26.95 Canada
Windows® 95 For Dummies®	by Andy Rathbone	ISBN: 1-56884-240-6	$19.99 USA/$26.99 Canada

PCS/HARDWARE

Illustrated Computer Dictionary For Dummies® 2nd Edition	by Dan Gookin & Wallace Wang	ISBN: 1-56884-218-X	$12.95 USA/$16.95 Canada
Upgrading and Fixing PCs For Dummies® 2nd Edition	by Andy Rathbone	ISBN: 1-56884-903-6	$19.99 USA/$26.99 Canada

PRESENTATION/AUTOCAD

AutoCAD For Dummies®	by Bud Smith	ISBN: 1-56884-191-4	$19.95 USA/$26.95 Canada
PowerPoint 4 For Windows® For Dummies®	by Doug Lowe	ISBN: 1-56884-161-2	$16.99 USA/$22.99 Canada

PROGRAMMING

Borland C++ For Dummies®	by Michael Hyman	ISBN: 1-56884-162-0	$19.95 USA/$26.95 Canada
C For Dummies® Volume 1	by Dan Gookin	ISBN: 1-878058-78-9	$19.95 USA/$26.95 Canada
C++ For Dummies®	by Stephen R. Davis	ISBN: 1-56884-163-9	$19.95 USA/$26.95 Canada
Delphi Programming For Dummies®	by Neil Rubenking	ISBN: 1-56884-200-7	$19.99 USA/$26.99 Canada
Mac® Programming For Dummies®	by Dan Parks Sydow	ISBN: 1-56884-173-6	$19.95 USA/$26.95 Canada
PowerBuilder 4 Programming For Dummies®	by Ted Coombs & Jason Coombs	ISBN: 1-56884-325-9	$19.99 USA/$26.99 Canada
QBasic Programming For Dummies®	by Douglas Hergert	ISBN: 1-56884-093-4	$19.95 USA/$26.95 Canada
Visual Basic 3 For Dummies®	by Wallace Wang	ISBN: 1-56884-076-4	$19.95 USA/$26.95 Canada
Visual Basic "X" For Dummies®	by Wallace Wang	ISBN: 1-56884-230-9	$19.99 USA/$26.99 Canada
Visual C++ 2 For Dummies®	by Michael Hyman & Bob Arnson	ISBN: 1-56884-328-3	$19.99 USA/$26.99 Canada
Windows® 95 Programming For Dummies®	by S. Randy Davis	ISBN: 1-56884-327-5	$19.99 USA/$26.99 Canada

SPREADSHEET

1-2-3 For Dummies®	by Greg Harvey	ISBN: 1-878058-60-6	$16.95 USA/$22.95 Canada
1-2-3 For Windows® 5 For Dummies® 2nd Edition	by John Walkenbach	ISBN: 1-56884-216-3	$16.95 USA/$22.95 Canada
Excel 5 For Macs® For Dummies®	by Greg Harvey	ISBN: 1-56884-186-8	$19.95 USA/$26.95 Canada
Excel For Dummies® 2nd Edition	by Greg Harvey	ISBN: 1-56884-050-0	$16.95 USA/$22.95 Canada
MORE 1-2-3 For DOS For Dummies®	by John Weingarten	ISBN: 1-56884-224-4	$19.99 USA/$26.99 Canada
MORE Excel 5 For Windows® For Dummies®	by Greg Harvey	ISBN: 1-56884-207-4	$19.95 USA/$26.95 Canada
Quattro Pro 6 For Windows® For Dummies®	by John Walkenbach	ISBN: 1-56884-174-4	$19.95 USA/$26.95 Canada
Quattro Pro For DOS For Dummies®	by John Walkenbach	ISBN: 1-56884-023-3	$16.95 USA/$22.95 Canada

UTILITIES

Norton Utilities 8 For Dummies®	by Beth Slick	ISBN: 1-56884-166-3	$19.95 USA/$26.95 Canada

VCRS/CAMCORDERS

VCRs & Camcorders For Dummies™	by Gordon McComb & Andy Rathbone	ISBN: 1-56884-229-5	$14.99 USA/$20.99 Canada

WORD PROCESSING

Ami Pro For Dummies®	by Jim Meade	ISBN: 1-56884-049-7	$19.95 USA/$26.95 Canada
MORE Word For Windows® 6 For Dummies®	by Doug Lowe	ISBN: 1-56884-165-5	$19.95 USA/$26.95 Canada
MORE WordPerfect® 6 For Windows® For Dummies®	by Margaret Levine Young & David C. Kay	ISBN: 1-56884-206-6	$19.95 USA/$26.95 Canada
MORE WordPerfect 6 For DOS For Dummies®	by Wallace Wang, edited by Dan Gookin	ISBN: 1-56884-047-0	$19.95 USA/$26.95 Canada
Word 6 For Macs® For Dummies®	by Dan Gookin	ISBN: 1-56884-190-6	$19.95 USA/$26.95 Canada
Word For Windows® 6 For Dummies®	by Dan Gookin	ISBN: 1-56884-075-6	$16.95 USA/$22.95 Canada
Word For Windows® For Dummies®	by Dan Gookin & Ray Werner	ISBN: 1-878058-86-X	$16.95 USA/$22.95 Canada
WordPerfect 6 For DOS For Dummies®	by Dan Gookin	ISBN: 1-878058-77-0	$16.95 USA/$22.95 Canada
WordPerfect® 6.1 For Windows® For Dummies® 2nd Edition	by Margaret Levine Young & David Kay	ISBN: 1-56884-243-0	$16.95 USA/$22.95 Canada
WordPerfect® For Dummies®	by Dan Gookin	ISBN: 1-878058-52-5	$16.95 USA/$22.95 Canada

Windows is a registered trademark of Microsoft Corporation. Mac is a registered trademark of Apple Computer. OS/2 is a registered trademark of IBM. UNIX is a registered trademark of AT&T. WordPerfect is a registered trademark of Novell. The "...For Dummies Book Series" logo, the IDG Books Worldwide logos, Dummies Press, and The Fun & Easy Way are trademarks, and ---- For Dummies and ... For Dummies are registered trademarks under exclusive license to IDG Books Worldwide, Inc., from International Data Group, Inc.

DUMMIES PRESS™ QUICK REFERENCES

BOOK SERIES FROM IDG

IDG BOOKS WORLDWIDE

10/31/95

Fun, Fast, & Cheap!™

NEW!

The Internet For Macs® For Dummies® Quick Reference
by Charles Seiter

ISBN: 1-56884-967-2
$9.99 USA/$12.99 Canada

NEW!

Windows® 95 For Dummies® Quick Reference
by Greg Harvey

ISBN: 1-56884-964-8
$9.99 USA/$12.99 Canada

SUPER STAR

Photoshop 3 For Macs® For Dummies® Quick Reference
by Deke McClelland

ISBN: 1-56884-968-0
$9.99 USA/$12.99 Canada

SUPER STAR

WordPerfect® For DOS For Dummies® Quick Reference
by Greg Harvey

ISBN: 1-56884-009-8
$8.95 USA/$12.95 Canada

Title	Author	ISBN	Price
DATABASE			
Access 2 For Dummies® Quick Reference	by Stuart J. Stuple	ISBN: 1-56884-167-1	$8.95 USA/$11.95 Canada
dBASE 5 For DOS For Dummies® Quick Reference	by Barrie Sosinsky	ISBN: 1-56884-954-0	$9.99 USA/$12.99 Canada
dBASE 5 For Windows® For Dummies® Quick Reference	by Stuart J. Stuple	ISBN: 1-56884-953-2	$9.99 USA/$12.99 Canada
Paradox 5 For Windows® For Dummies® Quick Reference	by Scott Palmer	ISBN: 1-56884-960-5	$9.99 USA/$12.99 Canada
DESKTOP PUBLISHING/ILLUSTRATION/GRAPHICS			
CorelDRAW! 5 For Dummies® Quick Reference	by Raymond E. Werner	ISBN: 1-56884-952-4	$9.99 USA/$12.99 Canada
Harvard Graphics For Windows® For Dummies® Quick Reference	by Raymond E. Werner	ISBN: 1-56884-962-1	$9.99 USA/$12.99 Canada
Photoshop 3 For Macs® For Dummies® Quick Reference	by Deke McClelland	ISBN: 1-56884-968-0	$9.99 USA/$12.99 Canada
FINANCE/PERSONAL FINANCE			
Quicken 4 For Windows® For Dummies® Quick Reference	by Stephen L. Nelson	ISBN: 1-56884-950-8	$9.95 USA/$12.95 Canada
GROUPWARE/INTEGRATED			
Microsoft® Office 4 For Windows® For Dummies® Quick Reference	by Doug Lowe	ISBN: 1-56884-958-3	$9.99 USA/$12.99 Canada
Microsoft® Works 3 For Windows® For Dummies® Quick Reference	by Michael Partington	ISBN: 1-56884-959-1	$9.99 USA/$12.99 Canada
INTERNET/COMMUNICATIONS/NETWORKING			
The Internet For Dummies® Quick Reference	by John R. Levine & Margaret Levine Young	ISBN: 1-56884-168-X	$8.95 USA/$11.95 Canada
MACINTOSH			
Macintosh® System 7.5 For Dummies® Quick Reference	by Stuart J. Stuple	ISBN: 1-56884-956-7	$9.99 USA/$12.99 Canada
OPERATING SYSTEMS:			
DOS			
DOS For Dummies® Quick Reference	by Greg Harvey	ISBN: 1-56884-007-1	$8.95 USA/$11.95 Canada
UNIX			
UNIX® For Dummies® Quick Reference	by John R. Levine & Margaret Levine Young	ISBN: 1-56884-094-2	$8.95 USA/$11.95 Canada
WINDOWS			
Windows® 3.1 For Dummies® Quick Reference, 2nd Edition	by Greg Harvey	ISBN: 1-56884-951-6	$8.95 USA/$11.95 Canada
PCs/HARDWARE			
Memory Management For Dummies® Quick Reference	by Doug Lowe	ISBN: 1-56884-362-3	$9.99 USA/$12.99 Canada
PRESENTATION/AUTOCAD			
AutoCAD For Dummies® Quick Reference	by Ellen Finkelstein	ISBN: 1-56884-198-1	$9.95 USA/$12.95 Canada
SPREADSHEET			
1-2-3 For Dummies® Quick Reference	by John Walkenbach	ISBN: 1-56884-027-6	$8.95 USA/$11.95 Canada
1-2-3 For Windows® 5 For Dummies® Quick Reference	by John Walkenbach	ISBN: 1-56884-957-5	$9.95 USA/$12.95 Canada
Excel For Windows® For Dummies® Quick Reference, 2nd Edition	by John Walkenbach	ISBN: 1-56884-096-9	$8.95 USA/$11.95 Canada
Quattro Pro 6 For Windows® For Dummies® Quick Reference	by Stuart J. Stuple	ISBN: 1-56884-172-8	$9.95 USA/$12.95 Canada
WORD PROCESSING			
Word For Windows® 6 For Dummies® Quick Reference	by George Lynch	ISBN: 1-56884-095-0	$8.95 USA/$11.95 Canada
Word For Windows® For Dummies® Quick Reference	by George Lynch	ISBN: 1-56884-029-2	$8.95 USA/$11.95 Canada
WordPerfect® 6.1 For Windows® For Dummies® Quick Reference, 2nd Edition	by Greg Harvey	ISBN: 1-56884-966-4	$9.99 USA/$12.99/Canada

Microsoft and Windows are registered trademarks of Microsoft Corporation. Mac and Macintosh are registered trademarks of Apple Computer. UNIX is a registered trademark of AT&T. WordPerfect is a registered trademark of Novell. The "...For Dummies Book Series" logo, the IDG Books Worldwide logos, Dummies Press, The Fun & Easy Way, and Fun, Fast, & Cheap! are trademarks, and ---- For Dummies and ... For Dummies are registered trademarks under exclusive license to IDG Books Worldwide, Inc., from International Data Group, Inc.

For scholastic requests & educational orders please call Educational Sales at 1. 800. 434. 2086

FOR MORE INFO OR TO ORDER, PLEASE CALL ▶ 800 762 2974

For volume discounts & special orders please call Tony Real, Special Sales, at 415. 655. 3048

P C P R E S S

IDG BOOKS WORLDWIDE

10/31/95

Windows® 3.1 SECRETS™
by Brian Livingston

ISBN: 1-878058-43-6
$39.95 USA/$52.95 Canada
Includes software.

MORE Windows® 3.1 SECRETS™
by Brian Livingston

ISBN: 1-56884-019-5
$39.95 USA/$52.95 Canada
Includes software.

Windows® GIZMOS™
by Brian Livingston & Margie Livingston

ISBN: 1-878058-66-5
$39.95 USA/$52.95 Canada
Includes software.

Windows® 3.1 Connectivity SECRETS™
by Runnoe Connally, David Rorabaugh, & Sheldon Hall

ISBN: 1-56884-030-6
$49.95 USA/$64.95 Canada
Includes software.

Windows® 3.1 Configuration SECRETS™
by Valda Hilley & James Blakely

ISBN: 1-56884-026-8
$49.95 USA/$64.95 Canada
Includes software.

Internet SECRETS™
by John Levine & Carol Baroudi

ISBN: 1-56884-452-2
$39.99 USA/$54.99 Canada
Includes software.

Internet GIZMOS™ For Windows®
by Joel Diamond, Howard Sobel, & Valda Hilley

ISBN: 1-56884-451-4
$39.99 USA/$54.99 Canada
Includes software.

Network Security SECRETS™
by David Stang & Sylvia Moon

ISBN: 1-56884-021-7
Int'l. ISBN: 1-56884-151-5
$49.95 USA/$64.95 Canada
Includes software.

PC SECRETS™
by Caroline M. Halliday

ISBN: 1-878058-49-5
$39.95 USA/$52.95 Canada
Includes software.

WordPerfect® 6 SECRETS™
by Roger C. Parker & David A. Holzgang

ISBN: 1-56884-040-3
$39.95 USA/$52.95 Canada
Includes software.

DOS 6 SECRETS™
by Robert D. Ainsbury

ISBN: 1-878058-70-3
$39.95 USA/$52.95 Canada
Includes software.

Paradox 4 Power Programming SECRETS,™ 2nd Edition
by Gregory B. Salcedo & Martin W. Rudy

ISBN: 1-878058-54-1
$44.95 USA/$59.95 Canada
Includes software.

Paradox 5 For Windows® Power Programming SECRETS™
by Gregory B. Salcedo & Martin W. Rudy

ISBN: 1-56884-085-3
$44.95 USA/$59.95 Canada
Includes software.

Hard Disk SECRETS™
by John M. Goodman, Ph.D.

ISBN: 1-878058-64-9
$39.95 USA/$52.95 Canada
Includes software.

WordPerfect® 6 For Windows® Tips & Techniques Revealed
by David A. Holzgang & Roger C. Parker

ISBN: 1-56884-202-3
$39.95 USA/$52.95 Canada
Includes software.

Excel 5 For Windows® Power Programming Techniques
by John Walkenbach

ISBN: 1-56884-303-8
$39.95 USA/$52.95 Canada
Includes software.

...SECRETS®

INFO WORLD TECHNICAL BOOKS

Windows is a registered trademark of Microsoft Corporation. WordPerfect is a registered trademark of Novell. ----SECRETS, ----GIZMOS, and the IDG Books Worldwide logos are trademarks, and ...SECRETS is a registered trademark under exclusive license to IDG Books Worldwide, Inc., from International Data Group, Inc.

For scholastic requests & educational orders please call Educational Sales, at 1. 800. 434. 2086

FOR MORE INFO OR TO ORDER, PLEASE CALL ▶ 800. 762. 2974

For volume discounts & special orders please call Tony Real, Special Sales, at 415. 655. 3048

P C   P R E S S

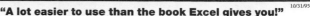

IDG
BOOKS
WORLDWIDE

10/31/95

"A lot easier to use than the book Excel gives you!"

Lisa Schmeckpeper, New Berlin, WI, on PC World Excel 5 For Windows Handbook

**Official Hayes Modem
Communications
Companion**
by Caroline M. Halliday

ISBN: 1-56884-072-1
$29.95 USA/$39.95 Canada
Includes software.

**1,001 Komputer Answers
from Kim Komando**
by Kim Komando

ISBN: 1-56884-460-3
$29.99 USA/$39.99 Canada
Includes software.

**PC World DOS 6
Handbook, 2nd Edition**
*by John Socha, Clint Hicks, &
Devra Hall*

ISBN: 1-878058-79-7
$34.95 USA/$44.95 Canada
Includes software.

**PC World Word
For Windows® 6 Handbook**
*by Brent Heslop
& David Angell*

ISBN: 1-56884-054-3
$34.95 USA/$44.95 Canada
Includes software.

**PC World Microsoft®
Access 2 Bible,
2nd Edition**
*by Cary N. Prague
& Michael R. Irwin*

ISBN: 1-56884-086-1
$39.95 USA/$52.95 Canada
Includes software.

**PC World Excel 5
For Windows® Handbook,
2nd Edition**
*by John Walkenbach
& Dave Maguiness*

ISBN: 1-56884-056-X
$34.95 USA/$44.95 Canada
Includes software.

**PC World WordPerfect® 6
Handbook**
by Greg Harvey

ISBN: 1-878058-80-0
$34.95 USA/$44.95 Canada
Includes software.

**QuarkXPress
For Windows® Designer
Handbook**
*by Barbara Assadi
& Galen Gruman*

ISBN: 1-878058-45-2
$29.95 USA/$39.95 Canada

**Official XTree
Companion, 3rd Edition**
by Beth Slick

ISBN: 1-878058-57-6
$19.95 USA/$26.95 Canada

**PC World DOS 6
Command Reference
and Problem Solver**
*by John Socha
& Devra Hall*

ISBN: 1-56884-055-1
$24.95 USA/$32.95 Canada

**Client/Server
Strategies™: A Survival
Guide for Corporate
Reengineers**
by David Vaskevitch

ISBN: 1-56884-064-0
$29.95 USA/$39.95 Canada

*"PC World Word
For Windows 6
Handbook is very
easy to follow with
lots of 'hands on'
examples. The
'Task at a Glance'
is very helpful!"*

Jacqueline Martens, Tacoma, WA

**"Thanks for publish-
ing this book! It's
the best money I've
spent this year!"**

*Robert D. Templeton,
Ft. Worth, TX, on MORE
Windows 3.1 SECRETS*

Microsoft and Windows are registered trademarks of Microsoft Corporation. WordPerfect is a registered trademark of Novell. ----STRATEGIES and the IDG Books Worldwide logos are trademarks under exclusive license to IDG Books Worldwide, Inc., from International Data Group, Inc.

For scholastic requests & educational orders please
call Educational Sales, at 1. 800. 434. 2086

FOR MORE INFO OR TO ORDER, PLEASE CALL ▶ 800 762 2974

For volume discounts & special orders please call
Tony Real, Special Sales, at 415. 655. 3048

Macworld
PRESS

MACWORLD® PRESS

Macworld
PRESS

10/31/95

Macworld® Mac® & Power Mac SECRETS,™ 2nd Edition
by David Pogue & Joseph Schorr

HOT!

This is the definitive Mac reference for those who want to become power users! Includes three disks with 9MB of software!

WINNERS 1994-95 TECHNICAL PUBLICATIONS AND ART COMPETITIONS OF THE SOCIETY FOR TECHNICAL COMMUNICATION

ISBN: 1-56884-175-2
$39.95 USA/$54.95 Canada

Includes 3 disks chock full of software.

NEWBRIDGE BOOK CLUB SELECTION

Macworld® Mac® FAQs™
by David Pogue

HOT!

Written by the hottest Macintosh author around, David Pogue, *Macworld Mac FAQs* gives users the ultimate Mac reference. Hundreds of Mac questions and answers side-by-side, right at your fingertips, and organized into six easy-to-reference sections with lots of sidebars and diagrams.

ISBN: 1-56884-480-8
$19.99 USA/$26.99 Canada

Macworld® System 7.5 Bible, 3rd Edition
by Lon Poole

ISBN: 1-56884-098-5
$29.95 USA/$39.95 Canada

NATIONAL BESTSELLER!

Macworld® ClarisWorks 3.0 Companion, 3rd Edition
by Steven A. Schwartz

ISBN: 1-56884-481-6
$24.99 USA/$34.99 Canada

NATIONAL BESTSELLER!

Macworld® Complete Mac® Handbook Plus Interactive CD, 3rd Edition
by Jim Heid

BMUG SPRING 1995 CHOICE PRODUCT

ISBN: 1-56884-192-2
$39.95 USA/$54.95 Canada

Includes an interactive CD-ROM.

NEWBRIDGE BOOK CLUB SELECTION

Macworld® Ultimate Mac® CD-ROM
by Jim Heid

ISBN: 1-56884-477-8
$19.99 USA/$26.99 Canada

CD-ROM includes version 2.0 of QuickTime, and over 65 MB of the best shareware, freeware, fonts, sounds, and more!

Macworld® Networking Bible, 2nd Edition
by Dave Kosiur & Joel M. Snyder

ISBN: 1-56884-194-9
$29.95 USA/$39.95 Canada

XI WINNER

Macworld® Photoshop 3 Bible, 2nd Edition
by Deke McClelland

ISBN: 1-56884-158-2
$39.95 USA/$54.95 Canada

Includes stunning CD-ROM with add-ons, digitized photos and more.

WINNERS 1994-95 TECHNICAL PUBLICATIONS AND ART COMPETITIONS OF THE SOCIETY FOR TECHNICAL COMMUNICATION

NEW!

Macworld® Photoshop 2.5 Bible
by Deke McClelland

ISBN: 1-56884-022-5
$29.95 USA/$39.95 Canada

NATIONAL BESTSELLER!

Macworld® FreeHand 4 Bible
by Deke McClelland

ISBN: 1-56884-170-1
$29.95 USA/$39.95 Canada

Macworld® Illustrator 5.0/5.5 Bible
by Ted Alspach

ISBN: 1-56884-097-7
$39.95 USA/$54.95 Canada

Includes CD-ROM with QuickTime tutorials.

Mac is a registered trademark of Apple Computer. Macworld is a registered trademark of International Data Group, Inc. ----SECRETS, and ----FAQs are trademarks under exclusive license to IDG Books Worldwide, Inc., from International Data Group, Inc.

For scholastic requests & educational orders please call Educational Sales, at 1. 800. 434. 2086

FOR MORE INFO OR TO ORDER, PLEASE CALL ▶ 800. 762. 2974

For volume discounts & special orders please call Tony Real, Special Sales, at 415. 655. 3048

"Macworld Complete Mac Handbook Plus CD covered everything I could think of and more!"*

Peter Tsakiris, New York, NY

"Very useful for PageMaker beginners and veterans alike— contains a wealth of tips and tricks to make you a faster, more powerful PageMaker user."

Paul Brainerd, President and founder, Aldus Corporation

"Thanks for the best computer book I've ever read—*Photoshop 2.5 Bible*. Best $30 I ever spent. I *love* the detailed index....Yours blows them all out of the water. This is a great book. We must enlighten the masses!"

Kevin Lisankie, Chicago, Illinois

"Macworld Guide to ClarisWorks 2 is the easiest computer book to read that I have ever found!"*

Steven Hanson, Lutz, FL

*"...thanks to the *Macworld Excel 5 Companion*, 2nd Edition occupying a permanent position next to my computer, I'll be able to tap more of Excel's power."*

Lauren Black, Lab Director, *Macworld* Magazine

Macworld® QuarkXPress 3.2/3.3 Bible
by Barbara Assadi & Galen Gruman

ISBN: 1-878058-85-1
$39.95 USA/$52.95 Canada

Includes disk with QuarkXPress XTensions and scripts.

Macworld® PageMaker 5 Bible
by Craig Danuloff

ISBN: 1-878058-84-3
$39.95 USA/$52.95 Canada

Includes 2 disks with PageMaker utilities, clip art, and more.

Macworld® FileMaker Pro 2.0/2.1 Bible
by Steven A. Schwartz

ISBN: 1-56884-201-5
$34.95 USA/$46.95 Canada

Includes disk with ready-to-run data bases.

Macworld® Word 6 Companion, 2nd Edition
by Jim Heid

ISBN: 1-56884-082-9
$24.95 USA/$34.95 Canada

NEWBRIDGE BOOK CLUB SELECTION

Macworld® Guide To Microsoft® Word 5/5.1
by Jim Heid

ISBN: 1-878058-39-8
$22.95 USA/$29.95 Canada

Macworld® ClarisWorks 2.0/2.1 Companion, 2nd Edition
by Steven A. Schwartz

ISBN: 1-56884-180-9
$24.95 USA/$34.95 Canada

Macworld® Guide To Microsoft® Works 3
by Barrie Sosinsky

ISBN: 1-878058-42-8
$22.95 USA/$29.95 Canada

Macworld® Excel 5 Companion, 2nd Edition
by Chris Van Buren & David Maguiness

ISBN: 1-56884-081-0
$24.95 USA/$34.95 Canada

NEWBRIDGE BOOK CLUB SELECTION

Macworld® Guide To Microsoft® Excel 4
by David Maguiness

ISBN: 1-878058-40-1
$22.95 USA/$29.95 Canada

Microsoft is a registered trademark of Microsoft Corporation. Macworld is a registered trademark of International Data Group, Inc.

For scholastic requests & educational orders please call Educational Sales, at 1. 800. 434. 2086

FOR MORE INFO OR TO ORDER, PLEASE CALL ▶ 800. 762. 2974

For volume discounts & special orders please call Tony Real, Special Sales, at 415. 655. 3048

IDG BOOKS WORLDWIDE

Order Center: **(800) 762-2974** *(8 a.m.–6 p.m., EST, weekdays)*

Quantity	ISBN	Title	Price	Total

Shipping & Handling Charges

	Description	First book	Each additional book	Total
Domestic	Normal	$4.50	$1.50	$
	Two Day Air	$8.50	$2.50	$
	Overnight	$18.00	$3.00	$
International	Surface	$8.00	$8.00	$
	Airmail	$16.00	$16.00	$
	DHL Air	$17.00	$17.00	$

*For large quantities call for shipping & handling charges.
**Prices are subject to change without notice.

Ship to:

Name _____

Company _____

Address _____

City/State/Zip _____

Daytime Phone _____

Payment: ☐ Check to IDG Books Worldwide (US Funds Only)

☐ VISA   ☐ MasterCard   ☐ American Express

Card # _____ Expires _____

Signature _____

Subtotal _____

CA residents add
applicable sales tax _____

IN, MA, and MD
residents add
5% sales tax _____

IL residents add
6.25% sales tax _____

RI residents add
7% sales tax _____

TX residents add
8.25% sales tax _____

Shipping _____

Total _____

Please send this order form to:
IDG Books Worldwide, Inc.
7260 Shadeland Station, Suite 100
Indianapolis, IN 46256

Allow up to 3 weeks for delivery.
Thank you!